THE BOOK OF LE BLANC

by

Nora Lee Clouatre Pollard

CLAITOR'S PUBLISHING DIVISION
Baton Rouge, La.

DEDICATION

Dedicated to:

The memory of my grandmother, Elmire
LeBlanc, born May 26, 1858, died September 11, 1937, who first stirred my interest
in my ancestors.

Compiled for:

My daughter, Barbara Anne Pollard, an
only child, who I feared would not know her
relatives.

Published for:

My only direct descendant, John Michael
Michelli.

With Love.

FOREWORD

For thirty-four years, I have attempted to trace direct and indirect ancestors and also the collateral lines of both. At times it has been hard work, but I must say that it has been a rewarding experience.

Not only have I learned a great deal, I have come in contact with so many wonderful people I would not have known had I not pursued my interest in Genealogy.

I started out with only a high-school education, but I feel that Genealogy has given me a well-rounded education. I have learned so much along the way: history, geography, math, reading skills, law, medicine, philosophy, psychology, religion, and of course, compassion, patience, and love, in so many forms.

I am so proud that most of my ancestors were those wonderful Acadians and I am so happy that I know who and what my people were. To say that they were brave and adventurous; devout and pious; courageous and daring; loving and happy does present a true picture of these people. But let us also remember that they were all of these things in spite of their misfortunes and extreme poverty.

Today we all live in a world of plenty compared to what they had, but I sometimes doubt that we value what we have and whether or not our ideals and motives are as high as theirs were. And are we as staunchly loyal to our families, our neighbors and our God?

I can never think of my Acadians without this picture in my mind, these families being driven from their homes, some separated from their loved ones, some old and sick, not knowing if or when they would meet again. Yet they had the presence of mind to take with them their records. These records were so important to them. The ones not written were carried in their hearts and minds and the older people were ever so careful to impart this knowledge to each new generation. A great deal of their life centered around this interest in keeping family records and stories alive and constantly in the forefront of their minds and in the minds of each new generation.

In my childhood this custom was still carried on. Even those who could not read or write managed to get and receive messages from families who moved from one place to another. Although travel was difficult, families managed to keep in touch. At times, weddings, funerals, and All Saint's Day were the only times of reunion. But what grand occasions these all were! At those times they learned what had happened to "our people", the marriages, the births, and alas, the deaths, all duly recorded and documented. I have tried to write it as I see it and I hope that it is the way you see it, too.

I have compiled the material, but this book would not have been possible without a great deal of help from so many interested parties. I want to express my deep gratitude to those of you who over the years have been interested in my work and have sent me so much valuable information.

And last but certainly not least, a personal note. My late husband, John Michael Pollard, was an ardent collector of old and unusual coins so he understood what my hobby meant to me. He was the first to encourage me and support me in this undertaking. His great pride in my work spurred me on whenever I lost interest. He came from a small family, so that at times he was overwhelmed at my many relations. He had only five first cousins and I had fifty-eight plus first cousins.

John Michael Pollard wanted me to complete this undertaking, so I know he is proud of me. Since true Acadians are very frank people, I will say that I am pleased, too.

Nora Lee Clouatre Pollard

ACKNOWLEDGEMENTS

My aunt and uncle, Mr. and Mrs. Anthony Gozales, who just celebrated their sixty-ninth wedding anniversary.

My great uncle, Joseph LeBlanc, who lived to be ninety-six years of age. Mrs. Leslie (Shirley) LeBlanc, Mrs. Cleve (Lee Anna) LeBlanc, Mrs. Albert A. Moskau, Miss Elizabeth Adele Stock of New Orleans. May and Desire LeBlanc of Donaldsonville. Louis and Maria LeBlanc, also of Donaldsonville and Bill and Modeste LeBlanc of Baton Rouge. Mr. and Mrs. Adam Dugas and Miss Leonie Clouatre of Baton Rouge. At times due to illness and unable to drive, my brother, Livingston J. Clouatre and my cousin, Melvin Dugas, would take me to courthouses, cemeteries, churches and relatives' homes. Also, Cheryl (Jex) LeBlanc for Index of Living Descendants.

I also want to thank: the Department of History and Archives of the Diocese of Baton Rouge; Mr. William King Hunt of the L.S.U. Genealogy Department; the late Sidney Marchand; the State Archives at Baton Rouge; the State Library; present and past pastors of St. Michael Church at Convent; St. James Church at St. James and Ascension Church at Donaldsonville; the following courthouses: Assumption Parish Courthouse at Napoleonville; Ascension Parish Courthouse at Donaldsonville; St. James Parish Courthouse at Convent; West Baton Rouge Parish Courthouse at Port Allen and Iberville Parish Courthouse at Plaquemine.

Special thanks to the typist, Miss Joyce Amedee, and to the photographer, Mr. Cleve LeBlanc, Jr.

CLEVELAND P. LE BLANC, SR.   LEE ANNA (LANDRY) LE BLANC

SHIRLEY (BRAUD) LE BLANC   LESLIE J. LE BLANC

TABLE OF CONTENTS

PART I

DANIEL LE BLANC and FRANÇOISE GAUDET

I. Daniel LeBlanc born about 1626 in de Martaize, France married about 1645 Francoise GAUDET (daughter of Jean Gaudet) born 1575

   A. Francoise LeBlanc born 1647 Port Royal, Acadia married 1671 Martin BLANCHARD (son of Jean Blanchard and Rodegonde LAMBERT)

      1. Francoise Blanchard born 1672 married 1692 Jean DOUCET (son of Pierre Doucet and Henriette PELLERET)
      2. Marie Blanchard born 1674
      3. Rene Blanchard born 1677 married c. 1703 Anne LANDRY (daughter of Rene Landry and Marie BERNARD)

         a. Rene Blanchard born 1705 married July 9, 1726 Marguerite TERRIOT
         b. Marie Blanchard born August 28, 1709 married November 5, 1731 Joseph TRAHAN
         c. Francois Blanchard born 1710
         d. Joseph Blanchard born January 6, 1712
         e. Francoise Blanche Blanchard born 1713
         f. Etienne Blanchard born 1719
         g. Rosalie Blanchard married Pierre MELANCON

   B. Jacque LeBlanc born 1651 Port Royal, Acadia and settled at St. Charles aux Mines, Grand Pre married 1673 Catherine HEBERT (daughter of Etienne Hebert of de Martaize, France and Marie GAUDET)

      1. Jean LeBlanc born 1674 married 1694 Marguerite RICHARD. Jean died June 10, 1747 at age 74 (SGA)

         a. Claude-Andre LeBlanc born 1696 married c. 1720 Madeleine BOUDROT (daughter of Francois Boudrot Madeleine BELIVEAU) This family at Isle St. Jean in 1752

            i. Joseph LeBlanc born 1722
            ii. Anne LeBlanc born 1725 married July 18, 1746 Claude TRAHAN (son of Alexandre Trahan and Marguerite LE JEUNE)
            iii. Marguerite LeBlanc born 1726; baptized December 17, 1726. (SGA)
            iv. Marie Josephe LeBlanc born 1728
            v. Andre LeBlanc born October 21, 1729; baptized October 31, 1729 (SGA)
            vi. Madeleine LeBlanc born 1732
            vii. Elizabeth LeBlanc born 1733
            viii. Charles LeBlanc born 1734
            ix. Genevieve LeBlanc born 1741
            x. Paul LeBlanc born 1742

         b. Pierre LeBlanc born 1699 married October 14, 1721 at Grand Pre Anne TERRIOT (daughter of Jean Terriot and Jeanne LANDRY)

   i. Francoise LeBlanc born November 7, 1723 married January 11, 1745 (SGA) Belonie BOURG (son of Alexandre Bourg and Marguerite MELANCON)
   ii. Marie Josephe LeBlanc baptized December 7, 1726 (SGA)
   iii. Anne LeBlanc baptized December 17, 1728 (SGA)
   iv. Agnes LeBlanc born August 30, 1732
   v. Marguerite Euphrosie LeBlanc born 1734
   vi. Pierre LeBlanc born May 6, 1736
   vii. Elizabeth LeBlanc born May 6, 1736
   viii. Charles LeBlanc born 1738
   ix. Anselme LeBlanc born October 16, 1740
   x. Joseph LeBlanc baptized February 17, 1731 (SGA)
   xi. Jean Pierre LeBlanc baptized April 11, 1726 (SGA)

c. Anne LeBlanc born 1701 married 1723 Joseph BOUDROT (son of Charles Boudrot and Marie CORPORON)
d. Francois LeBlanc born 1705 married c. 1728 Marie LA BAUVE (daughter of Rene LaBauve and Anne LE JEUNE) This family resided at Grand Pre

   i. Felicite LeBlanc born 1730
   ii. Simon LeBlanc born 1732
   iii. Joseph LeBlanc born January 17, 1735
   iv. Felicite LeBlanc born 1736
   v. Pierre LeBlanc born 1738
   vi. Anastasie LeBlanc born February 27, 1740 (SGA)
   vii. Marie Marguerite LeBlanc born April 14, 1744 (SGA)

e. Jean LeBlanc born 1707 married c. 1729 Marie TERRIOT (daughter of Claude Terriot and Agnes AUCOIN)

   i. Marie Josephe LeBlanc born October 6, 1730 (SGA)
   ii. Thomas LeBlanc born 1732
   iii. Joseph LeBlanc born 1734
   iv. Jean Baptiste LeBlanc born 1736
   v. Jean Claude LeBlanc born 1738
   vi. Marie LeBlanc born 1740

f. Jacques LeBlanc born 1709 married June 18, 1731 (SGA) Henriette DUPUIS (daughter of Martin Dupuis and Marie LANDRY)

   i. Marguerite Blanche LeBlanc born 1732
   ii. Joseph LeBlanc born 1734

g. Paul LeBlanc born February 20, 1711
h. Michel LeBlanc born October 7, 1720 married 1741 Marie Josephe TRAHAN

   i. Marie Josephe LeBlanc born January 12, 1742
   ii. Elizabeth LeBlanc born March 11, 1744

2

   iii. Joseph LeBlanc born October 28, 1746 married
     June 18, 1781 Marguerite LANDRY
    iv. Marguerite LeBlanc born 1748

  i. Charles LeBlanc born 1722 married 1744 Magdeleine
   VINCENT

    i. Charles LeBlanc born 1746

  j. Marie LeBlanc born February 17, 1711 married
   Charles GRANGER

2. Marguerite LeBlanc born 1675 married 1732 Francois
 CORMIER (son of Thomas Cormier and Magdeleine
 GIROUARD)

  a. Marie Cormier born 1693
  b. Pierre Cormier born 1695 married November 22, 1718
   Marie Anne CYR (daughter of Jean Cyr and Francoise
   MELANCON)

    i. Madeleine Cormier born 1719
    ii. Pierre Cormier born 1722
   iii. Jean Francois Cormier born 1724
    iv. Jean Baptiste Cormier born 1726
    v. Jean Cormier born 1732
    vi. Francoise Cormier born 1732
   vii. Francois Cormier born 1735
   viii. Rosalie Cormier born 1740
    ix. Pierre Cormier born 1741
    x. Marie Blanche Cormier born 1745

  c. Paul Cormier born 1696
  d. Marguerite Cormier born 1697
  e. Marie Cormier born 1699
  f. Anne Cormier born 1700
  g. Cecile Cormier born 1706
  h. Catherine Cormier born 1708
  i. Francois Cormier born 1710 married 1730 Anne CYR
   (daughter of Jean Cyr and Francoise MELANCON)

    i. Francois Cormier born 1731
    ii. Joseph Cormier born 1732
   iii. Marie Cormier born 1738
    iv. Pierre Cormier born 1740
    v. Jean Baptiste Cormier born 1742

  j. Joseph Cormier born 1712 married
        (1) November 24, 1733 Francoise
          CYR (daughter of Jean Cyr and
          Francoise MELANCON)

    i. Joseph Cormier born 1734
    ii. Jean Cormier born 1737

        (2) 1739 Marie ARSENAULT

   iii. Marie Josephe Cormier born 1740

        iv. Francois Cormier born 1741
         v. Marguerite Cormier born 1743
        vi. Rosalie Cormier born 1746
       vii. Osite Cormier born 1748

    k. Jean Cormier born 1718 married November 25, 1740
        at Beaubassin Madeleine HEBERT (daughter of
        Pierre Hebert and Marie Josephe BELON)

         i. Joseph Cormier born 1741
        ii. Marie Madeleine Cormier born 1746

3. Jacques LeBlanc born 1677 married 1707 Elizabeth
    BOUDROT (daughter of Charles Boudrot and Renee
    BOURG)

    a. Joseph LeBlanc born November 10, 1718 married
        November 26, 1742 at Grande Pre Magdeleine
        MELANCON (daughter of Paul Melancon and Marie
        TERRIOT)

         i. Etienne LeBlanc born September 2, 1743 mar-
             ried November 26, 1778 Marie-Amable RIVARD-
             LORANGER (daughter of Joseph Loranger and
             Genevieve COTE) Etienne died December 20,
             1834

             a) Etienne LeBlanc born 1779
             b) Marie-Amable LeBlanc born 1781
             c) Marguerite LeBlanc born 1783
             d) Jean Francois LeBlanc born 1785
             e) Charles LeBlanc born 1786
             f) Alexis LeBlanc born 1788
             g) Joseph LeBlanc born 1790
             h) Jean LeBlanc born 1795

        ii. Anselme LeBlanc born April 5, 1745
       iii. Marie Madeleine LeBlanc born February 4, 1748

    b. Pierre LeBlanc born 1719 married October 4, 1745
        Marie Madeleine BABIN (daughter of Joseph Babin
        and Angelique LANDRY)

         i. Marie Josephe LeBlanc born June 18, 1746
             married Pierre LANDRY (son of Pierre Landry
             Marie Josephe LE BLANC)
        ii. Marguerite Modeste LeBlanc born October 6,
             1747 married Germain BERGERON
       iii. Elizabeth LeBlanc born 1756
        iv. Francoise LeBlanc born 1756
         v. Charles LeBlanc born 1759
        vi. Anne Marie LeBlanc born 1762
       vii. Marie Suzanne LeBlanc born 1764
      viii. Anselme LeBlanc born 1767

    c. Jean Jacques LeBlanc born 1722 married 1755
        Marie HEON (daughter of Charles Heon and Anne
        CLEMENCEAU)

                          4

```
      i. Marie Victoire LeBlanc born 1758
     ii. Etienne LeBlanc born 1759
    iii. Marie Marthe LeBlanc born 1761
     iv. Francois Xavier LeBlanc born 1762
      v. Joseph Alexis LeBlanc born 1763
     vi. David LeBlanc born 1768
    vii. Amable LeBlanc born 1770
   viii. Marie Francoise LeBlanc born 1774
```

d. Marie LeBlanc born 1712 married November 18, 1737
   Paul AUCOIN (son of Martin Aucoin and Catherine
   TERRIO)

```
      i. Olivier Aucoin born 1738
     ii. Joseph Aucoin born 1740
    iii. Marie Aucoin born 1742
     iv. Pierre Paul Aucoin born 1743
      v. Mathurin Amand Aucoin born 1746
     vi. Jean Charles Aucoin born 1748
```

4. Marie LeBlanc born 1678 married 1700 Alexis CORMIER
   (son of Thomas Cormier and Madeleine GIROUARD)

a. Marie Cormier born c. 1700 married October 24,
   1716 Michel BOURG

```
      i. Michel Bourg born 1719
     ii. Pierre Bourg born 1722
    iii. Anne Bourg born 1725
     iv. Joseph Bourg born 1727
      v. Abraham Bourg born 1729
     vi. Jacques Bourg born 1732
    vii. Marie Bourg born 1733
   viii. Jean Bourg born 1734
     ix. Benony Bourg born 1735
      x. Madeleine Bourg born 1738
     xi. Pierre Bourg born 1739
```

b. Pierre Cormier born 1704 married Marguerite CYR
   (daughter of Jean Cyr and Francoise MELANCON)

```
      i. Francoise Cormier born 1724
     ii. Anne Cormier born 1728
    iii. Marie Josephe Cormier born 1733
     iv. Marguerite Cormier born 1734
      v. Jean Cormier born 1735
     vi. Rosalie Cormier born 1738
    vii. Pierre Cormier born 1742
   viii. Marie Madeleine Cormier born 1746
```

c. Madeleine Cormier born 1705 married February 16,
   1718 Charles BOURGEOIS
d. Agnes Cormier born 1706 married c. 1724 Paul CYR
   (son of Jean Cyr and Francoise MELANCON)

```
      i. Marie Cyr born 1724
```

       ii.   Jean Cyr born 1725
      iii.   Marguerite Cyr born 1727
       iv.   Francoise Cyr born 1734
        v.   Marie Josephe Cyr born 1741
       vi.   Francoise Marie Cyr born 1742
      vii.   Agnes Cyr born 1745

    e.   Marguerite Cormier born 1708
    f.   Jean Baptiste Cormier born 1710 married c. 1734
         Marie TERRIOT

         i.   Alexis Cormier born 1738
        ii.   Joseph Cormier born 1740
       iii.   Jean Cormier born 1743

    g.   Anne Cormier born 1712

5. Antoine LeBlanc born 1680
6. Anne LeBlanc born 1681 married c. 1692 Pierre BRAUD
    (son of Vincent Braud and Marie BOURG)

    a.   Joseph Braud born 1706 married c. 1738 Elizabeth
         THIBODEAUX (daughter of Michel Thibodeaux and
         Agnes DUGAS)

         i.   Marguerite Braud born 1738
        ii.   Joseph Braud born 1739 married c. 1761 Marie
              Anne PICOT
       iii.   Amand Braud born 1740 married c. 1764
              Madeleine DUPUY
        iv.   Joseph Samuel Braud born 1742
         v.   Jean-Anselme Braud born 1748

    b.   Catherine Braud born February 7, 1708 married
         September 30, 1732 Pierre SURET
    c.   Isabelle Braud born February 17, 1712 married
         1730 Jean BABINEAU dit Deslauriers (son of
         Nicholas Babineau and Marguerite GRANGER)

         i.   Marie Babineau born 1732
        ii.   Marguerite Babineau born 1733
       iii.   Isabelle Babineau born 1735
        iv.   Paul Babineau born 1740 married

                         (1)   July 21, 1768 Marguerite
                               RICHARD
                         (2)   Ludivine BELLIVEAU

         v.   Jean Babineau born 1747 married 1770 Anne
              BASTARCHE
        vi.   Sylvain Babineau born 1750
       vii.   Dominique Babineau born 1753

d. Pierre Braud born 1713 married c. 1745 Marie
    Josephe DUPUIS (daughter of Germain Dupuis and
    Marie GRANGER)

    i.   Marguerite Braud born 1745
    ii.   Madeleine Braud born 1748
    iii. Elizabeth Braud born 1755
    iv.   Joseph Braud born 1759
    v.   Jean Baptiste Braud born 1760

e. Paul Braud born 1717 married c. 1742 Marie Josephe
    LANDRY (daughter of Francois Landry and Marie
    Josephe DOUCET)

    i.   Joseph Braud born 1743
    ii.   Jean Braud born 1745
    iii. Anne Braud born 1747
    iv.   Marie Braud born 1751
    v.   Jean Baptiste Braud born 1755
    vi.   Elizabeth Braud born 1757

f. Brigitte Braud born 1719
g. Amand Braud born 1721 married February 4, 1743
    Madeleine LE BLANC(daughter of Francois LeBlanc
    and Jeanne HEBERT)

    i.   Anne Marie Braud born 1746
    ii.   Jean Baptiste Braud born 1748
    iii. Joseph Richard Braud born 1750
    iv.   Madeleine Braud born 1752
    v.   Marguerite Braud born 1754
    vi.   Marie Anne Ange Braud born 1758
    vii. Joseph Amand Braud born 1761

7. Catherine LeBlanc born 1682 married c. 1703 Pierre
CORMIER (son of Thomas Cormier and Madeleine GIROUARD)

a. Pierre Cormier born 1704 married July 17, 1730 at
    Grande Pre Cecile THIBODEAU (daughter of Jean
    Thibodeau and Marguerite HEBERT)

    i.   Jean Baptiste Cormier born 1732
    ii.   Pierre Cormier born 1733
    iii. Francois Cormier born 1738
    iv.   Michel Cormier born 1741
    v.   Marie Josephe Cormier born 1742
    vi.   Charles Cormier born 1744
    vii. Marie Cecile Cormier born 1745
    viii. Jacques Cormier born 1749
    ix.   Amand Cormier born 1750

b. Catherine Cormier born 1705 married 1725 Francois
    LANDRY (son of Antoine Landry and Marie Blanche
    LE BLANC)

c. Jean Baptiste Cormier born 1708 married August 11,
    1733 at Beaubassin Madeleine RICHARD (daughter of
    Martin Richard and Marguerite BOURG)

        i.   Jean Baptiste Cormier born 1734
       ii.   Marie Anne Cormier born 1736

   d.   Marguerite Cormier born 1718 married January 26,
        1734 at Beaubassin Jean CYR (son of Jean Cyr
        and Francoise MELANCON)

        i.   Joseph Cormier born 1735 married c. 1758
             Marguerite Blanche THIBODEAU
       ii.   Jean Baptiste Cormier born 1735 married
             February 12, 1767 Judith GUERETTE
      iii.   Paul Cormier born 1741
       iv.   Jacques Cormier born 1743
        v.   Pierre Cormier born 1744
       vi.   Francois Cormier born 1747 married February 19,
             1790 Marie Anne GUILBAUT
      vii.   Olivier Cormier born 1755
     viii.   Antoine Cormier born 1768

   e.   Francois Cormier born 1719 married July 12, 1742
        Anne CHIASSON (daughter of Jacques Chiasson and
        Marie ARSENAULT)

        i.   Basile Cormier born 1743
       ii.   Pierre Cormier born 1745
      iii.   Jean Cormier born 1747
       iv.   Guillaume Cormier born 1750

   f.   Marie Agnes Cormier born 1722 married c. 1746
        Joseph TERRIOT (son of Claude Terriot and
        Marguerite CORMIER)

        i.   Jacques Leon Terriot born 1747
       ii.   Anselme Terriot born 1748
      iii.   Charles Terriot born 1750
       iv.   Joseph Pierre Terriot born 1751
        v.   Marguerite Terriot born 1752
       vi.   Cecile Terriot born 1755
      vii.   Marie Anne Terriot born 1757
     viii.   Catherine Terriot born 1759
       ix.   Antoine Terriot born 1770

   g.   Marie Cormier born 1723 married March 13, 1743 at
        Beaubassin Claude BABIN (son of Claude Babin and
        Marguerite DUPUIS)

        i.   Osite Babin born 1745
       ii.   Claude Marie Babin born 1758
      iii.   Charles Andre Babin born 1760
       iv.   Augustin Amable Babin born 1762
        v.   Marie Therese Babin born 1764
       vi.   Jean Marie Babin born 1768

   h.   Anne Cormier married November 14, 1740 at Beau-
        bassin Antoine LANDRY (son of Jean Landry and
        Madeleine MELANCON)

      i.   Marie Landry born 1741
     ii. Jean Baptiste Landry born 1743
   iii. Josette Landry born 1745
    iv. Jacques Landry born 1746
     v. Anne Landry born 1748
    vi. Joseph Landry born 1750
   vii. Anastasie Landry born 1752

8. Genevieve LeBlanc born 1684
9. Pierre LeBlanc born 1685 married November 15, 1718 at Grande Pre Marie LANDRY (daughter of Rene Landry and Anne TERRIOT)

   a. Marie Madeleine LeBlanc born 1719 married February 16, 1745 Pierre MELANCON (son of Philippe Melancon and Marie DUGAS)
   b. Pierre LeBlanc born 1721 married 1742 Elizabeth HEBERT

      i.   Jean Baptiste LeBlanc born August 31, 1743
     ii. Pierre LeBlanc born 1744
   iii. Marguerite LeBlanc born February 1, 1745
    iv. Marie LeBlanc born January 5, 1747

   c. Jean Baptiste LeBlanc born 1723

10. Magdeleine LeBlanc born 1686 married October 12, 1711 Michel HACHE-GALLENT (son of Michel Hache and Anne CORMIER)

   a. Marie Hache born 1712
   b. Michel Hache born 1713 married
               (1) 1738 Anne Marie GRAVOIS (daughter of Joseph Gravois and Marie SIRE)

      i.   Michel Hache born 1738 married August 29, 1768 Anne MELANCON
     ii. Marie Josephe Hache born 1740
   iii. Felicite Hache born 1745
    iv. Reine Hache born 1748

               (2) June 2, 1749 Madeleine BLANCHARD (daughter of Rene Blanchard and Madeleine SAVOIE)

   c. Jean Hache born 1716 married 1740 Marguerite GRAVOIS (daughter of Joseph Gravois and Marie SIRE)

      i.   Marie Joseph Hache born 1741
     ii. Anne Hache born 1743
   iii. Marie Blanche Hache born 1745
    iv. Raphael Hache born 1748
     v. Marguerite Hache born February 15, 1760

   d. Madeleine Hache-Gallent born 1718 married 1738 Pierre SAULNIER (son of Pierre Saulnier and Madeleine COMMEAU)

  i. Anne Saulnier born 1739
  ii. Marie Madeleine Saulnier born 1739
 iii. Marie Saulnier born 1742
  iv. Francoise Saulnier born 1743

 e. Marie Anne Hache-Gallent born 1720 married

     (1) August 11, 1734 at Beaubassin Jean Baptiste SAVOIE (son of Francois Savoie and Marie RICHARD)

  i. Rosalie Savoie born 1741
  ii. Madeleine Savoie born 1745
 iii. Jean Baptiste Savoie born 1748
  iv. Francoise Savoie born 1750
  v. Madeleine Savoie born 1751
  vi. Pierre Savoie born 1752

     (2) July 20, 1744 Francois DOUCET (son of Francois Doucet and Marie POIRIER)

  i. Francois Doucet born 1745 married January 27, 1777 Genevieve BEAUDET (daughter of Joseph Michel Beaudet and Angelique BELANGER)

   a) Francois Doucet born 1778
   b) Francois d'Assise Doucet born 1779
   c) Marie Doucet born 1781
   d) Paul Doucet born 1783
   e) Theotiste Doucet born 1785
   f) Joseph Doucet born 1788
   g) Jean Baptiste Doucet born 1791
   h) Andre Doucet born 1793
   i) Marie Julie Doucet born 1796
   j) Marie Genevieve Doucet born 1798
   k) Angele Doucet born 1801

 f. Marguerite Hache-Gallent born 1722
 g. Francois Hache-Gallent born 1724
 h. Joseph Hache-Gallent born 1726
 i. Pierre Hache-Gallent born 1728 married 1748 Marguerite HEBERT (daughter of Pierre Hebert and Madeleine GAUDET)

  i. Pierre Hache born 1763
  ii. Marie Louise Hache born 1766

 j. Joseph Michel Hache-Gallent born 1731

11. Rene LeBlanc born 1686 at Grande Pre married c. 1708 Jeanne LANDRY (daughter of Claude Landry and Anne THIBODEAU)

 a. Claire LeBlanc born March 19, 1709; died November 21, 1725

b. Claude LeBlanc born August 8, 1710 married February 12, 1738 at Grand Pre Judith BENOIT (daughter of Pierre Benoit and Elizabeth LE JUGE)

    i. Marie LeBlanc born July 4, 1739
    ii. Charles LeBlanc born November 5, 1740
    iii. Marguerite LeBlanc born December 3, 1741
    iv. Madeleine LeBlanc born March 10, 1743
    v. Joseph LeBlanc born June 5, 1744
    vi. Anastasie LeBlanc born January 27, 1746
    vii. Jean Baptiste LeBlanc born July 4, 1748

c. Marie LeBlanc born 1713
d. Jean Baptiste LeBlanc born 1715 married July 31, 1731 at Grande Pre Marguerite HEBERT (daughter of Rene Hebert and Marie BOUDROT)

    i. Jean Mathurin LeBlanc baptized December 11, 1742
    ii. Pierre LeBlanc born August 21, 1746 married

        (1) October 19, 1772 Madeleine TRAHAN (daughter of Charles Trahan and Anne LANDRY)

        a) Madeleine LeBlanc born 1773
        b) Joseph LeBlanc born 1775
        c) Marguerite LeBlanc born 1777
        d) Pierre LeBlanc born 1779
        e) Elizabeth LeBlanc born 1782
        f) Genevieve LeBlanc born 1784
        g) Marie Anne LeBlanc born 1787
        h) Jean Baptiste LeBlanc born 1788
        i) Charles LeBlanc born 1791

        (2) March 31, 1801 Francoise GERMAIN (daughter of Joseph Germain and Francoise GUILBAUT)

        j) Francois LeBlanc born 1802
        k) Pierre LeBlanc born 1803

    iii. Jean LeBlanc born June 5, 1748
    iv. Marie Josephe LeBlanc born 1750
    v. Joseph LeBlanc born 1754
    vi. Marguerite LeBlanc born 1756
    vii. Elizabeth LeBlanc born 1758
    viii. Marie Anne LeBlanc born 1760
    ix. Madeleine LeBlanc born 1762
    x. Honore LeBlanc born 1764
    xi. Judith LeBlanc born 1766
    xii. Rosalie LeBlanc born 1769

e. Charles LeBlanc born 1717 married

                (1)   September 27, 1745 (SGA) Anne
                       BOUDROT (daughter of Claude
                       Boudrot and Catherine MEUNIER)

      i.   Madeleine LeBlanc born 1746
     ii.   Charles LeBlanc born May 15, 1748
   iii.   Marie LeBlanc born 1749

                (2)   1758 at Southhampton, England
                       Madeleine GAUTEROT (daughter
                       of Pierre Gauterot and Marie
                       BUJEAU)

     iv.   Joseph LeBlanc born 1759
      v.   Jean Baptiste LeBlanc born 1760
     vi.   Simon LeBlanc born 1762
    vii.   Francois LeBlanc born 1763
   viii.   Marguerite LeBlanc born 1764

f.   Francois LeBlanc born 1717 married c. 1745 at
     Beaubassin Madeleine CORMIER (daughter of Germain
     Cormier and Marie LE BLANC)

      i.   Marie Josephe LeBlanc born 1746
     ii.   Osite LeBlanc born 1748

g.   Pierre LeBlanc born 1718 married October 24, 1740
     at Grande Pre Claire BOUDROT (daughter of Claude
     Boudrot and Catherine MEUNIER)

      i.   Pierre LeBlanc baptized October 6, 1741
     ii.   Marie Blanche LeBlanc born June 10, 1743
   iii.   Elizabeth LeBlanc born July 8, 1745
   iv.   Joseph LeBlanc born April 18, 1747

h.   Marguerite LeBlanc born 1721 married Charles
     HEBERT (son of Rene Hebert and Marie BOUDROT)
i.   Rene LeBlanc born 1722 married c. 1746 Marie
     BABIN (daughter of Pierre Babin and Madeleine
     BOURG)

      i.   Charles LeBlanc born 1750
     ii.   Joseph LeBlanc born 1752
   iii.   Jean LeBlanc born 1756
   iv.   Marie LeBlanc born 1758

j.   Olivier LeBlanc born 1724 married November 23,
     1747 at Grande Pre Marie Josephe AUCOIN (daughter
     of Martin Aucoin and Elizabeth BOUDROT)
k.   Joseph LeBlanc born 1726 married

                (1)   August 2, 1750 at Grande Pre
                       Marguerite TRAHAN (daughter of
                       Pierre Trahan and Madeleine
                       COMEAU)

      i.   Jean Baptiste LeBlanc born 1752
     ii.   Marguerite Olive LeBlanc born 1754

                              (2) January 28, 1758 Anne HEBERT
                                  (daughter of Jean Hebert and
                                  Marguerite TRAHAN)

   iii. Marguerite Blanche LeBlanc born 1765
    iv. Marie Francoise LeBlanc born 1767
     v. Joseph Marin LeBlanc born 1768
    vi. Simon LeBlanc born 1771
   vii. Louis LeBlanc born 1771
  viii. Marie LeBlanc born 1771

1. Jean Baptiste LeBlanc married July 3, 1741
   Marguerite HEBERT (daughter of Rene Hebert and
   Marie BOUDROT)
m. Marie Madeleine LeBlanc married

                              (1) October 3, 1735 Michel PAERIE
                                  (son of Pierre Paerie and
                                  Agnes CORMIER)

                              (2) January 13, 1739 Charles HEBERT
                                  (son of Rene Hebert and Marie
                                  BOUDROT)

    i. Joseph Hilarin Hebert born 1739

                              (3) October 8, 1748 at Grande Pre
                                  Paul BENOIT (son of Paul
                                  Benoit and Anne TRAHAN)

   ii. Joseph Benoit born 1749
  iii. Agatha Benoit born 1751

n. Lucien LeBlanc born April 12, 1724

12. Francois LeBlanc born 1688 married September 19, 1712
    Marguerite BOUDROT (daughter of Claude Boudrot and
    Anne Marie THIBODEAU)

a. Francois LeBlanc born 1713 married 1738 Isabelle
   DUGAS. Francois died August 18, 1790.

    i. Marie LeBlanc born September 15, 1739; died
       August 5, 1744
   ii. Marie LeBlanc born March 2, 1942
  iii. Elizabeth LeBlanc born April 2, 1744
   iv. Francois LeBlanc born 1747
    v. Jean Baptiste LeBlanc born 1749
   vi. Marguerite LeBlanc born 1750
  vii. Francoise LeBlanc born 1756
 viii. Pierre LeBlanc born 1758
   ix. Anne LeBlanc born 1760
    x. Madeleine LeBlanc born 1764

b. Marie LeBlanc born 1714 married Paul AUCOIN
c. Joseph LeBlanc born November 1718 married 1740
   Madeleine GIROUARD (daughter of Pierre Girouard
   and Marie DOIRON)

     i.   Basile LeBlanc born 1741
    ii.   Joseph LeBlanc born 1743
  iii.   Marie LeBlanc born 1745
   iv.   Elizabeth LeBlanc born January 11, 1748
     v.   Marguerite LeBlanc born 1749
   vi.   Madeleine LeBlanc born 1751

d. Elizabeth LeBlanc born February 26, 1721
e. Charles LeBlanc born May 17, 1723 married c. 1750
    Marie BARILLOT

     i.   Pierre LeBlanc born 1751
    ii.   Joseph LeBlanc born 1753
  iii.   Marie LeBlanc born 1755
   iv.   Marguerite LeBlanc born 1759
     v.   Annette LeBlanc born 1760
   vi.   Isabelle LeBlanc born 1761
  vii.   Anne LeBlanc born 1762
 viii.   Charles LeBlanc born 1765
   ix.   Francois LeBlanc born 1766
    x.   Anastasie LeBlanc born 1769

f. Pierre LeBlanc born August 18, 1725 married
    c. 1760 Marie BOURGEOIS dit Lafond (daughter of
    Honore Bourgeois and Marie Jeanne RICHARD)

     i.   Marie LeBlanc born 1761
    ii.   Pierre LeBlanc born 1763
  iii.   Anne LeBlanc born 1765
   iv.   Etienne LeBlanc born 1767

g. Etienne (Antoine) LeBlanc baptized February 9,
    1728
h. Amand LeBlanc born January 7, 1731
i. Jacques LeBlanc born November 30, 1732 married
    c. 1758 in Philadelphia Natalie BRAULT

     i.   Marie LeBlanc born 1759
    ii.   Simon LeBlanc born 1760 married c. 1785
         Madeleine RICHARD

        a)   Timothee LeBlanc born 1788 married c. 1808
            Barbe GAUDET

  iii.   Isabella LeBlanc born 1762
   iv.   Marguerite LeBlanc born 1763
     v.   Anne LeBlanc born 1766
   vi.   Jacques LeBlanc born 1767
  vii.   Natalie LeBlanc born 1768

j. Simon LeBlanc born 1734 married c. 1771 Madeleine
    COMEAU

     i.   Marcelline LeBlanc born 1772

k. Marguerite LeBlanc born February 13, 1737
l. Elizabeth LeBlanc born 1739

13. Ignace LeBlanc born 1692
14. Bernard LeBlanc born 1694 married February 7, 1714 Marie BOURG (daughter of Alexandre Bourg and Marguerite MELANCON)

    a. Marie Madeleine LeBlanc born c. 1719

    b. Anne LeBlanc born c. 1723 married October 19, 1743 Charles LANDRY (son of Antoine Landry and Marie Blanche LE BLANC)

        i. Marguerite Landry born July 13, 1748

    c. Joseph LeBlanc born 1724 at Grande Pre married 1747 Marie Josephe DAIGRE (daughter of Olivier Daigre and Francoise GRANGER)

        i. Joseph LeBlanc born 1748

    d. Marguerite LeBlanc born February 13, 1728 at Grande Pre married July 16, 1748 Abraham DUGAS (son of Joseph Dugas and Marguerite RICHARD)

        i. Marie Dugas born 1749
        ii. Marguerite Dugas born 1750
      iii. Anne Dugas born 1752
       iv. Frnacoise Dugas born 1754
        v. Louise Dugas born 1756
      vi. Angelique Dugas born 1758

    e. Marie Madeleine LeBlanc born 1734
    f. Pierre LeBlanc born August 21, 1737

C. Etienne LeBlanc born 1656 in Acadia
D. Rene LeBlanc born 1657 married 1679 at Port Royal, Acadia Anne BOURGEOIS (daughter of Jacque Bourgeois and Jeanne TRAHAN) Rene died in 1734 at age 77; Anne died December 28, 1747 at age 87. Rene, Anne and their family moved to Grande Pre in 1682.

    1. Jacques LeBlanc born 1680 married October 8, 1702 Catherine LANDRY (daughter of Rene Landry and Marie BERNARD) Jacques died October, 1755; Catherine died Easter, 1754.

        a. Anne LeBlanc born 1704 married January 16, 1719 Jean GAUTEROT (son of Claude Gauterot and Marie TERRIOT) Jean died November 13, 1747

           i. Anne Gauterot born 1721
           ii. Euphrosie Gauterot born 1724 married January 23, 1741 Pierre GRANGER (son of Pierre Granger and Elizabeth GUILBAUD)
          iii. Marguerite Gauterot born 1729
           iv. Francois Gauterot born 1733
            v. Rose Gauterot born 1736

        b. Jean Jacques LeBlanc born 1705 married 1728 Madeleine TERRIOT (daughter of Germain Terriot and Anne BROUSSARD)

15

      i. Paul Honore LeBlanc born September 10, 1729
     ii. Joseph LeBlanc born January 18, 1731
    iii. Marie LeBlanc born 1732
    iv. Desire LeBlanc born February 16, 1734; died
         February 18, 1734 at age 2 days
      v. Anne LeBlanc born February 16, 1734
     vi. Francois LeBlanc born November 2, 1736
    vii. Jean Baptiste LeBlanc born December 20, 1740
   viii. Augustin Marie LeBlanc born June 5, 1742
     ix. Marie Blanche LeBlanc born April 1, 1744
      x. Ursule LeBlanc born October 21, 1739

c. Marie LeBlanc born 1706 married October 8, 1725
  at Grande Pre Charles GAUTEROT (son of Claude
  Gauterot and Marie TERRIOT)

      i. Joseph Gauterot born 1728
     ii. Paul Honore Gauterot born 1730
    iii. Amand Paul Gauterot born 1732
    iv. Charles Gauterot born 1734
     v. Simon Gauterot born 1736 married Magdelena
       BRO (daughter of Ambroise Braud and Marie
       Magdelaine MICHEL)

       a) Louis Gautreaux born 1766 married Janu-
         ary 2, 1786 in St. James Parish Marie
         Rose LE BLANC

          i) Pedro Pablo Gautreaux born December 5,
             1793 in St. James Parish
         ii) Maria Apollonia Gautreaux born Janu-
            ary, 1796
        iii) Maria Angela Gautreaux born March 9,
            1798
         iv) Margarita Domitilia Gautreaux born
            July 9, 1800
          v) Urbino Anatolio Gautreaux born
            March 15, 1803
         vi) Maria Doralize Gautreaux born May 12,
            1805

       b) Jean Baptiste Gautreaux born 1768 married

           (1) January 21, 1788 in St. James
              Parish Magdalen BRO (daughter
              of Jean Carlos Bro and Maria
              BENOIT)

          i) Clemence Gautreaux born July 15, 1796
            married February 22, 1814 Paul THIBO-
            DEAUX (son of Jean Charles Thibodeaux
            and Marie LANDRY) Clemence died Janu-
            ary 5, 1849

       c) Charles Gautreaux baptized June 3, 1770
         in St. James married

   (1) February 9, 1790, St. James,
     Louisiana, Marie Martha
     RICHARD (daughter of Damant
     Richard and Maria BRAUD)

 i) Valentine Gautreaux married May 9,
   1840, Ascension Parish, Eloise
   MARCHAND (daughter of Jean Baptiste
   Marchand and Eugenie VICNAIR)
 ii) Jose Perfecto Gautreaux born October 12, 1803, Ascension Parish
 iii) Marie Aime Gautreaux married May 15,
   1821, Ascension Parish, Francois
   LUCINTY (son of Vincent Lucinty and
   Therese MALONI) Native of Rome, Italy
 iv) J. Louis Gautreaux married October 27,
   1829, Ascension Parish, Marguerite
   LE BLANC (daughter of Sylvain LeBlanc
   and Rosalie LE BLANC)

   (2) January 26, 1818, St. James
     Parish, Constance MELANCON
     (daughter of Jacques Melancon
     and Elizabeth LANDRY)

d) Simon Gautreaux born August 22, 1772
  married

   (1) December 29, 1793, St. James
     Parish, Marie DUHON (daughter
     of Jean Duhon and Anne LE BLANC)
     Marie died December 13, 1808,
     Ascension Parish

 i) Marie Marcelline Gautreaux married
   April 29, 1811 Manuel Marcus MELANCON
   (son of Jacques Melancon and Elizabeth HENRY)
 ii) Alexandre Gautreaux married January 26,
   1829 Euphemie LE BLANC (daughter of
   Donat LeBlanc and Marie Josef MELANCON)
 iii) Elize Gautreaux married October, 1831
   Joseph HERNANDEZ
 iv) Maria Gautreaux born September 15,
   1802
 v) Marie Louise Gautreaux born May 12,
   1803

   (2) February 25, 1811 Henriette
     MELANCON (daughter of Jacques
     Melancon and Elizabeth LANDRY)

e) Marie Magdelena Gautreaux baptized January 1, 1775 married April 20, 1801
  Charles GAUTREAUX (son of Joseph Gautreaux
  and Anna PITRE) Native of France

     i) Urasie Modeste Gautreaux born 1805,
        Ascension Parish
    ii) Modeste Gautreaux amrried May 3, 1824,
        Ascension Parish, August ROGER (son
        of Joseph Roger and Magdelaine BABIN)

f) Anastasie Gautreaux married February 17,
   1800, St. James Parish, Jean Manuel BREAUX
   (son of Jean Charles Breaux and Marie
   BENOIT)

     i) Simon Athanase Breaux married Septem-
        ber 2, 1839, St. Gabriel, Louisiana,
        Marie Seraphine BROUSSARD (daughter
        of Firmin Broussard and Marie BREAUX)
        widow of J. B. KLING
    ii) Jean Charles Breaux married June 19,
        1843, Convent, Louisiana, Azelie
        GAUTREAUX (daughter of Urbain Gau-
        treaux and Marcellite GAUDIN)

g) Amand Gautreaux born 1779; died May 30,
   1828 at age 49

        (1) November 26, 1798, St. James
           Parish, Marie Francoise LANDRY
           (daughter of Marino Landry and
           Pelagie LANDRY)

     i) Francoise Azelie Gautreaux born Au-
        bust 29, 1802 married

        (1) May 7, 1827 Casimere GAUDIN
           (son of Edouard Gaudin and
           Marie Magdelaine LANDRY)

        (2) March 25, 1841 Joseph BOURK
           (son of Made Bourk and Rosalie
           MIRE)

    ii) Francoise Arthemise Gautreaux born
        January 1, 1800 married February 26,
        1821 Jean TERRIO (son of Oliver Terrio
        and Marie AUCOIN) Francoise died
        December 18, 1827
   iii) Marie Henriette Gautreaux born July 21,
        1805 married February 26, 1827 Joseph
        MELANCON (son of Joseph Melancon and
        Appolonise LE BLANC)
    iv) Carlos Valerio Gautreaux

        (2) July 8, 1811, St. James Par-
           ish, Marie MELANCON (daughter
           of Jacques Melancon and Isa-
           belle LANDRY)

v) Joseph Hercules (Eusebe) Gautreaux born February 7, 1828, Ascension Parish, married December 5, 1843 Marie Augustine LANOUX (daughter of Jacques Lanoux and Marguerite SAVOIE)

vi) Antoine Augustin Gautreaux born August 5, 1828 married April 23, 1850, Ascension Parish, Felonise LE BLANC (daughter of Jean Baptiste LeBlanc and Celonise GAUDET)

vii) Theotitte Melanie Gautreaux born March 20, 1824 married May 30, 1841, Ascension Parish, Valemon VILLENEUVE (son of Manuel Villeneuve and Eugenie LANDRY)

viii) Marie Emelina Gautreaux married January 30, 1837 Cyril GAUDIN (son of Seraphin Gaudin and Clementine LE BLANC)

h) Joseph Gautreaux married August 12, 1805 Henriette Adelaide LANDRY (daughter of Pierre Abraham Landry dit Pitre and Marguerite ALLAIN)

i) Joseph Gervais Gautreaux married January 7, 1828 Marie Louise LE BLANC (daughter of Donat LeBlanc and Marie MELANCON)

ii) Appoline Gautreaux married

(1) July 20, 1841 Joseph LE BLANC (son of Donat LeBlanc and Marie MELANCON)

(2) April 25, 1854 Joseph BABIN (son of Joseph Babin and ___)

iii) Marite Marguerite Gautreaux born April 8, 1814

iv) Simon Joseph Gautreaux born October 5, 1816

v) Joseph Richard Gautreaux born April 3, 1819

vi) Marie Justine Gautreaux born November 1, 1824

vii) Joseph Cyprien Gautreaux born October 3, 1829

i) Raphael Gautreaux married February 3, 1804 Marie Constance BRAUD (daughter of Joseph Braud and Marie AUCOIN)

i) Marie Louise Gautreaux born February 24, 1805 married February 11, 1839

19

Joseph REAU (son of Joseph Reau and
Marie MARAIS)

ii) **Simeon** Gautreaux married April 28, 1869,
East Ascension Parish, Elizabeth
GONZALES (daughter of Joseph Gonzales
and Andrea MARBIAS)

vi. Jean Gauterot born 1741
vii. Marie Madeleine Gauterot born 1744
viii. Jean Martin Gauterot born 1747

d. Jacques LeBlanc born September 21, 1708 at Pisiquid, Acadia married June 12, 1730, St. Charles
Parish, Acadia, Catherine Josephe FOREST (daughter of Pierre Forest and Cecile RICHARD) Listed
in Louisiana Census of 1769 in St. James Parish

i. Rene LeBlanc born 1733 married 1761 Anne
RICHARD

a) Hyacinthe LeBlanc born 1762
b) Clothilde LeBlanc born 1764
c) Domitille LeBlanc born 1765
d) Gaetan LeBlanc born 1765
e) Sabine LeBlanc born 1771

ii. Marcell LeBlanc born 1734 married November 10,
1760 at Ristigauche, Marie Josephe BREAU
(daughter of Joseph Breau and Ursule BOURG)
Marcell and Marie Josephe were in St. James
in 1769

a) Marguerite LeBlanc born 1763
b) Marie Josephe LeBlanc born 1766 married
September 21, 1784 Joseph MELANCON (son
of Alexandre Melancon and Osite HEBERT)
c) Osite Barbe LeBlanc born 1769
d) Sylvain LeBlanc born 1770
e) Angelique LeBlanc baptized May 2, 1772
f) Paul LeBlanc born 1776
g) Appolonia LeBlanc baptized January, 1778
Married November 22, 1796 Joseph MELANCON
(son of Santiago Melancon and Isabel
LANDRY)

iii. Marguerite LeBlanc born 1736 married April 8,
1768 Efreme BABIN (son of Paul Babin and
Marie LANDRY)
iv. Paul LeBlanc born 1740
v. Catherine LeBlanc born 1750
vi. Osite LeBlanc married January 25, 1771, St.
James Parish, Joseph BABIN (son of Jean
Baptiste Babin and Ursule LANDRY) Osite
died March 9, 1809 in Ascension Parish

e. Honore LeBlanc born November 1, 1710 married 1732
   Marie TRAHAN (daughter of Guillaume Trahan and
   Jacqueline BENOIT)

   i. Charles LeBlanc born 1734 married 1755 Anne
      LANDRY (daughter of Rene Landry and Marie
      Rose RIVET)

      a) Marie LeBlanc born 1763 at Liverpool
      b) Claude LeBlanc born 1765 at Morlaix

   ii. Raymond LeBlanc born 1742 married 1765 Marie
       TERRIOT (daughter of Pierre Terriot and
       Marie Josephe DUPUIS)
   iii. Agatha LeBlanc born 1744 married 1764 Paul
        DAIGRE (son of Olivier Daigre and Francoise
        GRANGER)

        a) Marie Jeanne Daigre born 1765, Morlaix,
           France

   iv. Paul LeBlanc born 1751
   v. Joseph LeBlanc born 1753

f. Madeleine LeBlanc born October 1, 1712 married
   February 8, 1729, Grande Pre, Acadia, Jean
   Baptiste MELANCON (son of Jean Melancon and
   Marguerite DUGAS)

   i. Paul Melancon born 1730; baptized October 21,
      1730 married Marie TERRIOT
   ii. Osite Melancon born September 21, 1732
   iii. Joseph Melancon born 1734
   iv. Charles Honore Melancon born 1738
   v. Marguerite Blanche Melancon born March 23,
      1741
   vi. Charles Melancon born March 22, 1743 married
       February 5, 1768 Felicite LANDRY (daughter of
       Rene Landry and Marie THERIOT)
   vii. Marie Rose Melancon born August 25, 1745
   viii. Madeleine Melancon born September 20, 1747
   ix. Jean Baptiste Melancon born December 12, 1736
   x. Felicite Melancon married November 10, 1788
      Bonaventure BABIN
   xi. Marie Melancon married February 5, 1768,
       Ascension Parish, Isaac LE BLANC (son of
       Desire LeBlanc and Marie Magdeleine LANDRY)

g. Marguerite LeBlanc born 1712 married October 8,
   1725, Grande Pre, Acadia, Joseph GRANGER (son of
   Rene Granger and Catherine LANDRY)

   i. Joseph Simon Granger born 1726
   ii. Jean Baptiste Granger born 1729
   iii. Armand Granger born 1734

      iv. Marie Marguerite Granger born 1736 married
          1753 Germain DUPUIS (son of Jean Dupuis and
          Marguerite RICHARD)

h. Francoise LeBlanc born 1716 married Charles
    GRANGER (son of Rene Granger and Marguerite
    TERRIOT)

      i. Marie Granger married 1757 Basile RICHARD
        (son of Michel Richard and Marie BOURGEOIS)

          a)   Joseph Richard born 1759
          b)   Jean Baptiste Richard born 1763
          c)   Jean Pierre Richard born 1766
          d)   Marie Anne Richard born 1768
          e)   Jean Marie Richard born 1770

     ii. Marguerite Granger married 1761 Charles DAIGRE

i. Charles LeBlanc born August 29, 1718 married
    September 26, 1741 Elizabeth THIBODEAUX (daughter
    of Jean Thibodeaux and Marguerite HEBÈRT)

      i. Marie Blanche LeBlanc born August 8, 1742
        Married 1758 Olivier DAIGRE (son of Olivier
        Daigre and Francoise GRANGER)
     ii. Marguerite LeBlanc born 1744 married 1764
        Joseph Ignace RICHARD (son of Pierre Richard
        and Marie Josephe LE BLANC)
   iii. Jean Baptiste LeBlanc born 1746
    iv. Olivier LeBlanc born 1748
     v. Marine LeBlanc born 1750
    vi. Anselme LeBlanc born 1752

j. Joseph LeBlanc born March 23, 1720 at Grande Pre
    married July 2, 1742 Elizabeth GAUDET (daughter
    of Bernard Gaudet and Elizabeth TERRIOT) Joseph
    died July 12, 1805 at age 86 in St. James Parish

      i. Marie Joseph LeBlanc born 1743 married Febru-
        ary 1, 1760 Athanase BREAUX (son of Ambroise
        Breaux and Marie MICHEL)

          a)   Anastasie Breaux born 1762
          b)   Joseph Breaux born 1763
          c)   Marie Breaux born 1765
          d)   Marie Breaux born 1770
          e)   Anne Breaux born 1772
          f)   Paul Breaux born 1775

     ii. Anne LeBlanc born 1748 married May 28, 1770
        Jean DUHON (son of Honore Duhon and Marie
        VINCENT)

          a)   Francois Duhon baptized June 23, 1771,
             St. James

iii. Joseph LeBlanc born 1750 married Marguerite
LE BLANC

a) Donat LeBlanc born 1779 married Marie
MELANCON. Donat died 1843 at age 64.

iv. Madeleine LeBlanc born 1753
v. Isabelle LeBlanc born 1754 married September 21, 1772 Simon LE BLANC (son of Etienne
LeBlanc and Elizabeth BOUDREAUX)

a) Benjamin LeBlanc born 1777 married September 8, 1806, Ascension Parish, Felicite
MORAIS (daughter of Joachim Morais and
Rosalie FOREST) Benjamin died October 17,
1817.

    i) Josephia Artemisa LeBlanc born January 27, 1816, Ascension Parish

b) Marie Magdelaine LeBlanc born October 25,
1775 married

      (1) February 7, 1774 Enselm
FOREST (son of Charles Forest
and Marguerite   _

    i) Louis Forest died July 21, 1799
   ii) Hypolite Forest died May 26, 1799

      (2) July 15, 1805 Hypolite
CARMOUCHE (son of Pierre Carmouche and Genevieve ROUSSEAU)

c) Hypolite LeBlanc born 1777 married August 4, 1805 Claire BARBAY (daughter of
Louis Barbay and Jeanne Charlotte FALGOUST) Claire was the widow of Honore
CHENET.

    i) Desire LeBlanc married January 21, 1836
Eugenie SENETTE (daughter of Eugene
Senette and Charlotte BARBAY)

d) Marguerite LeBlanc born January 25, 1780
e) Simon LeBlanc born June 24, 1781 married
March 1, 1802 Francoise LANDRY (daughter
of Francois Landry and Marie Rose DUGAS)
f) Louis LeBlanc born September 29, 1783
g) Baltazar LeBlanc born February 19, 1786
h) Celeste LeBlanc born May 27, 1788
i) Joseph LeBlanc married

      (1) February 17, 1797 Polonia
DUGAS (daughter of Francois
Dugas and Marguerite BABIN)

    i) Joseph Narcisse LeBlanc married September 19, 1819 Josephine LIRETTE

ii) Hypolite Eugene LeBlanc married February 4, 1822 Adeline BOUDREAUX (daughter of Simon Boudreaux and Celeste BABIN)

iii) Onesime LeBlanc married August 9, 1833 Eulalie LE BLANC (daughter of Lubin LeBlanc and Melanie AUCOIN)

iv) Marcille LeBlanc married February 9, 1835 Seraphine DAIGLE (daughter of Joseph Daigle and Magdelaine LE BLANC)

(2) June 18, 1810 Magdelaine BABIN (daughter of Aman Babin and Anastasie LANDRY) widow of Noel Miguel DUGAS

(3) May 4, 1812 Julie Clothilde DUGAS (daughter of Michel Dugas and Ann Sophie FOREST)

j) Etienne LeBlanc married

(1) February 15, 1813 Euphrosine LE BLANC (daughter of Marcel LeBlanc and Magdelaine BOURGEOIS)

(2) July 21, 1834 Eulalie LE BLANC (daughter of Joseph LeBlanc and Marie LANDRY

vi. Gilles LeBlanc born 1757 married

(1) February 2, 1781 Theotiste GAUDIN (daughter of Bonaventure Gaudin and Marguerite BERGERON)

Gilles died September 28, 1832 at age 75 in St. James

a) Desire LeBlanc born 1783 married May 4, 1807 Marcellite LE BLANC (daughter of Joseph LeBlanc and Pelagie DOIRON)

i) Desire LeBlanc born June 28, 1808
ii) Henriette LeBlanc born April 9, 1810
iii) Leon Silver LeBlanc born March 17, 1812
iv) Leonade LeBlanc born July 11, 1815

b) Constance LeBlanc born 1785 married

(1) July 28, 1798 Louis DUGAS (son of Carlos Dugas and Marguerite BROUSSARD)

(2) Francois BERNARD

23

Gilles LeBlanc ----- (2) December 21, 1783 Marine
                          LE BLANC (daughter of Desire
                          LeBlanc and Marie Magdelaine
                          LANDRY)

    c) Rosemond LeBlanc born March 28, 1789
       married

           (1) Marie Desiree BROU (daughter
               of Charles Brou and Julie
               PRINCE)

           (2) March 19, 1811 Francoise
               Marcellite BOURGEOIS (daugh-
               ter of Pierre Bourgeois and
               Marie BERGERON)

        i) Rosemond LeBlanc born 1817 married
           Virginia LANGLINAIS (daughter of
           Louis Langlinais and Aspasie BOUDREAUX)

    d) Nicholas Colin LeBlanc married January 21,
       1805 Constance BRAUX (daughter of Alexis
       Braux and Marie BRAUX)

        i) Nicholas LeBlanc born November 8, 1805
       ii) Edmond Gille LeBlanc born January 23,
           1808

           (3) September 26, 1816 Magdelaine
               BOURGEOIS (daughter of Michael
               Bourgeois and Anne LANDRY)
               widow of August GRAVOIS

  k. Judith LeBlanc born 1722 Grande Pre married Au-
     gust 6, 1742 Germain THIBODEAUX (son of Jean
     Thibodeaux and Marguerite HEBERT)

    i. Marie Thibodeaux born 1743
   ii. Elizabeth Thibodeaux born 1745
 iii. Anne Thibodeaux born 1747

1. Simon LeBlanc born 1723 married.

           (1) Marguerite BOURG (daughter of
               Jean Bourg and Francoise
               AUCOIN)

    i. Francoise LeBlanc born 1745 (In 1767 she was
      at religious Ursulines de Morlaix, France)
   ii. Jean LeBlanc born 1746
 iii. Basile LeBlanc born 1748
  iv. Simon LeBlanc born 1750

           (2) 1757 Marie TRAHAN (daughter
               of Joseph Trahan and Eliza-
               beth TERRIOT) widow of
               Francois GRANGER

        v.   Joseph LeBlanc born 1764
       vi.   Pierre Marie LeBlanc born 1766
      vii.   Marie Anne LeBlanc born 1769

   m. Catherine LeBlanc born February 2, 1725 married
       September 30, 1745 Jean Baptiste BABIN (son of
       Pierre Babin and Madeleine BOURG)

        i.   Marie Madeleine Babin born July 30, 1746
       ii.   Marie Josephe Babin born March 17, 1748

   n. Elizabeth LeBlanc baptized September 28, 1726
       married July 16, 1748 Simon LE BLANC (son of
       Joseph LeBlanc and Anne BOUDREAUX)

2. Francois LeBlanc born 1682 married c. 1705 Jeanne
    HEBERT

   a. Francois LeBlanc born 1706 married 1727 Anne
       BENOIT (daughter of Jean Benoit and Marie BOURG)

        i.   Joseph LeBlanc born 1728
       ii.   Anne LeBlanc born 1729
      iii.   Francois LeBlanc born 1730

   b. Jacques LeBlanc born 1707 married September 18,
       1727 Catherine LANDRY (daughter of Pierre Landry
       and Madeleine BROUSSARD)

        i.   Marie Madeleine LeBlanc born 1743
       ii.   Jean Baptiste LeBlanc born 1745
      iii.   Beloni LeBlanc born 1750

   c. Anne LeBlanc born January 16, 1708 married July 4,
       1729 Germain LANDRY (son of Germain Landry and
       Marie MELANCON)

        i.   Marie Joseph Landry born July 16, 1730
       ii.   Marguerite Landry born 1732
      iii.   Anne Landry born 1734
       iv.   Francois Landry born 1736
        v.   Charles Landry born November 8, 1741
       vi.   Magdeleine Landry born May 9, 1744
      vii.   Marie Landry born September 7, 1746

   d. Marie LeBlanc born January 23, 1810 married Janu-
       ary 14, 1727 Jean Baptiste THIBODEAUX (son of
       Jean Thibodeaux and Marguerite HEBERT)

        i.   Germain Thibodeaux born 1728 married

                  (1) 1752 Francoise PREJEAN

             a) Marie Rose Thibodeaux born 1757
             b) Joseph Jean Thibodeaux born 1759
             c) Jean David Thibodeaux born 1760

                  (2) 1765 Marie BABINEAU

                         25

        d) Amand Thibodeaux born 1766
        e) Henriette Thibodeaux born 1768
        f) Henry Rene Thecle Thibodeaux born 1770
        g) Marie Josephe Thibodeaux born 1772
        h) Madeleine Thibodeaux born 1773
        i) Isaac Thibodeaux born 1774

   ii. Marie Joseph Thibodeaux born 1729
  iii. Jean Baptiste Thibodeaux born 1731 married
        1755 Marie Anne Francoise BABIN (daughter of
        Jean Baptiste Babin and Marguerite TERRIOT)

        a) Marguerite Thibodeaux born 1757
        b) Marie Thibodeaux born 1758
        c) Etienne Thibodeaux born 1770
        d) Jean Francois Thibodeaux born 1773
        e) Joseph Thibodeaux born 1774

   iv. Olivier Thibodeaux born 1732 married Septem-
        ber 23, 1765 Madeleine POTHIER (daughter of
        Jean Pothier and Marie Josephe HEBERT

        a) Olivier Thibodeaux born 1766
        b) Paul Gregoire Thibodeaux born 1768
        c) Firmin Thibodeaux born 1770
        d) Madeleine Thibodeaux born 1771
        e) Paul Thibodeaux born 1774
        f) Toussaint Thibodeaux born 1775
        g) Georges Thibodeaux born 1781
        h) Jean Baptiste Thibodeaux born 1785
        i) Francois Thibodeaux born 1786

    v. Marie Josephe Thibodeaux born 1734
   vi. Anne Thibodeaux born 1736
  vii. Blanche Marguerite Thibodeaux born 1738
 viii. Marie Madeleine Thibodeaux born 1746
   ix. Francois Thibodeaux born 1748
    x. Marie Luce Thibodeaux born 1750

e. Joseph LeBlanc born August 24, 1712 married 1734
    Marie Josephe BOURG (daughter of Ambroise Bourg
    and Elizabeth MELANCON)

    i. Ambroise LeBlanc born December 19, 1737
   ii. Simon Joseph LeBlanc born 1740 married c. 1764
        Osite ARSENAULT (daughter of Francois Arsenault
        and Marguerite BERNARD)

        a) Therese LeBlanc born 1765
        b) Marguerite LeBlanc born 1768
        c) Charlotte LeBlanc born 1772

  iii. Joseph LeBlanc born 1744
   iv. Benony LeBlanc born 1749
    v. Charles LeBlanc born 1752
   vi. Lazare LeBlanc born 1755
  vii. Georges Robert LeBlanc born 1758

f. Marguerite LeBlanc born 1716 married May 28, 1733
    Charles HEBERT (son of Jacques Hebert and Margue-
    rite LANDRY)

    i. Osite Hebert born 1734

g. Cecile LeBlanc born September 27, 1717 married

    November 7, 1740 Charles LANDRY (son of Rene
    Landry and Anne TERRIOT)

h. Marie Josephe (Josette) LeBlanc born 1720 married
    October 29, 1737 Jean Baptiste LANDRY (son of Jean
    Baptiste Landry and Marguerite GAUTEROT)

    i. Jean Landry born 1739 married 1765 Marie DUGAS
        (daughter of Abraham Dugas and Marguerite
        LE BLANC)

        a) Marie Charlotte Landry born 1767
        b) Jean Antoine Landry born 1770
        c) Abraham Joseph Landry born 1771
        d) Angelique Landry born 1773
        e) Jeanne Landry born 1774

    ii.   Joseph Landry born 1741
    iii. Charles Landry born 1743
    iv.   Marie Landry born 1745 married 1766 Jean DUGAS
          (son of Abraham Dugas and Marguerite FOUGERE)
          a) Sylvain Dugas born 1766
          b) Cyprien Dugas born 1768
          c) Pulcherie Dugas born 1770
          d) Martial Dugas born 1771

    v.   Pierre Landry born 1747
    vi.   Rene Landry born 1748
    vii. Marguerite Landry born 1750
    viii. Gertrude Landry born 1759

i. Madeleine LeBlanc born 1722 married February 4,
    1743 Amand BREAUX (son of Pierre Breaux and Anne
    LE BLANC)

    i.   Anne Marie Breaux born 1746
    ii.   Jean Baptiste Breaux born 1748
    iii. Joseph Richard Breaux born 1750
    iv.   Madeleine Breaux born 1752
    v.   Marguerite Breaux born 1754
    vi.   Marie Anne Ange Breaux born 1758
    vii. Joseph Amand Breaux born 1761

j. Jean Baptiste LeBlanc baptized October 29,
    1725 married

                    (1) November 8, 1746 Marie LANDRY
                         (daughter of Jean Landry and
                         Madeleine MELANCON)

27

         i. Jean Baptiste LeBlanc born February 15, 1747
        ii. Joseph LeBlanc born August 6, 1748
       iii. Pierre LeBlanc born 1753

                     (2) 1758 Marguerite CELESTIN dit
                          Bellemere

         iv. Moise LeBlanc born 1761
          v. Joseph LeBlanc born 1766
         vi. Jacques Hypolite LeBlanc born 1768
        vii. Francoise Marie LeBlanc born 1770

    k. Beloni LeBlanc born October 23, 1729 married
        July 13, 1748 Marguerite HEBERT (daughter of
        Guillaume Hebert and Marie Josephe DUPUIS)

         i. Marguerite LeBlanc married

                     (1) Germain BERGERON
                     (2) Joseph GAUDET

3. Rene LeBlanc (Notary) born 1684 married

                     (1) July 30, 1709 Elizabeth
                          MELANCON (daughter of Pierre
                          Melancon and Marguerite
                          Mius D'ENTREMONT)

    a. Benjamin LeBlanc born April 6, 1711
    b. Marie Josephe LeBlanc born 1714 married April 27,
        1734 Joseph MEUNIER (son of Paul Meunier and
        Claire de SAINT-CASTIN)

         i. Maturin Meunier born March 4, 1743
        ii. Rene Meunier born November 2, 1744
       iii. Paul Meunier born July 24, 1747
         iv. Marie Josephe Meunier born 1735
          v. Claire Meunier born 1736
         vi. Joseph Amand Meunier born 1738
        vii. Isabelle Marguerite Meunier born 1740

    c. Elizabeth LeBlanc born 1718; baptized December 8,
        1718

                     (2) November 26, 1720 Marguerite
                          THIBAULT (daughter of Pierre
                          Thibault and Jeanne COMMEAU)

    d. Marguerite LeBlanc born July 25, 1721 married
        November 22, 1745 Joseph BABIN (son of Rene Babin
        and Elizabeth GAUTEROT)

         i. Joseph Barthelemy Babin born 1746
        ii. Jean Baptiste Babin born 1748

    e. Marie LeBlanc born July 25, 1721
    f. Anne Marie LeBlanc born July 25, 1721

g. Anne LeBlanc born September 20, 1724 married
November 23, 1744 Rene TERRIOT (son of Joseph
Terriot and Marguerite MELANCON)

   i. Joseph Terriot born 1748
  ii. Simon Terriot born 1749

h. Blanche LeBlanc baptized March 19, 1726 married
1762 Michel BONHOMME
i. Marie LeBlanc baptized March 19, 1726
j. Madeleine LeBlanc born October 17, 1727 married
June 7, 1746 Charles BROSSAR (son of Pierre
Brossar and Marguerite BOURG)
k. Rene LeBlanc born November 10, 1731
l. Simon LeBlanc born November 10, 1731
m. Francoise LeBlanc born May 1, 1734
n. Ursule LeBlanc born December 27, 1735 married
1758 at Quebec Jacque Christophe BABUTY
o. Marie Joseph LeBlanc born May 20, 1738
p. Pierre Benjamin LeBlanc born 1740 married 1760
Marie Anne DUGAS (daughter of Charles Dugas and
Anne LE BLANC)

     i. Benjamin LeBlanc born 1765
    ii. Scholastique LeBlanc born 1766
   iii. Charlotte LeBlanc born 1767
    iv. Luc LeBlanc born 1768
     v. Agatha Blanche LeBlanc born 1770
    vi. Monique LeBlanc born 1773
   vii. Desire LeBlanc born 1775
  viii. Theotiste LeBlanc born 1777
    ix. Hilaire LeBlanc born 1779
     x. Colette LeBlanc born 1780
    xi. Luce LeBlanc born 1783
   xii. Elizabeth LeBlanc born 1785
  xiii. Rufine LeBlanc born 1787

q. Esther LeBlanc born 1740 married Raymond BOURDAGES
r. Paul Marie LeBlanc born May 2, 1742
s. Jean Baptiste LeBlanc born June 5, 1744 married
1770 Marguerite BOUDREAU (daughter of Joseph
Boudreau and Rosalie ARSENAULT)
t. (Jeanne) Marie Joseph LeBlanc born April 5, 1748

4. Pierre LeBlanc born 1685 married October 26, 1711
Jeanne TERRIOT (daughter of Jean Terriot and Jeanne
LANDRY)

   a. Paul LeBlanc born 1712 married November 7, 1735
   Madeleine RICHARD (daughter of Michel Richard and
   Agnes BOURGEOIS)

     i. Marie LeBlanc born September 2, 1736
    ii. Paul Marie LeBlanc born November 20, 1741
   iii. Joseph Marie LeBlanc born August 28, 1744
    iv. Josephe Marie LeBlanc born January 17, 1746

b. Francoise LeBlanc born November 26, 1717; died
   November 27, 1743 at age 25
c. Jean Baptiste LeBlanc born 1720
d. Charles Honore LeBlanc born 1721 married August 16,
   1741 Anne HEBERT (daughter of Jacques Hebert and
   Marguerite LANDRY)
e. Elizabeth LeBlanc born 1723 married August 13,
   1748 Charles HEBERT (son of Guillaume Hebert and
   Marie Josephe DUPUY)
f. Jean Pierre LeBlanc born April 11, 1726 married
   c. 1746 Ozite MELANCON (daughter of Jean Baptiste
   Melancon and Magdelaine LE BLANC)

   i. Isaac LeBlanc born 1760 married November 16,
      1789, St. James, Marianne ARSENO (daughter of
      Joseph Arseno and Marie BERGERON. Isaac died
      July 25, 1810 in St. James

      a) Casimiro LeBlanc born December 17, 1789
      b) Marie Justine LeBlanc born December 17,
         1789
      c) Ademundo LeBlanc born November 20, 1790
      d) Sosthenes LeBlanc born October 20, 1795
      e) Celeste LeBlanc baptized March 30, 1794
      f) Domingo LeBlanc born August 5, 1797 mar-
         ried

         (1) Eugenie HAYDEL
         (2) February 13, 1821 Arthemise
             ROME (daughter of Abraham
             Rome and Jeanne BAUDOUIN)

      g) Silvester LeBlanc born December 29, 1803
      h) Nicolas LeBlanc born May 11, 1805
      i) Semer LeBlanc born April 20, 1808
      j) Etienne LeBlanc baptized December 10, 1803
      k) Isaac LeBlanc born December 22, 1809

   ii. Helene LeBlanc married March 4, 1786 Joseph
       BOURGEOIS (son of Jean Baptiste Bourgeois and
       Marie Magdelaine BOURG)
   iii. Jozine (Joseph) LeBlanc born 1763 married

        (1) Marguerite DUHON
        (2) January 7, 1801 Margarita
            BERNARD (daughter of Andre
            Bernard and Marguerite EDLEMON)

g. Daniel (David) LeBlanc born May 16, 1729
h. Joseph LeBlanc born September 25, 1733
i. Agnes LeBlanc born April 3, 1736
j. Anselm LeBlanc born October 16, 1740

5. Joseph LeBlanc born c. 1686
6. Etienne LeBlanc born c. 1686
7. Marie LeBlanc born c. 1687 married

                          (1) October 2, 1713 Jacques THERIOT
                               (son of Germain Theriot and
                               Anne RICHARD)

    a. Marie Terriot born 1718
    b. Anne Terriot born 1721
    c. Jean Baptiste Terriot born 1723
    d. Etienne Terriot born 1725; baptized January 1, 1725
        married 1747 Helene LANDRY

          i. Joseph Terriot born 1748
         ii. Francoise Terriot born 1751

                          (2) June 3, 1726 Marie Madeleine
                               ROBICHAUD (daughter of Prudent
                               Robichaud and Henriette PETI-
                               TIPAS)

    e. Henriette Terriot born 1727
    f. Jean Jacques Terriot born 1728
    g. Olivier Terriot·born 1730
    h. Pierre Terriot born 1733

 8. Jean Baptiste LeBlanc born c. 1688
 9. Victoire LeBlanc born c. 1689
10. Claude LeBlanc born 1691 married

                          (1) Marie TERRIOT
                          (2) May 4, 1718 Jeanne DUGAS
                               (daughter of Abraham Dugas
                               and Jeanne GUILBAUT) widow
                               of Jean RICHARD

    a. Felix LeBlanc born September 30, 1719 married
        October 10, 1742 Marie Josephe TERIOT (daughter
        of Jean Teriot and Magdeleine BOURG)

          i. Amand Francois LeBlanc born October 4, 1743
         ii. Marin LeBlanc born 1745
        iii. Etienne LeBlanc born 1748
         iv. Marie LeBlanc born 1752
          v. Joseph LeBlanc born 1752
         vi. Elizabeth LeBlanc born 1755

    b. Amand LeBlanc born September 30, 1719; died
        October 6, 1742 at about age 23
    c. Victor LeBlanc born 1721 married 1740 Marie AUCOIN

          i. Marie LeBlanc born 1741
         ii. Elizabeth LeBlanc born 1743
        iii. Olivier LeBlanc married November 7, 1790 Rosa
              RICHARD (daughter of Jean Richard and Margue-
              rite RICHARD)
         iv. Pierre LeBlanc married

                          (1) Anne LE BERT
                          (2) 1787 Genevieve RICHARD

                          31

d. Blanche LeBlanc born June 16, 1722 married February 27, 1745 Joseph RICHARD (son of Rene Richard and Marie Josephe Vincent BABIN)
e. Francois LeBlanc born c. 1723
f. Osite LeBlanc born September 23, 1724 married Francois ROBICHAU
g. Etienne LeBlanc born April 11, 1727
h. Marin LeBlanc born c. 1728 married July 2, 1748 Anne CORMIER (daughter of Pierre Cormier and Marguerite CYR)

    i. Madeleine LeBlanc born 1755
   ii. Marie LeBlanc born 1761

i. Alain LeBlanc born February 20, 1732 married 1756 Anne Marie BABIN (daughter of Claude Babin and Marguerite DUPUIS)
j. Alexis (Alexandre) LeBlanc born 1732
k. Martha LeBlanc born 1734
l. Marie Madeleine LeBlanc born August 21, 1739
m. Rose Osite LeBlanc married 1750 Jean PRINCE (son of Antoine Prince and Anne TRAHAN)

    i. Jean Prince born 1762 married January 24, 1785 Rosalie BOURG

E. Andre LeBlanc born 1659 married 1783 Marie DUGAS (daughter of Abraham Dugas and Marguerite Marie Judith DOUCET) Andre died May 4, 1743

1. Jean LeBlanc born 1684 married January 25, 1704 Jeanne BOURGEOIS (daughter of Guillaume Bourgeois and Marie Anne de MARTIGNON)

a. Jean LeBlanc born 1705 married July 9, 1726 Francoise BLANCHARD (daughter of Rene Blanchard and Anne LANDRY)

    i. Pierre LeBlanc born August 3, 1734 married 1758 Francoise TRAHAN (daughter of Joseph Trahan and Elizabeth TERRIOT)

       a) Marie LeBlanc born 1761
       b) Marguerige Genevieve LeBlanc born 1763
       c) Marie Therese LeBlanc born 1766
       d) Yves LeBlanc born 1766
       e) Simon LeBlanc born 1771

   ii. Anne LeBlanc born 1736 married 1758 Rene TRAHAN (son of Pierre Trahan and Jeanne DAIGLE) Anne died 1764 Morlaix, France

       a) Raphael Trahan born December 28, 1761

  iii. Alexis LeBlanc born February 1742
   iv. Charles LeBlanc born February 1745
    v. Marguerite LeBlanc born July 1746

b. Joseph LeBlanc born 1708 married July 18, 1730
    Madeleine LA LANDE (daughter of Pierre Lalande
    and Anne PRETIEUX) Joseph died 1756; Magdelaine
    died 1744.

    i.   Anne LeBlanc born June 1, 1731 married 1757
         Joseph Oliver HEBERT (son of Joseph Hebert
         and Madeleine TRAHAN)
    ii. Joseph LeBlanc born June 1, 1731 married 1760
         Marie Modeste HEBERT (daughter of Joseph
         Hebert and Madeleine TRAHAN)

         a) Marguerite Marie LeBlanc born 1763
         b) Simon LeBlanc born 1765
         c) Victoire Reine LeBlanc born 1766
         d) Marie Marguerite LeBlanc born 1768
         e) Joseph Mathurin LeBlanc born 1769
         f) Marie Jeanne LeBlanc born 1771
         g) Madeleine Felicite LeBlanc born 1772

    iii. Marguerite LeBlanc born 1732 married 1756
         Louis Athanase TRAHAN
    iv. Marie LeBlanc born 1735 married Anselme GUIDRY
    v.   Desire Gaspard LeBlanc born 1740
    vi. Blanche Cecile LeBlanc married 1765 Pierre
         LEVRON (son of Jean Baptiste Levron and
         Francoise LABAUVE)

         a) Martha Levron born 1766

c. Marie LeBlanc born February 17, 1711 married
    January 9, 1731 Alexandre of Belle Isle LE BORGNE
    (son of Alexandre Belle Isle LeBorgne and Marie
    Anastasie de SAINT CASTIN)

    i.   Marguerite Belisle born 1731
    ii.   Mathurin Belisle born 1732
    iii. Marie Rose Belisle born 1733
    iv.   Anastasie Belisle born 1734
    v.   Alexandre Belisle born 1736
    vi.   Jean Pierre Belisle born 1740
    vii. Josephe Marie Belisle born 1742
    viii. Mathurin Belisle born 1744

d. Pierre LeBlanc born 1715 married November 18, 1737
    Marguerite GAUTROT (daughter of Charles Gautrot
    and Magdeleine BLANCHARD)

    i.   Marie Madeleine LeBlanc born 1739
    ii.   Jean Baptiste LeBlanc born September 2, 1747
    iii. Elizabeth LeBlanc married Joseph CAILLOUET

e. Desire LeBlanc born 1717 married 1740 Marie
    Madeleine LANDRY (daughter of Jean Landry and
    Claire LE BLANC) Desire died March 15, 1777 in
    Ascension Parish. This family was in Louisiana
    prior to 1768 and will be Part II of this book.

    i.   Simon LeBlanc born 1741 married
                    (1) Marie Josephe LANDRY
                    (2) November 9, 1767 Ann ARCENEAUX
   ii.   Isaac LeBlanc born 1746 married
                    (1) February 5, 1768 Marie MELANCON
                    (2) May 21, 1782 Marguerite BABIN
  iii.   Marie Martha LeBlanc born 1748 married
                    (1) February 7, 1768 Jacques
                         LA CHAUSSE
                    (2) April 30, 1770 Paul BRAUD
   iv.   Jerome LeBlanc born 1749 married Madeleine
         LANDRY; Jerome died August 24, 1789 age 40
    v.   Isabel LeBlanc born 1751 married April 18,
         1775 Joseph LANDRY; Isabel died September 1,
         1777 age 26
   vi.   Desire LeBlanc born 1753
  vii.   Anne Marine LeBlanc born 1758 married
                    (1) February 19, 1775 Joseph
                         BABIN
                    (2) December 21, 1783 Gille
                         LE BLANC
 viii.   Benjamin LeBlanc born 1760 married February 19,
         1775 Rosalie BABIN
   ix.   Ozitte LeBlanc born 1760 married January 7,
         1778 Etienne LE BLANC
    x.   Enselm LeBlanc born 1769 married December 27,
         1784 Marie Madeleine BABIN
   xi.   Gregoire LeBlanc born 1769 married April 23,
         1787 Marie Barbe BABIN

 f. Sylvain LeBlanc born November 5, 1719 married 1743
     Anne LE PRINCE (daughter of Antoine LePrince and
     Anne TRAHAN)

    i.   Marguerite LeBlanc born February 10, 1748
   ii.   Marie LeBlanc born 1754
  iii.   Anastasie LeBlanc born 1760
   iv.   Marie Modeste LeBlanc born 1761

 g. Claude LeBlanc born April 11, 1723 married
                    (1) 1748 Marie Josephe LONGUESPEE
                         (daughter of Louis Longuespee
                         and Anne BRASSEAU)

    i.   Jean de Dieu LeBlanc born 1752
   ii.   Helene LeBlanc born 1759
                    (2) 1760 Marie GUIDRY (widow of
                         Benjamin MIUS)

34

        iii.   Joseph LeBlanc born 1760
        iv.   Pierre LeBlanc born 1762

    h.   Marguerite LeBlanc born November 15, 1724 married

                    (1)   November 1745 Pierre TRAHAN
                          (son of Pierre Trahan and
                          Marguerite COMEAU)
                    (2)   Felix BOUDROT (son of Pierre
                          Boudrot and Madeleine COMMEAU)

    i.   Marie Josephe LeBlanc born 1729 married 1748
         Felix BOUDROT (son of Francois Boudrot and Ange-
         lique DOIRON)

        i.   Felicite Boudrot born 1754
       ii.   Joseph Simon Boudrot

    j.   Anne LeBlanc born February 6, 1732 married Joseph
         BUJEAUX (BUJOL) (son of Joseph Bujeaux and Marie
         Joseph LANDRY)

        i.   Marguerite Bujeaux (BUJOL) born 1751 married

                    (1)   Joseph CONSTANT
                    (2)   February 8, 1780 Don Juan
                          VIVES (son of Juan Vives and
                          Francisca PLANEZ)

       ii.   Augustin Bujol born 1753 married February 7,
             1774 Gertrude LANDRY (daughter of Joseph
             Landry and Marie BOURQUE)
      iii.   Perpetue Bujol born 1755 married February 13,
             1773 Paul PROVOST (son of Nicolas Provost and
             Yve DUHON)
       iv.   Anne Bujol born 1757 married November 25, 1779
             Joseph LANDRY (son of Etienne Landry and Marie
             Josephe BOURG) widower of Isabel LeBlanc
        v.   Marie Magdelaine Bujol born 1761 married
             February 15, 1784 August VERRET (son of Nicolas
             Verret and Marie CANTRELL)
       vi.   Joseph Bujol born 1769

2.   Marie LeBlanc born 1692 married c. 1703 Germain CORMIER
     (son of Thomas Cormier and Madeleine GIROUARD)

    a.   Pierre Cormier born 1705 married

                    (1)   Anne Marie PITRE

        i.   Pierre Cormier born 1729
       ii.   Marguerite Cormier born 1733
      iii.   Jacques Cormier born 1740

                    (2)   January 18, 1742 Jeanne
                          THIBODEAU (daughter of Pierre
                          Thibodeau and Anne Marie AUCOIN)

  iv. Marie Blanche Cormier born 1742
   v. Charles Cormier born 1744

 b. Anne Cormier born 1706
 c. Marie Cormier born 1708
 d. Marguerite Cormier born 1709 married 1732 Maurice
   COMMEAU (son of Pierre Commeau and Jeanne BOURG)

   i. Oliver Commeau born 1733
   ii. Catherine Commeau born 1741
  iii. Madeleine Commeau born 1742

 e. Michel Cormier born 1710
 f. Madeleine Cormier born 1712
 g. Germain Cormier born 1713 married January 30, 1741
   Anne GAUDET (daughter of Guillaume Gaudet and
   Marie BOUDROT)

   i. Pierre Poncy Cormier born 1741
   ii. Marie Madeleine Cormier born 1743
  iii. Charles Cormier born 1745

 h. Catherine Cormier born 1714
 i. Jean Baptiste Cormier born 1715 married 1740
   Marie HUGON (daughter of Louis Hugon and Marie
   BOURGEOIS)

   i. Jean Baptiste Cormier born 1742

 j. Jean Cormier born 1716
 k. Pierre Cormier born 1720 married February 25, 1745
   Marie DOUCET

   i. Raphael Cormier born 1744

 l. Marie Madeleine Germain Cormier born 1722
 m. Francois Cormier born 1724 married February 19,
   1748 Madeleine DOUCET (daughter of Francois
   Doucet and Marie POIRIER)

   i. Madeleine Cormier born 1748
   ii. Pierre Cormier born 1751
  iii. Felix Cormier born 1753
   iv. Marie Cormier born 1755
   v. Francois Cormier born 1758

 n. Charles Cormier born 1726 married November 9, 1778
   Madeleine LE BLANC (daughter of Francois LeBlanc
   and Jeanne HEBERT   widow of Amand BRAUD

3. Pierre LeBlanc born 1689 married c. 1714 Elizabeth
 BOUDROT

 a. Paul LeBlanc born 1716 married August 27, 1743
   Elizabeth GAUTEROT (daughter of Paul Gauterot and
   Marie BUJEAUD)

        i.   Marie Blanche LeBlanc baptized May 6, 1745
       ii.   Francoise LeBlanc born May 3, 1747
    b.   Anne LeBlanc born May 17, 1719
    c.   Jean LeBlanc born March 12, 1722
    d.   Marguerite LeBlanc born November 6, 1727
    e.   Elizabeth LeBlanc married November 16, 1734
         Joseph DUPUIS (son of Martin Dupuis and Marie
         LANDRY)

        i.   Pierre Dupuis born 1735
       ii.   Marie Madeleine Dupuis born 1737
      iii.   Marie Joseph Dupuis born 1742
       iv.   Osite Dupuis born 1744
        v.   Jean Baptiste Dupuis born 1747

4.   Anne LeBlanc born 1692
5.   Claude LeBlanc born 1696
6.   Jacques LeBlanc born 1701 married

                        (1)   November 14, 1718 Catherine
                              BOUDROT (daughter of Claude
                              Boudrot and Catherine MEUNIER)

     Jacques died January 10, 1743

    a.   Marie Josephe LeBlanc born October 1, 1719 married
         July 24, 1742 Pierre LE JEUNE (son of Pierre
         LeJeune and Jeanne BENOIT)

        i.   David LeJeune born 1745
       ii.   Anselme LeJeune born 1746
      iii.   Anne LeJeune born 1749
       iv.   Marie Blanche LeJeune born 1751

                        (2)   October 15, 1731 Marguerite
                              LANOUE (daughter of Louis
                              Lanoue and Marie RIMBAULT)

    b.   Joseph Abel LeBlanc born July 26, 1733
    c.   Bonaventure LeBlanc born 1734
    d.   Helvidge (Ludivine) LeBlanc born January 4, 1737
    e.   Anselme LeBlanc born Decmeber 13, 1739
    f.   Anastasie LeBlanc born June 23, 1742

7.   Joseph LeBlanc born 1704 married July 29, 1726 Marie
     GRANGER (daughter of Jacques Granger and Marie
     GIROUARD)

    a.   Marie Josephe LeBlanc baptized May 13, 1730
    b.   Anne Marie LeBlanc born September 24, 1732
    c.   Marie Joseph LeBlanc born 1734
    d.   Madeleine LeBlanc born 1739

8.   Charles LeBlanc born September 29, 1707 married Octo-
     ber 23, 1730 Marie Joseph FLAN (Blanc) (daughter of
     Jean Francois Flan and Marie DUPUIS)

                              37

a. Charles LeBlanc born September 11, 1731
b. Joseph LeBlanc born January 5, 1734
c. Marin LeBlanc born February 27, 1736
d. Etienne LeBlanc born October 20, 1741
e. Marie Josephe LeBlanc born March 4, 1746

9. Claire LeBlanc born June 1, 1710 married April 30, 1726 Joseph ROBACHEAUX (son of Charles Robacheaux and Marie BOURG)

a. Joseph Robacheaux born 1728 married 1750 Marie MICHEL
b. Marie Blanche Robacheaux born 1731
c. Marie Josephe Robacheaux born 1733
d. Pierre Robacheaux born 1735 married 1760 Anne MICHEL (widow of Francois LeBlanc)

     i. Anne Blanche Robacheaux (ROBICHAUD) born 1762
    ii. Marie Rose Robichaud born 1763
   iii. Joseph Seruan Robichaud born 1765
    iv. Olive Victoire Robichaud born 1767
     v. Pierre Robichaud born 1768
    vi. Ignace Robichaud born 1768
   vii. Marthe Elizabeth Robichaud born 1770
  viii. Jean Louis Robichaud born 1770
    ix. Jacques Cyrille Robichaud born 1776

e. Anne Theodose Robichaud born 1736
f. Francoise Robichaud born 1739
g. Marguerite Pelagie Robichaud born 1744
h. Michel Robichaud born 1746 married 1766 Francoise LANDRY

     i. Jean Michel Robichaud born 1767
    ii. Pierre Marie Robichaud born 1769
   iii. Anne Marie Robichaud born 1770
    iv. Marguerite Theodose Robichaud born 1772
     v. Jean Baptiste Michel Robichaud born 1776
    vi. Francoise Josephe Robichaud born 1778
   vii. Tharsile Robichaud born 1780
  viii. Blanche Robichaud born 1784
    ix. Marie Francoise Robichaud born 1784

i. Isidore Robichaud born 1747 married April 4, 1769 Marguerite BOUDROT (daughter of Basile Boudrot and Marguerite GIROUARD)

     i. Jean Isidore Robichaud born 1770
    ii. Marie Marguerite Robichaud born 1772
   iii. Angelique Rosalie Robichaud born 1773
    iv. Jean Baptiste Robichaud born 1774
     v. Pierre Serve Robichaud born 1776
    vi. Marguerite Adelaide Robichaud born 1777
   vii. Charles Robichaud born 1778
  viii. Helene Robichaud born 1783

<pre>
        ix. Andre Robichaud born 1786
         x. Francoise Antoine Robichaud born 1788
        xi. Nicolas Robichaud born 1790
       xii. Francois Antoinette Robichaud born 1790
      xiii. Maxime Robichaud born 1792
</pre>

   j. Jean Baptiste Robichaud born 1751 married Febru-
       ary 4, 1773 Felicite SIRE (daughter of Jean Sire
       and Marie Josephe HEBERT)

<pre>
         i. Jean Baptiste Robichaud born 1774
        ii. Claire Felicite Robichaud born 1775
       iii. Jean Marie Robichaud born 1775
        iv. Julie Robichaud born 1776
         v. Elizabeth Anastasie Robichaud born 1777
        vi. David Robichaud born 1777
       vii. Marie Modeste Robichaud born 1778
      viii. Vincent Robichaud born 1783
        ix. Paul Robichaud born 1784
</pre>

   k. Charles Robichaud born 1753

F. Antoine LeBlanc born 1662 married c. 1680 Marie BOURGEOIS
(daughter of Jacob Bourgeois and Jeanne TRAHAN)

   1. Antoine LeBlanc born 1681 married c. 1701 Anne Jeanne
       LANDRY (daughter of Antoine Landry and Marie THIBODEAU)

       a. Antoine LeBlanc born 1702 married July 16, 1726
           Marie BABIN (daughter of Charles Babin and
           Madeleine RICHARD)

<pre>
             i. Son of Antoine LeBlanc baptized and buried
                 October 2, 1741
            ii. Jean Baptiste LeBlanc born 1730
           iii. Pierre LeBlanc born 1731
            iv. Simon LeBlanc born 1733
             v. Elizabeth Ann LeBlanc born December 10, 1735;
                 died November 1, 1748 at age 13 years (SGA)
            vi. Marguerite LeBlanc born October 2, 1739
           vii. Madeleine Blanche LeBlanc born April 24, 1743
</pre>

       b. Paul LeBlanc born October 11, 1707 married Novem-
           ber 13, 1730 Madeliene FOREST (daughter of Pierre
           Forest and Cecile RICHARD)

<pre>
             i. Anastasie LeBlanc born 1732
            ii. Marie Blanche LeBlanc born October 6, 1736
           iii. Olivier LeBlanc born 1739
            iv. Jean Baptiste LeBlanc born March 12, 1742
             v. Lucie Josephe LeBlanc born December 12, 1744
                 married September 28, 1767 Joseph DOUCET (son
                 of Joseph Doucet and Marie Anne BOURG)

                 a) Marie Josephe Doucet born 1766
                 b) Joseph Doucet
</pre>

     vi. Anne LeBlanc born February 7, 1747

  c. Anne Marie LeBlanc born January 15, 1712 married
     August 6, 1733 Joseph RICHARD (son of Michael
     Richard and Agnes BOURGEOIS)
  d. Marie Josephe LeBlanc born 1715 married 1740
     Pierre RICHARD (son of Pierre Richard and Made-
     leine GIROUARD)

     i.   Marie Richard born 1741 married 1760 Amable
        HEBERT (son of Jean Hebert and Marguerite
        TRAHAN)
     ii. Joseph Ignace Richard born 1743 married 1764
        Marguerite LE BLANC (daughter of Charles
        LeBlanc and Elizabeth THIBODEAU)
    iii. Jean Charles Richard born 1745
     iv. Catherine Richard born 1747 married Simon
        TRAHAN
     v.   Brigitte Richard born 1749
     vi. Simon Richard born 1752
    vii. Anselme Richard born 1756

  e. Brigitte LeBlanc born January 23, 1710 married
     October 14, 1728 Claude GRANGER (son of Rene
     Granger and Marguerite TERIOT)

     i.   Marie Josephe Granger born 1729 married 1748
        Jean Baptiste DUPUIS
     ii. Joseph Granger born 1732 married 1757 Elizabeth
        TERRIOT
    iii. Marie Madeleine Granger born 1738 married 1767
        Jean Baptiste DESPREZ
     iv. Mathurin Granger born 1740.
     v.   Marguerite Granger born 1744
     vi. Charles Granger born 1748
    vii. Jean Baptiste Granger born 1751

  f. Simon LeBlanc born 1722 married c. 1745 Marguerite
     TERRIOT (daughter of Claude Terriot and Agnes
     AUCOIN)

     i.   Marguerite LeBlanc born Decmeber 13, 1744
     ii. Jean LeBlanc born 1754

  g. Marguerite LeBlanc born 1723
  h. Olivier LeBlanc baptized July 7, 1726
  i. Blanche LeBlanc born 1730; died July 9, 1730 at
     age 9 months

2. Charles LeBlanc born 1683 married c. 1708 Marie
    GAUTEROT (daughter of Claude Gauterot and Marie THERIOT)

  a. Anne LeBlanc born January 30, 1710 married June 26,
     1730 Jacques RICHARD (son of Pierre Richard and
     Marguerite LANDRY)

     i.   Joseph Richard born 1731
     ii. Charles Ignace Richard born 1733

b. Madeleine LeBlanc born 1719 married c. 1740 Paul
   RICHARD (son of Pierre Richard and Marguerite
   LANDRY)

   i.   Mathurin Richard born June 18, 1741
   ii. Amans Richard born March 1, 1744
   iii. Marie Magdeleine Richard born October 8, 1746
   iv. Pierre Richard born 1748
   v.   Jacques Richard born 1750

c. Mathurin LeBlanc born 1722 married October 16,
   1747 Elizabeth BABIN (daughter of Jean Babin and
   Marguerite TERIOT)
d. Pierre LeBlanc born August 18, 1725
e. Marguerite Charlotte LeBlanc married February 21,
   1735 Joseph RICHARD (son of Pierre Richard and
   Marguerite LANDRY)

   i.   Marguerite Richard born 1735
   ii. Antoine Etienne Richard born 1738
   iii. Simon Richard born December 2, 1740
   iv. Francois Richard born September 19, 1743
   v.   Marie Blanche Richard born 1746
   vi. Joseph Richard born 1749
   vii. Jean Charles Richard born 1766

f. Elizabeth LeBlanc married June 30, 1732 Abraham
   LANDRY (son of Abraham Landry and Marie GUILBAUT)

   i.   Mathurin Landry born 1733
   ii. Joseph Landry dit a Petit Abram born 1740 mar-
        ried

             (1) Madeleine GAUDIN
             (2) August 10, 1768 Anne GRANGER
                  (daughter of Pierre Granger
                  and Ufrosine GAUTROS)
             (3) Marie Madeleine BRAUD

   iii. Etienne Landry dit LeJeune born 1743 married
        May 12, 1776 Brigit TRAHAN (daughter of
        Charles Trahan and Brigit LANDRY)
   iv. Simon Landry born 1745 married Marguerite
        BABIN (daughter of Germain Babin and Margue-
        rite LANDRY)
   v.   Natalie Landry born 1746
   vi. Anastasie Landry born 1747 married Aman BABIN;
        died August 18, 1795 at age 48
   vii. Marie Landry born 1750 married February 5,
        1768 Joseph BABIN (son of Joseph Babin and
        Anne THERIOT)
   viii. Pierre Abraham Landry dit Pitre born 1751
        married Marguerite ALLAIN;

3. Pierre Gustave LeBlanc dit Pinault born 1685 married
February 16, 1711 Francoise LANDRY (daughter of
Antoine Landry and Marie THIBODEAU)

   a. Agnes LeBlanc born March 15, 1712 married October 15, 1735 Pierre GAUTREAU (son of Francois
Gautreau and Louise AUCOIN)

      i. Agnes Gautreau born 1734
     ii. Charles Gautreau born 1739 married 1763
Madeleine MELANCON

         a) Jean Charles Gautreau born 1764
         b) Jean Pierre Gautreau born 1766
         c) Marie Madeleine Gautreau born 1767
         d) Joseph Benoit Gautreau born 1768

    iii. Theo Gautreau born 1738
     iv. Basile Gautreau born 1741
      v. Marie Josephe Gautreau born 1745
     vi. Rose Gautreau born 1747 married August 18, 1767
Paul GAUDET (son of Augustin Gaudet and Agnes
CHIASSON)

         a) Apolonie Rose Gaudet born 1768
         b) Anne Gaudet born 1771
         c) Marie Gaudet born 1773

   b. Anne LeBlanc born 1718; baptized March 6, 1718
married January 7, 1739 Charles DUGAS (son of
Joseph Dugas and Marguerite RICHARD)

      i. Charles Dugas born 1739
     ii. Anne Dugas born 1740
    iii. Joseph Dugas born 1742
     iv. Pierre Dugas born 1742
      v. Amand Herculin Dugas born 1743
     vi. Helene Dugas born 1750
    vii. Marthe Dugas born 1755

   c. Theodore LeBlanc born 1719 married June 4, 1740
Marie CORMIER (daughter of Francois Cormier and
Marie Genevieve LE BLANC)

      i. Marie Madeleine LeBlanc born 1741
     ii. Rosalie LeBlanc born 1745

   d. Angelique LeBlanc born May 27, 1722
   e. Marie Madeleine LeBlanc born 1723
   f. Augustin LeBlanc born November 25, 1724 married
1752 Francoise HEBERT (daughter of Jean Baptiste
Hebert and Elizabeth GRANGER); died July 13, 1786

      i. Jean LeBlanc born 1753
     ii. Augustin LeBlanc born 1755
    iii. Charles LeBlanc born 1758

      iv. Joseph LeBlanc born 1760
       v. Elizabeth LeBlanc born 1762
      vi. Etienne LeBlanc born 1763
    vii. Rosalie LeBlanc born 1766

g. Joseph LeBlanc born February 11, 1726
h. Francoise LeBlanc born July 27, 1727
i. Marie LeBlanc born April 6, 1729 married July 10, 1748 Francois GAUTEROT (son of Francois Gauterot and Louise AUCOIN)

       i. Jean Baptiste Gauterot born 1749
      ii. Joseph Gauterot born 1751

j. Marguerite Monique LeBlanc born 1734
k. Pierre Hilaire LeBlanc born 1739 married 1763 Marie Elizabeth HEBERT (daughter of Pierre Hebert and Elizabeth DUPUIS)

       i. Pierre LeBlanc born 1764
      ii. Marie Claire LeBlanc born 1768
    iii. Jean LeBlanc born 1771
     iv. Elizabeth LeBlanc born 1772

l. Pierre Raymond LeBlanc born January 7, 1731
m. Ursule LeBlanc married February, 1740 Joseph BROSSAR (son of Pierre Brossar and Marie BOURG)

       i. Joseph Brossar (Broussard) born February 26, 1741
      ii. Jean Baptiste Broussard born January 14, 1742
    iii. Charles Broussard born April 11, 1743
     iv. Marie Broussard born September 2, 1744

n. Marie Rose LeBlanc born March 25, 1732 married 1762 Jean Baptiste HEBERT (son of Jean Baptiste Hebert and Elizabeth GRANGER)

       i. Honore Hebert born 1763
      ii. Francoise Hebert born 1766
    iii. Marie Rose Hebert born 1768
     iv. Marguerite Hebert born 1770

4. Marie (Blanche) LeBlanc born 1688 married c. 1706 Antoine LANDRY (son of Antoine Landry and Marie THIBODEAU)

a. Francoise Landry born 1707
b. Paul Landry born 1708 married October 20, 1732 Marie Josephe Hebert (daughter of Guillaume Hebert and Marie Josephe DUPUIS)

       i. Marie Landry born 1744

c. Francois Landry born November 10, 1709
d. Pierre Landry born December 10, 1711
e. Alexis Landry born 1717

f. Joseph Landry born 1720
g. Charles Landry born 1722
h. Jean Baptiste Landry born 1724
i. Michel Landry born April 29, 1726
j. Amand Landry born 1728
k. Marie Josephe Landry born 1734

5. Jean LeBlanc dit Des Sapins born 1691 married February 4, 1715 Anne LANDRY (daughter of Rene Landry and Anne THERRIOT)

    a. Jean Baptiste LeBlanc born 1716 married January 11, 1745 Marguerite MELANCON (daughter of Joseph Melancon and Marguerite LE BLANC)

        i. Jean Baptiste LeBlanc born 1746

    b. Gregoire LeBlanc born September 24, 1720
    c. Simon Pierre LeBlanc born 1721
    d. Marine LeBlanc born 1724
    e. Blaise LeBlanc baptized February 28, 1725 married September 7, 1747 Marie Josephe MELANCON (daughter of Joseph Melancon and Marguerite LE BLANC)

        i. Marguerite LeBlanc born June 19, 1748

    f. Marguerite LeBlanc born December 29, 1733
    g. Marianne (Marine) LeBlanc born 1736 married 1756 Joseph BABIN (son of Claude Babin and Marguerite DUPUIS)

        i. Joseph Nicaise Babin born 1757
       ii. Bonaventure Babin born 1759
      iii. Marie Theotiste Babin born 1761
      iv. Marie Victoire Babin born 1763
       v. Francois Laurent Babin born 1766
      vi. Pierre Moise Babin born 1768
     vii. Anne Marguerite Babin born 1770
    viii. Mathurin Babin born 1773

6. Jacques LeBlanc born 1693 married 1716 Cecile DUPUIS

    a. Helene LeBlanc born November 24, 1717 married November 26, 1742 Honore LANDRY (son of Rene Landry and Madeleine MELANCON)

        i. Anselme Landry born September 17, 1743
       ii. Jean Baptiste Landry born December 10, 1744

    b. Marie Madeleine LeBlanc born December 17, 1720 married 1748 Anselme LANDRY (son of Rene Landry and Madeleine MELANCON)

        i. Jean Pierre Landry born 1751

    c. Jean Jacques LeBlanc born January 22, 1723
    d. Francoise LeBlanc born March 3, 1726
    e. Jean Pierre LeBlanc born 1727

f. Joseph LeBlanc born December 11, 1729
g. Dominique LeBlanc born October 29, 1731
h. Casimir LeBlanc born March 3, 1736

7. Joseph LeBlanc born 1697 married February 13, 1719
    Anne BOURG (daughter of Alexandre Bourg and Margue-
    rite MELANCON)

    a. Joseph LeBlanc born 1721 married

                    (1) 1745 Marie LANDRY (daughter of
                         Pierre Landry and Marie BABIN)

        i.   Joseph LeBlanc born September 16, 1746
       ii.   Simon LeBlanc born January 5, 1748
      iii.   Jean Baptiste LeBlanc born 1750

                    (2) 1752 Marguerite LE BLANC
                         (daughter of Claude LeBlanc
                         and Marguerite DUPUIS)
                    (3) Angelique DAIGRE (daughter of
                         Bernard Daigre and Angelique
                         RICHARD)

       iv.   Moise LeBlanc born 1762
        v.   Jean LeBlanc born 1764
       vi.   Firmin LeBlanc born 1766
      vii.   Anselme LeBlanc born 1767
     viii.   Paul LeBlanc born 1768
       ix.   Charles Ignace LeBlanc born 1768
        x.   Euphrosine LeBlanc born 1770
       xi.   Victor LeBlanc born 1772
      xii.   Augustin LeBlanc born 1774
     xiii.   Angelique LeBlanc born 1776

    b. Marguerite LeBlanc born June 14, 1723 married
        Joseph DUGAS (son of Abraham Dugas and Marguerite
        RICHARD)

        i.   Marie Dugas married 1765 Jean LANDRY (son of
              Jean Baptiste Landry and Marie Josephe LE BLANC)
       ii.   Marguerite Dugas married 1763 Jean CYR (son of
              Jean Cyr and Anne BOURGEOIS)

              a)   Jean Cyr born 1764
              b)   Fabien Cyr born 1766
              c)   Joseph Cyr born 1768
              d)   Xavier Cyr born 1770
              e)   Marie Josephe Cyr born 1773

      iii.   Angelique Dugas married 1762 Jacques CYR (son
              of Pierre Cyr and Madeleine POIRIER)

              a)   Marie Adelaide Cyr born 1764
              b)   Anastasie Cyr born 1766
              c)   Amand Cyr born 1768
              d)   Jacques Cyr born 1771

        e) Marie Francoise Cyr born 1773
        f) Jean Baptiste Cyr born 1776

    c. Simon LeBlanc born March 4, 1726 married July 16,
        1748 Elizabeth LE BLANC (daughter of Jacques
        LeBlanc and Catherine LANDRY)
    d. Olivier LeBlanc born February 18, 1729 married
        1750 Marguerite LE BLANC (daughter of Jacques
        LeBlanc and Henriette DUPUIS)
    e. Alexandre LeBlanc born July 1, 1732 married 1752
        Marguerite BOUDROT (daughter of Joseph Boudrot
        and Marguerite DUGAS)

        i.   Alexandre LeBlanc born April 6, 1760
        ii.   Polycarpe LeBlanc born 1762
        iii. Simon LeBlanc born 1766
        iv.   Charles LeBlanc born 1770
        v.   Joseph LeBlanc born 1772

    f. Paul LeBlanc born 1734 married 1758 Anne DE LATOU
        (daughter of Charles de Latour and Marguerite
        RICHARD) Paul died May 21, 1771

        i.   Charles Andre LeBlanc baptized November 30,
              1761
        ii.   Etienne LeBlanc born 1762
        iii. Joseph LeBlanc born 1764
        iv.   Anne Adelaide LeBlanc born 1766
        v.   Marie Xavier Josephe LeBlanc born 1768

    g. Anne LeBlanc born 1740 married 1760 Joseph Nicola
        GAUTHIER (son of Nicolas Gauthier and Marie ALAIN

        i.   Victoire Gauthier born 1763
        ii.   Charlotte Gauthier born 1765
        iii. Nicolas Joseph Gauthier born 1768
        iv.   Anselme Gauthier born 1772
        v.   Simon Gauthier born 1774

8. Marguerite LeBlanc born 1699 married 1721 Joseph
    MELANCON (son of Philippe Melancon and Marie DUGAS)

    a. Joseph Melancon born 1721
    b. Marguerite Melancon born 1722
    c. Alexandre Melancon born 1723 married Osite HEBERT
    d. Ursule Melancon baptized November 15, 1724
    e. Honore Melancon born 1725 married M.Josephe BRAUD
    f. Marie Joseph Melancon born 1726
    g. Amand Melancon born October 14, 1728 married 1755
        Anne BABIN
    h. Jean Melancon born November 1730

9. Rene LeBlanc born 1701 married c. 1721 Anne THERIOT
    (daughter of Germain Theriot and Anne RICHARD)

a. Etienne LeBlanc born November 11, 1722 married
   October 1, 1742 Elizabeth BOUDROT (daughter of
   Claude Boudrot and Catherine HEBERT)

    i. Marie LeBlanc born July 24, 1743
    ii. Simon Joseph LeBlanc born Decmeber 16, 1744
   married September 21, 1772 Elizabeth LE BLANC
   (daughter of Joseph LeBlanc and Elizabeth
   GAUTROT)
    iii. Anne LeBlanc born July 19, 1746
    iv. Marguerite LeBlanc born March 22, 1748 married
   Joseph LE BLANC
    v. Etienne LeBlanc born 1751 married January 7,
   1778 Ozite LE BLANC (daughter of Desire
   LeBlanc and Marie Magdeleine LANDRY)
    vi. Mathurin LeBlanc born 1754 married May 4, 1778
   Rosalie TERRIO
    vii. Madeleine LeBlanc born 1758 married

        (1) Joseph Landry (son of Abraham
            Landry and Marguerite LE BLANC)
        (2) September 8, 1787 Henry
            ROBICHAUX
        (3) Jacques LAMOTHE

    viii. Joseph LeBlanc born 1761
    ix. Marie LeBlanc born 1765

b. Claire LeBlanc married June 5, 1744 Joseph LEGER
   (son of Jacques Leger and Anne AMIRAULT)

    i. Anastasie Leger born 1754
    ii. Rosalie Leger born 1764
    iii. Francois Henri Leger born 1767

c. Francoise LeBlanc married January 11, 1745 Benony
   BOURG (son of Alexandre Bourg and Marguerite
   MELANCON)

    i. Marguerite Bourg born 1745
    ii. Jean Baptiste Bourg born 1747

d. Anne LeBlanc born May 22, 1728
e. Anastasie LeBlanc baptized July 20, 1730
f. Elizabeth LeBlanc born 1732
g. Rose LeBlanc born 1734
h. Simon Joseph LeBlanc born January 30, 1737
i. Jean Baptiste LeBlanc born 1739
j. Pierre Victor LeBlanc born 1742 married August 29,
   1768 Marguerite SAULNIER

    i. Joseph Ignace LeBlanc born 1766
    ii. Marguerite LeBlanc born 1767
    iii. Marie LeBlanc born 1770
    iv. Simon LeBlanc born 1771
    v. Hilarion LeBlanc born 1778

    vi.   Nicolas LeBlanc born 1780
   vii.   Francois LeBlanc born 1782

   k.   Rene LeBlanc born c. 1752 married Marguerite
        TRAHAN

10. Elizabeth LeBlanc born 1703 married 1722 Charles
     DUPUIS (son of Pierre Dupuis and Madeliene LANDRY)

     a.   Jean Charles Dupuis born 1724 married February 10,
          1747 Marie GAUTROT
     b.   Cyprien Dupuis born August 2, 1726
     c.   Marie Dupuis born January 1, 1729
     d.   Amand Dupuis born 1731
     e.   Anne Dupuis born 1733
     f.   Judith Dupuis born 1735
     g.   Marguerite Dupuis born 1738
     h.   Joseph Dupuis born 1742
     i.   Rosalie Dupuis born February 17, 1745
     j.   Jean Baptiste Dupuis born June 22, 1748

11. Francois LeBlanc born 1714 married c. 1739 Isabelle
     DUGAS

     a.   Marie LeBlanc born September 15, 1739
     b.   Joseph LeBlanc born 1741
     c.   Marie LeBlanc born March 2, 1742
     d.   Elizabeth LeBlanc born April 2, 1744
     e.   Marie LeBlanc born 1746
     f.   Isabelle LeBlanc born 1748
     g.   Francois LeBlanc born 1750

G. Pierre LeBlanc born 1664 married

                       (1) 1684 Marie THERIOT (daughter
                            of Claude Theriot and Fran-
                            coise GAUTEROT)

     Pierre died November 4, 1717 at Port Royal, Acadia

     1. Pierre LeBlanc born 1685

                       (2) c. 1699 Madeleine BOURG

     2. Joseph LeBlanc born 1701 married January 20, 1721
         Marguerite BOURGEOIS (daughter of Germain Bourgeois
         and Magdeleine DUGAS)

         a.   Madeleine LeBlanc born 1721 married July 22, 1743
              Joseph RICHARD (son of Rene Richard and Marguerite
              THERIOT)

              i.   Michel Richard born 1744
             ii.   Marie Blanche Richard born 1746
            iii.   Felicite Richard born 1748
             iv.   Joseph Richard born 1749
              v.   Madeleine Richard born 1750

        vi.   Basile Richard born 1751
       vii.   Rosalie Richard born 1757

   b. Joseph LeBlanc born 1726 married 1746 Cecile
       Claire BENOIT (daughter of Claude Benoit and
       Jeanne HEBERT)

         i.   Joseph LeBlanc born 1747
        ii.   Marguerite LeBlanc born 1750
       iii.   Pierre LeBlanc born 1753
        iv.   Marie LeBlanc born 1757

   c. Basile LeBlanc born 1727 married November 27, 1752
       Anne RICHARD (daughter of Rene Richard and Margue-
       rite TERRIOT)

         i.   Joseph LeBlanc born 1754
        ii.   Marie Ann LeBlanc born 1756

   d. Pierre LeBlanc born 1729
   e. Marie Josephe LeBlanc born 1731
   f. Felicite LeBlanc born 1733 married

                      (1)   November 29, 1753 Charles
                            RICHARD (son of Rene Richard
                            and Marguerite TERRIOT)

         i.   Joseph Richard born 1755

                      (2)   November 18, 1762 Joseph
                            BELIVEAU (son of Charles Beli-
                            veau and Anne DUGAS)

        ii.   Charles Beliveau born 1764
       iii.   Jean Beliveau born 1768

   g. Cajetan LeBlanc born 1736
   h. Rose LeBlanc born 1739
   i. Anne LeBlanc born 1742

3. Jean Simon LeBlanc born 1703 married November 23, 1722
   Jeanne DUPUIS (daughter of Jean Dupuis and Anne RICHARD)

   a. Jean LeBlanc born 1724 married January 19, 1750
       Marie Josephe LANDRY (daughter of Charles Landry
       and Marie Josephe SAVOIE)

         i.   Marie Anne LeBlanc born 1751
        ii.   Marguerite LeBlanc born 1752
       iii.   Scholastique LeBlanc born 1754
        iv.   Jean Joseph LeBlanc born 1755
         v.   Marie Seraphine LeBlanc born 1757
        vi.   Pierre Marie LeBlanc born 1759
       vii.   Marie Jeanne LeBlanc born 1762
      viii.   Marie Charlotte LeBlanc born 1766
        ix.   Marie Louise LeBlanc born 1769

   b. Nathalie LeBlanc born 1727 married February 19,
       1748 Joseph GIROUARD

c. Joseph LeBlanc born 1729 married January 20, 1755 Marguerite ROBICHAUX (daughter of Louis Robichaux and Jeanne BOURGEOIS)

   i. Marie LeBlanc born 1755
  ii. Marie Marguerite LeBlanc born 1760
 iii. Louis Edouard LeBlanc born 1762

d. Pierre LeBlanc born 1735
e. Amand LeBlanc born 1738
f. Madeleine LeBlanc born 1741
g. Marie Josephe LeBlanc born 1744
h. Isabelle LeBlanc married June 9, 1749 Pierre FORET

4. Anne LeBlanc married January 2, 1719 Joseph BOURGEOIS (son of Germain Bourgeois and Magdeleine DUGAS)

a. Judith Bourgeois born 1720
b. Joseph Gregoire Bourgeois born 1722 married

> (1) February 10, 1749 Catherine COMEAU (daughter of Abraham Comeau and Marguerite PITRE)

   i. Marguerite Bourgeois born 1752
  ii. Joseph Gregoire Bourgeois born 1753 married February 3, 1777 Marie Seraphine LE BLANC (daughter of Jean Simon LeBlanc and Marie LANDRY)
 iii. Jean Baptiste Bourgeois born 1755
  iv. Joseph Bourgeois born 1756
   v. Jean Francois Bourgeois born 1758
  vi. Marie Bourgeois born 1762
 vii. Marie Isabelle Bourgeois born 1765

> (2) June 20, 1774 Therese HUBERT (widow of Francois PRECOURT)

c. Bonaventure Bourgeois born 1725
d. Felicite Bourgeois born 1727 married February 3, 1750 Pierre PRINCE (son of Jean Prince and Jeanne Jeanne BLANCHARD)

   i. Anne Prince born 1750
  ii. Isabelle Prince

e. Perpetue Bourgeois born 1729 married February 10, 1749 Rene RICHARD (son of Rene Richard and Marguerite TERRIOT)

   i. Joseph Richard born 1749
  ii. Marie Madeleine Richard born 1765
 iii. Pierre Alexis Richard born 1766
  iv. Modeste Richard born 1768

f. Ludivine Bourgeois born 1732
g. Pepin Gauthier Bourgeois born 1734 married 1783 Marie POIRIER (widow of Oliver THIBODEAU)

    h.   Ludivine Bourgeois born 1735
    i.   Petronille Bourgeois born 1736 married June 26,
         1754 Antoine BENOIT (son of Claude Benoit and
         Jeanne HEBERT)
    j.   Joseph Thimotee Bourgeois born 1739 married 1769
         Elizabeth QUINIET (daughter of Guillaume Quiniet
         and Louise ROBICHAUD)
    k.   Elizabeth Bourgeois born 1742
    l.   Anne Seraphine Bourgeois born 1744
    m.   Marguerite Bourgeois born 1746

5. Marie LeBlanc married November 24, 1721 Claude
    BOURGEOIS (son of Germain Bourgeois and Magdeleine
    DUGAS)

    a.   Pierre Benjamin Bourgeois born 1726 married

                    (4)   Anne LE BLANC
                    (5)   Anne THIBODEAU

    b.   Marie Madeleine Bourgeois born 1728 married Novem-
         ber 28, 1752 Joseph Prudent ROBICHAUD (son of
         Joseph Robichaud and Marie FOREST)
    c.   Anastasie Bourgeois born 1730
    d.   Elizabeth Bourgeois born 1730 married 1760 Poly-
         carpe ROBICHAUD (son of Joseph Robichaud and
         Marie FOREST)

         i.   Marie Ursule Robichaud born   1762

    e.   Joseph Abel Bourgeois born 1733 married Septem-
         ber 28, 1767 (married civilly 1762) Marguerite
         DOUCET

         i.   Jean Baptiste Bourgeois born 1763
        ii.   Marie Josephe Bourgeois born 1765
       iii.   Joseph Bourgeois born 1768
        iv.   Marie Marguerite Bourgeois born 1771
         v.   Pierre Bourgeois born 1774
        vi.   Elizabeth Bourgeois born 1776
       vii.   Joseph Bourgeois born 1779

    f.   Amand Bourgeois born 1735 married July 26, 1767
         (married civilly 1766) Marguerite DUGAS (daugh-
         ter of Claude Dugas and Marie Josephe MELANCON)

         i.   Marie Anne Bourgeois born 1767
        ii.   Marie Josephe Bourgeois born 1768
       iii.   Abraham Bourgeois born 1770
        iv.   Marie Marguerite Bourgeois born 1772
         v.   Claude Bourgeois born 1774
        vi.   Marie Angelique Bourgeois born 1774
       vii.   Marie Esther Bourgeois born 1776
      viii.   Jean Baptiste Bourgeois born 1778
        ix.   Joseph Bourgeois born 1780

g. Amable Bourgeois born 1737 married July 26, 1767 (married civilly 1760) Louise RICHARD (daughter of Jean Baptiste Richard and Marguerite ROBICHAUD)
h. Gertrude Bourgeois born 1738
i. Marguerite Bourgeois born 1741
j. Nathalie Bourgeois born 1743
k. Germain Bourgeois born 1749 married June 10, 1776 Ludivine Elizabeth BELLIVEAU (daughter of Charles Belliveau and Osite DUGAS)

6. Pierre LeBlanc born 1709
7. Paul LeBlanc born 1716 married October 6, 1732 Marie Josephe RICHARD (daughter of Rene Richard and Marguerite BENOIT)

   a. Joseph LeBlanc born 1733
   b. Charles Gregoire LeBlanc born 1734 married 1762 Theotiste BELIVEAU (daughter of Pierre Beliveau and Jeanne GAUDET)

      i. Charles Ignace LeBlanc born 1763
      ii. Joseph Bonaventure LeBlanc born 1766
      iii. Marie Anne LeBlanc born 1766
      iv. Isaac LeBlanc born 1768
      v. Pierre LeBlanc born 1770
      vi. Firmin LeBlanc born 1772
      vii. Paul LeBlanc born 1788

   c. Pierre LeBlanc born 1736
   d. Bonaventure LeBlanc born 1738 married 1763 Rose BELLIVEAU (daughter of Pierre Belliveau and Jeanne GAUDET)

      i. Jean Isaac LeBlanc born 1767
      ii. Rosalie LeBlanc born 1768
      iii. Pierre LeBlanc born 1771
      iv. Anne LeBlanc born 1773
      v. Collette LeBlanc born 1775
      vi. Joseph LeBlanc born 1780
      vii. Amand LeBlanc born 1782

   e. Amand LeBlanc born 1740
   f. Nathalie LeBlanc born 1742
   g. Joseph LeBlanc born 1744
   h. Paul LeBlanc born 1745 married October 10, 1774 Marie HEBERT (daughter of Paul Hebert and Anne THIBODEAU)

      i. Marie LeBlanc born 1775
      ii. Jean Baptiste LeBlanc born 1776
      iii. Esther LeBlanc born 1779
      iv. Marguerite LeBlanc born 1781
      v. Marie Louise LeBlanc born 1783
      vi. Francois LeBlanc born 1785
      vii. Marguerite LeBlanc born 1786

        viii.   Marie Josephe LeBlanc born 1788
          ix.   Joseph LeBlanc born 1790
           x.   Marie Judith LeBlanc born 1792
          xi.   Marie Pelagie LeBlanc born 1794
         xii.   Paul LeBlanc born 1795

    i.   Basile LeBlanc born 1748 married

                    (1)   1768 Marie LANDRY

            i.   Jean Edouard LeBlanc born 1769

                    (2)   January 24, 1780 Marguerite
                          AMIRAULT (daughter of Francois
                          Amirault and Marguerite
                          ROBICHAUD)

    j.   Marie Josephe LeBlanc born 1749
    k.   Francois LeBlanc born 1751 married 1778 Marie
         Josephe PICHET

            i.   Francois LeBlanc born 1781
           ii.   Simon LeBlanc born 1785
          iii.   Joseph LeBlanc born 1787

    l.   Jean Baptiste LeBlanc born 1754

8. Madeleine LeBlanc born 1714
9. Charles LeBlanc born 1716 married January 10, 1735
    Madeleine GIROUARD (daughter of Francois Girouard
    and Anne BOURGEOIS)

    a.   Anne Gertrude LeBlanc born 1735
    b.   Charles LeBlanc born 1738
    c.   Pierre LeBlanc born 1740 married 1766 Marguerite
         BELLIVEAU (daughter of Jean Belliveau and
         Madeleine GAUDET)

            i.   Pierre LeBlanc born 1767
           ii.   Marin LeBlanc born 1770
          iii.   Amable LeBlanc born 1772

    d.   Madeleine LeBlanc born 1743
    e.   Marie Modeste LeBlanc born 1744 married 1768
         Frederic BELLIVEAU (son of Jean Belliveau and
         Marie Madeleine GAUDET)

            i.   Frederic Belliveau born 1769
           ii.   Marie Scholastique Belliveau born 1771
          iii.   Anselme Belliveau born 1776
           iv.   Madeleine Belliveau born 1778
            v.   Scholastique Belliveau
           vi.   Helene Belliveau born 1780
          vii.   Joseph Belliveau born 1783
         viii.   Francois Belliveau born 1786
           ix.   Suzanne Belliveau born 1790
            x.   Monique Belliveau born 1793

                        53

f. Felicite LeBlanc born 1746
g. Rose Prexede LeBlanc born 1749
h. Joseph LeBlanc born 1750

NOTE: Those entries indicated (SGA) indicate that the event hap-
       pened in Acadia but the record is found in the St. Gabriel
       Church records in the Archives of the Diocese of Baton
       Rouge.

PART II

DESIRE LE BLANC and MARIE MAGDELIENE LANDRY

FOUR GENERATION ANCESTOR CHART

```
                                                    8. Daniel LeBlanc
                                                    b.              ca. 1626
                                                    p.b.Martinaize, France
                         4. Andre LeBlanc           m.
                         b.            ca. 1659     p.m.
                         p.b. Port Royal, Acadia    d.
                         m.                         p.d.
                         p.m.
                         d.                         9. Francoise Gaudet
                         p.d.                       b.              ca. 1623
                                                    p.b.Martinaize, France
     2. Jean LeBlanc                                d.
     b.           ca. 1685                          p.d.
     p.b. Acadia
     m.
     p.m.                                           10.Abraham Dugas (gunsmith)
     d.                                             b.              ca. 1616
     p.d.                                           p.b.LaChausse, France
                                                    m.
                         5. Marie Dugas             p.m.
                         b.            ca. 1665     d.
                         p.b. Port Royal, Acadia    p.d.
                         d.
                         p.d.                       11.Marguerite Doucet
                                                    b.
                                                    p.b.
                                                    d.
  1. Desire LeBlanc                                 p.d.
  b.            ca. 1717
  p.b. Grand Pre, Acadia
  m.            ca. 1740                            12.Jacob Bourgeois (druggist)
  p.m. Acadia                                       b.              ca. 1618
  d. 15 March 1777                                  p.b. France
  p.d. Donaldsonville                               m.
                         6. Guillaume Bourgeois     p.m.
                         b.            ca. 1653     d.
                         p.b.Port Royal, Acadia     p.d.
                         m.            ca. 1786
                         p.m.                       13.Jeanne Trahan
                         d.                         b.              ca. 1631
                         p.d.                       p.b. France
                                                    d.
     3. Jeanne Bourgeois                            p.d.
     b.           ca. 1687
     p.b. Acadia
     d.                                             14.
     p.d.                                           b.
                                                    p.b.
                                                    m.
                         7. Marie Anne de Martignon p.m.
                         b.                         d.
                         p.b.                       p.d.
                         d.
                         p.d.                       15.
                                                    b.
                                                    p.b.
  Marie Magdelaine Landry                           d.
  Spouse of #1                                      p.d.
```

I. Desire LeBlanc (son of Jean LeBlanc and Jeanne BOURGEOIS)
    born 1717, Grande Pre, Acadia, married 1740 in Acadia Marie
    Magdeleine LANDRY (daughter of Jean Landry and Claire LE BLANC)
    born 1723 in Acadia. Desire died in Ascension Parish, Louisi-
    ana on March 15, 1777 at age 60.

    The family of Desire LeBlanc were natives of Acadia and were
    deported in 1755. They moved to Maryland, then to Louisiana
    arriving in about 1767. On August 9, 1778 the widow Marie
    Landry caused to be sold the estate of Desire LeBlanc (de-
    ceased). The estate was sold at the Church door. They owned
    a place Right Bank Mississippi River, 8 arpents between
    Joseph BUJOL and Jerome LE BLANC. It was sold to Simon, a
    son (C-269). This is the upper portion of Evan Hall Planta-
    tion. Marie Landry thereafter married Pierre LANDRY dit
    PIERROT a Jacque.

    A. Simon LeBlanc born 1741 in Grande Pre, Acadia married
        November 9, 1767, Ascension Parish, Anne ARCENEAUX (daugh-
        ter of Jean Arceneaux and Marie HEBERT). Simon died
        September 3, 1780 at age 39. He had been married previous-
        ly to Marie Joseph LANDRY. Anne Arceneaux was the widow
        of Bartheleme BERGERON and had a daughter, Marguerite, who
        was 4 years old when Anne married Simon. Anne died Au-
        gust 20, 1811 in St. James Parish, Louisiana.

        1. Marie Ann LeBlanc born 1768
        2. Antoine Alexandre LeBlanc baptized June 2, 1770 in St.
            James, Louisiana, married June 27, 1791 in Ascension
            Marie Clemence DUPUIS (daughter of Antoine Dupuis and
            Marie Anne GODIN).

            a. Edward LeBlanc married July 2, 1810 in Ascension
                Marcelite LA CHASSE (daughter of Philippe La-
                Chasse and Pelagie RICHARD).

                i.   Clete LeBlanc born December 20, 1818
                      St. Martinville, Louisiana
                ii.   Norbert LeBlanc born January 11, 1822
                      Lafayette, Louisiana
                iii. Clementine Celime LeBlanc born May 18, 1822
                      Lafayette, Louisiana married February 16, 1833
                      in St. Martinville, Louisiana Paul Emile BOUTTE
                      (son of Francois Boutte and Marie Celeste
                      GONSOULIN).
                iv.   Marie Marcelite LeBlanc born December 18, 1823
                      St. Martinville, Louisiana; married Simon
                      LE BLANC
                v.   Marguerite Melise LeBlanc born January 24, 1824
                      Lafayette, Louisiana
                vi.   Felicite LeBlanc born October 30, 1827
                      St. Martinville, Louisiana
                vii. Pelagie LeBlanc born May 21, 1829
                      St. Martinville, Louisiana

55

viii. Amelite LeBlanc born July 15, 1831
St. Martinville, Louisiana
ix. Edward LeBlanc married 1837 Seraphine ROY
(daughter of Charles Roy and Marie THERIOT)

    a) Amelie LeBlanc baptized August 20, 1838
at age 3 months, Lafayette, Louisiana
    b) Clementine LeBlanc born April 26, 1845
Lafayette, Louisiana
    c) Clarisse LeBlanc born February 12, 1848
Lafayette, Louisiana

b. Norbert LeBlanc married

    (1) August 13, 1816, St. Martin-
ville, Louisiana, Josephine
BROUSSARD

i. Simon LeBlanc born April 28, 1822
St. Martinville, Louisiana

    (2) February 9, 1824, St. Martin-
ville, Louisiana, Euphemie
LE BLANC (daughter of Benjamin
LeBlanc and Scholastique BRAUX)

ii. Elisa LeBlanc born December 12, 1825
St. Martinville, Louisiana
iii. Benjamin LeBlanc born March 5, 1829
Lafayette, Louisiana
iv. Scholastique Celestine LeBlanc born April 4,
1831, St. Martinville, Louisiana
v. Scholastique LeBlanc born December 20, 1832
St. Martinville, Louisiana
vi. Auguste LeBlanc born January 18, 1840
New Iberia, Louisiana

c. Clementina LeBlanc born May 30, 1794; baptized
October 12, 1794 in St. James, Louisiana
d. Carmelite LeBlanc born March 13, 1796; baptized
March 21, 1796 in St. James, Louisiana
e. Clette LeBlanc married January 7, 1822 in St.
James, Louisiana, Marie Melanie RICHARD (daughter
of Michel Richard and Rosalie MICHEL)

i. Antoine LeBlanc born December 3, 1822
St. James, Louisiana
ii. Clete LeBlanc born June 12, 1826
Lafayette, Louisiana
iii. Richard LeBlanc born May 29, 1828
St. Martinville, Louisiana
iv. Celeste Elodie LeBlanc born June 28, 1830
Convent, Louisiana
v. Michel LeBlanc born March 16, 1832
St. Martinville, Louisiana

        vi.   Eloy LeBlanc born 1833; baptized October 11,
              1835 at age 18 months, Lafayette, Louisiana
       vii.   Raymond Villere LeBlanc baptized April 26,
              1838, Lafayette, Louisiana
      viii.   Desire LeBlanc born 1838
              Lafayette, Louisiana

    3. Ann Constance LeBlanc baptized April 3, 1774, St. James,
        Louisiana married May 18, 1790, St. James, James Pierre
        RICHARD (son of Jean Richard and Rosalie BOURGEOIS);
        died in 1816
    4. Edward LeBlanc born May 2, 1772 (first child baptized
        in Ascension Church on August 30, 1772)
    5. Henriette LeBlanc married June 13, 1796, Ascension,
        Paul Hypolite BABIN (son of Joseph Babin and Marine
        LE BLANC)
    6. Benjamin LeBlanc married November 19, 1804, St. James,
        Scholastique BRAUD (daughter of Armand Braud and Mag-
        deleine CLOUATRE)

        a.   Anne Hortense LeBlanc born September 1, 1805;
             baptized February 16, 1806, St. James, Louisiana
        b.   Euphamie LeBlanc born March 30, 1807; baptized
             June 24, 1807, St. James, Louisiana
        c.   Simon Drozin LeBlanc born March 3, 1809; baptized
             April 24, 1809, St. James, Louisiana
        d.   Marie Constance LeBlanc born June 8, 1811; bap-
             tized February 1, 1812, St. James, Louisiana
        e.   Simon LeBlanc born August 29, 1813; baptized
             April 24, 1814, St. James, Louisiana
        f.   Modeste LeBlanc born June 15, 1817
             St. Martinville, Louisiana

B. Madeliene LE BLANC born 1742; died prior to 1767
C. Isaac LE BLANC born 1746, Grande Pre, Acadia, married

                        (1)   February 5, 1768, Ascension
                              Parish, Marie Rose MELANCON
                              (daughter of Jean Baptiste
                              Melancon and Madeleine LE BLANC)

    Isaac died June 21, 1794 at age 47 in Ascension Parish;
    Marie Rose died December 12, 1781 in Ascension Parish

    1. Joseph Isaac LeBlanc born 1769 married May 21, 1792
        in Ascension Parish Anne Martha BLANCHARD (daughter
        of Joseph Blanchard and Marie Josephe LANDRY)

        a.   Isaac Colin LeBlanc married April 6, 1816 in As-
             cension Parish Seraphine LANDRY (daughter of
             Pierre Landry and Marie Francoise HEBERT) Sera-
             phine died April 25, 1852 at age 60 in Ascension
             Parish

             i.   Bazile Camille LeBlanc born June 14, 1825;
                  baptized September 11, 1825 in Ascension

married November 10, 1851, Ascension Parish,
Nesida TERRIO (daughter of Jean Baptiste
Terrio and Azilda RICHARD)

   ii. Joseph Carville LeBlanc born August 18, 1827;
baptized November 18, 1827 in Ascension Parish,
married January 18, 1851 Marie Emma CIRE
(daughter of Pierre Cire and ZocaideMOROY)

      a) Francois Samuel LeBlanc born September 16,
1852; baptized October 31, 1852, Ascension

      b) Marie Amanda LeBlanc born September 13,
1855; baptized October 14, 1855, Ascension

      c) Marie Cecile Cire LeBlanc born November 24,
1857; baptized December 30, 1857, Ascension, married October 5, 1875, Ascension
Parish Edgard FORTIER (son of Lessant
Fortier and Hirma BRAUD)

      d) Anne Eugenie LeBlanc born February 21,
1859; baptized March 1, 1859, Ascension

      e) Louis A. LeBlanc born April 18, 1861;
baptized April 20, 1861, Ascension

  iii. Francoise Carmelite LeBlanc born April 26, 1831;
baptized April 7, 1833, Ascension, married
October 8, 1853, Ascension Parish, Theodule
CIRE (son of Pierre Cire and Zocaide MOROY)

   iv. Alphonse Amedee LeBlanc born October 5, 1833;
baptized May 9, 1834, Ascension

    v. Joseph Amadeo LeBlanc born October 5, 1833;
baptized May 9, 1834, Ascension

   vi. Isaac Aulime LeBlanc married July 12, 1841 in
Ascension Elvina BABIN (daughter of Landry
Babin and Marie Louise LANDRY)

  vii. Pierre Emile LeBlanc married February 3, 1842
in Ascension Parish Zulma LE BLANC (daughter
of Edouard LeBlanc and Gertrude MOLLERE)

 viii. Felix LeBlanc married June 5, 1855 in Ascension Aimee Desiree LANDRY (daughter of
Joseph Jules Landry and Aimee BLANCHARD)

b. Arthemise LeBlanc baptized May 23, 1799, Ascension,
married February 10, 1817 Simon Nabor BRAUD (son
of Jerome Raymond Braud and Rosalie LANDRY)
Arthemise died June 7, 1833, Ascension Parish

    i. Martha Anaise Braud born September 14, 1825;
baptized October 16, 1825, Ascension

   ii. Joseph Adelard Braud born October 27, 1827;
baptized October 26, 1828, Ascension

  iii. Marie Eveline Braud born July 10, 1820; baptized October 23, 1820, Ascension

   iv. Estelle Braud born August 18, 1832; baptized
October 18, 1832, Ascension, married August 19,
1851 in Ascension Camille COMES (son of Hubert

Comes and Ferande LE BLANC)
    v. Jean Gustave Braud born January 13, 1843; baptized July 25, 1843, Ascension

c. Joseph Dermon LeBlanc married May 20, 1817 in Ascension Marie Delphine LANDRY (daughter of Joseph Landry and Anne BUJOL)

    i. Marie Hermina LeBlanc married

        (1) August 21, 1834 in Ascension Valmont BLANCHARD (son of Victor Blanchard and Magdelaine RICHARD)
        (2) July 20, 1850 Isidore LAFARGUE (son of Joseph Lafargue and Marie DUBARD)

    ii. Dermond LeBlanc married January 22, 1841 in Ascension Elise COMES (daughter of Marcelin Comes and Arthemise BRAUD)

        a) Narcisse Faron LeBlanc born October 27, 1829; baptized November 3, 1829 in Ascension
        b) Marie Martha Cecile LeBlanc born September 2, 1842; baptized October 2, 1842 in Ascension
        c) Marie Phelomine Alice LeBlanc born July 4, 1844; baptized August 13, 1844 in Ascension
        d) Marie Marguerite Lisa LeBlanc born October 12, 1846; baptized January 17, 1847 in Ascension
        e) Marie Lore Antonia LeBlanc born June 27, 1849; baptized August 5, 1849 in Ascension

    iii. Denis Valcour LeBlanc born October 3, 1823; baptized October 28, 1823 in Ascension
    iv. Theresa Celeste LeBlanc born September 14, 1828; baptized March 18, 1829 in Ascension
    v. Elvina LeBlanc married September 26, 1853 in Ascension Ambroise ROUGEAU (son of Jean Rougeau and Jeanne DUCAST)
    vi. Justine Samuel LeBlanc born September 26, 1834; baptized March 22, 1835 in Ascension
    vii. Elizabeth Cecilia LeBlanc born November 21, 1836; baptized March 25, 1837 in Ascension married 1856 in Ascension Edouard GAUDIN (son of Edouard Gaudin and Lize GAUDET)

d. Edward LeBlanc born January 5, 1798; baptized March 25, 1798 in Ascension married March 5, 1821 in Ascension Gertrude MOLLERE (daughter of Louis Mollere and Anne LANDRY) born September 4, 1804; baptized November 19, 1804 in Ascension

i. Marie Zulma LeBlanc born August 16, 1823;
baptized October 12, 1823 in Ascension married February 3, 1842 in Ascension Pierre
Emile LE BLANC (son of Isaac Colin LeBlanc
and Seraphine LANDRY)
ii. Jean Adolph LeBlanc born August 8, 1825; baptized October 2, 1825 in Ascension married
April 13, 1850 in Ascension Marie Marguerite
LE BLANC (daughter of Privot LeBlanc and
Marie LE BLANC)
iii. Dominique Ernest LeBlanc baptized September 30,
1827 in Ascension married July 7, 1857 in
Ascension Marie Eliza TERRIO

    a) Joseph Camille LeBlanc born September 8,
1858; baptized September 27, 1858 in Ascension married

        (1) February 23, 1886 in Ascension
Georgina DUGAS (daughter of
Lazare Dugas and Laure GRAVOIS)
        (2) July 15, 1891 in Ascension
Lily COMSTOCK (adopted daugh-
ter of John Comstock)

    b) Emmanuel Edgar LeBlanc born December 25,
1859; baptized January 5, 1860 in Ascension
    c) Vizida LeBlanc married February 5, 1880
Prosper GANEL
    d) Marie L. LeBlanc born October 9, 1861;
baptized October 21, 1861 in Ascension
    e) Marie L. L. LeBlanc born November 4, 1863;
baptized November 12, 1863 in Ascension
    f) Mary Lorina LeBlanc born April 18, 1865;
baptized May 6, 1865 in Ascension
    g) Marie Lise LeBlanc born October 14, 1867;
baptized October 28, 1867 in Ascension
married April 2, 1891 in Ascension Bruno
BABIN
    h) Marie Olivia LeBlanc born March 28, 1870;
baptized April 6, 1870 in Ascension married March 13, 1892 in Ascension Jacques
LAVIGNE (son of Jacques Lavigne and
Ernestine DUGAS)
    i) Jean Baptiste LeBlanc born December 9,
1872; baptized December 31, 1872 in Ascension

iv. Marie Gracieuse LeBlanc born September 6, 1829;
baptized November 8, 1829 in Ascension
v. Marie Ernestine LeBlanc born January 16, 1832;
baptized April 1, 1832 in Ascension married
January 21, 1851 in Ascension Hypolite VIALA

(son of Jean Pierre Viala and Euphemie COMEAUX)
    vi.   Joseph Edouard LeBlanc born February 17, 1834;
           baptized May 29, 1834 in Ascension
   vii.   Louis Dernand LeBlanc born May 21, 1836; bap-
           tized May 27, 1836 in Ascension
  viii.   Narcisse Octave LeBlanc born November 18, 1838;
           baptized November 20, 1838 in Ascension
    ix.   Pierre Emile Amadeo LeBlanc born August 30,
           1840; baptized September 20, 1843 in Ascension
     x.   Prosper Alfred LeBlanc born June 20, 1842;
           baptized November 26, 1842 in Ascension mar-
           ried October 5, 1881 Marie ROTEAU

  e.   Marie Aurelia LeBlanc born November, 1800; bap-
        tized November 4, 1800 in Ascension married
        April 20, 1837 Jean Baptiste TUSSON (widower of
        Elizabeth LE BLANC)
  f.   Marguerite Eleonor LeBlanc born October 27, 1801
        St. Gabriel
  g.   Elizabeth LeBlanc married November 12, 1822 in
        St. Gabriel, Louisiana Jean Baptiste TUSSON (son
        of Jean Baptiste Tusson and Catherine GOURINGER)

      i.   Marie Louise Enest Tusson born September 10,
            1825; baptized September 27, 1825 in Ascen-
            sion
     ii.   Anne Ernestine Tusson born January 27, 1827;
            baptized April 12, 1827 in Ascension
    iii.   Philippe Ernest Tusson born April 9, 1831;
            baptized April 10, 1831 in Ascension
     iv.   Joseph Pierre Rene Tusson born March 5, 1841;
            baptized November 1, 1841 in Ascension

2. Dermon LeBlanc born 1771 Ascension married June 2,
    1794 Marguerite RICHARD (daughter of Joseph Richard
    and Anna LANDRY) Dermon died August 26, 1794 in
    Ascension Parish
3. Marie Sophie LeBlanc born June 21, 1774 Ascension mar-
    ried August 5, 1793 at St. Gabriel Pierre Isadore
    BLANCHARD (son of Joseph Blanchard and Marie Josephe
    LANDRY) born October 12, 1772 in St. Gabriel, Louisiana

  a.   Gilbert Blanchard
  b.   Enselm Blanchard married Marie Ester LE BLANC
  c.   Marie Marthe Blanchard
  d.   Marie Arthemise Blanched; died in infancy
  e.   Eloi Blanchard married January 15, 1821 Louise
        LE BLANC
  f.   Josephine Blanchard married June 23, 1826 in As-
        cension Parish Onezime LE BLANC (son of Donat
        LeBlanc and Marie MELANCON)

4. Marguerite Felicite LeBlanc born November 23, 1775 in
    Ascension married October 2, 1795 William HATKINSON

(son of William Hatkinson and Catherine VAN STOCK)
born 1764; died October 9, 1823 in Ascension. Marguerite died November 8, 1811 at age 35 in Ascension

    a. Isaac Hatkinson married February 8, 1819 in As-
cension Marie Constance LANDRY (daughter of Jean
Landry and Marie Joseph BLANCHARD) Isaac died
September 9, 1834 at age 38

        i. John Alfred Hatkinson married January 28, 1838
in Ascension Mary Clementine BOUQUOI (daughter
of John Bouquoi and Josephine BOURGEOIS)

    b. Marie Adele Hatkinson born 1801 in Ascension mar-
ried May 14, 1821 in Ascension Parish Jean Baptiste
MOLLERE (son of Louis Mollere and Anne Poulonne
LANDRY) Adele died October 9, 1837 at age 36 in
Ascension Parish

        i. Anne Michaele Mollere born April 10, 1824;
baptized July 25, 1824 in Ascension married
July 10, 1839 Jean Baptiste David ISRAEL (son
of Solomon Israel and Rebecca ISREAL)
       ii. Ozite Amelie Mollere born January 28, 1826;
baptized April 24, 1826 in Ascension
     iii. Marie Adele Mollere born January 27, 1829;
baptized April 15, 1829 in Ascension
      iv. Jean Bienvenu Mollere born February 27, 1831;
baptized June 16, 1831 in Ascension
       v. Felicite Elizabeth Mollere born July 10, 1833;
baptized November 18, 1833 in Ascension

    c. Helene Hatkinson married December 27, 1823 in As-
cension William Crammond RANDELL (son of Thomas
Randell and Isabel RENSHAW)

        i. Thomas Lafayette Randell born November 11, 1824;
baptized June 21, 1825 in Ascension

5. Jean Baptiste LeBlanc married March, 1801 in St.
Gabriel, Louisiana Rosalie HEBERT (daughter of Pierre
Hebert and Isabel LE BLANC)

                      (2) May 21, 1782 in Ascension
Marguerite BABIN (daughter of
Jean Baptiste Babin and Ursule
LANDRY) born 1748 in Acadia;
Marguerite died October 8, 1815

6. Charles Pierre LeBlanc born May 9, 1783; baptized
June 1, 1783 in Ascension married January 23, 1804
Marguerite Adelaide LANDRY (daughter of Hyacinthe
Landry and Marguerite LANDRY)

    a. Marguerite Carmelite LeBlanc married 1824 August
Francois LE COQ of Nantes, France

7. Ozite LeBlanc baptized December 13, 1785 in Ascension married April 9, 1804 Nicholas LANDRY (son of Silvain Landry and Anne Marguerite BABIN)

   a. Leocade Landry married January 23, 1826 _____ BABIN (son of Simon Sifrin Babin and Marguerite LANDRY)

8. Marie Magdeleine LeBlanc born November 12, 1785 married April 16, 1804 in Ascension Jerome MELANCON (son of Joseph Melancon and Marguerite LANDRY) Marie Magdeleine died October 28, 1815 in Ascension

   a. William Melancon died February 9, 1805 Ascension
   b. Jeanette Melancon married February 6, 1829 in Ascension Sifrin BABIN (son of Sifrin Babin and Marguerite LANDRY)

      i. Jerome Emile Babin born January 8, 1830; baptized July 11, 1830 in Ascension
      ii. Edouard Babin born April 21, 1832; baptized May 1, 1832 in Ascension
      iii. Marie Elmire Babin born April 12, 1834; baptized August 6, 1834 in Ascension
      iv. Aimee Marguerite Babin born September 5, 1836; baptized February 2, 1837 in Ascension
      v. Felix Babin born July 14, 1842; baptized July 21, 1842 in Ascension

   c. Clarisse Melancon married August 3, 1829 in Ascension Vital Trasimond BABIN (son of Alexander Eusebe Babin and Magdeleine LE BLANC)

9. Barthelemi LeBlanc baptized August 18, 1787 in Ascension married

   (1) May 20, 1810 Constance BLANCHARD (daughter of Firmin Blanchard and Marie Magdeleine BUJOL) Constance was the widow of Paul LE BLANC

   a. Narcisse Faron LeBlanc (child of Paul LeBlanc and Constance Blanchard) married February 16, 1829 in Ascension Coralie LANDRY (daughter of Victor Landry and Jeanette MELANCON); died April 30, 1852 at age 47 in Ascension; Coralie died January 23, 1846 in Ascension

      i. Narcisse Faron LeBlanc born October 27, 1829; baptized November 3, 1829 in Ascension
      ii. Anne Constance LeBlanc born January 28, 1832; baptized February 18, 1832 in Ascension
      iii. Anne Euphrasie LeBlanc born March 5, 1836; baptized April 20, 1836 in Ascension
      iv. Joseph Elzear LeBlanc born May 10, 1837; baptized June 21, 1837 in Ascension

     v.   Elisa LeBlanc born June 28, 1838; baptized
September 5, 1838 in Ascension
    vi.   Camile Joseph Adam LeBlanc born February 28,
1841; baptized March 13, 1841 in Ascension
   vii.   Joseph Francois LeBlanc born March 17, 1842;
baptized April 3, 1824 in Ascension
  viii.   Marie Estelle LeBlanc born October 19, 1843;
baptized February 13, 1844 in Ascension; died
December 11, 1847 at age 4
    ix.   Anne Coralie LeBlanc born July 13, 1845; bap-
tized August 6, 1845 in Ascension

        (2) May 20, 1817 in Ascension
              Anne LANDRY (daughter of Jean
              Landry and Anna MORAN)

5. Isaac LeBlanc born October 8, 1789; died prior to 1794
6. Marie Constance LeBlanc died September 3, 1797

D. Marie Martha LeBlanc born 1748 Grande Pre, Acadia married

        (1) February 7, 1768 in St. James,
              Louisiana Jacque LA CHAUSSE.
              Jacque died 1769 in St. James

On April 30, 1770, Marie Marthe LeBlanc, widow of Jacque
LaChasse abandoned to His Majesty and to Jeasonne a track
of land 23 LNO. declaring she could not occupy said land
and maintain the "Chemin Royaux".

On April 13, 1779 Judice made inventory of estate of
Jacque LaChasse, being a place RBMR abt 22 LNO ab. Armand
Prejean, bel. by Basil Prejean (A-1)

1. Jacque LaChausse died April 25, 1790 at age 20 in
St. James

        (2) April 30, 1770 Paul BRAUD (son
              of Baptiste Braud and Eliza-
              beth HENRY) born 1745 in
              Acadia; Paul died January 7,
              1797 in Ascension

On May 15, 1782, Commandant Judice made inventory of es-
tate of Marie Marthe LeBlanc, who left by Paul Braud:
Jerome, Simon, Etienne, Marie Madeleine and Marie Henrietta.
They owned a place, RMBR, bet. Baptist Braud and Baptist
Landry, house sur aaul, 28'x16', surrounded and covered
with pickets (A-481)

2. Jerome Raymond Braud baptized August 28, 1772 in Ascension married August 6, 1792 in Ascension Anastasie
Rosalie LANDRY (daughter of Mathurin Landry and Anne
LANDRY) born December 25, 1772 in Ascension. Jerome
died September 13, 1829

a. Marthe Arthemise Braud married November 28, 1816
    in Ascension Marcelin COMES (son of Joseph Comes
    and Marie LANDRY) Marcelin died September 28,
    1835 at age 45

    i.   Elise Comes married January 22, 1841 in As-
         cension Dermond LE BLANC (son of Joseph
         LeBlanc and Martha BLANCHARD)
    ii. Josephe Marie Rosalie Comes born September 2,
         1824; baptized September 3, 1824 in Ascension
    iii. Joseph Jerome Jackson Comes born June 22, 1829;
         baptized June 23, 1829 in Ascension married
         Leontine LE BLANC
    iv. Marie Estelle Comes born May 18, 1831;baptized
         June 11, 1831 in Ascension married August 5,
         1854 in Ascension Joseph VINCENT (son of Gil-
         bert Vincent and Henrietta COMES)
    v.   Louis Marcellin Comes born October 18, 1835;
         baptized November 15, 1835 in Ascension

b. Simon Nabor Braud married February 10, 1817 in
    Ascension Marie Arthemise LE BLANC (daughter of
    Joseph LeBlanc and Anne Marthe BLANCHARD)

    i.   Martha Anaiz Braud born September 14, 1825;
         baptized October 16, 1825 in Ascension
    ii. Joseph Adelard Braud born October 27, 1827;
         baptized October 26, 1829 in Ascension
    iii. Marie Evelina Braud born July 19, 1830; bap-
         tized October 23, 1830 in Ascension
    iv. Estelle Braud born August 18, 1832; baptized
         October 18, 1832 in Ascension married Au-
         gust 19, 1851 in Ascension Camile COMES (son
         of Hubert Comes and Ferande LE BLANC)
    v.   Jean Gustave Braud born January 13, 1843; bap-
         tized May 25, 1843 in Ascension

c. Etienne Anaclet Braud married March 5, 1820 in
    Ascension Appoline LANDRY (daughter of Simon
    Bellamy Landry and Marie Jeanette SAUBIN)

    i.   Joseph Marcellin Braud born September 4, 1827;
         baptized March 20, 1827 in Ascension married
         November 29, 1853 in Ascension Emelie BLOUIN
         (daughter of Zenon Blouin and Emelie LE BLANC)
    ii. Marie Braud born March 10, 1838; baptized
         March 15, 1838 in Ascension
    iii. Norbert Adolphe Braud born December 10, 1829;
         baptized December 10, 1829 in Ascension
    iv. Jean Rene Braud born March 22, 1831; baptized
         April 2, 1831 in Ascension
    v.   Andre Reymond Braud born November 30, 1833;
         baptized November 30, 1833 in Ascension
    vi. Virginia Anastasie Braud born June 7, 1835;
         baptized June 7, 1835 in Ascension

vii. Jules Joseph Braud born June 11, 1837; baptized June 18, 1837 in Ascension
viii. Pierre Etienne Braud born April 25, 1839; baptized May 5, 1839 in Ascension
ix. Marie Josephine Eugenie Braud born Augsut 14, 1841; baptized August 17, 1841 in Ascension
x. Jerome Arthur Braud born October 19, 1844; baptized February 16, 1845 in Ascension
xi. Marie Matilde Braud born June 13, 1846; baptized July 26, 1846 in Ascension
xii. Julienne Antonia Braud born June 2, 1850; baptized June 3, 1850 in Ascension

d. Marie Aspasie Braud married January 17, 1825 in Ascension Ferdinand TERRIO (son of Oliver Terrio and Marie AUCOIN)

i. Marie Elodie Terrio born October 23, 1825; baptized April 29, 1826 in Ascension
ii. Marie Helene Honorine Terrio born March 1, 1829; baptized March 4, 1829 in Ascension
iii. Marie Rosalie Lisida Terrio born January 18, 1831; baptized February 20, 1831 in Ascension
iv. Edouard Severin Terrio born February 11, 1823; baptized February 17, 1823 in Ascension

e. Euphemia Delia Braud married January 17, 1825 in Ascension Leon Narcisse LE BLANC (son of Gregoire LeBlanc and Marie Barbe BABIN)

i. Joseph Leonard LeBlanc born February 14, 1826; baptized April 8, 1826 in Ascenson
ii. Joseph Camille LeBlanc born January 13, 1828; baptized March 16, 1828 in Ascension
iii. Jules Norbert LeBlanc born June 10, 1830; baptized June 13, 1830 in Ascension
iv. Joseph Auguste LeBlanc born May 12, 1832; baptized June 16, 1832 in Ascension
v. Mary Leontine LeBlanc born July 30, 1834; baptized November 1, 1834 in Ascension
vi. Pierre Hercules LeBlanc born November 9, 1837; baptized April 14, 1838 in Ascension
vii. Marie Rosalie LeBlanc born October 18, 1839; baptized January 5, 1840 in Ascension
viii. Marie Augustine LeBlanc born July 8, 1843; baptized August 20, 1843 in Ascension
ix. Joseph Leon LeBlanc born April 9, 1846; baptized June 3, 1846 in Ascension
x. Marie Leonie LeBlanc born April 9, 1846; baptized June 3, 1846 in Ascension
xi. Joseph Adam Arthrmise LeBlanc born January 21, 1849; baptized January 22, 1849 in Ascension
xii. Louis Benjamine LeBlanc born November 7, 1855; baptized November 21, 1855 in Ascension

f. J. Adelard Braud married 1838 in Ascension Hen-
    rietta LANDRY (daughter of Narcisse Landry and
    Henrietta BLANCHARD)

3. Anselm (Simon) Braud born April 20, 1773 in Ascension
    married May 7, 1794 in St. James Parish Marguerite
    RICHARD (daughter of Juan Marie Richard and Rosa
    BOURGEOIS)

4. Marie Magdeleine Braud born January 8, 1775 in Ascen-
    sion; baptized February 19, 1775 married

                        (1) November 24, 1792 Guillaume
                             Raphael LANDRY (son of Joseph
                             Landry and Anne GRANGER)

    a. Marie Eugenie Landry married June 10, 1814 Joseph
        Gideon DUPUY (son of Antoine Dupuy and Marguerite
        BOUDRAUX)
    b. Marie Delphine Landry married April 5, 1817 Edward
        DUPUY (son of Joseph Dupuy and Ludovine LANDRY)
        of Iberville
    c. Melanie Genevieve Landry married February 11, 1822
        Elie Narcisse LANDRY
    d. Arthemise Landry married February 2, 1825 Onezime
        BABIN (son of Macimillian Babin and Julie DUGAS)

                        (2) September 1, 1825 Alexander
                             Eusebe BABIN (widower of Anne
                             DUHON and Magdeliene LE BLANC)

5. Etienne Braud born November 4, 1776; baptized Febru-
    ary 11, 1777 in Ascension married February 21, 1797
    in Ascension Victoire BABIN (daughter of Charles
    Babin and Magdeleine BABIN) born 1779. Etienne died
    September 18, 1820; Victoire died October 24, 1819 in
    Ascension

    a. Simon Braud
    b. Laurent Braud married February 27, 1827 Magdeleine
        _____(widow of Charles Joseph BABIN)
    c. Pierre Edmond Braud married February 25, 1827 in
        Ascension Adele Marceline DUGAS (daughter of Jerome
        Dugas and Isabel BABIN)

6. Hypolite Armand Braud born September 2, 1778; baptized
    September 20, 1778 in Ascension; died September 13,
    1780 at age 2
7. Pierre Anselme Braud born April 28, 1780; baptized
    April 29, 1780 in Ascension
8. Marie Henriette Braud born September 19, 1781; bap-
    tized September 19, 1781 in Ascension; died in infancy

E. Jerome LeBlanc born 1749 in Grande Pre, Acadia married
    Marie Magdeleine LANDRY (daughter of Joseph Landry and
    Marie Joseph BOURG) born 1747. Jerome died August 24, 1789

at age 40 in Ascension; Marie Magdeleine died October 5, 1800 at age 53 in Ascension.

F. Isabel LeBlanc born 1751 in Grande Pre, Acadia married April 18, 1775 in Ascension Joseph LANDRY (son of Joseph Etienne Landry and Marie Josephe BOURG). Joseph Landry was the first American Commandant in Ascension Parish. He also served as a Justice of the Peace, State Representative and State Senator. Isabel died September 1, 1777 at age 26 in Ascension Parish. After her death Joseph married a second time on November 25, 1779 Anna BUJOL (daughter of Joseph Bujol and Anne LE BLANC). Joseph died October 10, 1814 in Ascension. The Landry monument is located on the left side of the entrance of Ascension Cemetery, Donaldsonville, Louisiana.

1. Louis Landry born May 12, 1776 married

      (1) January 10, 1803 Carmelite VIVES (daughter of Dr. Juan Vives of Spain and Marguerite BUJOL)

Louis Landry died June 21, 1831 at age 60

a. Amanda Landry born 1825 married Jerome Kleibert GAUDET. Amanda died 1885

    i. Jerome Louis Gaudet born 1852 in Convent, Louisiana married Evaline CAGNOLATTI. Jerome was District Attorney of Ascension and St. James Parishes

b. Carmelite Landry married August CONSTANT

    i. Carmelite Constant married July 10, 1821 in Ascension Judge Ben WINCHESTER

      (2) January 12, 1824 in Ascension Clemence LESSARD (daughter of Jean Baptiste Lessard and Madeleine Marie LAROTE) widow of Butler GILBERT

G. Desire LeBlanc born about 1753 in Grande Pre, Acadia listed on 1769 Census of Ascension Parish

H. Marine LeBlanc born 1758 in Acadia married

      (1) February 19, 1775 in Ascension Parish Joseph BABIN dit DIOS (son of Pierre Babin and Anne FOREST)

Marine died September 8, 1789 at age 55 in Ascension; Joseph Babin died February 1, 1782 in Ascension. On May 7, 1782 an inventory of the estate of Joseph Babin was made, and we note a place, RBMR, between Pierre

Landry and Charles Lincour, house sur saul, 20' front
gallery, 6' covered surrounded and floored above and be-
low with pickets (A-499). Place sold to Benjamine
LeBlanc, December 7, 1783 (C-535). Benjamine was Marine's
brother.

1. Paul Babin born November 20, 1775 in Ascension
2. Charles Babin born May 12, 1777 in Ascension
3. Benjamine Babin married May 15, 1797 in St. James
   Felicite RICHARD (daughter of Jean Richard and Rosa
   BOURGEOIS)

   a. Joseph Babin born March 24, 1799 in St. James
   b. Josephine Babin born June 2, 1803 in St. James
   c. Marie Doralize Babin born January 4, 1806 in
      St. James

4. Jerome Babin
5. Bonaventure Babin married November 8, 1788 in Ascension Parish Felicite LANDRY (widow of Charles
   MELANCON)

   a. Casimir Babin born September 8, 1789 in Ascension

6. Anne Marguerite Babin married Valentine Dosite RICHARD

                        (2) December 21, 1783 in Ascension
                             Gille LE BLANC (son of Joseph
                             LeBlanc and Elizabeth GAUDIN)
                             born 1754 in Acadia. Gille
                             died September 28, 1832 in
                             St. James

7. Nicolas LeBlanc married January 21, 1805 in St. James
   Marie Constance BRAUX (daughter of Alexis Braux and
   Marie BRAUX)

   a. Nicolas LeBlanc born November 8, 1805; baptized
      May 20, 1806 in St. James married January 24, 1833
      Marie Helene PROVOST (daughter of Godfroi Provost
      and Anne LE BLANC)

      i. Nicolas Colin LeBlanc born October 2, 1841
         in New Iberia

   b. Edmond Gille LeBlanc born January 23, 1808; bap-
      tized April 18, 1808 in St. James

8. Rosemond LeBlanc born March 28, 1789; baptized September 27, 1789 in St. James married

                        (1) June 19, 1809 in St. James
                             Marie Desiree BROU (daughter
                             of Charles Brou and Julie
                             PRINCE)

                        (2) March 19, 1811 at St. Michael
                             Church, Convent Francoise Mar-
                             cellite BOURGEOIS (daughter of

Pierre Bourgeois and Marie
BERGERON)

    a. Edouard LeBlanc born December 12, 1813; baptized
       1816, St. Michael Church, Convent, Louisiana mar-
       ried May 8, 1838 Hortiste PATIN
    b. Amelie LeBlanc married Charles DURAND

I. Ozite LeBlanc born 1760, Maryland, New England, married
January 7, 1778 in St. James Etienne LE BLANC (son of
Etienne LeBlanc and Isabel BOUDREAUX) Isabel died Janu-
ary 7, 1808 in Ascension

    1. Anne Catherine LeBlanc born September 25, 1778; bap-
       tized December 25, 1778 in Ascension
    2. Edouard LeBlanc born June 4, 1780; baptized October 8,
       1780 in Ascension
    3. Anne Celeste LeBlanc born November 14, 1782; baptized
       December 1, 1782 in Ascension married January 2, 1809
       in Ascension Gregoire Sifroy LE BLANC (son of Enselm
       LeBlanc and Magdeleine BABIN) Anne Celeste died
       March 25, 1814 in Ascension Parish
    4. Marcelina LeBlanc born November 25, 1790; baptized
       June 9, 1791 in St. James
    5. Andre LeBlanc married February 10, 1812 in Assumption
       Marguerite LANDRY

        a. Marie Azema LeBlanc married January 22, 1835
           Anselme MOLLERE (son of Joseph Mollere and
           Henriette BLANCHARD)

    6. Etienne Privot LeBlanc born July 22, 1793; baptized
       March 19, 1797 in St. James
    7. Gustave LeBlanc born October 6, 1795; baptized Novem-
       ber 22, 1795 in St. James; buried October 2, 1798 in
       St. James
    8. Manette LeBlanc married July 25, 1808 in Assumption
       Jean Francois ST. MARTIN (son of Claude St. Martin
       and Alexandrine GOUSSEL)

J. Benjamine Desire LeBlanc born 1760 in Maryland married
July 12, 1790 in Ascension Rosalie BABIN (daughter of
Joseph Babin and Ozite LE BLANC) Benjamine Desire died
February 18, 1804 at age 44 in Ascension Parish

    1. Anne Marie Mannette LeBlanc born May 20, 1791; baptized
       March 18, 1792 in Ascension married

                 (1) November 19, 1807 Pierre
                     DUPOVILLE (son of Jean Dupo-
                     ville and _____ DUBALLO)
                 (2) November 19, 1811 in Ascension
                     Pierre AYRAUD (son of Pierre
                     Ayraud and Catherine MARTIN)

2. Benjamine Desire LeBlanc born November 14, 1796; baptized March 26, 1797 in Ascension married June 9, 1817 in Ascension Marguerite Felonise DUGAS (daughter of Miguel Noel Dugas and Magdeleine BABIN) born 1798 in Ascension. Marguerite died January 10, 1871 in Ascension

NOTE: This family constitutes Part III of this book

    a. Joseph LeBlanc born March 30, 1818; baptized October 19, 1818 in Ascension married August 21, 1848 at St. Michael Church, Convent, Louisiana Amelia WEBRE (daughter of Christophe Webre and Felicie ROME)

        i. Joseph Desire LeBlanc born August 12, 1849 married in Ascension Parish

            (1) December 29, 1872 Elizabeth DENOUX
            (2) February 18, 1895 Jeanette RUIZ

        Joseph died 1928 in New Orleans at age 79.

        ii. Pierre Christophe LeBlanc born April 29, 1852 in Ascension married January 19, 1875 Amanda DUGAS. Pierre Christophe died May 28, 1938 at age 86 and is buried in Donaldsonville

        iii. Phelonise Althee LeBlanc born June 4, 1854 in Ascension; died about age 16 and buried in Donaldsonville

        iv. Frederick Hubert LeBlanc born April 2, 1856 in Ascension; died at age 21 and buried in Donaldsonville

        v. Marie Elmire LeBlanc born May 26, 1858 in Ascension married 1875 Leon CLOUATRE. Marie Elmire died September 11, 1937 at age 79 and buried in Donaldsonville

        vi. Joseph Telasmar LeBlanc born April 1, 1860 in Ascension married October 12, 1885 Victoria DUGAS. Joseph died February 10, 1940 at age 80 and buried in Donaldsonville

        vii. Michel Ernest LeBlanc born February 2, 1863 in Ascension married July 15, 1885 in Assumption Carlotta DEOCURRO. Michel died October 23, 1945 at age 82 and buried in Donaldsonville

        viii. Christine Amelia LeBlanc born January 18, 1865 in Ascension married January 11, 1883 Valentine LANDRY. Christine died March 29, 1929 at age 64 and buried in Donaldsonville

        ix. Marie Emelia LeBlanc born October 3, 1868 in Ascension. Died at about age 4 and buried in Donaldsonville

x. Benjamine Constant LeBlanc born December 12, 1870 in Ascension; died April 3, 1877 at age 6 and buried in Donaldsonville

xi. Joseph LeBlanc born April 3, 1872 married January 27, 1903 Ernestine LIRETTE; died January 26, 1967 at age 95 and buried in Donaldsonville

b. Rosalie LeBlanc born September 16, 1820; baptized April 6, 1821 in Ascension married February 22, 1841 in Ascension Leon LESSARD (son of Jean Baptiste Lessard, Jr. and Josephine LE BLANC)

i. Joseph Leon Lessard born December 19, 1842; baptized January 6, 1843 in Ascension married August 10, 1863 in Ascension Marie MORALES (daughter of Perique Morales and Elizabeth ALBARADO)

ii. Rosalie Desiree Lessard born October 21, 1845; baptized March 28, 1846 in Ascension

iii. Amanda Phelomine Lessard born August 12, 1847; baptized October 11, 1847 in Ascension

c. Magdeleine Adelaine LeBlanc born June 7, 1823; baptized January 6, 1825 in Ascension married February 3, 1840 in Ascension Valentine HEBERT (son of Joseph Eloi Hebert and Angelique HEBERT) native of Iberville

i. Faustin Hebert born February 15, 1841; baptized February 15, 1841 in Ascension

ii. Valentine Hebert born May 22, 1842; baptized August 13, 1842 in Ascension

iii. Theodore Hebert born January 11, 1845; baptized February 15, 1845 in Ascension

iv. Joseph Octave Hebert born July 2, 1848; baptized March 10, 1849 in Ascension

v. Madelaine Octavie Hebert born July 11, 1850; baptized October 16, 1850 in Ascension

vi. Hubert Gustave Hebert born May 6, 1855; baptized August 6, 1855 in Ascension

d. Joseph Theodule LeBlanc born October 7, 1827; baptized November 5, 1828 in Ascension married August 25, 1857 in St. Gabriel, Louisiana Estelle BRAUD (daughter of Drouzin Braud and Magdelaine DENEOU) Joseph died September 4, 1873 in Ascension; Estelle died February 2, 1869 at age 36

i. Mathieu Theodule LeBlanc born September 21, 1858; baptized November 19, 1858 in Ascension; died before 1874

ii. Rigobert Aulime LeBlanc born January 4, 1861; baptized April 12, 1861 in Ascension

72

        iii.   Madeleine LeBlanc born November 7, 1862; baptized January 24, 1863 in Ascension; died before 1874

        iv.   Jules Ovide LeBlanc born June 19, 1864; baptized August 2, 1864 in Ascension

         v.   Eve LeBlanc (named in succession)

    e.   Trasimond LeBlanc born January 11, 1831; baptized January 17, 1831 in Ascension

3.   Narcisse LeBlanc born January 17, 1800 in Ascension

4.   Joseph LeBlanc born March 19, 1801 in Ascension married

        (1)   February 23, 1822 Marie Clemence BABIN (daughter of Alexander Eusebe Babin and Anne DUHON)

        (2)   February 14, 1825 Marguerite Modeste BABIN (daughter of Jacque Babin and Marie Francoise LANDRY)

        (3)   February 9, 1858 in Ascension Emelite LANDRY (daughter of Paul Landry and Francoise HEBERT)

K.   Enselm LeBlanc born 1763 in Maryland, New England married Magdeleine BABIN (daughter of Efreme Babin and Marguerite LE BLANC) Enselm died February 1, 1797 at age 34 in Ascension Parish

1.   Gregoire Sifrin LeBlanc born May 27, 1788 in Ascension married January 2, 1809 Celeste LE BLANC (daughter of Etienne LeBlanc and Ozite LE BLANC)

2.   Marie Judith LeBlanc married November 6, 1809 Joseph BLANCHARD (son of Firmin Blanchard and Magdeleine BUJOL) Marie Judith died July 6, 1839 at age 46

3.   Santiago Valery LeBlanc

L.   Gregoire LeBlanc married April 21, 1787 in Ascension Marie Barbe BABIN (daughter of Olivier Babin and Marie Madeleine BRAUD) Gregoire died May 11, 1824 in Ascension at age 55

1.   Desire LeBlanc born April 23, 1787 in Ascension married December 26, 1810 in Ascension Carmelite LANOUX (daughter of Pierre Lanoux and Catherine LE BLANC)

2.   Marie Clemence LeBlanc married May 7, 1810 in Ascension Ursin LANDRY (son of Joseph Landry and Anna BUJOL)

3.   Rosemond LeBlanc married

        (1)   November 30, 1816 Clothilde BUJOL (daughter of Jean Bujol and Marie BOURG)

a. Carmelite LeBlanc married February 24, 1835 in
    Ascension Robert SCOTT (son of Robert Scott and
    Susanne TYLER)

> (2) November 16, 1826 Marie LANDRY
>   (daughter of Jean Landry and
>   Marie Josephe BLANCHARD)
> (3) October 25, 1830 in Ascension
>   Emilie MIGANO (daughter of
>   Michel Migano and Rosalie ___)

4. Geralde Marie LeBlanc married February 3, 1817 in As-
    cension Hubert COMES (son of Joseph Comes and Marie
    LANDRY)
5. Marie Hortense LeBlanc married October 2, 1820 in
    Ascension Pierre COMEAU (son of Jean Charles Comeau
    and Anne Catherine BOUCHE)

a. Pierre Comeau married April 19, 1858 in Baton
    Rouge Virginia ALTAZIN (daughter of Achille
    Altazin and Louise Sara KRAIG)

6. Lessin LeBlanc married

> (1) January 27, 1823 Clarice
>   GRAVOIS (daughter of Jean
>   Gravois and Marie BOURG)

a. Marie Elizabeth LeBlanc born November 3, 1823;
    baptized November 13, 1823 in Ascension
b. Jean Baptiste Lessin LeBlanc born July 2, 1825;
    baptized September 4, 1825 in Ascension

> (2) October 5, 1829 in Ascension
>   Eugenie BORNE (daughter of
>   Benjamin Borne and Rose Aime
>   LAURENT)

c. Joseph Numa LeBlanc born March 11, 1831; baptized
    April 16, 1831 in Ascension married January 26,
    1856 in Ascension Justine OUBRE (daughter of
    Pierre Oubre and Justine GUEDRY)
d. Rose Eliza LeBlanc born September 12, 1833; bap-
    tized December 8, 1833 in Ascension
e. Pierre Felix LeBlanc born February 23, 1836; bap-
    tized February 23, 1836 in Ascension
f. Marie Cecile LeBlanc born January 15, 1838; bap-
    tized February 17, 1838 in Ascension married Janu-
    ary 13, 1855 in Ascension Manuel CABALLERO (son of
    Joseph Caballero and Leonoda DIEPA)
g. Marie Adolphine LeBlanc born November 14, 1839;
    baptized November 18, 1839 in Ascension married

> (1) September 14, 1854 in Ascen-
>   sion Emile PICOU (son of Zenon
>   Picou and Antoinette Anne
>   MELANCON)

          (2) May 8, 1867 in Assumption
               Antoine ALEMAN (son of Barthar
               Aleman and Josie CABALLERO)

   h. Marie Athenaise LeBlanc born November 10, 1847;
      baptized November 11, 1847 in Ascension
   i. Jean Baptiste LeBlanc born July 14, 1857; baptized
      August 8, 1857 in Ascension

7. Leon Narcisse LeBlanc married January 17, 1825 in As-
    cension Euphemie Delia BRAUD (daughter of Jerome Ray-
    mond Braud and Anastasie Rosalie LANDRY)

   a. Joseph Leonard LeBlanc born February 14, 1826;
      baptized April 8, 1826 in Ascension
   b. Joseph Camille LeBlanc born January 13, 1828; bap-
      tized March 16, 1828 in Ascension
   c. Jules Norbert LeBlanc born June 10, 1830; baptized
      June 13, 1830 in Ascension
   d. Joseph Auguste LeBlanc born May 12, 1832; baptized
      June 16, 1832 in Ascension
   e. Mary Leontine LeBlanc born July 30, 1834; baptized
      July 1,1834 in Ascension
   f. Pierre Hercules LeBlanc born November 9, 1837; bap-
      tized April 11, 1838 in Ascension
   g. Marie Rosalie LeBlanc born October 18, 1839; bap-
      tized January 5, 1840 in Ascension
   h. Marie Augustine LeBlanc born July 8, 1843; baptiz-
      ed August 20, 1843 in Ascension
   i. Joseph Leon LeBlanc born April 8, 1846; baptized
      June 3, 1846 in Ascension
   j. Marie Leonie LeBlanc born April 9, 1846; baptized
      August 23, 1846 in Ascension
   k. Joseph Adam LeBlanc born January 21, 1849; bap-
      tized January 22, 1849 in Ascension
   l. Louis Benjamin LeBlanc born November 7, 1855; bap-
      tized November 21, 1855 in Ascension

8. Privot LeBlanc married May 20, 1832 in Ascension Marie
    LE BLANC (daughter of Sylvain LeBlanc and Marguerite
    GAUDIN) widow of Celestin PREJEAN

   a. Marguerite LeBlanc born April 7, 1835; baptized
      July 16, 1835 at St. Michael Church, Convent,
      Louisiana

9. Catherine LeBlanc

PART III

JOSEPH BENJAMIN LE BLANC and AMELIA WEBRE

FOUR GENERATION ANCESTOR CHART

8. Desire LeBlanc
b.   1717
p.b. Grand Pre, Acadia
m.   1740
p.m.
d.15 March 1777
p.d. Ascension Parish

4.Benjamine LeBlanc
b.   1760
p.b.Maryland, New England
m. 12 June 1790
p.m. Ascension Parish
d. 18 February 1804
p.d.Ascension Parish

9.Marie Magdelaine Landry
b.   1723
p.b. Acadia
d.14 October 1786
p.d. Ascension Parish

2.Benjamine Desire LeBlanc
b. 14 October 1796
p.b.Ascension Parish
m. 9 June 1817
p.m.Ascension Parish
d. 30 December 1853
p.d.Ascension Parish

10.Joseph Oliver Babin
b.   1743
p.b. Acadia
m.
p.m.
d.9 March 1809
p.d. Ascension Parish

5.Rosalie Babin
b.   1760
p.b. New England
d. 3 October 1840
p.d. Ascension Parish

11.Ozite LeBlanc
b.   1748
p.b. Acadia
d.27 June 1813
p.d. Ascension Parish

1 Joseph Benjamin LeBlanc
b. 30 March 1818
p.b. Ascension Parish
m.21 August 1848
p.m. Convent, La.
d. 8 May 1871
p.d. Ascension Parish

12.Francois Dugas
b.   ca. 1753
p.b. St. Ann, Quebec
m.   28 June 1768
p.m. Ascension Parish
d.
p.d. Ascension Parish

6.Miguel Noel Dugas
b. 25 December 1775
p.b. Ascension Parish
m. 12 February 1798
p.m. Ascension Parish
d. 25 July 1807
p.d. Ascension Parish

13.Marguerite Babin
b.
p.b.Pisiquid, Acadia
d.9 March 1807
p.d. Ascension Parish

3.Marguerite Felonise Dugas
b.
p.b.
d. 19 January 1871
p.d. Ascension Parish

14.Aman Babin
b.   1742
p.b. Acadia
m.
p.m.
d.11 March 1808
p.d. Ascension Parish

7.Magdelaine Babin
b. Bt. 1 January 1777
p.b. St. James Parish
d. 23 September 1810
p.d. Ascension Parish

15.Anastasie Landry
b.   1743
p.b. Acadia
d.18 August 1795
p.d. Ascension Parish

Amelia Webre
Spouse of #1

FOUR GENERATION ANCESTOR CHART

```
                                             8.Juan Webre
                                             b.              ca. 1725
                                             p.b.
                                             m.              ca. 1753
                   4. Jean Michael Webre     p.m.
                   b.              1766      d. 30 May 1787
                   p.b.                      p.d.St. John the Baptist
                   m. 4 January 1791
                   p.m. St. John the Baptist 9.Maria Catherina Tregre
                   d. 22 July 1829           b.              ca. 1723
                   p.d. St. John the Baptist p.b.
 2. Christophe Webre                         d. 25 November 1813
 b. 24 January 1799                          p.d.St. John the Baptist
 p.b.St. John the Baptist
 m. 18 September 1820
 p.m.  St. James, Louisiana                  10.Nicholas Haydel
 d. 12 June 1855                             b.
 p.d. St. James Parish                       p.b.St. Charles Parish
                                             m.              ca. 1760
                   5. Francoise Haydel       p.m.
                   b.              1769      d. February 1777
                   p.b.                      p.d.St. John the Baptist
                   d.  18 March 1824
                   p.d. St. John the Baptist 11.Perrine LeRoux
                                             b.
                                             p.b.
                                             d.Succession, 16 May 1803
                                             p.d.St. John the Baptist
 1 Amelia Webre
 b. 12 March 1829
 p.b. St. John the Baptist                   12.Juan Rome
 m.21 August 1848                            b.
 p.m. Convent, La.                           p.b.
 d. 26 November 1882                         m. 8 August 1752
 p.d.. Ascension Parish                      p.m.
                   6. Abraham Rome           d.
                   b.              1764      p.d.
                   p.b. St. Charles Parish
                   m.              1790
                   p.m.                      13. Marguerite Oubre
                   d. 5 August 1827          b.              ca. 1730
                   p.d. St. James Parish     p.b.
                                             d. 14 March 1829
 3 Felicite Rome                             p.d. Convent, La.
 b. 30 January 1804
 p.b. St. James Parish
 d. 13 November 1832                         14. Nicholas Baudouin
 p.d. St. James Parish                       b.
                                             p.b.
                                             m.
                   7. Jeanne Baudouin        p.m. St. Charles Parish
                   b.              1761      d.
                   p.b. St. Charles Parish   p.d.
                   d. 1 April 1816
                   p.d. St. John the Baptist 15.Marguerite Breaux
                                             b. Bt. 11 August 1750
                                             p.b. St. Charles Parish
 Joseph Benjamin LeBlanc                     d.
 Spouse of #1                                p.d.
```

FAMILY GROUP RECORD

ENTER ALL DATA IN THIS ORDER:
DATES: 14 Apr 1794

NAMES: WATSON, John Henry
PLACES: Sharon, Wndsr, Vrmn

To indicate that a child is an ancestor of the family representative, place an "X" behind the number pertaining to that child.

HUSBAND: Jean Michel Webre

	Date	Place
Born	24 January 1799	St. John the Baptist Parish, Louisiana
Chr.		
Marr.	(1) 18 September 1820	St. James Parish, Louisiana
Died	12 June 1855	Convent, Louisiana
Bur.		St. Michael Church Cemetery, Convent, Louisiana

HUSBAND'S FATHER: Jean Michel Webre
HUSBAND'S MOTHER: Francoise Haydel
HUSBAND'S OTHER WIVES: (2) 16 February 1835 Melasie TASSIN (daughter of Antoine Tassin and Melanie Staver)

WIFE: (1) ROME, Felicie

	Date	Place
Born	30 January 1804	St. James, Louisiana
Chr.		
Died	13 November 1832 age 28	St. James, Louisiana
Bur.		

WIFE'S FATHER: Abraham Rome
WIFE'S MOTHER: Jeanne Baudouin
WIFE'S OTHER HUSBANDS:

CHILDREN

SEX M/F	SURNAME (CAPITALIZED) GIVEN NAMES	WHEN BORN DAY	MONTH	YEAR	WHERE BORN TOWN	COUNTY	STATE OR COUNTRY	DATE OF FIRST MARRIAGE / TO WHOM	WHEN DIED DAY MONTH YEAR
1	WEBRE, Catherine								
2									
3	WEBRE, Emilien	19	Mar.	1825	Edgard	St. John	La.	25 Jan. 1847 Marie Emma LE BLANC	
4	WEBRE, Amelia (Aurelie)	12	Mar.	1829	Edgard	St. John	La.	21 Aug. 1848 Joseph LE BLANC	26 Nov. 1882
5	WEBRE, Philogene	22	Dec.	1830	St. James	St. James	La.	1856	
6	WEBRE, Euphrosine	4	Sept.	1832	St. James	St. James	La.	Antoine HAYDEL	1856
	Children from second marriage:								
7	WEBRE, Jean Verenand	13	Dec.	1835	St. James	St. James	La.		
8	WEBRE, Antoine	20	Aug.	1837	St. James	St. James	La.	1864	
9	WEBRE, Louis Theophile	10	Feb.	1841	Donaldsonville	Ascension	La.	1867 Mirza LOUPE	
10	WEBRE, Michel Eugene	1	Apr.	1844	Donaldsonville	Ascension	La.	1867 Cecile BAUDRY	
11	WEBRE, Joseph	22	Sept.	1846	Convent	St. James	La.	1869 Alice ROUSSEL	

SOURCES OF INFORMATION:

OTHER MARRIAGES:

I. Joseph Benjamin LeBlanc (son of Benjamin Desire LeBlanc and
    Marguerite Felonise DUGAS) born March 30, 1818 and baptized
    October 19, 1818 in Ascension Church, Donaldsonville; mar-
    ried August 21, 1848 in St. Michael Church, Convent to
    Amelia WEBRE (daughter of Christophe Webre and Felicie ROME)
    born March 12, 1829 and baptized July 3, 1829 in St. John the
    Baptist Church, Edgard. Joseph died in 1878 and Amelia died
    November 27, 1882. Both are buried in Ascension Cemetery.

AMELIE WEBRE LE BLANC
(1829 - 1882)

76

THE LE BLANC FAMILY HOME

The LeBlanc family home is located at Brusly McCall, Ascension Parish, Louisiana. All of the LeBlanc children were born in this house. Joseph LeBlanc and Amelia Webre LeBlanc both died there. At that time the house and property were bought by Christophe and Telasmar and the house was cut in half and each took half the land. The half-houses were added onto by each son. The half bought by Telasmar is still in his family; their daughter, May LeBlanc, is living there. May is married to Desire LeBlanc.

FOUR GENERATION ANCESTOR CHART

8.
b.
p.b.
m.
p.m.
d.
p.d.

4. Pierre Denoux
b.
p.b.
m.
p.m.
d.
p.d.

9.
b.
p.b.
d.
p.d.

2. Henry Denoux
b.
p.b.
m. 29 August 1836
p.m.Ascension Parish
d.
p.d.

10.
b.
p.b.
m.
p.m.
d.
p.d.

5. Marie Louise LeGrange
b.
p.b.
d.
p.d.

11.
b.
p.b.
d.
p.d.

1 Elizabeth Denoux
b.   1850
p.b.Ascension
m. 20 December 1873
p.m. Ascension
d.   1890
p.d. .Ascension Parish

12. Bernard Capdeville
b.
p.b.
m.
p.m.
d.
p.d.

6.Ferdinand Capdeville
b.
p.b.
m.
p.m.
d.
p.d.

13.
b.
p.b.
d.
p.d.

3 Felicite Capdeville
b.
p.b.
d.
p.d.

14.
b.
p.b.
m.
p.m.
d.
p.d.

7. Elizabeth Melancon
b.
p.b.
d.
p.d.

15.
b.
p.b.
d.
p.d.

Joseph Desire LeBlanc
Spouse of #1

A. Joseph Desire LeBlanc born August 12, 1849 and baptized
    September 26, 1849 in St. Michael Church, Convent; mar-
    ried in Ascension Church, Donaldsonville

                          (1) December 29, 1873 Elizabeth
                               DENOUX (daughter of Henry
                               Denoux and Felicite CAPDEVILLE)

JOSEPH DESIRE LE BLANC
      (1849 - 1928)

ELIZABETH DENOUX
   (1850 - 1890)

FOUR GENERATION ANCESTOR CHART

                                          8.
                                          b.
                                          p.b.
                                          m.
          4. Cyril Landry   p.m.
          b.   d.
          p.b.   p.d.
          m. 11 January 1870
          p.m. Assumption Parish   9.
          d.   b.
          p.d.   p.b.
  2. Joseph (Majo) Landry   d.
  b.   p.d.
  p.b. Assumption Parish
  m. 7 February 1871
  p.m. St. Elizabeth Church   10.
  d.   b.
  p.d.   p.b.
                                          m.
          5. Marcellite Gravois   p.m.
          b.   d.
          p.b.   p.d.
          d.
          p.d.   11.
                                          b.
                                          p.b.
                                          d.
  1 Ernestine Landry   p.d.
  b.   1875
  p.b.
  m. 12 February 1895   12.
  p.m.   b.
  d.   1946   p.b.
  p.d. Baton Rouge   m.
          6. Adrien LeBlanc   p.m.
          b.   d.
          p.b.   p.d.
          m.
          p.m.   13.
          d.   b.
          p.d.   p.b.
  3. Adrienne LeBlanc   d.
  b.   p.d.
  p.b.
  d.   14.
  p.d.   b.
                                          p.b.
                                          m.
          7. Eliza Landry   p.m.
          b.   d.
          p.b.   p.d.
          d.
          p.d.   15.
                                          b.
  Ulysses LeBlanc   p.b.
  Spouse of #1   d.
                                          p.d.

1. Ulyssis LeBlanc born December 12, 1874 at Brusly Mc-
    Call (Ascension Parish) married February 12, 1895 in
    Ascension Church Ernestine LANDRY (daughter of Joseph
    Landry and Adrienne LE BLANC) born 1875. Ulyssis
    died February 14, 1944 and Ernestine died in 1946.
    Both are buried in Roselawn Cemetery, Baton Rouge, La.

ULYSSIS LE BLANC
(1874 - 1944)

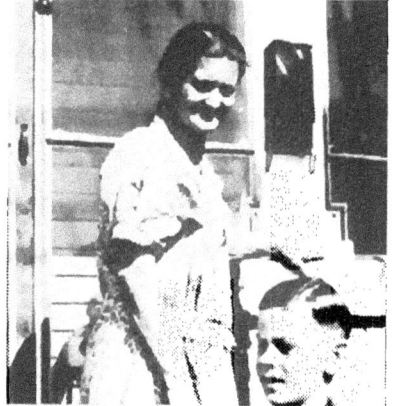

ERNESTINE LANDRY
(1875 - 1946)

a. Ulysses Ernest LeBlanc born November 7, 1895 in
    Assumption Parish married October 26, 1920 in
    St. James Church, St. James to Eula BRIGNAC
    (daughter of Pierre Brignac and Leontine MONTZ)
    born June 18, 1901. Ulysses died October 23,
    1971 in New Orleans.

    i. Evelyn Mae LeBlanc born August 4, 1921 in
        New Orleans married Lucien DARMOY.

        a) Linda Darmoy born December 9, 1947 mar-
            ried E. John ANDREWS

            i) Karyn Andrews born March 10, 1970 in
                Juneau, Alaska

        b) Janis Darmoy born July 26, 1952
        c) Bryan Darmoy born May 21, 1954

    ii. Irwin E. LeBlanc born December 18, 1925 in
         New Orleans married Marge Boryczka DUNKIRK
         of New York

a) Carol Ann LeBlanc born June 17, 1946
   married Claude JOHNSON of Mobile, Alabama
b) Jeffrey LeBlanc born November 1, 1951

b. Euzleien LeBlanc born March 22, 1897 in Ascension
   Parish married March 21, 1918 in Thibodaux Anita
   LEONARD (daughter of Jacques Leonard and Theressa
   GROS) born September 23, 1897 in Lockport, La.

   i. Joy LeBlanc born August 29, 1922 in Baton
      Rouge married Dalton L. SAMSON (son of Alias
      Samson and Lillian LORIO) of Pointe Coupee

      a) Randall J. Samson born July 24, 1947 in
         Baton Rouge married June 1, 1966 Carolyn
         HILBOUN (daughter· of George Philip Hil-
         boun and Edith BIRDNEAU) born December 16,
         1948 in Junction City, Arkansas

         i) Christine Samson born November 19,
            1967 in Pointe Coupee
        ii) Pamela Ann Samson born June 26, 1969
            in Baton Rouge

      b) Mary Ann Samson born May 28, 1957
      c) Valerie Samson born April 20, 1960

c. Virginia Jean LeBlanc born July 8, 1899 in Ascension Parish married Linus LANDRY (son of LaCroix
   Landry and Clemence LE BLANC) born February, 1904
   in New Orleans, La. Virginia died December 14,
   1968; Linus died January 29, 1936. There were no
   children.

d. Paul Virginia LeBlanc born July 8, 1901 in Ascension Parish married Myra BESSONET of Assumption
   Parish

   i. Wanda Fay LeBlanc born ca. 1930 in Baton Rouge

e. Rose Adolphine LeBlanc born June 17, 1903 in Ascension Parish married August 10, 1922 in Smoke
   Bend to Norman HIDALGO (son of Adrian Hidalgo and
   Hermena CARBO) born February 8, 1900. Norman
   died November 13, 1967 in Baton Rouge, La.

   i. Rose Mary Hidalgo born June 25, 1923 in Baton
      Rouge married Ivy THOMPSON (now divorced)

      a) Ivy Thompson born March 9, 1941 (adopted
         by grandparents and now carries the name
         Hidalgo) married July 21, 1962 in Baton
         Rouge to Linda CAIN (daughter of Hollis
         Cain and Dorothy SAMSON) born January 24,
         1945 in Baton Rouge, La.

         i) Kevin Allen Hidalgo born May 25, 1963
        ii) Karolyn Denise Hidalgo born October 5,
            1965

80

f. Clarence Anthony LeBlanc born June 13, 1906 and
    baptized July 4, 1906 in St. Francis of Assisi
    Church, Smoke Bend married January 31, 1930 to
    Hilda ROUSSEAU (daughter of Marcelan Rousseau
    and Adele DUPRE) Clarence died October 2, 1964
    in Baton Rouge and buried in Resthaven Cemetery,
    Baton Rouge, La.

    i. Allen Huey LeBlanc born December 1, 1931 in
        Baton Rouge married April 27, 1957 in St.
        Agnes Church, Baton Rouge to Jewel Mae BECK
        (daughter of Jewel Storm Beck and Pauline
        GRANGER) born November 12, 1934.

        a) Stayce Renee LeBlanc born February 25, 1959
        b) Lindsey Allen LeBlanc born October 24, 1963

g. Clara LeBlanc born June 30, 1907; died at age 5

h. Richard Etienne LeBlanc born August 3, 1909 in As-
    cension Parish married April 25, 1936 to Adeline
    POURCIAU (daughter of Joseph Hebrard Pourciau and
    Eugenie SOLARI) born March 4, 1910 of Iberville

    i. Richard Etienne LeBlanc, Jr. born October 20,
        1940 in Baton Rouge married at St. George
        Church, Baton Rouge to Marie Louise VINCENT
        (daughter of Walter B. Vincent and Edna
        WATSON) of Livingston Parish

        a) Tina Marie LeBlanc born November 16, 1963
        b) Delaine Michelle LeBlanc born March 23,
            1971 in Baton Rouge.

i. Marguerite Eloise LeBlanc born July 20, 1911 in
    Ascension Parish married November 6, 1937 in
    Sacred Heart Church, Baton Rouge to Maurice
    LE BLANC (son of Etienne LeBlanc and Espedia
    BROUSSARD) born January 26, 1910, Lafayette, La.

      i. Dian LeBlanc born September 8, 1938, single
     ii. Patricia LeBlanc born March 17, 1944, single
    iii. Robert LeBlanc born December 12, 1947, single

j. Marguerite Emma LeBlanc born November 13, 1913
    married May 23, 1931 Edwin J. ALEMAN (son of
    Sidney Aleman and Emily CARBO) Edwin, Sr. died
    November 18, 1954 at age 46; buried in Shreveport,
    Louisiana

     i. Edwin J. Aleman, Jr. born December 26, 1932
    ii. Donald Robert Aleman born October 29, 1934
         in Baton Rouge married Clara Kate WARNER

        a) Stephanie Aleman born June 21, 1957
            Shreveport
        b) Darlene Aleman born February 18, 1959

  c) Dondra Aleman born May 27, 1963
    Shreveport

iii. Ernestine Aleman born August 4, 1938 in Shreve-
  port married May 10, 1962 in Bossier City
  Walter E. TEDDER (son of Malvin B. Tedder and
  Hettie Augusta RESTER) born January 27, 1934
  Natalbany, Louisiana

  a) Warren Dean Tedder born September 16, 1964
    Shreveport
  b) Wal Bryant Tedder born March 18, 1967
    Shreveport

iv. Gene Raymond Aleman born August 7, 1943
  Shreveport

FOUR GENERATION ANCESTOR CHART

8.
b.
p.b.
m.
p.m.
d.
p.d.

4. Cyril Landry
b.
p.b.
m. 11 January 1870
p.m. Assumptión Parish
d.
p.d.

9.
b.
p.b.
d.
p.d.

2. Joseph Landry
b.
p.b.
m.
p.m.
d.
p.d.

10.
b.
p.b.
m.
p.m.
d.
p.d.

5. Marcellite Gravois
b.
p.b.
d.
p.d.

11.
b.
p.b.
d.
p.d.

1. LaCroix Landry
b.   1873
p.b. Ascension Parish
m. 23 April 1895
p.m. Smoke Bend, La.
d. 17 December 1936
p.d. New Orleans

12.
b.
p.b.
m.
p.m.
d.
p.d.

6. Adrien LeBlanc
b.
p.b.
m.
p.m.
d.
p.d.

13.
b.
p.b.
d.
p.d.

3. Adrienne LeBlanc
b.
p.b.
d.
p.d.

14.
b.
p.b.
m.
p.m.
d.
p.d.

7. Eliza Landry
b.
p.b.
d.
p.d.

15.
b.
p.b.
d.
p.d.

Clemence LeBlanc
Spouse of #1

k. Lucille Alma LeBlanc born November 13, 1913 and died at age 4 years

l. Alice LeBlanc born May 21, 1915 and died at age 6 months

2. Clemence LeBlanc born November 6, 1876 in Ascension Parish and married at age 19

      (1) April 23, 1895 in Ascension Parish to LaCroix LANDRY (son of Joseph Landry and Aderian LE BLANC)born in 1873 and died December 17, 1936, New Orleans, La.

LA CROIX LANDRY
(1873 - 1936)

CLEMENCE LE BLANC
(1876 - 1950)

FRANK W. WILLIAMS, SR.
(- 1941)

Clemence took her two sisters, Ernestine and Amelia, as their mother had died. She died November 28, 1950 and is buried in St. Mary's Cemetery, New Orleans, La.

a. Achille Valentine Landry born February 14, 1896 in Belle Rose married

83

     (1) Aline YOUNG who died Decem-
       ber 6, 1922 at age 25

There were no children born of Achille's first
marriage.

     (2) July 23, 1924 in New Orleans
       Orelia BARRIENT (daughter of
       Frank Barrient and Leonie
       LE BLANC)

 i. Frank J. Landry born January 24, 1926 in New
   Orleans married September 17, 1949 Grace
   WEBSTER. Frank died October 9, 1968. There
   were no children born.
 ii. Lee J. Landry born September 24, 1927 in New
   Orleans and died in June, 1929 at the age of
   2 years in New Orleans

     (3) Bertha GRIFFIN

There were no children born of Achille's third
marriage.

b. Adele Landry born May 7, 1897 in Belle Rose married November 2, 1921 in New Orleans Conrad
  STOCK, Sr. (son of John Stock and Mary SNYDER)
  born December 20, 1879 in New Orleans. Conrad
  died April 6, 1932 in New Orleans.

 i. Mary Louise Stock born July 29, 1922 in New
   Orleans
 ii. Freida Julia Stock born February 25, 1924 in
   New Orleans married April 10, 1945 John G.
   MARFORD (son of Garrett Marford and Margaret
   TRESS). John died April 19, 1968 in Bethesda,
   Maryland.

   a) Michael C. Marford born April 29, 1947
   b) Janice Marford born January 8, 1949
   c) John G. Marford, Jr. born July 6, 1950

 iii. Elizabeth Adelle Stock born April 25, 1926
 iv. Conrad Stock, Jr. born June 10, 1930 married
   October 29, 1971 in New Orleans to Jean
   WELDING (daughter of Martin Welding and
   Myrtle _____) born June 2, 1938 in New Orleans

c. Elizabeth Landry died an infant in 1899
d. George Landry died in 1908 at age 7 years
e. Edna Landry born February 6, 1902 in New Orleans
  married June 4, 1924 Charles Daniel STEIB, Sr.

 i. Charles D. Steib, Jr. born November 12, 1925
   in New Orleans married in Laurel, Mississippi
   December 24, 1955 Elizabeth SIMMONS (daughter
   of Roy L. Simmons and Jessie Gladys JOHNSON)
   born October 9, 1932 in Amite, La.

        a) Jill Elaine Steib born March 13, 1959
        b) Julie Elizabeth Steib born March 13, 1959
        c) Charles Daniel Steib, III born June 5, 1957
        d) Courtney Andrew Steib born December 29, 1961

f. Linus Landry born February 1904 in New Orleans married about 1925 Virginia Jean LE BLANC (daughter of Ulyssis LeBlanc and Ernestine LANDRY) born July 8, 1899. Linus died January 26, 1936 and is buried in Lafayette Cemetery #2 in New Orleans. Virginia died December 14, 1968 and is buried in Roselawn Cemetery in Baton Rouge

        (2) Frank Wilford WILLIAMS who died in 1941 and is buried in Carrollton Cemetery in New Orleans

g. Frank Wilford (Nookie) Williams, Jr. born November 8, 1912 in New Orleans and married June 12, 1948 Velma SIMON (daughter of Joseph Simon and Lena SCIONEAUX) born July 5, 1910 in Vacherie

h. Walter Thomas Williams born April 24, 1914 in New Orleans married September 19, 1937 Melvina PINTOT (daughter of Firmin John Pintot and Julia NUNEZ) born February 24, 1916 in New Orleans

    i. Palmira Williams born December 12, 1940 in New Orleans married Gerald HAUSWALD born July 23, 1936 in New Orleans

        a) Jay Hauswald born November 28, 1962 in New Orleans
        b) Shawn Hauswald born November 25, 1966 in New Orleans

    ii. Linda Williams born October 25, 1945 in New Orleans married Michael A. NEVLE (son of Gus Nevle and Nellie _____) born March 8, 1941

        a) Michael A. Nevle, Jr. born May 28, 1965 in New Orleans
        b) Rebecca Nevle born June 1, 1967 in New Orleans

    iii. Walter Thomas Williams born November 3, 1952 in New Orleans

i. Palmira Williams born 1916 in New Orleans; died in 1927 at age 11 and buried in St. Mary's Cemetery, New Orleans

3. Marie Ernestine LeBlanc born January 18, 1881 in Ascension Parish married about 1900 George LE BLANC (son of Alcee (Alcide) LeBlanc and Marie RODRIGUE) Ernestine died February 27, 1954; George died June 11, 1964; buried Greenwood Cemetery, New Orleans

FOUR GENERATION ANCESTOR CHART

8. Joseph LeBlanc
b.
p.b.
m.
p.m.
d.
p.d.

4.Valery Cyprien LeBlanc
b.
p.b.
m. 28 May 1821
p.m.Assumption Parish
d.
p.d.

9.Marie Josephe Landry
b.
p.b.
d.
p.d.

2.Alcee (Alcide) LeBlanc
b.
p.b.
m.
p.m.
d.
p.d.

10.Raphael Landry
b.
p.b.
m.
p.m.
d.
p.d.

5.Hortense Landry
b.
p.b.
d.
p.d.

11.Marguerite Richard
b.
p.b.
d.
p.d.

1.George P. LeBlanc
b.
p.b. Assumption Parish
m.   1900
p.m. Ascension Parish
d. 11 June 1964
p.d. New Orleans, La.

12.Antoine Rodrigue
b.
p.b.
m.
p.m.
d.
p.d.

6. Laurent Rodrigue
b.
p.b.
m. 26 May 1834
p.m. Assumption Parish
d.
p.d.

13.Sebastianne Acosta
b.
p.b.
d.
p.d.

3.Marie Rodrigue
b.
p.b.
d.
p.d.

14.Antoine Vega
b.
p.b.
m. 2 July 1816
p.m.Ascension Parish
d.
p.d.

7. Marie Vega
b.
p.b.
d.
p.d.

15.Marie Ruiz
b.
p.b.
d.
p.d.

Ernestine LeBlanc
Spouse of #1

MARIE ERNESTINE LE BLANC   GEORGE P. LE BLANC
(1881 - 1954)   (- 1964)

    a. Daniel Leah LeBlanc born December 27, 1902 in As-
        cension Parish married about 1927 Anna SPOHRER
        (daughter of Eugene Spohrer and Mammie DILLON)
        born September 22, 1904. Daniel died April 9,
        1962 in New Orleans
    b. Elizabeth LeBlanc born May 2, 1904 in Ascension
        Parish married April 11, 1934 in New Orleans
        John Shearer BARKER (son of Charles Edward Barker
        and Laura M. SHEARER) born December 20, 1902 in
        New Orleans

  4. Eli LeBlanc born December 20, 1882 in Ascension Parish
     married November 30, 1910 in New Orleans Cecilia Mary
     PIQUE (daughter of Charles John Pique and Mary GOETTE)
     born May 14, 1883. Eli died in November, 1947;
     Cecilia died September 3, 1964. Both are buried in
     Soniat #1 Cemetery, New Orleans

    a. Alvin Joseph LeBlanc born September 13, 1911 in
        New Orleans married in June, 1940 Ethel HEIGLE
        (daughter of George Heigle and Ethel ROBERTS)
        Alvin died November 23, 1963 and is buried in
        Metairie Cemetery, New Orleans

        i. Alvin Joseph LeBlanc, Jr. born in 1942

    b. Eli Edmund LeBlanc born May 2, 1918 in New Orleans
        married March 30, 1940 Mildred KEENE (daughter of
        Philip James Keene and Wilda Mae RUSHING) born
        November 25, 1917 in New Orleans

        i. Douglas Philip LeBlanc born September 17, 1942
           in New Orleans married December 28, 1963

FOUR GENERATION ANCESTOR CHART

4. Ferdinand Collet
b.
p.b.
m.
p.m.
d.
p.d.

2. Andrea Ferdinand Collet
b. 4 February 1854
p.b. Ascension Parish
m. 19 April 1881
p.m. Ascension Parish
d. 29 November 1926
p.d. Donaldsonville, La.

5. Amalie LeBlanc ·
b.
p.b.
d.
p.d.

1 Adine Ann Collet
b. 28 December 1882
p.b. Ascension Parish
m. 22 September 1909
p.m. Smoke Bend
d. 5 October 1959
p.d. Bur. Ascension Cemetery

6. Leon U. Landry
b.
p.b.
m. 17 January 1853
p.m. Ascension Parish
d.
p.d.

3. Marie Ozilphie Landry
b.   1863
p.b.
d. June 1936
p.d. Bur. Donaldsonville

7. Advelina Landry
b.
p.b.
d.
p.d.

Mederick LeBlanc
Spouse of #1

8.
b.
p.b.
m.
p.m.
d.
p.d.

9.
b.
p.b.
d.
p.d.

10.
b.
p.b.
m.
p.m.
d.
p.d.

11.
b.
p.b.
d.
p.d.

12. August Hyacinth Landry
b.
p.b.
m.
p.m.
d.
p.d.

13. Marguerite Eugenie Babin
b.
p.b.
d.
p.d.

14. Simonet Landry
b.
p.b.
m.
p.m.
d.
p.d.

15. Bethilde Landry
b.
p.b.
d.
p.d.

FOUR GENERATION ANCESTOR CHART

8.
b.
p.b.
m.
p.m.
d.
p.d.

4. Manuel Ruiz
b.
p.b.
m.
p.m.
d.
p.d.

9.
b.
p.b.
d.
p.d.

2. Antonio Ruiz
b.
p.b.
m. 31 July 1860
p.m. Ascension Parish
d.
p.d.

10.
b.
p.b.
m.
p.m.
d.
p.d.

5. Maria Monson
b.
p.b.
d.
p.d.

11.
b.
p.b.
d.
p.d.

1. Jeanette Ruiz
b.
p.b.
m. 18 February 1895
p.m.
d. 1921
p.d.. Donaldsonville, La. (burial)

12. Joseph Hernandez
b.
p.b.
m.
p.m.
d.
p.d.

6. Estéve Hernandez
b.
p.b.
m.
p.m.
d.
p.d.

13. Jeanne Truxillo
b.
p.b.
d.
p.d.

3. Antoinette Hernandez
b.
p.b.
d. c. 1900
p.d. Ascension Parish

14. Silvestre Ramirez
b.
p.b.
m.
p.m.
d.
p.d.

7. Rosalia Ramirez
b.
p.b.
d.
p.d.

15. Antonia Mora
b.
p.b.
d.
p.d.

Joseph Desire LeBlanc
Spouse of #1

A. Joseph Desire LeBlanc married

>(2) February 18, 1895 in Ascension
>Jeanette RUIZ (daughter of
>Antoine Ruiz and Antoinette
>HERNANDEZ) widow of Antoine
>RODRIGUEZ

DESIRE LE BLANC
(1849 - 1928)

JEANETTE RUIZ
(- 1921)

Veronica LA GARDE (daughter of Lawrence
LaGarde and Veronica BAGGETT)

a) Sean Michael LeBlanc born October 19, 1964
b) Steven Mark LeBlanc born June 7, 1966
c) Sheryl Ann LeBlanc born November 12, 1967
d) Shannon Michelle LeBlanc born May 15, 1971

ii. Barbara Ellie LeBlanc born July 27, 1943 in
New Orleans married October 12, 1967 Robert
Lee BARNHILL (son of Leonard T. Barnhill and
Rose HUTTA) born May 15, 1942 in Michigan

a) Brett Talmadge Barnhill born September 29,
1971 in New Orleans

5. Mederick LeBlanc born June 19, 1884 in Ascension Par-
ish married September 22, 1909 in Smoke Bend Adine
COLLET (daughter of Andres Ferdinand Collet and Marie
Olzelphia LANDRY) born December 28, 1882. Mederick
died October 5, 1959 and Adine died December 5, 1936.
Mederick is buried in Greenoaks Memorial Park, Baton
Rouge; Adine is buried in the Collet family tomb in
Ascension Cemetery, Donaldsonville

MEDERICK LE BLANC
(1884 - 1959)

ADINE COLLET
(1882 - 1936)

87

a. Mederick LeBlanc, Jr. born September 24, 1910 in
   Ascension Parish married Carrie Elizabeth MELANCON
   (daughter of Ernest Thomas Melancon and Eva
   BURLETT) born July 16, 1910

   i. Joseph LeBlanc born July 5, 1931 in Baton
   Rouge; died at birth and buried in Donaldsonville

  ii. Betty Joyce LeBlanc born July 3, 1933 in Baton
   Rouge and married January 24, 1953 to Leland
   TURNER (son of Willie D. Turner and Mildred
   CARNEY)

 iii. Carol Joseph LeBlanc born November 8, 1934 in
   Baton Rouge married

      (1) Marie ROCKHOLT of England

    a) Mark LeBlanc born in 1957
    b) Gary LeBlanc born in 1959
    c) Ann LeBlanc born October 13, 1961

      (2) Dolores BURGUIERES

There were no children born of the second marriage.

b. Florence LeBlanc born January 28, 1912 in Ascension
   Parish married December 19, 1936 to Leonard Paul
   BOUDREAUX (son of Anthel P. Boudreaux and Mathilde
   FALCON) born September 27, 1907 in Labadieville.
   Florence died September 10, 1968 and Leonard died
   March 31, 1967.

c. Aline LeBlanc born March 8, 1913 in Ascension
   Parish; died January 29, 1932 and buried in Ascension Cemetery

d. Lee Leonard LeBlanc born August 12, 1914 in Ascen-
   sion Parish married May 10, 1940 in Baton Rouge to
   Lois Leonide VALENTINE (daughter of Leo Craig
   Valentine and Bertha Kay KENT)

   i. Donnyl Lois LeBlanc born December 1, 1941
   married

      (1) November 12, 1960 to Sedgie
   Frank MELANCON

There were no children born of this marriage

      (2) December 24, 1966 to James
   Mark BOLLINGER, Jr. (son of
   James Mark Bollinger, Sr. and
   Myrtle Prudent TYSEN) born
   February 22, 1935

    a) Jayme Michel Bollinger born February 25,
   1968 in Baton Rouge

ii. Jerilyn Lee LeBlanc born August 9, 1945 in
Baton Rouge married George Allen LEE (son of
George Allen Lee, Sr. and Lucille CARLTON)

a) Jeffrey Alan Lee born May 16, 1965; died
May 23, 1965
b) Dana Alane Lee born June 25, 1966
c) Jeffrey Alan Lee born January 5, 1970

iii. Dale Leonard LeBlanc born November 16, 1947
in Baton Rouge married

(1) Gayle LANDRY (daughter of
Willard Joseph Landry and
Christine CALLENDER)

a) Joseph Lee LeBlanc

(2) Cynthia Brown

b) Dale Leonard LeBlanc born August 23, 1968

iv. Sharon Leonide LeBlanc born September 15, 1949
in Baton Rouge married Van Paul DUHON (son of
Lloyd Francis Duhon and Dorothy SIMONEAUX)
born March 21, 1949

a) Darla Ann Duhon born March 15, 1968 in
Baton Rouge

e. Velma LeBlanc born September 14, 1915 in Ascension
Parish married July 13, 1946 in Lakeland, La. Shel-
ton Joseph GAUTREAUX (son of Florian Joseph Gautreaux
and Anisette YOUNG) born September 14, 1915

i. Arlene Ann Gautreaux born August 23, 1947 in
Baton Rouge married January 8, 1972 in St.
Louis King of France Church, Baton Rouge
Donald WYATT (son of Albert John Wyatt and
Lois THURMOND) born December 3, 1950 in Houston,
Texas. Donald served in the United States
Army from 1969 to 1971
ii. Charmine Marie Gautreaux born April 16, 1952
in Baton Rouge married October 23, 1961 in St.
Louis King of France Church, Baton Rouge John
Walter NEPTUNE (son of John William Neptune, Jr.
and Althea ZAMMIT) born October 14, 1951
iii. Janell Elizabeth Gautreaux born June 7, 1954

f. Jenny V. LeBlanc born May 18, 1922 in Ascension
Parish married L. J. STOREY (son of Allison
Lafayette Storey and Jessie PERKINS) born February 24, 1919 in Philadelphia, Mississippi. L. J.
served in the United States Army from 1942 to 1945

i. Susan Marie Storey born October 27, 1954 in
Baton Rouge married March 6, 1971 Clyde A.

FOUR GENERATION ANCESTOR CHART

8.
b.
p.b.
m.
p.m.
d.
p.d.

4. Ferdinand Collet
b.
p.b.
m.
p.m.
d.
p.d.

9.
b.
p.b.
d.
p.d.

2. Andrea Ferdinand Collet
b.   4 February 1854
p.b. Ascension Parish
m.   19 April 1881
p.m. Ascension Parish
d.   29 November 1926
p.d. Donaldsonville, La.

10.
b.
p.b.
m.
p.m.
d.
p.d.

5. Amalie LeBlanc
b.
p.b.
d.
p.d.

11.
b.
p.b.
d.
p.d.

1 Modeste Collet
b. 30 November 1890
p.b. Ascension Parish
m. 7 October 1912
p.m. Smoke Bend, La.
d.
p.d.

12. August Hyacinth Landry
b.
p.b.
m.
p.m.
d.
p.d.

6. Leon U. Landry
b.
p.b.
m. 17 January 1853
p.m. Ascension Parish
d.
p.d.

13. Marguerite Eugenie Babin
b.
p.b.
d.
p.d.

3 Marie Ozilphie Landry
b.   1863
p.b.
d.   June 1936
p.d. Bur. Donaldsonville, La.

14. Simonet Landry
b.
p.b.
m.
p.m.
d.
p.d.

7. Advelina Landry
b.
p.b.
d.
p.d.

15. Bethilde Landry
b.
p.b.
d.
p.d.

Willie Joseph LeBlanc
Spouse of #1

HONEY (son of Sherman Lamar Honey and Joyce
HEINE) born December 2, 1949
ii.   Lorreta Ann Storey born April 8, 1960 in
Baton Rouge

6.   William LeBlanc (Willie Joseph) born April 1, 1886 in
Ascension Parish married October 7, 1912 in Smoke
Bend Modeste Anne COLLET (daughter of Andres Ferdinand
Collet and Marie Olzelphia LANDRY) born November 30,
1890. William died September 11, 1972 in Baton Rouge
and is buried in Greenoaks Memorial Park, Baton Rouge

WILLIAM LE BLANC   MODESTE   COLLET
(1886 - 1972)   (1890 -   )

a.   Sadie Marie LeBlanc born October 22, 1913 in Ascension Parish married July 27, 1935 in St.
Anthony Church, Baton Rouge, La. John CARONA (son
of Salvador Carona and Josephine AUGUST) born
November 2, 1912

i.   William Joseph Carona born September 24, 1939
in Baton Rouge married June 6, 1959 in Sacred

Heart Church, Baton Rouge, La. Patricia DANNA
(daughter of Ralph Anthony Danna and Juanita
AUGUSTA) born December 28, 1940 in Baton
Rouge. William graduated from the Loyola
University School of Dentistry on May 23, 1963.
He served in the U. S. Naval Reserve from 1963
to 1965.

WILLIAM J. CARONA, D.D.S.
(1939 -   )

    a) Deborah Ann Carona born September 16, 1960
       in Baton Rouge
    b) Sherri Lynn Carona born November 2, 1963
       in San Diego, California
    c) Nancy Jean Carona born June 10, 1965 in
       Baton Rouge

b. Effie Cecile LeBlanc born January 28, 1920 in As-
cension Parish married October 5, 1939 in St.
Anthony Church, Baton Rouge, La. Price Henry
CARNEY (son of Ben C. Carney and Laura PRICE)
born September 18, 1919 in Lawrence County, Jayess,
Mississippi

    i. Henry Carol Carney born March 20, 1942 in
       Baton Rouge married March 19, 1961 Jeanette
       GOUDEAU (daughter of Harris Goudeau and
       Blanche MIX) born January 9, 1944 in Baton
       Rouge

a) Pamela Carney born December 14, 1961 in
Baton Rouge

b) Karen Carney born January 26, 1967 in
Baton Rouge

ii. Darline Ann Carney born May 30, 1946 in Baton
Rouge married November 14, 1964 in Sacred
Heart Church, Baton Rouge, La. Raymond MONTZ
(son of Claude Montz, Jr. and Marion DUGAS)
born August 22, 1944 in New Orleans

a) Michelle Denise Montz born April 22, 1966
in Jacksonville, North Carolina

b) Rachelle Darlene Montz born July 1, 1968
in Baton Rouge, La.

iii. Gary Lee Carney born January 15, 1954 in Baton
Rouge

iv. Emery James Carney born June 7, 1956 in Baton
Rouge

c. Dolores Rita LeBlanc born June 16, 1931 in Baton
Rouge married February 27, 1949 in St. Anthony
Church, Baton Rouge, La. Francis Gene BEHRNES
(son of William Henry Behrnes and Sena KNAPP)
born October 12, 1928 in Baton Rouge, La.

i. Robert Gerald Behrnes born June 25, 1953 in
Baton Rouge married May 19, 1972 in St.
Anthony Church, Baton Rouge, La. Tanya Marie
LANDRY (daughter of Wayne Landry and   )

7. Amelia LeBlanc born November 7, 1888 in Ascension
    Parish married John E. DAVIS of Houston, Texas.
    Amelia died in 1940 and is buried in Houston.

AMELIA LE BLANC and JOHN E. DAVIS
(1888 - 1940)   (-   )

FOUR GENERATION ANCESTOR CHART

8. Benjamine Desire LeBlanc
b. 14 October 1796
p.b. Ascension Parish
m. 9 June 1817
p.m. Ascension Parish
d. 30 December 1853
p.d. Ascension Parish

4. Joseph LeBlanc
b. 30 March 1818
p.b. Ascension Parish
m. 21 August 1848
p.m. St. James Parish
d. 8 May 1871
p.d. Ascension Parish

9. Marguerite Felonise Dugas
b.
p.b. Ascension Parish
d. 10 January 1871
p.d. Ascension Parish

2. Telasmar LeBlanc
b. 1 April 1860
p.b. Brusly McCall, La.
m. 2 October 1885
p.m. Ascension Parish
d. 10 February 1940
p.d. Bur. Ascension Cemetery
Donaldsonville, La.

10. Christophe Webre
b. 24 January 1799
p.b. St. John the Baptist
m. 18 September 1820
p.m. Convent, La.
d. 12 June 1855
p.d. St. James Parish

5. Amelia Webre
b. 12 March 1829
p.b. St. John the Baptist
d. 26 November 1882
p.d. Ascension Parish

11. Felicite Rome
b. 30 January 1804
p.b. St. James Parish
d. 13 November 1832
p.d. St. James Parish

1. May LeBlanc
b. 9 May 1900
p.b. Brusly McCall, La.
m. 22 May 1918
p.m. Bay St. Louis, Miss.
d.
p.d..

12. Pierre Trasimond Dugas
b. ca. 1816
p.b.
m. 26 June 1837
p.m. Ascension Parish
d.
p.d.

6. Pierre Trasimond Dugas
b. 27 April 1843
p.b. Brusly McCall, La.
m. 13 January 1866
p.m. Ascension Parish
d.
p.d. Ascension Parish

13. Melanie Denoux
b. ca. 1822
p.b.
d.
p.d.

3. Victoria Dugas
b. 7 September 1869
p.b. Brusly McCall, La.
d. 19 February 1936
p.d. Bur. Ascension Cemetery
Donaldsonville, La.

14. Henry Denoux
b. ca. 1816
p.b.
m. 29 August 1836
p.m. Ascension Parish
d.
p.d.

7. Felicite Denoux
b. ca. 1846
p.b. Ascension Parish
d.
p.d. Ascension Parish

15. Felicite Capdeville
b.
p.b.
d.
p.d.

Desire LeBlanc
Spouse of #1

8. Desire LeBlanc born September 12, 1895 in Ascension
    Parish married May 22, 1918 in Bay St. Louis, Missis-
    sippi May LE BLANC (daughter of Telasmar LeBlanc and
    Victoria DUGAS) born May 9, 1900 in Ascension Parish

DESIRE LE BLANC   MAY LE BLANC
  (1895 -   )   (1900 -   )

BETTY LE BLANC   BERNICE LE BLANC   ROMSEY J. LE BLANC

a. Romsey Joseph LeBlanc born May 15, 1919 in Ascen-
    sion Parish married Helen CAMBRE (daughter of
    Joseph D. Cambre and Helen ARCENEAUX) of St.
    Gabriel

    i. Janet Marie LeBlanc born March 16, 1944 mar-
        ried Luther Conley JUBAN, Jr. (son of Luther
        Conley Juban, Sr. and Maxine PETERS)

        a) Joan Alison Juban born June 8, 1968 in
            Baton Rouge, La.
        b) Christopher Conley Juban born August 10,
            1970 in Baton Rouge, La.

ii. Randy Joseph LeBlanc, Jr. born February 7,
1960 in Baton Rouge, La.

b. Bernice LeBlanc born May 17, 1920 in Ascension
Parish married November 28, 1945 in St. Agnes
Church, Baton Rouge to Leo Leonce GUIDRY (son of
Leonce Leo Guidry and Ella Marie ARCENEAUX) born
May 17, 1920 in Ascension Parish

i. Wayne Edward Guidry born March 17, 1947 in
Baton Rouge married April 16, 1971 in Baton
Rouge to Suzanne HURST (daughter of Carl
Hurst and Ella BARRIS) born June 29, 1940 in
Savannah, Georgia. Wayne entered the United
States Air Force in Baton Rouge on May 13,
1966 and was separated March 12, 1970.
ii. Gayle Ann Guidry born April 19, 1959 in Baton
Rouge, La.

c. Mary Elizabeth (Betty) LeBlanc born September 13,
1933 in Baton Rouge married November 13, 1955 in
St. Agnes Church, Baton Rouge to Achille Paul
DENOUX (son of Achille Joseph Denoux and Ella
LANOIX) born September 23, 1931 in Ascension
Parish

i. Kelvin Paul Denoux born June 10, 1957
ii. Rodney Joseph Denoux born March 3, 1959
iii. Glenn Edward Denoux born January 29, 1962
iv. Scott David Denoux born August 3, 1971

FOUR GENERATION ANCESTOR CHART

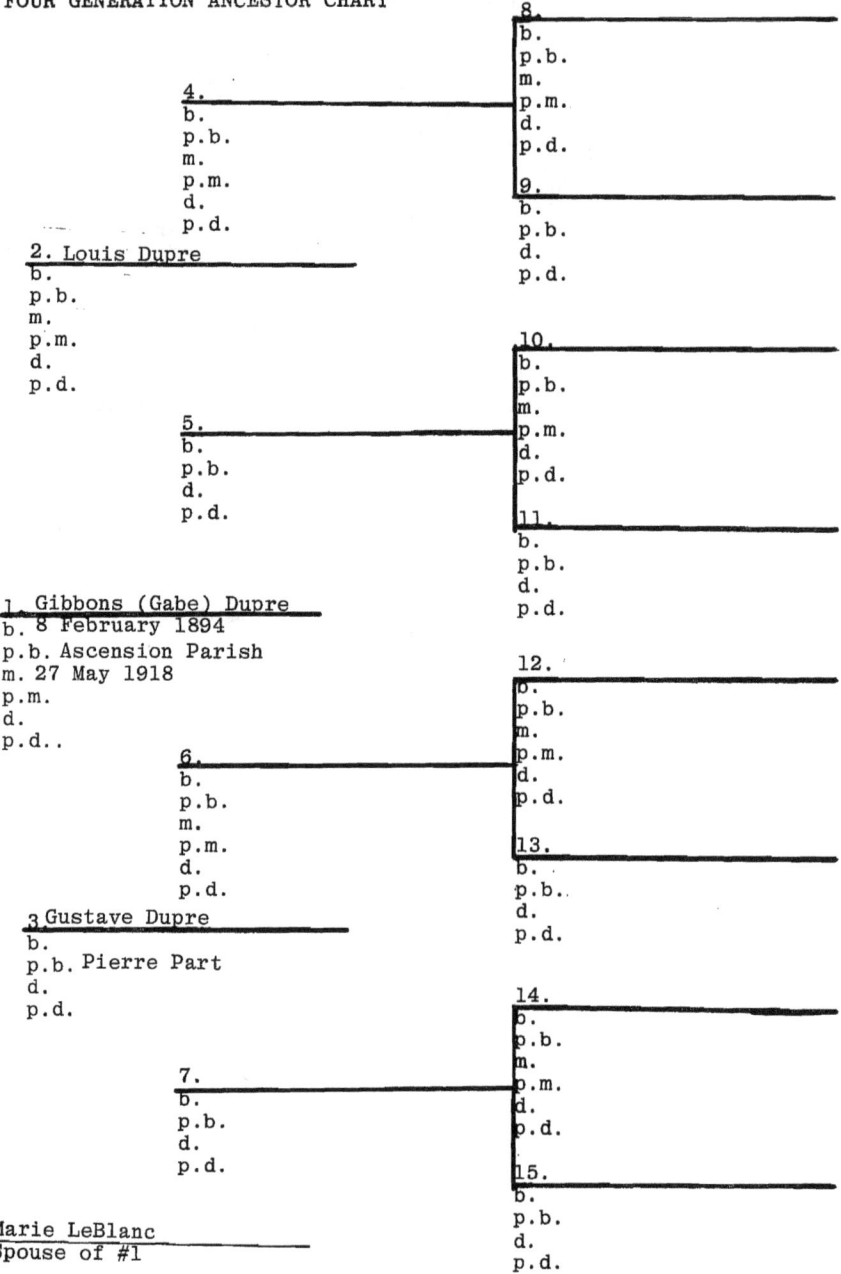

8.
b.
p.b.
m.
4.   p.m.
b.   d.
p.b.   p.d.
m.
p.m.   9.
d.   b.
    p.d.   p.b.
2. Louis Dupre   d.
b.   p.d.
p.b.
m.
p.m.   10.
d.   b.
p.d.   p.b.
                                        m.
5.   p.m.
b.   d.
p.b.   p.d.
d.
p.d.   11.
                                        b.
                                        p.b.
                                        d.
1. Gibbons (Gabe) Dupre   p.d.
b. 8 February 1894
p.b. Ascension Parish
m. 27 May 1918   12.
p.m.   b.
d.   p.b.
p.d..   m.
6.   p.m.
b.   d.
p.b.   p.d.
m.
p.m.   13.
d.   b.
    p.d.   p.b.
3 Gustave Dupre   d.
b.   p.d.
p.b. Pierre Part
d.
p.d.   14.
                                        b.
                                        p.b.
                                        m.
7.   p.m.
b.   d.
p.b.   p.d.
d.
p.d.   15.
                                        b.
                                        p.b.
Marie LeBlanc   d.
Spouse of #1   p.d.

9. Marie LeBlanc born August 10, 1896 in Ascension Par-
    ish married May 27, 1918 in Ascension to Gibbons
    (Gabe) DUPRE (son of Louis Dupre and Gustave DUPRE)
    of Pierre Part born February 8, 1894. Marie died
    November 10, 1960 in Ascension. After the death of
    Marie in 1960, Gabe was married to Lucy BERNARD
    on April 15, 1961 in Assumption Parish.

GIBBONS DUPRE   MARIE   LE BLANC
(1894   )   (1896 - 1960)

a. Jeanette Dupre born September 23, 1919 in Ascen-
    sion Parish married January 30, 1940 in St. Eliza-
    beth Church, Paincourtville to Pierre Morris
    LE BLANC (son of Renaud LeBlanc and Emma LANDRY)
    born December 22, 1917, Brusly St. Martin, La.

    i. Joan Jeanette LeBlanc born February 2, 1942
        married February 25, 1972 (second marriage)
        to Paul GIAMBRONE, Jr. (son of Paul Giambrone
        and Eloise VARIANI) born April 28, 1939.

Children of Joan Jeanette's first marriage:
a) Janell Bergeron born November 6, 1962
b) Gwen Bergeron born December 6, 1964

Children of Paul Giambrone's first marriage:
Joy Giambrone born January 21, 1959
Charles Giambrone born March 29, 1960
Debra Giambrone born May 18, 1961

ii. Leslie LeBlanc born December 20, 1942
iii. Tracy Arthur LeBlanc born July 5, 1946 married August 13, 1966 in St. Elizabeth Church, Paincourtville to Diane Mary LE BLANC (daughter of Joseph Felix LeBlanc and Marilyn Theresa LE BLANC) born December 25, 1946 in New Orleans

   a) Becky Ann LeBlanc born July 14, 1967 in Thibodaux
   b) Laurie Marie LeBlanc born September 17, 1968 in Thibodaux
   c) John Michael LeBlanc born August 27, 1971

iv. Pamela Ann LeBlanc born August 31, 1952

b. Leslie Dupre born May 27, 1920 in Ascension Parish married in 1942 in a Lutheran Church in New Orleans to Adelaide HAYDEL (daughter of Premilas J. Haydel and Claudia Marie LANDRY) born October 27, 1922

   i. Arvid Dupre born May 31, 1947 in New Orleans married August 3, 1968 in St. Christopher Church, Metairie, to Carolyn Ann ASPRION (daughter of Owen Adolph Asprion and Dorothy MARRON) born November 18, 1948

      a) Wade Michael Dupre born August 18, 1969 in New Orleans

   ii. Dennis Dupre born May 25, 1951 in New Orleans

c. Audrey Dupre born January 18, 1922 in Ascension Parish married in 1945 to Lugger CEDOTAL (son of Eugene Cedotal and   HUGH)

   i. Aubery Cedotal born April, 1949
   ii. Adele Marie Cedotal born September, 1951

d. Mary Lee Dupre born August 14, 1924 in Ascension Parish married July 18, 1945 in St. Joseph Church, Pierre Part to Davis A. VERRETTE (son of Herbert Verrette and Edith COMEAUX) born June 22, 1925 in Pierre Part, La.

   i. David A. Verrette, Jr. born March 29, 1950 in New Orleans
   ii. Craig J. Verrette born July 3, 1955
   iii. Brian Paul Verrette born August 25, 1957

97

e. Woodrow Joseph (Bosco) Dupre born August 17, 1925
    in Assumption Parish married June 15, 1947 in
    Pierre Part Violet Bernadette LEONARD (daughter
    of Dozelien Joseph Leonard and Hortence OCKMAN)
    born October 30, 1930 in Assumption Parish

    i. Claudia Marie Dupre born October 2, 1950 in
        Pierre Part married August 1, 1964 Wayne
        Joseph LAMBERT (son of Calvin Lambert and
        Ozelia ACKLIN) born November 10, 1948 in
        Napoleonville, La.

        a) Troy Joseph Lambert born February 27, 1965
            in Napoleonville, La.
        b) Todd Anthony Lambert born September 12,
            1967 in Pierre Part, La.
        c) Michelle Bernadette Lambert born Septem-
            ber 27, 1970 in Donaldsonville, La.

    ii. Charlotte Marie Dupre born October 16, 1954
        married October 24, 1970 Brent Paul GAUTREAUX
        (son of Ervin Paul Gautreaux and Mary Louise
        MILLER) born September 1, 1950 in Charenton,
        La.

        a) Tiffany Ann Gautreaux born December 3,
            1971 in Donaldsonville, La.

    iii. Clint Anthony Dupre born October 29, 1960 in
         Pierre Part, La.

f. Rita Mae Dupre born October 26, 1926 in Ascension
    Parish married August 23, 1945 Rivest Raymond
    THIBODEAUX (son of Robert Thibodeaux and Zulma
    DAIGRE) born in Thibodaux. Rivest served in the
    United States Army from LaFourche Parish. He
    died February 18, 1972 and is buried in St. Joseph
    Cemetery, Thibodaux, La.

    i. Abbegail Marie Thibodeaux born August 29, 1947
        in Thibodaux married November 19, 1966 William
        FORTNER, Jr. (son of William Fortner, Sr. and
        Doris VALO) born November 20, 1947 in Biloxi,
        Mississippi

        a) Kay Marie Fortner born October 5, 1967 in
            Thibodaux

    ii. Trudy Rita Thibodeaux born November 9, 1950
        married Robert Patrick BRAUD (son of Charles
        Braud, Jr. and Dorothy NAVVERRE)

        a) Tiffany Ann Braud born March 16, 1969 in
            Thibodaux, La.
        b) Celeste Leigh Braud born September 24,
            1971 in Thibodaux

        iii.   Raymond Ralph Thibodeaux born July 16, 1953
        iv.   Mark Thibodeaux born September 24, 1958

   g.   Kenneth Dupre born July 21, 1938 in Ascension
       Parish married Maxine MC GOVERN (daughter of
       Cornelius McGovern and Florence ZEIGE) born
       July 1, 1939

      i.   Kendra Ann Dupre born October 17, 1958
     ii.   Kenneth J. Dupre, Jr. born April 29, 1969

10. Joseph LeBlanc died at age 12
11. Theodule LeBlanc born April 26, 1900 in Ascension
    Parish married May 24, 1924 to Maria GUILLOT (daugh-
    ter of Evariste Guillot and Lydia BRAUD) of Assumption
    Parish born August 27, 1905 in Pierre Part, La.
    Theodule died February 9, 1972 in Pierre Part and is
    buried in the St. Joseph Church Cemetery

FOUR GENERATION ANCESTOR CHART

8.
b.
p.b.
m.
4. Joseph Ursin Guillot
p.m.
b.
d.
p.b.
p.d.
m.
p.m.
d.
9.
p.d.
b.
p.b.
2. Evariste Guillot
d.
b.
p.d.
p.b. Pierre Part
m. 8 February 1888
p.m. Pierre Part
d.
10.
p.d.
b.
p.b.
m.
5. Josephine Daigle
p.m.
b.
d.
p.b.
p.d.
d.
p.d.
11.
b.
p.b.
d.
1 Maria Guillot
p.d.
b. 28 August 1905
p.b. Pierre Part
m. 24 May 1924
12.
p.m.
b.
d.
p.b.
p.d..
m.
6. Joseph Braud
p.m.
b.
d.
p.b.
p.d.
m.
p.m.
13.
d.
b.
p.d.
p.b.
d.
3 Lydia Braud
p.d.
b.
p.b. Pierre Part
d.
14.
p.d.
b.
p.b.
m.
7. Zulma Simoneaux
p.m.
b.
d.
p.b.
p.d.
d.
p.d.
15.
b.
p.b.
Theodule LeBlanc
d.
Spouse of #1
p.d.

THEODULE LE BLANC   MARIA GUILLOT
(1900 - 1972)   (1905 -   )

a. Eura Mae LeBlanc born April 19, 1925 in Pierre
Part married December 15, 1942 to Minas HEBERT
(son of Nicholas Hebert and   ) born
October 9, 1919. Minas died November 25, 1968.

  i. Gaynel Hebert born March 3, 1944 married
May 1, 1965 in Pierre Part to Donald HOLLAND
(son of Arthur L. Holland, Sr. and Minnie
Helen WESLEY) born May 13, 1940 in Weiss, La.
Donald served in the United States Air Force
from 1959 to 1963

    a) Donna Rae Holland born November 8, 1965
in Napoleonville
    b) Paula Marie Holland born July 31, 1968
in Baton Rouge

  ii. Rita Mae Hebert born April 16, 1945 in Pierre
Part married June 12, 1965 Frank Joseph MIS-
TRETTA (son of Salvatore Mistretta and
Angelina REGIRA) born December 6, 1935 in
Ascension Parish

100

a) Samuel Mistretta born August 3, 1967 in Donaldsonville, La.
b) Adrienne Mistretta born February 18, 1969, in Donaldsonville, La.

iii. Jennifer Hebert born October 6, 1946 in Pierre Part married May 30, 1970 Timothy Joseph GAUTREAUX (son of Desire Robert Gautreaux and Edna Bernadette FOUNERETTE) born April 24, 1943 in Pierre Part, La.

a) Bennett Paul Gautreaux born April 21, 1971 in Paincourtville, La.

iv. Abigail Hebert born April 28, 1949 in Pierre Part married September 10, 1967 Gerald John BRAUD (son of Desire Braud and Gersie RODRIGUE) born July 20, 1945 in Pierre Part, La.

a) Samantha Mary Braud born July 29, 1968 in Pierre Part
b) Gerald John Braud, Jr. born July 30, 1969 in Pierre Part

v. Ronnie Hebert born January 16, 1954; died in May, 1964 at age 4 months

b. Mercedes LeBlanc born September 26, 1926 in Pierre Part married Roland Alexander COMEAUX born August 16, 1926

i. Mervin Alex Comeaux born November 9, 1949 in Pierre Part
ii. Nelson Joseph Comeaux born December 28, 1953 in Pierre Part
iii. Eric George Comeaux born February 26, 1957 in Pierre Part
iv. Rhonda Mercedes Comeaux born July 13, 1961 in Pierre Part

c. Murphy Louis LeBlanc born March 11, 1928 in Pierre Part married September 22, 1951 in Morgan City Alberta VERRETT (daughter of Curtis Verrett and Althea DAIGLE) born July 18, 1933, Terrebonne Parish

i. Merenda Theresa LeBlanc born June 30, 1952 in New Orleans married October 10, 1970 Wayne PENNISON (son of Raymond Pennison and Melba ESTAVE)

a) Shawn Michael Pennison born June 23, 1971 in Morgan City

ii. Rodney Paul LeBlanc born February 20, 1954 in Morgan City
iii. Kimberly Marie LeBlanc born September 30, 1956 in Morgan City

d. Raymond LeBlanc born April 29, 1929 in Assumption Parish married February 16, 1955 to Hortense CROCHET (daughter of Armond Crochet and Mercedes MC CARTHY) born May 16, 1935 in Pierre Part, La.

    i. Kathleen LeBlanc born July 16, 1956 in Paincourtville
    ii. Vincent LeBlanc born December 30, 1957 in Pierre Part
    iii. Mark Everyest LeBlanc born May 30, 1959 in Pierre Part
    iv. Mathilda LeBlanc born April 5, 1961 in Morgan City

e. Agnes Elizabeth LeBlanc born October 4, 1930 in Pierre Part married Leo Paul RICHARD, Sr. (son of Albert Richard and Lellie HEBERT) born November 19, 1928 in Belle Rose

    i. Leo Paul Richard, Jr. born December 31, 1952
    ii. Margaret Ann Richard born March 30, 1954
    iii. Sandra Marie Richard born July 6, 1955
    iv. Jo Ann Richard born December 18, 1958
    v. Reggie Mark Richard born April 18, 1960
    vi. Rene Joseph Richard born May 14, 1961
    vii. Randel John Richard born July 31, 1962
    viii. Richard Joseph Richard born June 18, 1965

f. Eloise Marie LeBlanc born May 19, 1932 in Assumption Parish married Charles G. LANDRY (son of Collise Landry and Angelic Cecily CALLAHAN) born July 1, 1928

    i. Carolyn Marie Landry born October 25, 1950 in White Castle
    ii. Debra Ann Landry born May 16, 1952 in White Castle
    iii. Charles Gerard Landry born April 21, 1954 in White Castle
    iv. Angelic Cecile Landry born August 16, 1958 in Donaldsonville
    v. Lisa Ann Landry born April 20, 1960 in White Castle
    vi. Camille Joseph Landry born December 16, 1964 in White Castle
    vii. Antoine Joseph Landry born November 28, 1965 in White Castle

g. Gladys Marie LeBlanc born September 7, 1934 in Assumption Parish married August 30, 1952 Robert J. ALLEMAN, Sr. (son of David Alleman and Regina DUGAS) born May 20, 1929 in Assumption Parish

    i. Maria Lynne Alleman born November 23, 1954 in Paincourtville

    ii. Timothy Joseph Alleman born April 15, 1956 in Paincourtville

  iii. Robert Joseph Alleman, Jr. born May 31, 1958 in Paincourtville

   iv. Regina Mae Alleman born May 8, 1964 in Paincourtville

h. Mary Jane LeBlanc born March 27, 1936 in Assumption Parish married April 26, 1950 Edwin Joseph DUGAS (son of Philip Joseph Dugas and Marie MABILE) born April 3, 1932 in Assumption Parish

     i. Ramona Ann Dguas born February 21, 1954 in Belle Rose, La. married Whitney James SIMONEAUX

    ii. Melissa Ann Dugas born April 18, 1957 in Donaldsonville

  iii. Patricia Jane Dugas born December 16, 1959 in Donaldsonville

   iv. Julie Marie Dugas born February 23, 1964 in Belle Rose

i. Anna Rose LeBlanc born May 30, 1940 in Pierre Part married Leonard THERIOT (son of Rene Theriot and Estelle LANDRY) born September 13, 1939 in Pierre Part

     i. Rodrick Joseph Theriot born December 26, 1958 in Pierre Part

    ii. Carl Louis Theriot born December 22, 1960 in Pierre Part

  iii. Diana Marie Theriot born September 9, 1962 in Pierre Part

   iv. Rachel Ann Theriot born November 28, 1963 in Pierre Part

    v. Stacey Elizabeth Theriot born March 26, 1969 in Pierre Part

j. Dianne LeBlanc born in 1941 in Pierre Part, La.

FOUR GENERATION ANCESTOR CHART

8. Francois Dugas
b.   ca. 1753
p.b. St. Anne, Quebec
m. 28 June 1768
p.m. Ascension Parish
d.
p.d.

4. Miguel Noel Dugas
b. 25 December 1775
p.b. Ascension Parish
m. 12 February 1798
p.m. Ascension
d. 25 July 1807
p.d. Ascension Parish

9. Marguerite Babin
b.
p.b. Pisiquid, Acadia
d. 9 March 1807
p.d. Ascension Parish

2. Trasimond Dugas, Sr.
b.   ca. 1816
p.b. Ascension Parish
m. 26 March 1837
p.m. Ascension Parish
d.
p.d.

10. Amand Babin
b.   ca. 1742
p.b. Acadia
m.
p.m.
d. 11 March 1808
p.d. Ascension Parish

5. Magdelaine Babin
b. Bt. 1 January 1777
p.b. St. James Parish
d. 23 December 1810
p.d. Ascension Parish

11. Marie Anastasie Landry
b.   ca. 1743
p.b. Acadia
d. 18 August 1795
p.d. Ascension Parish

1.   Amanda Dugas
b. 1 March 1856
p.b. Ascension Parish
m. 19 January 1875
p.m. Ascension Parish
d. 27 January 1923
p.d.. Ascension Parish

12.
b.
p.b.
m.
p.m.
d.
p.d.

6. Pierre Deneau
b.
p.b.
m.
p.m.
d.
p.d.

13.
b.
p.b.
d.
p.d.

3. Melanie Deneau
b.   ca. 1822
p.b. Ascension Parish
d.
p.d.

14.
b.
p.b.
m.
p.m.
d.
p.d.

7. Marie Louise Lagrange
b.
p.b.
d.
p.d.

15.
b.
p.b.
d.
p.d.

Pierre Christophe LeBlanc
Spouse of #1

B. Pierre Christophe LeBlanc born April 29, 1852 in Ascension
    Parish married January 19, 1875 at the home of the bride's
    parents in Donaldsonville to Marie Amanda DUGAS (daughter
    of Trasimond Dugas and Melanie DENOUX) born March 1, 1856
    in Ascension Parish. Pierre Christophe died May 28, 1938
    and Marie Amanda died January 27, 1923. Both are buried
    in Ascension Cemetery, Donaldsonville.

CHRISTOPHE LE BLANC
(1852 - 1938)

AMANDA   DUGAS
(1856 - 1923)

1. Mary Leontine LeBlanc born December 29, 1875 in Ascen-
    sion Parish married April 27, 1893 in Ascension Church
    Nestor Louis LANDRY (son of Joseph Landry and Adrienne
    LE BLANC) born February 29, 1872 in Paincourtville.
    Nestor was a sugar boiler and blacksmith. He died
    February 12, 1940. Mary Leontine died September 16,
    1968. Both are buried in St. Mary's Cemetery, New
    Orleans

FOUR GENERATION ANCESTOR CHART

8.
b.
p.b.
m.
p.m.
d.
p.d.

9.
b.
p.b.
d.
p.d.

4. Cyril Landry
b.
p.b.
m. 11 January 1870
p.m. Assumption Parish
d.
p.d.

2. Joseph Telesphore Landry
b.
p.b. Assumption Parish
m. 7 February 1871
p.m. St. Elizabeth Church
d.
p.d.

10.
b.
p.b.
m.
p.m.
d.
p.d.

11.
b.
p.b.
d.
p.d.

5. Marcellite Gravois
b.
p.b.
d.
p.d.

1. Nestor Louis Landry
b. 29 February 1872
p.b. Paincourtville
m. 27 April 1893
p.m. Ascension Parish
d. 12 February 1940
p.d. New Orleans

12.
b.
p.b.
m.
p.m.
d.
p.d.

13.
b.
p.b.
d.
p.d.

6. Adrien LeBlanc
b.
p.b.
m.
p.m.
d.
p.d.

3. Adrienne LeBlanc
b.
p.b.
d.
p.d.

14.
b.
p.b.
m.
p.m.
d.
p.d.

15.
b.
p.b.
d.
p.d.

7. Eliza Landry
b.
p.b.
d.
p.d.

Leontine LeBlanc
Spouse of #1

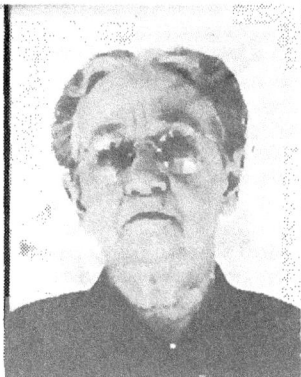

LEONTINE LE BLANC   NESTOR LOUIS LANDRY
(1875 - 1968)   (1871 - 1940)

a. O'Neil Joseph Landry born February 1, 1894 in As-
cension Parish and married August 24, 1916 in
St. Joseph Church, Grosse Tete, to Felicitee
SCHUBERT (daughter of Bartholemy Schubert and
Marie OURSO) born December 19, 1895. O'Neil died
December 25, 1951 and is buried in Greenlawn Ceme-
tery, New Orleans.

    i. O'Neil Raymond Landry born June 21, 1923 in
New Orleans married August 31, 1961 in New
Orleans to Myrle Cecilia HOTARD (daughter of
Al J. Hotard and Willemina FISCHER) born
September 8, 1931. O'Neil was inducted into
the United States Army in Orleans Parish in
1943 and served until 1946. He saw duty in
Italy.

b. Edward Joseph (Eddie) Landry born December 3, 1897
in Donaldsonville married June 8, 1921 in New
Orleans to Theresa Gladys FORURIA (daugher of
Frank Foruria, Sr. and Freda SCHREINER) born
June 11, 1902. Eddie was inducted into the United
States Navy in Detroit, Michigan in April 31, 1917
and was discharged in New Orleans on September, 1919.
He was an Electrician 2nd class and served in France,
England and Ireland in WWI.

105

i.   Edward Joseph Landry, Jr. born February 16, 1922
       in New Orleans (Jefferson Parish). Edward died
       the same day having lived only two hours.

c.   Helen Marie Landry born January 6, 1896 in Donald-
      sonville married January 8, 1917 to James (Jim)
      GRAY (son of James Gray of Dublin, Ireland and
      Kathryn REYNOLDS of Steven's Point, Wisconsin)
      born June 22, 1881. Jim was a high school teacher
      and owned and operated Gray Lumber Company in New
      Orleans until his death on June 3, 1955.

      i.   John James (Jimmy) Gray born October 29, 1917
             in Tallahassee, Florida married August 3, 1946
             in New Orleans to Beryl May MAYER (daughter of
             Lester Emanuel Mayer and Ilma Marie MAHE) born
             March 7, 1916. Jimmy was an insurance agent
             and a graduate of Auburn University in Alabama.

             a)   Nancy Marie Gray born July 13, 1947 in New
                   Orleans married May 8, 1970 to Michael
                   McGrath DURAN (son of Richard G. Duran, Sr.
                   and Grace A. Werling) born November 25,
                   1949 in New Orleans. Michael attended the
                   United States Naval Academy in the summer
                   of 1967. He obtained his B.A. degree in
                   English from Louisiana State University at
                   New Orleans (1967-1971); his M.A. degree
                   in Comparative Literature from the Univer-
                   sity of Maine(1971-1973). He is currently
                   teaching assistant in the English Depart-
                   ment at the University of Maine
                   Nancy obtained her B.A. degree in French
                   from Louisiana State University at New
                   Orleans (1966-1970); studied at the Uni-
                   versite de Nice in France in the summer
                   of 1968; obtained her M.A. degree in
                   French from the University of Maine (1971-
                   1973). She is currently teaching assistant
                   in the Department of Foreign Languages and
                   Classics.

             b)   Beryl Ann Gray born December 8, 1948 in
                   New Orleans married October 31, 1964 to
                   Thomas Davenport (Tommy) KERR (son of Roy
                   Darnell Kerr and Dolores LABRANO) born
                   September 23, 1945 in Mexico City, Mexico.

                   i)   Debra Ann Kerr born August 2, 1965
                  ii)   Roy Darnell Kerr born October 19, 1966

             c)   John James (J. J.) Gray, Jr. born August 25,
                   1951 in New Orleans married September 22,
                   1972 to Valerie Ann BOUDREAUX (daughter of

Francis Gibbons Boudreaux and Mary KOCH)
born October 27, 1953 in New Orleans. J.J.
is presently a student at Louisiana State
University at New Orleans.

ii. Helen Marie Gray born July 18, 1919 (known as
"Little Nell") married October 29, 1942 in
Tuskegee, Alabama to Thomas Calvin FENN, Sr.
(son of Edgar James Fenn and Sarah MORTON)
born November 25, 1914 in Union Springs, Alabama. Little Nell is a graduate of the University of Alabama.

a) Mary Helen Fenn born December 26, 1944 in
Montgomery, Alabama
b) Thomas Calvin Fenn, Jr. born December 28,
1945 married August 18, 1966 to Eugenie
Norton SMITH-T (daughter of F. B. Smith-T, Jr.
and Susan Jane NORTON)

i) Eugenia Smith-T Fenn born August 6,
1968
ii) Helen Marie Fenn born December 31,
1970

c) Edgar James Fenn born March 19, 1950

d. Sidney Joseph Landry, Sr. born August 8, 1900 in
Donaldsonville married October 24, 1925 in Grosse
Tete to Orilia Marie AMEDEE (daughter of Fabien
Amedee and Honorine GRANIER) born January 25, 1905
in Vacherie, St. James Parish. Sidney was a gal-
vanizer. He died March 26, 1966 and is buried
in Garden of Memories Cemetery in Jefferson Parish.

i. Sidney Joseph Landry, Jr. born June 25, 1927
in Rosedale, Iberville Parish, married January 15, 1949 in New Orleans to Shirley Mae
BERNOS (daughter of Louis Bernos and Josephine
LA SALLE) born June 11, 1928. S. J. is shop
supervisor for Parish Lumber Company, Baton
Rouge.

a) David Joseph Landry born November 19, 1949
b) Dennis Raymond Landry born February 12, 1951
c) Melanie Anne Landry born August 7, 1955

e. Lillian Landry born August 3, 1902 in Donaldsonville married

(1) February 12, 1927 in Ascension
Parish to John LE BLANC (son
of Joseph LeBlanc and Laurie
LANDRY); died March, 1944.

i. Ellis Nestor LeBlanc born May 31, 1928 in New
Orleans married January 31, 1953 to Shirley

Ann BENOIT (daughter of Hector Allen Benoit
and Maritte Marie GAUBERT) born January 6,
1930 in Gretna, Jefferson Parish. Ellis is a
rate clerk for a freight line. He was inducted
into the United States Coast Guard in Orleans
Parish on November 1, 1948 and discharged on
April 30, 1952.

    a) Pamela Rose LeBlanc born November 3, 1955
in Jefferson Parish
    b) Ellis Nestor LeBlanc, Jr. born June 10,
1959
    c) Darren James LeBlanc born June 22, 1960

        (2) December 24, 1952, St. Bernard
Parish, Lloyd Gerard GUERIN
(son of Frank Gerard Guerin
and Mary Agnes BERGERON) born
April 10, 1919 in Pointe
Coupee Parish

f. Joseph Nestor Landry born October 19, 1909 in
Ascension Parish married January 14, 1931 in New
Orleans Anna Rita LEAHY (daughter of Thomas Leahy
and Mary DONLON) born November 17, 1908 in New
Orleans

    i. Nestor Joseph Landry born February 21, 1932 in
New Orleans married November 5, 1949 Elise
Peggy HEFFLER (daughter of Casper Heffler, a
native of Germany, and Beatrice Elenore PEAR-
SON of Bloomington, Illinois) born March 25,
1932. Nestor is employed at Avondale Shipyard

        a) Susan Clare Landry born August 26, 1957
in New Orleans
        b) Shelley Clare Landry born April 29, 1960
in New Orleans

    ii. Joanne Marie Landry born October 28, 1934 in
New Orleans married November 15, 1952 in New
Orleans Max Clifford CANNON, Jr. (son of Max
Clifford Cannon, Sr. and Kate Lee SIMS) born
February 1, 1932 in Charlotte, North Carolina.
Max is an architect.

        a) Max Clifford Cannon, III born August 15,
1954 in Lake Charles and presently a student at Tulane University, New Orleans
        b) Rhonda Jean Cannon born June 1, 1958 in
New Orleans

    iii. Gail Lillian Landry born Augsut 3, 1936 in
New Orleans married

        (1) August 26, 1954 in New Orleans

Wayne Ernest STOLTZ (son of
Edward William Stoltz and Olga
Albertine SCHWALL) born Decem-
ber 26, 1933 in New Orleans

a) Wayne Ernest Stoltz, Jr. born October 20,
1955 in New Orleans
b) Christopher Stephen Stoltz born May 21,
1957 in New Orleans
c) Martin Edward Stoltz born May 13, 1960 in
New Orleans

(2) July 16, 1965 Walter John
BARTHE, Jr. (son of Walter J.
Barthe, Sr. and   )

iv. Kathleen Margaret Landry born April 30, 1946
in New Orleans married July 20, 1968 in New
Orleans Robert Hass MOSELEY (son of Robert
Lester Moseley, native of Cuba, and Dorothy
Elizabeth YAUN, of Atlanta, Georgia) born
November 26, 1946 in New Orleans.

v. Debra Maria Landry born August 15, 1953 in
New Orleans married December 28, 1971 in New
Orleans Don Joseph DAVEZAC (son of Ramon Arvin
Davezac and Dorothy Mary HOCK) born August 13,
1951 in New Orleans

2. Joseph Constance LeBlanc born August 7, 1877 in Ascension Parish; died August 16, 1877 and buried in Ascension Cemetery in Donaldsonville

FOUR GENERATION ANCESTOR CHART

```
                                               8.
                                               b.
                                               p.b.
                                               m.
                    4.                          p.m.
                    b.                          d.
                    p.b.                        p.d.
                    m.
                    p.m.                        9.
                    d.                          b.
                    p.d.                        p.b.
      2. John (Joseph) Barrient                 d.
      b.                                         p.d.
      p.b.
      m.
      p.m.                                       10.
      d.                                         b.
      p.d. Bur. Ascension                        p.b.
                                                 m.
                    5.                           p.m.
                    b.                           d.
                    p.b.                         p.d.
                    d.
                    p.d.                         11.
                                                 b.
                                                 p.b.
                                                 d.
  1. Francois (Frank) Barrient                   p.d.
  b. 16 April 1871
  p.b. Ascension Parish
  m. 19 April 1899                               12.
  p.m. Ascension Parish                          b.
  d. 22 February 1936                            p.b.
  p.d. Ascension Parish                          m.
                    6.                           p.m.
                    b.                           d.
                    p.b.                         p.d.
                    m.
                    p.m.                         13.
                    d.                           b.
                    p.d.                         p.b.
      3. Carmelite Albares                        d.
      b.                                         p.d.
      p.b.
      d.
      p.d. Bur. Ascension                        14.
                                                 b.
                                                 p.b.
                                                 m.
                    7.                           p.m.
                    b.                           d.
                    p.b.                         p.d.
                    d.
                    p.d.                         15.
                                                 b.
                                                 p.b.
  Leonie LeBlanc                                 d.
  Spouse of #1                                   p.d.
```

3. Leonie LeBlanc born February 8, 1880 in Ascension
    Parish married April 19, 1899 in Ascension Parish to
    Frank Joseph BARRIENT (son of Joseph Barrient and
    Carmelite ALBAREZ) born October 16, 1871. Frank died
    February 22, 1936 and is buried in Ascension Cemetery.

LEONIE LE BLANC   FRANK J. BARRIENT
(1880 -   )   (1871 - 1936)

a. Edith Marie Barrient born July 2, 1902 in Ascen-
    sion Parish married

                    (1) January 31, 1924 in Ascension
                         Church Earl Joseph DOMINIQUE
                         (son of Lawrence Dominique and
                         Mamie LE BLANC) born May 15,
                         1901 in Belle Rose, La. Earl
                         died December 15, 1941 in New
                         Orleans

            i. Edith Marie Dominique born February 15, 1925
                in Assumption Parish married February 4, 1945
                Philip Joseph LE BLANC, Jr. (son of Philip J.
                LeBlanc, Sr. and Noemie GARCIA) born August 5,

110

1925 in St. James Parish

    a) Ronald Philip LeBlanc born July 30, 1946 married Dorothy Jane HOOD born January 18, 1945.

        i) Carey Eugene LeBlanc born May 11, 1965 in Napoleonville
      ii) Keith Michael LeBlanc born July 28, 1967 in Biloxi, Mississippi

    b) Daniel Felix LeBlanc born October 14, 1952 married February 5, 1972 in Ascension Parish to Dianne Elizabeth COLLIER (daughter of Frederick Collier and Maxine POIRIE)
    c) Alisia Ann LeBlanc born August 20, 1957

  ii. Elizabeth Marie Dominique born February 7, 1927 in New Orleans, La.
  iii. Earl Joseph Dominique, Jr. born February 15, 1932 in New Orleans married July 27, 1951 in Texarkana, Arkansas to Annie Jane ALLUMS (daughter of James Theodore Allums, Sr. and Connie Bee FITE) born November 7, 1931 in Carthage, Texas

    a) Earl Joseph Dominique, III born July 27, 1953 in Shreveport
    b) Bruce Anthony Dominique born January 11, 1955 in Shreveport, La.
    c) Penny Marie Dominique born June 16, 1956
    d) Pamela Ann Dominique born October 2, 1957
    e) Jason Paul Dominique born September 10, 1969

  iv. Daniel Felix Dominique born November 29, 1935 in New Orleans; died August 12, 1952 in New Orleans
        (2) August 3, 1944 in Ascension Church, Donaldsonville to Rene GRAVOIS.

No children were born of Edith's second marriage

b. Laura Marie Barrient born May 30, 1904 in Ascension Parish married May 30, 1933 to Walter Allou d'HEMECOURT (son of Jules Allou d'Hemecourt and Marie del NODAL) born December 19, 1900. Walter died September 27, 1943 in New Orleans.

c. Orelia Marie Barrient born February 23, 1906 in Ascension Parish married

        (1) July 23, 1924 in New Orleans to Achille LANDRY (son of LaCroix Landry and Clemence LE BLANC)

    i. Frank J. Landry born January 24, 1926 in New
        Orleans, La. married September 17, 1949 Grace
        WEBSTER. Frank died October 9, 1968
   ii. Lee J. Landry born September 24, 1927 in New
        Orleans; died June 7, 1929 in New Orleans

            (2) Paul HOLGATE of Scranton,
                 Pennsylvania; died May 1, 1941
                 in New Orleans

d. Leo Joseph Barrient, Sr. born July 22, 1907 in
    Ascension Parish married in 1936 in Gonzales
    Melva HARVEY. Leo died in 1944

    i. Leo Joseph Barrient, Jr. born 1937 in New
        Orleans

e. Generes J. Barrient born April 6, 1909 in Ascen-
    sion Parish married June 29, 1932 in Smoke Bend
    Melba Philomine VERON (daughter of O'Neil F. Veron
    and Stella Marie BRASSET) born September 18, 1910.
    Generes died April 11, 1955 and is buried in As-
    cension Cemetery, Donaldsonville

    i. Stella Marie Barrient born November 28, 1933
        in Ascension Parish married

            (1) April 14, 1953 Douglas Spor
                 HAYWARD, Sr. (son of William C.
                 Hayward and Helene REUSS) born
                 January 18, 1927 in New Orleans

        a) Douglas Spor Hayward, Jr. born February 4,
           1955 in Donaldsonville

            (2) Lawrence Joseph ANDERMAN (son
                 of Emile Anderman and Celine
                 THERIOT) born November 25, 1925
                 in Convent, La.

        b) Lawrence Joseph Anderman, Jr. born Novem-
           ber 24, 1964 in White Castle, La.

   ii. Aldridge Paul Barrient born March 15, 1935 in
        Ascension Parish married September 14, 1956
        in Smoke Bend Derlie FALCON (daughter of
        Leonard Falcon and Nelia OUFNAC) born June 15,
        1936 in White Castle, La.

        a) Dirk Paul Barrient born August 14, 1959
           in White Castle
        b) Keely Francis Barrient born March 29, 1961
        c) Deidre Marie Barrient born March 22, 1964

  iii. Frankie Ann Barrient born September 14, 1938 in
        Ascension married Leonard THERIOT (son of
        Frank J. Theriot and Ada ALLEMAN) born May 5,
        1936 in Paincourtville. Leonard died Septem-
        ber 24, 1960 in Smoke Bend

iv. Percy Joseph Barrient born June 15, 1940 in
Ascension married August 8, 1958 in Mississippi
to Margie Ann MURPHY (daughter of Jack Murphy
and Christine STEER) born July 18, 1938 in
Brookhaven, Mississippi

   a) Debra Barrient born January 15, 1960 in
   Donaldsonville, La.
   b) Steve Jasper Barrient born October 17, 1961
   in Baton Rouge, La.
   c) Christopher J. Barrient born July 23, 1971
   in Baton Rouge, La.

v. Lee Jude Barrient born December 24, 1941 in
Ascension married June 8, 1960 Shirley BURGESS
(daughter of Samuel Franklin Burgess and
Gladys DETILLIER) born October 5, 1939 in New
Orleans. Lee Jude was a State Highway Patrol-
man for Ascension Parish. He was killed in an
automobile accident while on duty in Port
Allen, La. (West Baton Rouge Parish) on August 29, 1969 and is buried in the Barrient
Family tomb, Ascension Cemetery, Donaldsonville, La.

   a) Mary Lee Barrient born September 25, 1961
   in New Orleans
   b) Lee Jude Barrient born March 31, 1967 in
   Lutcher, La.

vi. Leonie Ann Barrient born March 18, 1947 in
Ascension married October 15, 1966 Robert
John HIDALGO, Jr. (son of Robert John Hidalgo
and Lillian RODRIGUE) born July 10, 1941 in
Ascension

   a) Robert John Hidalgo, III born May 28,
   1968 in Donaldsonville

vii. Frank Joseph Barrient born September 21, 1950
in Ascension married July 3, 1971 in Smoke
Bend Margaret Ann FALCON (daughter of Lee
Adam Falcon and Mercedes Theresa LANOIX) born
September 29, 1951 in Donaldsonville, La.

f. Ernest Joseph Barrient born October 24, 1911 in
Ascension; died December 19, 1911 and buried in
Ascension Cemetery, Donaldsonville
g. Lawless Joseph Barrient born January 22, 1912 in
Ascension married January 7, 1938 in Smoke Bend
Florence Mae SCARABIN (daughter of John Frank
Scarabin and Mary Magdeline REESE) born June 30,

1916 in Apalachicola, Florida. Lawless died
October 25, 1948 and is buried in Ascension Cemetery. Florence married again to Al SWINDALL

i. Carolyn Fay Barrientos (Barrient) born November 4, 1938 in Apalachicola, Florida married
June 3, 1958 in Tallahassee, Florida Edwin
LeGrand WILLIAMS, Jr. (son of Edwin L. Williams
and Doris Louella CASON)born June 1, 1937.

a) Edwin LeGrand Williams, III born February 16, 1960 in Tallahassee, Florida
b) Joseph Cason Williams born September 19,
1962 in Rome, Georgia
c) Virginia Grace Williams born February 25,
1972 in Valdosta, Georgia

ii. Mary Ann Barrientos (Barrient) born November 14,
1940 in Apalachicola, Florida married February 27, 1959 in Tallahassee, Florida Robert
Madison MOYE, Jr. (Son of Robert M. Moye, Sr.
and Mary Lillian SMITH) born October 1, 1939.

a) Robert Michael Moye born September 6, 1960
in Gainesville, Florida
b) William Bruce Moye born March 28, 1962 in
Gainesville, Florida
c) Richmond Maurice Moye born February 22,
1963 in Live Oak, Florida
d) Thomas Madison Moye born January 10, 1966
in Panama City, Florida
e) David Alan Moye born January 25, 1967 in
Valdosta, Georgia

iii. Lawless Joseph Barrientos (Barrient) born
February 21, 1947 in Port St. Joe, Florida
married October 3, 1968 in Hawaii Alice Marie
SMITH (daughter of Isaac Earl Smith and
Dorotha Mae HAWKINS) born December 26, 1949.
Lawless served as a Second Lieutenant in the
United States Army from 1966 to 1967 and as
a Captain in the Reserves from 1967 to 1969.
He received his B.S. degree from Florida
State University

a) Shelly Lynn Barrientos born November 24,
1971 in Tallahassee, Florida

h. Edna Marie Barrient born March 8, 1914 in Ascen-
sion married November 16, 1935 to Earl Joseph
TERRIO (son of Ernest Terrio and Anna Elizabeth
ZIMMER) born November 3, 1910 in Ascension

i. Barbara Ann Terrio born November 13, 1936 married January 18, 1959 to Helmuth J. MONTZ, Jr.

114

(son of Helmuth J. Montz, Sr. and Mable
LASSEIGNE) born July 18, 1935.

    a)   Lisa Ann Montz born September 23, 1960
    b)   Robin Ann Montz born August 20, 1962
    c)   Khristine Ann Montz born December 3; 1966
    d)   Scott Joseph Montz born December 21, 1968

ii.   Margaret Ann Terrio born December 18, 1938
married January 17, 1960 to Robert J. POCHE
(son of Leonard Poche and Helene ARCENEAUX)
born February 12, 1939

    a)   Michael Shane Poche born May 5, 1962
    b)   David Paul Poche born November 27, 1965

iii.   Beryl Terrio born July 31, 1944 married
April 27, 1968 to Richard Anthony ROME (son
of Frozine Rome and Noemie BECNEL) born
April 15, 1943.

    a)   Monique Ann Rome born June 7, 1971

iv.   Anna Elizabeth Terrio born June 8, 1946 married September 2, 1972 to Gerald M. BERTHELOT
(son of Moise Berthelot and Marie LOBELL) born
October 4, 1949.

i.   Alice Marie Barrient born February 14, 1916 in
Ascension married October 20, 1935 to Elmore
Joseph BRIGNAC (son of Washington Brignac and
Odell HYMEL) born September 6, 1913 in Lutcher.
Elmore Brignac died March 4, 1969 at age 56.

i.   Ronald James Brignac born June 16, 1937 married February 8, 1961 to Edith TABOR. Ronald
died June 2, 1963 at age 26.

    a)   Ronald James Brignac, II born September 12,
        1961 in New Orleans
    b)   Arlene Evelyn Brignac born November 22,
        1962 in New Orleans

Ronald served in the United States Navy. He
was inducted in New Orleans in June, 1955 and
was discharged in New Orleans in June, 1959.
He served in Newfoundland and the Aleutian
Islands.

ii.   Ruth Marie Brignac born October 22, 1939 married June 18, 1960 to John Elvin MUNSTER (son
of Ernest Munster and Christine van RANKIN)
born September 30, 1941.

    a)   John Elvin Munster, II born March 15, 1961
    b)   Donna Marie Munster born February 6, 1964

iii. Alice Mae Brignac born September 25, 1942 married Wyle HEATH

j. Olive Ann Barrient born November 3, 1918 married December 12, 1937 in New Orleans Ernest S. BESNARD (son of Ernest Oscar Besnard and America SIRES) born August 8, 1913 in New Orleans, La.

   i. Olive Glynn Besnard born April 3, 1940 in New Orleans married

      (1) August 29, 1959 in New Orleans Edward GRYGO (son of John Grygo, native of Poland, and Anne GORSKI of Cleveland, Ohio) born May 17, 1927 in Erie, Pennsylvania. Edward served in the United States Marines from March, 1945 to Novmeber 30, 1965. He was discharged in New Orleans with the rank of Master Sergeant. He fought in major battles in WWII

    a) Olive Glynn Anne Grygo born October 8, 1960 in New Orleans

    b) Michael Edward Grygo born August 17, 1963 in New Orleans

      (2) April 19, 1969 in New Orleans Raymon H. ÇAPRIOTTI (son of Enrico Capriotti and Mary Marie ANSCANI) Parents: natives of Italy

    c) Tanya Marie Capriotti born February 1, 1970 in New Orleans, La.

   ii. Sharon Yvette Besnard born December 28, 1944 married January 27, 1963 Craig J. LILES (son of Roy Liles of Kentwood and Marie CLEMENT of Destrahan) born October 25, 1942

   iii. Malcum Ernest Besnard born January 9, 1947 in New Orleans married October 30, 1965 Dianne CARTULLO (daughter of Joseph Cartullo of Boston, Massachusetts and Edella HOFFA of Humble, Texas) born May 9, 1946

    a) Tracey Dianne Besnard born August 18, 1967

    b) Malcom Todd Besnard born June 30, 1970

k. Hubert Joseph (Bosco) Barrient born February 29, 1920 in Ascension Parish married October 12, 1946 in New Orleans Lea Mary LAVIGNE (daughter of Robert Lavigne of Ponchatoula and Lea POCHE of St. James) born March 13, 1918 in Ponchatoula, La.

Hubert served in the United States Army from 1941 until 1945. He served in Italy, France, Africa and Germany.

    i.   Linda Marie Barrient born July 15, 1947 in New Orleans

   ii.   Vera Francis Barrient born July 2, 1949 in New Orleans married Lonnie SEAGER (son of A. J. Seager and   ) from Utah

        a) Tiffany Angle Seager born June 6, 1970 in New Orleans

1. Dorothea Carmel Barrient born July 5, 1921 in Assumption Parish married June 13, 1943 in New Orleans Albert Alfred MOSKAU, Sr. (son of August E. Moskau and Sadie Jane O'BRIEN) born March 23, 1923 in New Orleans. Albert was inducted into the service in Orleans Parish on June 27, 1943 and was discharged November 28, 1945. He served in the Philippines, Guadecanal and the South Pacific

    i.   Albert Alfred Moskau, Jr. born February 28, 1944 in New Orleans married June 3, 1967 in St. Matthew Church, Metairie, La. Georgia Ann FRENTZ (daughter of George Frentz and Velma Louise EMBOULAS) born April 2, 1949 in New Orleans. Albert attended Southeastern Louisiana University in Hammond for 3 years; Louisiana State University at New Orleans for 1 year; is a student at Tulane University and will graduate in 1973 in Advertising. He was inducted into the United States Air Force (specia forces) in New Orleans on October 28, 1965 and was discharged at Travis Air Force Base, California on October 20, 1969. He served in the Canal Zone, Taiwan, Vietnam, Okinawi, the Philippines, Thailand, Japan, Peru and Bolivia.

        a) Albert August Moskau, III born September 7, 1968 in New Orleans

   ii.   Larry James Moskau born May 28, 1948 in New Orleans married June 26, 1971 in Hammond, La. Roberta Lea EAKER (daughter of Robert Lee Eaker and Helen Agusta SCOTT) born May 15, 1950 in Vicksburg, Mississippi. Larry graduated from Southeastern Louisiana University on May 27, 1972

        a) Larry James Moskau, II born January 13, 1972 in Hammond

  iii.   Chris David Moskau born October 18, 1954 in New Orleans. Presently attending Southeastern Louisiana University in Hammond

   iv.   Timothy Carl Moskau born May 6, 1960

FOUR GENERATION ANCESTOR CHART

<pre>
                                                8.
                                                b.
                                                p.b.
                        4. Firmin Aucoin   m.
                        b.   p.m.
                        p.b.   d.
                        m.   ca. 1850   p.d.
                        p.m.
                        d.   9.
                        p.d.   b.
                                                 p.b.
        2. Camille Aucoin   d.
        b.   p.d.
        p.b.
        m. 20 April 1871
        p.m. Ascension Parish   10.
        d.   b.
        p.d. Assumption Parish   p.b.
                                                  m.
                        5. Irma Hebert   p.m.
                        b.   d.
                        p.b.   p.d.
                        d.
                        p.d.   11.
                                                  b.
                                                  p.b.
                                                  d.
1. Alcide Firmin Aucoin   p.d.
b. 18 September 1873
p.b.Plattenville
m. 27 January 1902   12. Augustin Aucoin
p.m. Ascension   b.
d.   p.b.
p.d..   m.
                6. Joseph Augustin Aucoin p.m.
                b.   d.
                p.b.   p.d.
                m. 19 February 1849
                p.m. Assumption Parish   13. Henrietta Gautreaux
                d.   b.
                p.d.   p.b.
                                           d.
        3.Ptolemie Aucoin   p.d.
        b.
        p.b.
        d.   14. Laurent Giroir
        p.d.   b.
                                         p.b.
                                         m.
                        7. Pamela Giroir p.m.
                        b.   d.
                        p.b.   p.d.
                        d.
                        p.d.   15. Anne Hebert
                                         b.
                                         p.b.
Alice LeBlanc   d.
Spouse of #1   p.d.
</pre>

4. Alice LeBlanc born December 6, 1882 in Ascension Parish married January 27, 1902 in Donaldsonville Alcide AUCOIN (son of Camille Aucoin and Ptolemie AUCOIN) born September 18, 1873 in Plattenville, La. Alice died November 22, 1920 and is buried in Donaldsonville Alcide was an automobile mechanic.

ALICE LE BLANC
(1882 - 1920)

There were no children born of Alice's marriage with Alcide Aucoin.

FOUR GENERATION ANCESTOR CHART

```
                                            8.
                                            b.
                                            p.b.
            4. Joseph Hebert                m.
            b.                              p.m.
            p.b.                            d.
            m.                              p.d.
            p.m.
            d.                              9.
            p.d.                            b.
    2. Mesmin Hebert                        p.b.
    b. 15 December 1860                     d.
    p.b. Pierre Part                        p.d.
    m. 5 February 1881
    p.m. Pierre Part, La.
    d. 5 May 1929                           10.
    p.d.Bur. Maringouin                     b.
                                            p.b.
                                            m.
            5. Marie Hebert                 p.m.
            b.                              d.
            p.b.                            p.d.
            d.
            p.d.                            11.
                                            b.
                                            p.b.
                                            d.
1. Marie Lucille Hebert                     p.d.
b. 9 November 1889
p.b. Napoleonville
m. 25 January 1909                          12. Gaudefroy Breaud
p.m. White Castle                           b.
d. 11 November 1971                         p.b.
p.d. Bur. Maringouin                        m.
            6. Gerville Breaux              p.m.
            b.                              d.
            p.b.                            p.d.
            m. 8 February 1846
            p.m. Paincourtville, La.        13. Rosalie Coupel
            d.                              b.
            p.d.                            p.b.
                                            d.
    3. Adeline Breaux                       p.d.
    b. 15 August 1861
    p.b. Pierre Part
    d. 14 January 1925                      14. Polumire Landry
    p.d. Bur. Maringouin                    b.
                                            p.b.
                                            m.
            7. Elina Landry                 p.m.
            b.                              d.
            p.b. Pierre Part, La.           p.d.
            d.
            p.d. Pierre Part, La.           15. Elisa Landry
                                            b.
                                            p.b.
Lessin LeBlanc                              d.
Spouse of #1                                p.d.
```

5. Joseph Lessin LeBlanc born February 13, 1885 in Ascension Parish married January 25, 1909 in White Castle Marie Lucille HEBERT (daughter of Mesmin Hebert and Adeline BREAUX) born November 9, 1889 in Napoleonville. Lessie died May 1, 1933 in Maringouin; Lucille died November 11, 1971 in Baton Rouge. Both are buried in Immaculate Heart of Mary Cemetery in Maringouin

LESSIN LE BLANC
(1885 - 1933)

LUCILLE HEBERT
(1889 - 1971)

a. Nolan Julien LeBlanc born January 9, 1910 in Ascension Parish married

 (1) November 11, 1932 in Livonia Nelma Rita GUIDROZ (daughter of Elie Guidroz and Mary Etna DE BELEVUE of Marksville) born August 16, 1914 in Livonia, La.

 i. Barbara Jean LeBlanc born December 11, 1933 in Livonia married December 22, 1955 in Livonia John BRODNAX born February 4, 1922 in Alexandria La. John died March 5, 1971 in Alexandria and is buried in Boyce Louisiana. Johnny served

119

in the United States Navy in WWII. He was
inducted from Alexandria and served in the
South Pacific. Barbara graduated in 1971
from Louisiana State University with a Mas-
ters Degree in Education. She is teaching
at Livonia High School, Livonia, La.

a) Roan Marie Brodnax born October 1, 1956
    in Baton Rouge
b) David Lynn Brodnax born June 22, 1958 in
    Baton Rouge
c) Von Allen Brodnax born July 14, 1961 in
    Baton Rouge
d) Paul Wayne Brodnax born April 28, 1964 in
    New Iberia, La.

ii. Betty Joyce LeBlanc born November 5, 1935 in
Baton Rouge married

(1) February 11, 1956 in Baton
     Rouge Steve Otis RICHARDSON,
     Jr. (son of Steve Otis Richard-
     son, Sr. and Leona COATES) born
     January 7, 1935 in Raleigh,
     North Carolina

a) Steven Otis Richardson born December 14,
    1956 in Baton Rouge
b) Joie DeEtte Richardson born April 30,
    1959 in Baton Rouge

(2) December 25, 1971 in Las Vegas,
     Nevada William Daniel WATTS

iii. Hubert O'Neil LeBlanc born September 18, 1937
in Lake Providence married November 17, 1961
in Indianapolis, Indiana Mary Francis PAGE
(daughter of Ben Clyde Page, a native of Bar-
ren County, Kentucky, and Amy PEDIGO, of Met-
calfe, Kentucky) born June 4, 1943 in Indianapolis, Indiana. Hubert served in the United
States Army having been inducted on January 31,
1955 and separated January 31, 1958. He is
presently employed at Dow Chemical Corporation
and served 17 months in Korea.

a) Jeffery Allen LeBlanc born November 19,
    1969 in Baton Rouge
b) Paige Michelle LeBlanc born March 24, 1971
    in Baton Rouge

iv. Celeste Marie LeBlanc born August 31, 1945 in
Lake Providence married

(1) February 12, 1966 in St.
     Agnes Church, Baton Rouge, La.

William Woodrow SHARKEY, Jr.
(son of William W. Sharkey
and Addie HERTZLER) of Slaugh-
ter, La.

(2) February 19, 1972 in Hammond
James Edward LAYRISSON (son of
Louis Edward Layrisson and Inez
PARKER) born January 2, 1942 in
New Orleans. James is Principal
of Springfield High School,
Springfield, Louisiana

Celeste graduated from the University of
Southwestern Louisiana with a degree in education

a) Jean Paul Layrisson born September 3, 1965
(child of James E. Layrisson's first marriage)

Second marriage of   (2) Mary DE ARMOND
Nolan LeBlanc

b. Norman Joseph LeBlanc born November 5, 1911 in
Bayou Goula married November 5, 1933 in Livonia
Mary Ellen GRIMMER (daughter of John Oscar Grimmer and Ellen Julia KEATY) born October 7, 1913
on Grimmer Plantation, Livonia, La. Norman is a
retired jockey and horse trainer and Mary Ellen
is organist at St. Francis Xavier Cabrini Church
in Livonia

i. Carolyn Rodney LeBlanc born November 24, 1934
in Maringouin, La. married October 6, 1956 in
Livonia Lyle Sanderson RINKER (son of Lyle E.
Rinker and Lida Jane SANDERSON) born January 31, 1931 in Tulsa, Oklahoma. Lyle is a
graduate of Tulane University in Industrial
Engineering

a) Joanne Rinker born May 5, 1958 in New
Orleans
b) John Sanderson Rinker born January 29,
1961 in Tulsa, Oklahoma
c) James Robert Rinker born April 6, 1964
in Tulsa
d) Jerri Ann Rinker born March 13, 1968 in
Kansas City, Missouri

ii. Norma Dell LeBlanc born December 9, 1935 in
Maringouin married August 17, 1957 in Livonia
Wallace Joseph OLINDE (son of Roger Blaise
Olinde and Laure DUREL of New Roads, La.) born
July 23, 1932. Wallace is a druggist in Mon-
roe; Norma Dell is a graduate of the Hotel Dieu

121

School of Nursing and is presently attending
Northeastern Louisiana University in Monroe.

   a) Wallace Joseph Olinde, Jr. born May 15,
       1958 in New Iberia
   b) Mary Ellen Olinde born October 4, 1959 in
       Monroe
   c) Larry Thomas Olinde born November 23, 1960
   d) Roger Blaise Olinde born January 14, 1962
   e) Kurt David Olinde born August 14, 1963
   f) Dianne Carol Olinde born November 2, 1964

iii. Dinah Lee LeBlanc born April 23, 1937 in
     Maringouin, Louisiana married February 24,
     1973 at St. Francis Xavier Cabrini Catholic
     Church, Livonia, Louisiana Henry Reuben
     WALLACE, native of Sullivan, Wisconsin. He
     is a honeybee farmer

iv. Charles Michael LeBlanc born May 6, 1939 at
     the Grimmer Plantation at Livonia, Louisiana,
     Pointe Coupee Parish, married September 27,
     1967 in St. Ann Catholic Church, Morganza,
     Louisiana Jacqueline Mary TUMINELLO (daughter
     of James Robert Tuminello and Rosa PURPERA)
     born December 8, 1939 in Morganza, Louisiana

   a) Charles Michael LeBlanc, Jr. born June 5,
       1968 in Baton Rouge, La.
   b) Janet Lynn LeBlanc born May 16, 1969 in
       Baton Rouge, La.
   c) Lori Suzanne LeBlanc born August 25,
       1970 in Baton Rouge, La.
   d) Ron Vincent LeBlanc born June 29, 1972
       in Baton Rouge, La.

c. Clifton Pierre LeBlanc born January 24, 1915 in
   Maringouin, Louisiana. He died February 12,
   1952 in New Orleans and is buried in Immaculate
   Heart of Mary Cemetery, Maringouin, Louisiana,
   Iberville Parish. At the time of his death he
   was employed at the New Orleans Louisiana Fair
   Grounds race track

d. Cleveland Paul LeBlanc born August 16, 1917 in
   Maringouin, Louisiana. Cleve was inducted into
   the United States Army in New Orleans, Louisiana
   on February 26, 1942. He was honorably discharged at Fort Sam Houston, Texas on September 21, 1945. He served in the southern Philippines, New Guinea, Luzon, Ryukyus and the
   Aleutian Islands. Decorations and citations
   included Philippine Liberation Medal with two
   bronze stars and the Good Conduct Medal as well

the Asiatic-Pacific Campaign medal with five
bronze stars.

> (1) August 29, 1937 Helen Rita
> AMEDEE (daughter of Fabien
> Amedee and Honorine GRANIER)
> born April 9, 1922 in Rose-
> dale, Louisiana

i. Terrell Anne LeBlanc bornNovember 16, 1938 in
Rosedale, Louisiana married November 16, 1958
George Joseph HARRIS (son of Isidore Harris
and Rita Marie BELLMORE) born February 20,
1933 in New Orleans, Louisiana

> a) Stephen George Harris born March 6, 1965
> in Metairie (Jefferson Parish) Louisiana
> b) Staci Elizabeth Harris born March 6,
> 1965 in Metairie, Louisiana
> c) Julie Rita Harris born November 30, 1967
> d) Paul Matthew Harris born June 8, 1971

CLEVELAND PAUL LE BLANC, SR.   LEE ANNA (LANDRY) LEBLANC
(1917 -   )   (1929 -   )

(2) August 4, 1947 to Lee Anna
LANDRY (daughter of Albert
Pierre Landry and Jeanne Marie
MABILE) born February 6, 1929
in Maringouin.

ii. Cleveland Paul LeBlanc, Jr. born May 27, 1948
in Baton Rouge married June 13, 1970 to Cheryl
JEX (daughter of Sterling Mark Jex, Sr. and
Betty Bernice OSTLER) born April 12, 1951 in
Spanish Fork, Utah. Cheryl is employed as a
secretary with the Louisiana State Department
of Education. Cleve was inducted into the
United States Navy in Orleans Parish on Sep-
tember 4, 1968 and was separated June 10, 1970
at Bremerton, Washington. He served in Viet
Nam and Korea and is presently at student at
Louisiana State University studying Industrial
Technology. Cleve, Jr. and Cheryl were mar-
ried at Ft. Benton, King County, Washington

iii. Linda Diane LeBlanc born January 21, 1950 in
New Orleans married January 31, 1970 in Baton
Rouge to David Joseph PIZZOLATO (son of Jacob
Pizzalato and Elma Marie TALBOT) born August 9,
1947 in Donaldsonville. David was inducted
into the United States Army on September 25,
1967. He served in Panama, the Canal Zone,
Viet Nam and is presently serving in Germany.
He plans to make a career of the Army.

a) David Joseph Pizzalato, Jr. born February 26, 1971 at Fort Sam Houston, Texas
b) Amy Lee Pizzalato born May 31, 1972 in
Baton Rouge, La.

iv. Peggy Darleen LeBlanc born March 5, 1954 in
New Orleans, La. She will be married on De-
cember 1, 1973 to Gary William TRUAX (son of
Wright William Truax and Francis FOTE)
v. James Brent LeBlanc born February 12, 1956 in
New Orleans, La.

e. Hubert Wyley LeBlanc born January 9, 1920 in Rosedale married June 29, 1957 in Detroit, Michigan
Adelaide VON BERGEN of Brussels, Belgium. Hubert
is a retired jockey.

i. Dominique Marie LeBlanc born February 21, 1958
in Detroit, Michigan

f. Euclid Thomas LeBlanc born March 7, 1922 in Rosedale, now a retired jockey, married

(1) 1941 to Ann GLASS

124

(2) 1946 Constance Ann SHEEHAN
(daughter of John Jefferson
Sheehan and Myrtle COWDREY)
born March 1, 1920 in Springfield, Missouri

i. Rickey Thomas LeBlanc born December 14, 1948
in Miami Beach, Florida married March 4, 1968
in Los Angeles, California Linda Lee AMUNDSON
(daughter of Milton Clair Amundson and Mary
Elizabeth CORUBBA) born May 9, 1950. Rickey
is a landscape gardner and a minister in the
Jehovah Witness

a) Cammie Kay LeBlanc born October 15, 1968
in Los Angeles, California
b) Teara Michelle LeBlanc born January 28,
1970 in Arcadia, California
c) Rickey Thomas LeBlanc, Jr. born August 25,
1971 in Monrovia, California

g. Helen Marie LeBlanc born March 24, 1924 in Maringouin married December 25, 1943 in Maringouin
Hubert Joseph BLANCHARD (son of Henry Joseph
Blanchard and Elda Marie LANDRY) born November 5,
1921 at Valverda, Louisiana

i. John Carl Blanchard born August 15, 1945 in
Vincennes, Indiana married April 17, 1971 in
Maringouin Margaret Dianne CASHIO (daughter
of Joseph Cashio and Margaret Juanita JONES)
born November 14, 1952. John Carl is an
operator with Ethyl Corporation

a) Trohn Peter Blanchard born March 24, 1973
in Baton Rouge

ii. Donna Marie Blanchard born June 11, 1948 in
Baton Rouge married April 1, 1967 in Grosse
Tete, La. Robert Charles JERRIE born Febru-
ary 12, 1948 in Gallon, Ohio

a) Robert Troy Jerrie born July 12, 1968 in
Litchfield,Minnesota
b) Tami Marie Jerrie born September 22, 1969
in Baton Rouge, La.

iii. Trudy Ann Blanchard born October 25, 1954 in
New Roads, La.
iv. Michel Todd Blanchard born January 11, 1966
in Baton Rouge

h. Charles Ray LeBlanc born March 14, 1927 in Marin-
gouin married in New Orleans January 12, 1948
Nancy Lee SNEE (daughter of Donald James Snee and
Christine BIBBINS) born October 6, 1927 in New

125

Orleans . Charles Ray is an official at a New
Orleans racetrack and is a retired jockey

   i. Thomas Allen LeBlanc born October 5, 1948 in
New York City married March 29, 1969 in New
Orleans Sheila Ann PERK (daughter of Dibert
Joseph Perk and Dessie TOUPS) Thomas served
in the United States Air Force from 1969 to
1972

   ii. James Donald LeBlanc born December 16, 1950 in
New Orleans

   iii. Charles Ray LeBlanc, Jr. born January 18, 1961
in Jefferson Parish

i. Anna Mae LeBlanc born May 4, 1929 in Maringouin
married June 10, 1951 in St. Anthony Church, Baton
Rouge Francis William COUVILLION (son of Louis
Supharien Couvillion and Margaret MAYEAUX) born
July 15, 1924 in Baton Rouge, La. Francis is a
carpenter and superintendent with L. W. Eaton,
Contractor. He served in the United States Navy
from January 25, 1943 to January 17, 1946. He
was a deep sea diver and saw action in major bat-
bles in the Pacific in WWII

   i. Clifton Thomas Couvillion born March 28, 1952
in Baton Rouge

   ii. Karen Elizabeth Couvillion born April 4, 1953

   iii. Cheryl Ann Couvillion born March 13, 1956

   iv. Gwendolyn Frances Couvillion born July 31, 1961

6. Joissant Cyril LeBlanc born January 28, 1887 in As-
cension Parish married May 18, 1910 in Smoke Bend
Jeanne Marie ALANZO (daughter of Cleophas Joseph
Alanzo and Adele DUGAS) born October 26, 1892 in Smoke
Bend. Joissant died July 25, 1965 and Jeanne Marie
died July 30, 1961. Both are buried in Westlawn
Cemetery in Gretna, La.

   a. Anna Adele LeBlanc born October 1, 1912 in Ascension; died at age of 2 months

   b. Alfred John LeBlanc born March 3, 1914 in New
Orleans married August 6, 1935 in New Orleans
Eva Mae JENKINS (daughter of Willie Lee Jenkins
and Tensey Estelle COX) born September 7, 1914 in
Washington Parish, La.

     i. Dorothy Estelle LeBlanc born November 3, 1936
in New Orleans married November 18, 1953 in
New Orleans Honora ESKINE (son of Honore Pete
Eskine and Eule Marie BERGERON) born May 5,
1934 in New Orleans. Honora is a railroad
engineer

FOUR GENERATION ANCESTOR CHART

```
                                                        8.
                                                        b.
                                                        p.b.
                        4. Xavier Alanzo                m.
                        b.                               p.m.
                        p.b.Spain, via Canary            d.
                        m.              Islands          p.b.
                        p.m.New Orleans                  9.
                        d.                               b.
                        p.d.New Orleans                  p.b.
          2. Cleophas  Joseph Alanzo                     d.
          b.                                             p.d.
          p.b.
          m. ca. 1890
          p.m.New Orleans                               10.
          d.                                             b.
          p.d.                                           p.b.
                                                         m.
                           5.                            p.m.
                           b.                            d.
                           p.b.                          p.d.
                           d.
                           p.d.                          11.
                                                         b.
                                                         p.b.
                                                         d.
          1  Jeanne Alanzo                               p.d.
          b. 26 October 1892
          p.b. Smoke Bend
          m. 18 May 1910                                12.
          p.m. Smoke Bend                                b.
          d. 30 July 1961                                p.b.
          p.d. New Orleans                               m.
                          6.                             p.m.
                           b.                            d.
                           p.b.                          p.d.
                           m.
                           p.m.                          13.
                           d.                            b.
                           p.d.                          p.b.
                                                         d.
             3 Adele  Dugas                              p.d.
             b.
             p.b.
             d.                                          14.
             p.d.                                        b.
                                                         p.b.
                                                         m.
                           7.                            p.m.
                           b.                            d.
                           p.b.                          p.d.
                           d.
                           p.d.                          15.
                                                         b.
          Joissant LeBlanc                               p.b.
          Spouse of #1                                   d.
                                                         p.d.
```

ALFRED
(1887 – 1965)

MILTON EUGENE
JOISANT LE BLANC
(1887 – 1965)

ROBERT CLEOPHAS
JEANNE ALANZO
(1892 – 1961)

ROY
VERLIN

127

       a) Roy Michael Eskine born November 28, 1955
          In New Orleans
       b) Rachael Eskine born October 6, 1966 in
          New Orleans

  ii. Vada Mae LeBlanc born June 18, 1939 in New
     Orleans married September 2, 1954 in New Or-
     leans Herbert Ned ROGERS (son of Camille Jean
     Rogers and Priscillia Marie DEMSTER of Vacherie
     born May 27, 1939 in Wallace, La. Herbert is
     an electrician

       a) John Craig Rogers born September 21, 1955
          in New Orleans
       b) Scott Paul Rogers born October 13, 1963
          in New Orleans
       c) Jane Lynn Rogers born March 11, 1964 in
          New Orleans

  iii. Richard Patrick LeBlanc born July 20, 1945 in
     New Orleans married June 2, 1963 in New Orleans
     Geraldine DAVIS, a native of Mississippi

       a) Richard Patrick LeBlanc, Jr. born Novem-
          ber 1, 1964 in New Orleans
       b) Lorraine LeBlanc born in 1968 in New Orlean

c. Cleophas Joseph (Lucky) LeBlanc born July 9, 1916
  in Ascension married October 9, 1937 in New Orléans
  Nathalie Irene CHESNUT (daughter of Nathaniel Chesnut and Irene MARQUES, natives of Morgan City) born
  July 18, 1920 in New Orleans

  i. Linda Ann LeBlanc born June 19, 1939 in New
     Orleans married June 6, 1959 in New Orleans
     Ronnie Joseph BLANCHARD born May 9, 1937

       a) Cynthia June Blanchard born March 5, 1960
          in New Orleans
       b) David Michael Blanchard born June 13, 1961
          in New Orleans
       c) Gregory Paul Blanchard born August 16,1963
          in New Orleans
       d) Douglas Gerald Blanchard born September 21,
          1964 in New Orleans

  ii. Janet Lee LeBlanc born July 22, 1940 in New
     Orleans married May 5, 1962 in New Orleans
     Ronald Francis SCHULTE born May 13, 1937

       a) Anne Elaine Schulte born November 5, 1962
          in New Orleans

       b) Ellen Marie Schulte born December 1, 1963
          in New Orleans
       c) Michele Rae Schulte born May 27, 1967 in
          New Orleans

      d) Antoine Joseph Schulte born June 14, 1968
          in New Orleans
      e) Amy Margaret Schulte born August 9, 1970
          in New Orleans

iii. Cleo Raye LeBlanc born December 19, 1941 in
     New Orleans
iv. Peggy Lou LeBlanc born May 29, 1943 in New
     Orleans married June 29, 1963 in New Orleans
     Frederick Lewis LE BLANC born May 14, 1942

      a) Wayne Michael LeBlanc born March 12, 1964
          in New Orleans
      b) Rebecca Ann LeBlanc born March 22, 1965
          in New Orleans
      c) Mark Stephen LeBlanc born February 26,
          1967 in New Orleans

v. Ruth Marie LeBlanc born September 23, 1947 in
     New Orleans
vi. Joseph Cleophas LeBlanc born December 14, 1948
     in New Orleans Married February 21, 1970 in
     Mobile, Alabama Mary Catherine LE BLANC (daugh-
     ter of Eugene LeBlanc and Lola Jean CHERNICK)
     born August 20, 1947 in Chicago, Illinois.
     Cleophas served in the Special Forces (Green
     Beret) with the United States Army in the
     Viet Nam conflict. He is presently a student
     in pre-med at Louisiana State University at
     New Orleans
vii. Nathaniel Chesnut LeBlanc born September 24,
     1950 in New Orleans married September 21,
     1970 in New Orleans Alma DUFOUR

      a) Heidi Lynn LeBlanc born September 28, 1971
          in New Orleans

viii. Raymond Michael LeBlanc born September 25, 1952
     in New Orleans
ix. Jeanne Irene LeBlanc born June 23, 1958 in New
     Orleans

d. Eugene Joseph (Gene) LeBlanc born October 9, 1918
   in Ascension Parish married April 27, 1946 in
   Chicago, Illinois Lola Joan CHERNICK (daughter of
   Joseph Chernick and Lillian MAGGENTI) born October 30, 1920 in Chicago, Illinois

    i. Mary Catherine LeBlanc born August 20, 1947
      in Chicago married February 21, 1970 in Mobile
      Alabama Joseph Cleophas LE BLANC (son of
      Cleophas J. LeBlanc and Nathalie Irene CHESNUT)
      born December 14, 1948 in New Orleans
    ii. Donna Jean LeBlanc born October 16, 1948 in
      Chicago, Illinois married September 5, 1970

Charles FITZPATRICK
    iii. Douglas Eugene LeBlanc born December 26, 1950
        in Chicago, Illinois married August 14, 1971
        Shirley _____
    iv. Wayne Michael LeBlanc born January 3, 1952 in
        Chicago, Illinois
    v. Russell Clifford LeBlanc born July 21, 1955
        in Chicago, Illinois
    vi. Brian Alan LeBlanc born July 6, 1959 in Chica-
        go, Illinois
  e. Roy James LeBlanc born December 24, 1920 in Rose-
    dale married March 19, 1943 in Washington, D. C.
    Ethel PACKETT born March 11, 1921 in Jenkins,
    Kentucky
    i. Roy Jefferies LeBlanc born January 22, 1944
        in Daytona Beach, Florida
    ii. Paul Michael LeBlanc born October 18, 1945 in
        Daytona Beach married March 11, 1967 in New
        Orleans Maureen Lee HESS (daughter of Howard
        Harley Hess and Mary Louise LIPSCOMB) born
        May 22, 1946 in New Orleans
        a) Michele Maureen LeBlanc born June 19, 1971
  f. Hazel LeBlanc born in 1922 in Lutcher; died in 1924
  g. Verlin Marie LeBlanc born August 3, 1925 in Lutcher
    married September 11, 1942 in New Orleans Lawrence
    Edward NIELSEN (son of Edward Joseph Nielsen and
    Elizabeth Lillian GLANCEY) born May 31, 1920 in
    New Orleans. Lawrence was inducted into the
    United States Air Force on December 4, 1941 in New
    Orleans and was discharged November 19, 1945
    i. Leonard Lawrence Nielsen born December 15, 1944
        in New Orleans married January 27, 1966 in New
        Orleans Susan NEBLE (daughter of Robert Mark
        Neble and Will Ell Juanita LIGON) born Septem-
        ber 11, 1945 in New Orleans. Leonard served
        in the United States Air Force from August 6,
        1965 to January 31, 1969
        a) Mark Edward Nielsen born September 15, 1969
        in New Orleans
        b) Paul Christopher Nielsen born November 5,
        1971 in New Orleans
    ii. Marsha Marie Nielsen born May 16, 1947 in New
        Orleans married April 27, 1968 in New Orleans
        Johnny Robert KIRKSEY, Jr. (son of Johnny
        Robert Kirksey, Sr. and Curcis CONNELL) born
        October 24, 1947 in Boyle, Mississippi
        a) Melinda Marie Kirksey born September 8,
        1969 in New Orleans

b) Barbara Ann Kirksey born May 5, 1972 in New Orleans

h. Marie LeBlanc born in July 1926 in Lutcher; died at age 6 days

i. Milton James LeBlanc born July 19, 1927 in Lutcher, La. married October 21, 1953 in St. Louis Cathedral, New Orleans, La. Diane BROWN (daughter of Floyd Joseph Brown and Pauline D'ANTONI) born October 11, 1929 in New Orleans, La.

   i. Nedra Gerard LeBlanc born August 6, 1955 in Orleans Parish

  ii. Nadine Gerard LeBlanc born August 6, 1958 in Jefferson Parish

j. Robert Raymond LeBlanc born July 29, 1932 in New Orleans married September 2, 1959 in Gretna Jacqueline Vera HACKER (daughter of John Joseph Hacker and Vera Rose MINX) born October 8, 1938 in New Orleans. Robert served in the United States Army

   i. Stephen Bryan LeBlanc born April 25, 1960 in New Orleans

  ii. Virginia Carol LeBlanc born January 6, 1962 in New Orleans

iii. Deborah Marie LeBlanc born May 21, 1963 in New Orleans

Robert Raymond was recently appointed Director of the Louisiana Tourist Commission and has assumed his post as Louisiana's top travel executive. He has a background in marketing, trade exhibit and display, and hotel convention sales.

FOUR GENERATION ANCESTOR CHART

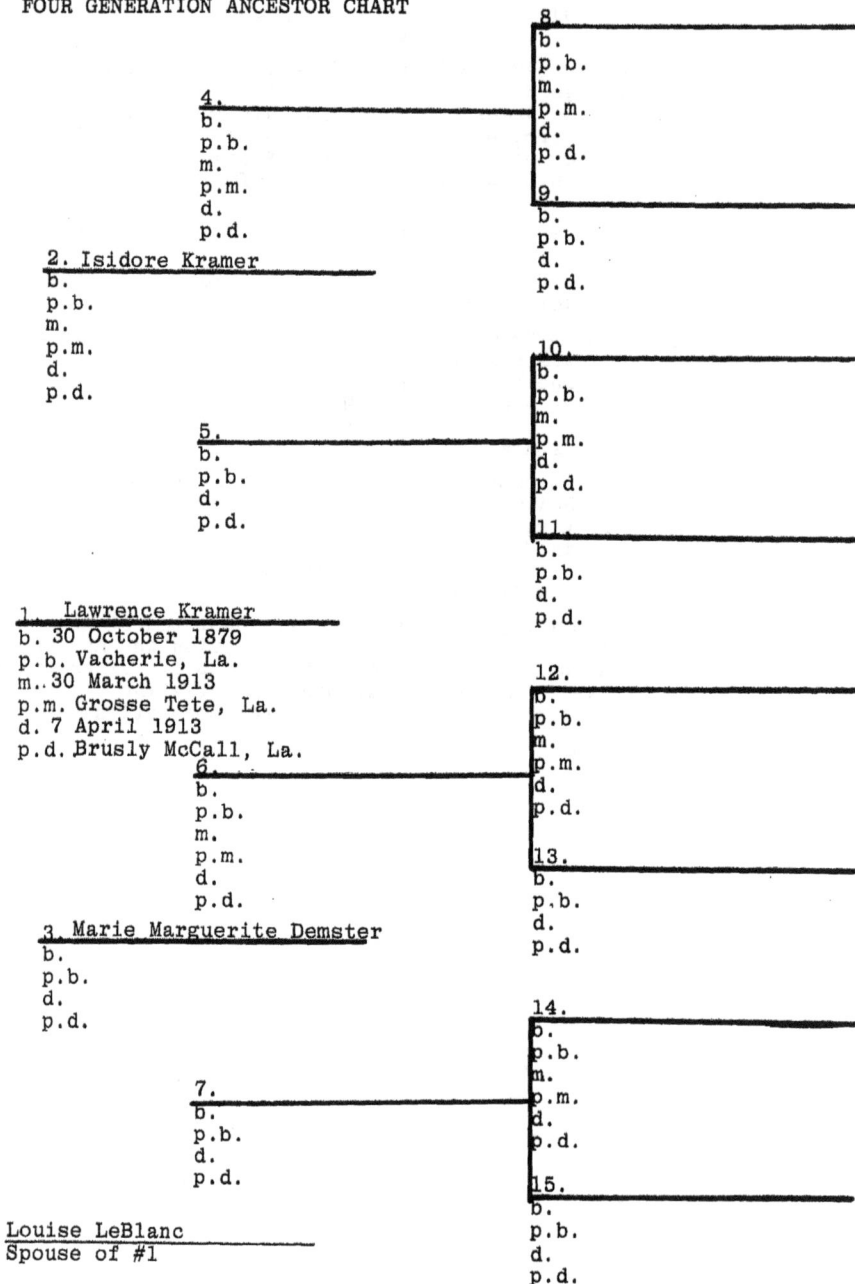

```
                                                    8.
                                                    b.
                                                    p.b.
                                                    m.
                          4.                        p.m.
                          b.                        d.
                          p.b.                      p.d.
                          m.
                          p.m.                      9.
                          d.                        b.
                          p.d.                      p.b.
     2. Isidore Kramer                              d.
     b.                                             p.d.
     p.b.
     m.
     p.m.                                           10.
     d.                                             b.
     p.d.                                           p.b.
                                                    m.
                          5.                        p.m.
                          b.                        d.
                          p.b.                      p.d.
                          d.
                          p.d.                      11.
                                                    b.
                                                    p.b.
     1.   Lawrence Kramer                           d.
     b. 30 October 1879                             p.d.
     p.b. Vacherie, La.
     m.. 30 March 1913
     p.m. Grosse Tete, La.                          12.
     d. 7 April 1913                                b.
     p.d. Brusly McCall, La.                        p.b.
                          6.                        m.
                          b.                        p.m.
                          p.b.                      d.
                          m.                        p.d.
                          p.m.
                          d.                        13.
                          p.d.                      b.
                                                    p.b.
     3. Marie Marguerite Demster                    d.
     b.                                             p.d.
     p.b.
     d.
     p.d.                                           14.
                                                    b.
                                                    p.b.
                                                    m.
                          7.                        p.m.
                          b.                        d.
                          p.b.                      p.d.
                          d.
                          p.d.                      15.
                                                    b.
     Louise LeBlanc                                 p.b.
     Spouse of #1                                   d.
                                                    p.d.
```

7. Louise LeBlanc born April 21, 1889 in Ascension Parish married March 30, 1913 in Grosse Tete to Lawrence KRAMER (son of Isidore Kramer and Marie DEMPSTER). Louise died on March 16, 1915 and is buried in Marin-gouin. Lawrence died April 7, 1913 having been struck by lightning while cutting logs in the woods with his father-in-law 8 days after he was married.

LOUISE LE BLANC
(1889 - 1915)

FOUR GENERATION ANCESTOR CHART

8.
b.
p.b.
m.
p.m.
d.
p.d.

4. Rosine Muenier Marshal
b.   ca. 1840
p.b. France-came to La.
m.   1866 via New Orleans
p.m.
d.   ca. 1901
p.d. Bur. Plaquemine

9.
b.
p.b.
d.
p.d.

2. Auguste Marshal
b. 14 July 1861
p.b. France
m.
p.m.
d. 14 January 1933
p.d. Plaquemine

10.
b.
p.b.
m.
p.m.
d.
p.d.

5.
b.
p.b.
d.
p.d.

11.
b.
p.b.
d.
p.d.

1. Ollie Marshal
b. 9 October 1898
p.b. Plaquemine, La.
m. 10 May 1916
p.m. Plaquemine
d. 7 February 1946
p.d. Plaquemine

12.
b.
p.b.
m.
p.m.
d.
p.d.

6.
b.
p.b.
m.
p.m.
d.
p.d.

13.
b.
p.b.
d.
p.d.

3. Hilda Viguet
b. 26 September 1864
p.b. Brusly, La.
d. 12 February 1923
p.d. Plaquemine

14.
b.
p.b.
m.
p.m.
d.
p.d.

7.
b.
p.b.
d.
p.d.

15.
b.
p.b.
d.
p.d.

Lawrence LeBlanc
Spouse of #1

8. Lawrence LeBlanc born August 10, 1892 in Ascension
Parish married

(1) May 10, 1916 in Plaquemine
Olive Mary MARSHAL (daughter
of August Marshal and Hilda
VIGES) born October 9, 1898
in Plaquemine, La. Died February 7, 1946 in Plaquemine
La.

OLIVE MARY MARSHAL
(1898 - 1946)

LAWRENCE   LE BLANC
(1892 - 1968)

MANASSA GARDNER
(-   )

a. Charles Edward LeBlanc born May 28, 1917 in Plaquemine married December 13, 1940 in Plaquemine
Iris Agatha LANDRY (daughter of George Landry and
Henriette NEAL) born November 17, 1920 in Plaquemine, La.

133

    i. Dianne Mary LeBlanc born March 10, 1943 in
        Plaquemine married October 1, 1966 in Pla-
        quemine Verner COMEAUX (manager of Home Ap-
        pliances, Plaquemine)

        a) Shannon Elizabeth Comeaux born October 12,
            1969 in Plaquemine, La.

   ii. Robert Neal LeBlanc born May 27, 1948 in Pla-
        quemine married December 18, 1971 in Metairie,
        La. Sheri Lee LESTER

b. Mildred Ann LeBlanc born May 3, 1927 in Plaquemine
    married March 24, 1946 in Plaquemine Vernon
    William MC LAUGHLIN (son of Roscoe Clifton Mc
    Laughlin of Glendo, Wyoming and Ellen WILLIAMS of
    Maryville, Missouri) born January 16, 1923 in
    Dillon, Montana

     i. Karen Ann McLaughlin born September 20, 1951
         in Dillon, Montana
    ii. Kathleen Marie McLaughlin born October 11, 1956
         in Plaquemine, La.
   iii. Laurie Ann McLaughlin born February 6, 1960
         in Plaquemine, La.

    Vernon McLaughlin was inducted into the service
    of the United States in Dillon, Montana on March 1,
    1943 and was separated at Fort Lewis, Washington
    on February 17, 1946. He saw service in the Philip-
    pines, Ryukyus and Japan

                    (2) January 22, 1953 in Iberville
                         Parish Manassa GARDNER (widow
                         Sellers)

    There were no children born of Lawrence's second
    marriage

FOUR GENERATION ANCESTOR CHART

8.
b.
p.b.
m.
p.m.
d.
p.d.

4. Rosine Muenier Marshal
b.   ca. 1840
p.b.France-came to La. via
m. New Orleans in 1866
p.m.
d.   ca. 1901
p.d.Bur. Plaquemine

9.
b.
p.b.
d.
p.d.

2. August Marshal
b. 14 July 1861
p.b. France
m.
p.m.
d. 14 January 1933
p.d. Bur. Plaquemine

10.
b.
p.b.
m.
p.m.
d.
p.d.

5.
b.
p.b.
d.
p.d.

11.
b.
p.b.
d.
p.d.

1. Agnes Celestine Marshal
b. 2 December 1900
p.b. Plaquemine
m. 3 October 1918
p.m. Plaquemine
d.
p.d..

12.
b.
p.b.
m.
p.m.
d.
p.d.

6.
b.
p.b.
m.
p.m.
d.
p.d.

13.
b.
p.b.
d.
p.d.

3. Hilda Viguet
b. 26 September 1864
p.b. Brusly, La.
d. 12 February 1923
p.d. Bur. Plaquemine

14.
b.
p.b.
m.
p.m.
d.
p.d.

7.
b.
p.b.
d.
p.d.

15.
b.
p.b.
d.
p.d.

Jimmie LeBlanc
Spouse of #1

9. Jimmie LeBlanc born June 28, 1898 in Ascension Parish, married October 3, 1918 in Plaquemine to Agnes Celestine MARSHAL (daughter of August Marshal and Hilda VIGES) born December 2, 1900. Jimmie was with his father and brother-in-law, Lawrence Kramer, who was killed by lightning while cutting logs in the woods. He is a retired employee of the city of Plaquemine.

JIMMIE LE BLANC
(1898 -   )

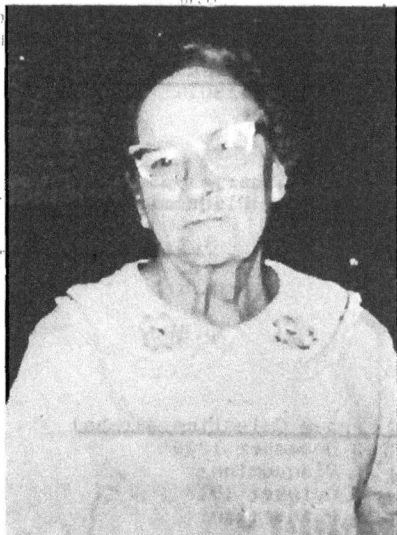

AGNES MARSHAL
(1900 -   )

a. Thomas LeBlanc born April 19, 1921 in Plaquemine married September 29, 1941 in Savanah, Georgia to Fanny Dorothy GOUDEAUX (daughter of Alcee P. Goudeaux and Jennie G. FRIOUX) born December 6, 1921. Thomas enlisted in the Army Air Force in 1939 at Barksdale Field, Louisiana and retired at McCord Air Force Base, Seattle, Washington in 1960 with the rank of M/Sgt. He saw service in New Guinea, Japan, Hawaii and Lybia. Thomas born in Plaquemine

1. Jonathan Thomas LeBlanc born December 3, 1945 in Miami, Florida married September 11, 1965 in Lake Bistineau, Louisiana to Shirley Annette MC COY (daughter of O. T. McCoy and Donie Elorvine WELCH) born January 19, 1943 in Ringgold, Louisiana.

135

             a) Sherry Carlene LeBlanc born June 21, 1966 in Shreveport

             b) Jonathan Thomas LeBlanc, Jr. born June 28, 1967

             c) William David LeBlanc born June 16, 1970

     ii. Darell Mark LeBlanc born May 28, 1948 in Plaquemine married Linda Earline IELANO (daughter of Luther Earl Ielano and Bobbie Jean FOY) born August 27, 1949 in Monroe, Louisiana

             a) Nicole Evett LeBlanc born June 2, 1970 in Shreveport, Louisiana

    iii. Mark LeBlanc born July 18, 1954 in Tacoma, Washington

  b. Helen LeBlanc born February 13, 1925 in Plaquemine; died February 14, 1925

  c. Gloria LeBlanc born April 27, 1927 in Plaquemine married November 18, 1945 in Plaquemine George J. RAMIREZ (son of James B. Ramirez and Lucille BOUDREAUX) born March 31, 1926. George is a farmer on Milly Plantation, Plaquemine, Louisiana

     i. Julie Ann Ramirez born September 9, 1946 in Plaquemine

    ii. George Joseph Ramirez, Jr. born April 15, 1952 in Plaquemine married March 4, 1972 in Plaquemine Wallace Aulena DANEHOWER (daughter of Justus H. Danehower and Shirley MARCOTTE) born December 19, 1954 in Moreauville, Louisiana

  d. Catherine LeBlanc born October 8, 1929 in Plaquemine; died April 12, 1930

C. Phelonise Althee LeBlanc born June 4, 1854 in Ascension; died about age 16 and buried in Ascension Cemetery, Donaldsonville, La.

D. Frederick Hubert LeBlanc born April 2, 1856 in Ascension; died at age 21 and buried in Ascension Cemetery, Donaldsonville, La.

FOUR GENERATION ANCESTOR CHART

8. Joseph Clouatre
b. 1760 St. Mary County
p.b. New England (USA)
m. 27 June 1785
p.m. St. James Parish
d. February 1841
p.d. St. James Parish

4. George Jerome Clouatre
b. 18 November 1799
p.b. St. James Parish
m. 27 January 1818
p.m. St. James Parish
d. 8 November 1847
p.d. St. James Parish

9. Maria Poirier
b. 1770
p.b. Parents natives of Acad
d. 15 March 1800
p.d. St. James Parish

2. Joseph Clouatre
b. 15 November 1819
p.b. St. James Parish
m. 22 January 1849
p.m. St. Michael Church
d.
p.d. St. James Parish

10 Amand Bourgeois
b. Bt. 1 March 1772
p.b. St. James Parish
m. 27 November 1792
p.m. St. James Parish
d. 5 November 1805
p.d. St. James Parish

5. Melite Bourgeois
b. 16 March 1796
p.b. St. James Parish
d. 4 November 1880
p.d. St. James Parish

11 Scholastic Arseneaux
b. Bt. 16 February 1772
p.b. St. James Parish
d.
p.d. St. James Parish

1. Leon Joseph Clouatre
b. 27 July 1851
p.b. St. James Parish, La.
m. 2 February 1875
p.m. Ascension Parish
d. 25 October 1926
p.d. Bur. Ascension Cemetery

12 Abraham Rome
b.   ca. 1764
p.b. St. Charles Parish
m.   ca. 1790
p.m.
d. 5 August 1827, age 63
p.d. St. James Parish

6. Nicholas Rome
b. 3 December 1795
p.b. St. James Parish
m. 7 January 1817
p.m. St. John the Baptist
d. 25 March 1835 (succession)
p.d. St. Mary Parish

13 Jeanne Baudouin
b.   ca. 1761
p.b. St. Charles Parish
d. 1 April 1816
p.d. St. James Parish

3. Marie Ezilda Rome
b. 22 June 1823
p.b. St. John the Baptist
d. 18 October 1853
p.d. Convent, La.

14 Jean Michel Webre
b.   ca. 1766
p.b. St. John the Baptist
m. 4 January 1791
p.m. St. John the Baptist
d. 22 July 1820
p.d. St. John the Baptist

7. Eurasie Webre
b.   ca. 1797
p.b. St. John the Baptist
d. 26 March 1881
p.d. St. James Parish

15. Francoise Haydel
b.   ca. 1769
p.b. St. John the Baptist
d. 18 March 1824, age 55
p.d. St. John the Baptist

Elmire LeBlanc
Spouse of #1

E. Marie Elmire LeBlanc born May 26, 1858 in Ascension Par-
    ish married February 2, 1875 in Ascension Parish (at home)
    Leon Joseph CLOUATRE (son of Joseph Clouatre and Marie
    Ezilda ROME) born July 27, 1851 at Union, St. James Par-
    ish. Leon Clouatre died October 25, 1926 in Belle Rose,
    Louisiana, Assumption Parish; Elmire died September 11,
    1937 at Denham Springs, Louisiana, Livingston Parish.
    Both are buried in Ascension Cemetery, Donaldsonville, La.
    Leon and Elmire made their home with their daughter, Philo-
    mine and husband Adam Dugas (from 1912 until their deaths)

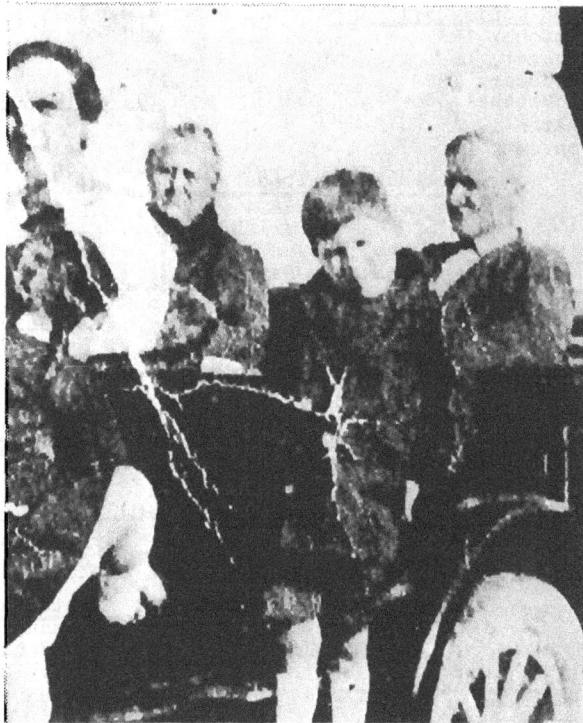

ELMIRE LE BLANC   LEON CLOUATRE
(1858 - 1937)   (1851 - 1926)
    Seated left: PHILOMENE (CLOUATRE) DUGAS
        Children: ANNIE and MELVIN DUGAS
1. Joseph Clouatre born April, 1878 in Ascension Parish;
    died October 22, 1878 and buried Ascension Cemetery.

137

FOUR GENERATION ANCESTOR CHART

8. Jean Baptiste Caillouet
b. 8 September 1789
p.b. St. James Parish
m. 4 May 1821 (civil 1812)
p.m. St. Michael, Convent, La.
d. 27 July 1864
p.d. Convent, La.

4. Joseph Florian Caillouet
b. 5 October 1820
p.b. Convent, La.
m. 3 February 1845
p.m. St. Michael, Convent
d. 22 February 1898
p.d. St. Landry Parish

9. Josephine Margarita Hebert
b. 12 September 1792
p.b. St. James, La.
d. 6 July 1833
p.d. Convent, La.

2. Joseph Louis Caillouet
b. 29 October 1851
p.b. Convent, La.
m. 24 February 1876
p.m. St. Michael, Convent, La.
d. 9 March 1925
p.d. Convent, La.

10 Charles Paul Thibodeaux
b. 30 April 1794
p.b. St. James Parish
m. 22 February 1814
p.m. St. James, La.
d. 8 February 1865
p.d. Convent, La.

5. Seraphine Thibodeaux
b. 14 September 1824
p.b. St. James Parish
d. 1 June 1898
p.d. St. Landry Parish

11 Marie Clemence Gautreaux
b. 15 July 1796
p.b. Ascension Parish
d. 5 June 1849
p.d. Convent, La.

1 Anna Marie Caillouet
b. 4 September 1894
p.b. Convent, La.
m. 3 July 1912
p.m. St. Michael, Convent, La.
d. 1 July 1968
p.d. Baton Rouge

12. Joseph Norbert Landry
b. 17 September 1799
p.b. St. James, La.
m. 5 July 1825
p.m. St. Michael, Convent, La.
d. 19 February 1866
p.d. Convent, La.

6. Norbert Sylvere Landry
b. 27 July 1830
p.b. Convent, La.
m. 17 April 1849
p.m. St. Michael, Convent
d. 8 December 1891
p.d. Convent, La.

13. Anastasie Poche
b. 22 January 1806
p.b. St. John the Baptist
d. 18 May 1871
p.d. Convent, La.

3. Corinne Landry
b. 27 May 1854
p.b. Convent, La.
d. 17 July 1933
p.d. Convent, La.

14. Evariste Oubre
b. 2 March 1802
p.b. St. James Parish
m. 21 February 1832
p.m. St. Michael, Convent, La.
d. 12 July 1841
p.d. Convent, La.

7. Marie Irma Oubre
b. 16 February 1833
p.b. Convent, La.
d. 24 October 1919
p.d. Convent, La.

15. Charlotte Dufresne
b. 27 February 1804
p.b. St. James, La.
d. 23 March 1858
p.d. Convent, La.

Livingston J. Clouatre
Spouse of #1

FAMILY GROUP RECORD

ENTER ALL DATA IN THIS ORDER:
DATES: 14 Apr 1794
NAMES: WATSON, John Henry
PLACES: Sharon, Wndsr, Vrmn

To indicate that a child is an ancestor of the family representative, place an "X" behind the number pertaining to that child.

HUSBAND: CAILLOUET, Joseph Louis

	Date	Place
Born	29 October 1851	Convent, St. James Parish, Louisiana
Chr.	1 December 1851	St. Michael Church, Convent, La.
Marr.	24 February 1876	St. Michael Church, Convent, La.
Died	9 March 1925	Convent, Louisiana
Bur.	11 March 1925	St. Michael Church Cemetery, Convent, Louisiana

HUSBAND'S FATHER: Joseph Florian Caillouet
HUSBAND'S MOTHER: Marie Seraphine Thibodeaux
HUSBAND'S OTHER WIVES:

WIFE: LANDRY, Marie Corinne

	Date	Place
Born	11 June 1851	Convent, St. James Parish, Louisiana
Chr.	29 July 1854	St. Michael Church, Convent, La.
Died	17 July 1933	Convent, Louisiana
Bur.	19 July 1933	St. Michael Church Cemetery, Convent, Louisiana

WIFE'S FATHER: Norbert Sylvere Landry
WIFE'S MOTHER: Marie Irma Oubre
WIFE'S OTHER HUSBANDS:

CHILDREN

M/F	Given Names (SURNAME)	When Born (Day Month Year)	Where Born (Town)	County	State	Date of First Marriage / To Whom	When Died (Day Month Year)
1	CAILLOUET, Constance	28 Dec. 1876	Convent	St. James	La.	5 June 1901 / Philomene LANDRY	14 Feb. 1947
2	CAILLOUET, Joseph Francis	3 Dec. 1878	Convent	St. James	La.	26 April 1900 / Honore LAMBERT	10 July 1961
3	CAILLOUET, Maria Philomene	29 June 1880	Convent	St. James	La.	18 June 1905 / Alice GUIDRY	26 Oct. 1957
4	CAILLOUET, George Joseph	29 June 1883	Convent	St. James	La.	21 August 1912 / Elista GAUDIN	20 Dec. 1957
5	CAILLOUET, Willie Joseph	29 June 1885	Convent	St. James	La.	2 March 1908 / Henry BOURGEOIS	16 Aug. 1961
6	CAILLOUET, Josephine Corinne	28 Nov. 1888	Convent	St. James	La.	3 July 1912 / Livingston CLOUATRE	1 July 1968
7	CAILLOUET, Anna Marie	4 Sept. 1894	Convent	St. James	La.		Feb. 1877
8							
9							
10							
11							

SOURCES OF INFORMATION

Standing: Livingston, Jr. Chester Calvin   Leon   Leslie
Seated: Elmo LIVINGSTON CLOUATRE ANNA CAILLOUET Nora Lee (Clouatre)

138

2. Livingston Joseph Clouatre born July 14, 1880 in As-
    cension Parish married July 3, 1912 in St. Michael's
    Church, Convent, La. to Anna Marie CAILLOUET (daughter
    of Joseph Louis Caillouet and Marie Corinne LANDRY)
    born September 4, 1894 in Convent, La. Livingston died
    February 14, 1964 and Anna died July 1, 1968. in Baton
    Rouge and are buried in Greenoaks Memorial Park. Liv-
    ingston Clouatre was a carpenter; Anna was a practical
    nurse. They made their home at 3434 Plank Road, Baton
    Rouge, La. from 1918 to 1964 at which time Anna made
    her home at 3471 Winnebago until 1968.

    a. Elmo Joseph Clouatre born July 6, 1913 in Burton,
        St. James Parish, married January 10, 1938 in New
        Orleans Margie SIMMONS, born March 25, 1905 in
        New Orleans
    b. Nora Lee Clouatre born January 22, 1915 in Ascen-
        sion Parish married July 13, 1936 in St. Anthony
        Church, Baton Rouge, La. John Michael POLLARD
        (son of Michael William Pollard and Ruth Nora
        ALTAZIN) born September 20, 1914 in Baton Rouge.
        J. M. died March 23, 1969 and is buried in Green-
        oaks Memorial Park, Baton Rouge, La. He was em-
        ployed at Esso Standard Oil Company from April,
        1936 until his death in 1969. Nora Lee was mana-
        ger of Baton Rouge Flower Shop from 1940 to 1950
        and designer at Hunt's Flowers from 1950 to 1960.

NORA LEE CLOUATRE   JOHN MICHAEL POLLARD
(1915 -   )   (1914 - 1969)

i. Barbara Anne Pollard born February 23, 1938 in
    Baton Rouge married October 15, 1957 in West
    Baton Rouge Parish Victor Raymond MICHELLI
    (son of Dominick Michelli and Antonia ROPPOLO,
    natives of Sicily)born February 16, 1920 in
    Baton Rouge. Victor died March 26, 1968 in
    Baton Rouge and is buried in Greenoaks Memo-
    rial Park. Victor enlisted in the United State
    Navy on April 30, 1942 and was discharged on
    November 5, 1945. At the time of his death
    he was a Sargeant with the Baton Rouge City
    Police force.

BARBARA ANNE POLLARD   VICTOR RAYMOND MICHELLI
      (1938 -   )   (1920 - 1968)

a) John Michael Michelli born January 24, 1959
    in Baton Rouge
b) Nora Lee Michelli born March 13, 1963 in
    Baton Rouge; died April 11, 1963. She is
    buried in Greenoaks Memorial Park.

Victor Michelli was previously married

          (1) February 16, 1941 Jeanette
               JOHNSON (daughter of Charles W.
               Johnson and Amanda GARIN)
          (2) Hilda HARRELL of Osyka, Missis-
               sippi

Children born of this second marriage:
Victoria Marie Michelli born January 17, 1947 in
Baton Rouge
Victor Raymond Michelli, II born May 4, 1951 in
Baton Rouge

141

JOHN MICHAEL (MIKE) MICHELLI
(1959 -   )

c. Livingston Joseph Clouatre, Jr. born September 8, 1916 in Garyville, Louisiana married April 15, 1936 in St. Anthony Church, Baton Rouge Josie BRAUD (daughter of Henry Estress Braud and Bernice Louise ARBOUR) born March 19, 1917 in Baton Rouge. Livingston retired in 1972 from Ethyl Corporation. He was employed there since 1936

    i. Livingston Joseph Clouatre, III born December 18, 1936 in Baton Rouge married

           (1) Bobbie Sue WILLIAMS

    a) Reva Darleen Clouatre born in June, 1960 in Baton Rouge
    b) Nina Marie Clouatre born December 19, 1962

           (2) Emily Jane SINOR (daughter of Howard Earl Sinor and Beverly Merrill BOURGEOIS)

    c) Amy Jane Clouatre born September 26, 1970 in New Orleans

Livingston served in the United States Navy from June 22, 1954 to 1958

    ii. Patricia June Clouatre born May 11, 1938 in Baton Rouge married

           (1) February 4, 1956 in Our Lady of Mercy Church, Baton Rouge David STEECE

    a) Theresa Ann Steece born August 6, 1957 in Baton Rouge

           (2) June 5, 1960 Scott Vincent HOOT of Effingham, Illinois

    b) Scott Vincent Hoot, Jr. born November 18, 1961 in East St. Louis, Illinois
    c) Dawn Marie Hoot born April 30, 1963 in East St. Louis, Illinois

           (3) David STEECE

    d) Anne Louise Steece born October 27, 1965 in New Orleans

           (4) Glen BASS

    e) Richard Lee Bass born December 30, 1967 in Baton Rouge

    iii. Henry Estress Clouatre born August 25, 1940 in Baton Rouge
    iv. Carolyn Ann Clouatre born August 18, 1943 in Baton Rouge married December 15, 1968 in Donaldsonville Victor DE LOUISE (son of Michel

DeLouise and Mary REGIRA) born December 15,
1933 in Donaldsonville, La.

a) Lisa Marie DeLouise born July 22, 1971 in
Baton. Rouge; baptized in Smoke Bend, La.

Victor DeLouise was previously married to
Rosemary OSBORNE (daughter of A. Z. Osborne
and Vita VIRGO) Children of this first mar-
riage are:
Stephanie DeLouise born August 19, 1954 in
Opelousas, La.
Andre Michael DeLouise born January 5, 1957
in Donaldsonville, La.
Dale Mark DeLouise born November 8, 1957 in
Baton Rouge, La.
Gregory DeLouise born August 14, 1962

v. Gene Raymond Clouatre born December 12, 1944
in Baton Rouge married June 15, 1963 Sandra
Diane CLARK (daughter of Walter Hugh Clark
and Ruby Pearl COBURN) born December 8, 1946
in Houston, Texas

a) John Walter Clouatre born March 26, 1964
in Baton Rouge, La.
b) Jason Wade Clouatre born January 13, 1967
in Baton Rouge, La.
c) Gena Diane Clouatre born May 17, 1969 in
Baton Rouge, La.
d) Sherilyn Clouatre born October 30, 1971
in Baton Rouge, La.

vi. Margie Louise Clouatre born January 2, 1946 in
Baton Rouge married October 2, 1965 in St.
Gerard Church, Baton Rouge William Lloyd WILSON
(son of Buford Wilson and Dorothy Margaret
LLOYD) born February 13, 1941 in McComb, Miss.

a) William Lloyd Wilson, Jr. born June 24,
1966 in Baton Rouge
b) Vicki Lynn Wilson born May 28, 1967
c) David Lawrence Wilson born June 5, 1968

vii. Celeste Clouatre born March 23, 1948 in Baton
Rouge married January 7, 1967 in St. Gerard
Church, Baton Rouge Don J. MYERS (son of
Edward J. Myers and Opal MC MILLS) born Febru-
ary 7, 1946

a) Brandon Lee Myers born December 2, 1972 in
Baton Rouge

viii. Jacqueline Jo Clouatre born December 15, 1949
in Baton Rouge married in 1968 Terrell Travis
KING (son of Clifford Augusta King and Ida V.
BOSEMAN) born February 11, 1945 in Baton Rouge

a) Troy Lynn King born January 3, 1969 in Baton Rouge

b) Chad Michael King born October 21, 1970

Terrell King was previously married and there was one child:

Terrell Travis King, Jr. born October 19, 1966

ix. Gerard Ray Clouatre born July 2, 1953 in Baton Rouge married Geraldine MICHELLI (daughter of Peter Michelli and Mildred ALBERADO) born November 28, 1955 in Baton Rouge

a) Erick Clouatre born January 18, 1973

b) Clint Clouatre born January 18, 1973

x. Debra Jean Clouatre born November 24, 1954 in Baton Rouge married August 19, 1972 in St. Louis King of France Church, Baton Rouge Bruce Gerard BLANCHARD (son of Carroll J. Blanchard and Palace Mae GUILFOU) born November 16, 1952 in Donaldsonville

xi. John Michael Clouatre born March 14, 1957 in Baton Rouge; died May 16, 1960 and buried in Roselawn Cemetery, Baton Rouge.

d. Celeste Marie Clouatre born November 28, 1917 in Convent, St. James Parish; died October 21, 1918 and buried in Ascension Cemetery, Donaldsonville

e. Chester Joseph Clouatre born October 22, 1919 in Baton Rouge married October 20, 1946 in St. John Cathedral, Lafayette, Lucille DUHON (daughter of George Paul Duhon and Irma Emily DOUCET) born October 12, 1920. Chester was employed with Pacific Naval Air Base Construction Company and stationed at Midway Island from December 7, 1941 until his return to the United States in March, 1942. He entered the United States Navy on September 12, 1942 and was discharged October 13, 1945 He served in major battles in the Pacific. He is presently employed at Ethyl Corporation since July 12, 1946

i. Lynn Louise Clouatre born November 10, 1961 in Baton Rouge. Adopted, age 3 days.

f. Lloyd Benjamin Clouatre born November 19, 1920 in Baton Rouge; died March 27, 1921 of whooping cough. He is buried in Ascension Cemetery, Donaldsonville

g. Leslie Joseph Clouatre born December 11, 1921 in Baton Rouge married

(1) December 23, 1944 in New Jersey Dorothy Anne WEIST (daughter of

George Weist and Mary GURCHAK)
born December 23, 1924 in
Jersey City, New Jersey

    i. Robert Raymond Clouatre born February 5, 1946
in Baton Rouge

    ii. Vicki Lynn Clouatre born April 20, 1948 in
Jersey City, New Jersey

    iii. Denise Louise Clouatre born November 28, 1953
Married August 12, 1972 in Avenel, New Jersey
Joseph CORIO, Jr. (son of Joseph Corio, Sr.
and Jeanette HENRY) born March 15, 1952 in
New Jersey

    iv. Leslie George Clouatre born July 4, 1955

        (2) Jeanette HENRY (widow of
Joseph Corio)

    v. Brian Clouatre born September 21, 1968 in
Sayreville, New Jersey

Leslie entered the United States Navy on August 11,
1942 from East Baton Rouge Parish and retired
after twenty years service on February 8, 1962.
He is an electrician.

h. Joseph Ivy Clouatre born May 20, 1924 in Baton
Rouge; died August 19, 1924 and buried in Ascension Cemetery, Donaldsonville

i. Calvin Joseph Clouatre born September 16, 1930 in
Baton Rouge married April 14, 1951 in St. Anthony
Church, Baton Rouge Gracie JANNEY (daughter of
Roy Janney and Dina DELATTE) born March 17, 1932.
Calvin served in the United States Army from
February 7, 1951 to February 6, 1954. He is an
electrician and district distributor for AMWAY
Products.

    i. Calvin Joseph Clouatre, Jr. born January 12,
1953 in El Paso, Texas married April 18, 1971
Monica Elaine BURNETT (daughter of James F.
Burnett, Jr. and Mary Lee Merle ABBOTT) born
February 9, 1949 in New Roads, La.

        a) Calvin Joseph Clouatre, III born Decem-
ber 14, 1971 in Baton Rouge

    ii. Dena Ann Clouatre born January 3, 1955 in
Baton Rouge married December 29, 1972 Dennis
Steve BERTHELOT (son of Dennie Paul Berthelot
and Helen Faye WALLACE) born September 22,
1953 in New Orleans

    iii. Christopher (Chris) Clouatre born December 16,
1959 in Baton Rouge

    iv. Danette Clouatre born March 29, 1962 in Baton
Rouge

146

j. Marion Leon Clouatre born December 4, 1933 in
    Baton Rouge married June 4, 1955 in St. Anthony
    Church, Baton Rouge Geraldine Frances HANKS
    (daughter of Alcide Hanks and Laurence MONTE)
    born July 13, 1937 in Lafayette, La.

    i.   Randel Michael Clouatre born August 17, 1957
         in Baton Rouge
    ii. Donna Denise Clouatre born February 2, 1960
         in Baton Rouge
    iii. Diane Clouatre born September 9, 1963 in
         Baton Rouge
    iv. Raymond Clouatre born August 6, 1967 in Baton
         Rouge

    Marion Leon served in the United States Navy from
    July 15, 1953 to August 6, 1956. He is employed
    at Allied Chemical Corporation, Baton Rouge, La.

8. Ferdinand Rodriguez
b.
p.b.
m.
p.m.
d.
p.d.

4. Fernando E. Rodriguez
b.
p.b.
m. 24 November 1817
p.m. Assumption Parish

9. Marie Perera
b.
p.b.
d.
p.d.

2. Mathias Rodrigue
b.   ca. 1828
p.b.
m.
d. June 1912
p.d. Ascension Parish

10. Joseph Gonzales
b.
p.b.
m.
p.m.
d.
p.d.

5. Catalina Gonzales
b.
p.b.
d.
p.d.

11. Catalina Rodriguez
b.
p.b.
d.
p.d.

1 Catherine Rodrigue
b. 25 August 1884
p.b. Ascension Parish
m. 6 April 1904
p.m. Smoke Bend
d. 1 September 1963
p.d. Bur. Plaquemine, La.

12. Mariono Pastor
b.
p.b. Viscoye, Spain
m.
p.m.
d.
p.d.

6. Francisco Pastor
b.
p.b.
m. 12 June 1848
p.m. Ascension Parish
d.
p.d.

13. Francoise Munci
b.
p.b.
d.
p.d.

3. Rosalie Clementine Pastor
b. 16 December 1849
p.b. Ascension Parish
d.
p.d.

14. Antoine Falcon
b.
p.b.
m.
p.m.
d.
p.d.

7. Rosalie Falcon
b.
p.b.
d.
p.d.

15. Marie Dominguez
b.
p.b.
d.
p.d.

Frederick Clouatre
Spouse of #1

3. Frederick (Pete) Clouatre born March 31, 1883 in As-
    cension Parish married April 6, 1904 in St. Francis
    of Assisi Church, Smoke Bend, to Catherine RODRIGUE
    (daughter of Mathias Rodrigue and Rosalie PASTOR)
    born August 25, 1884 in Ascension Parish. Pete died
    February 19, 1967 in White Castle as did Catherine
    on September 1, 1963. Both are buried in Plaquemine.
    Pete was a blacksmith.

CATHERINE RODRIGUE   FREDERICK (PETE) CLOUATRE
    (1884 - 1963)   (1883 - 1967)

a. Evella Clouatre born November 6, 1908 in Ascension
    Parish married Jake C. RODOSTA (son of Anthony C.
    Rodosta and Ursula CALCAGNO) born November 6, 1902
    in Iberville Parish (adopted)

    i. Catherine Lucille Rodosta born June 23, 1930 in
        White Castle married June 10, 1950 in Iberville
        Parish Calvin James BAJON (son of Omer Bajon
        and Maud LE BLANC) born May 30, 1924 in White
        Castle

        a) Calvin James Bajon, Jr. born July 14, 1951
            in White Castle married December 18, 1972
            in Livingston Parish Jerry Valleau HICKEL
            (daughter of Ned Hickel and Geraldine
            LEEBURN) born September 8, 1953 in Baton
            Rouge
        b) Craig Lewis Bajon born December 9, 1953
            in White Castle
        c) Laurie Ann Bajon born April 2, 1955 in
            White Castle
        d) Christine Marie Bajon born July 22, 1956
            in White Castle
        e) Jeffrey Joseph Bajon born September 18,
            1959 in White Castle

    ii. Patricia Ann Rodosta born June 12, 1934 in
        White Castle married December 20, 1953 in
        Iberville Parish Wilmer W. WALKER, Jr. (son
        of Wilmer W. Walker, Sr. and Hilda BARBAY)
        born July 14, 1933 in Iberville Parish

        a) Clint Paul Walker born September 25, 1956
        b) Matt Andrew Walter born November 29, 1959
        c) Richard Tracy Walker born January 2, 1962

            All children were born in White Castle, La.

    iii. Frederick Gerard Rodosta born November 29,
         1940 in White Castle married June 19, 1945 in
         New Orleans Priscilla Ann RAMSEY (daughter of
         Felix Johnson Ramsey and Nell GILBERT) born
         January 27, 1943 in Albany, Georgia

        a) Frederick Gerard Rodosta born April 19,
            1966 in Staten Island, New York
        b) Nicola Genia Rodosta born July 21, 1969
            Staten Island, New York
        c) Ashley Rae Rodosta born March 3, 1972 in
            Opelousas, Louisiana

4. Leonie Clouatre born November 10, 1884 on Souvenir Plantation in Ascension Parish. At the age of 12 she made her home with her mother's sister, Cecile LeBlanc, who married Valentine Landry. From 1930 to 1950 she worked in the Waguespack home in Donaldsonville (until the children of this family were grown). In 1950 she made her home with her sister, Philomine Clouatre, who married Adam Dugas. They live in Baton Rouge.

LEONIE CLOUATRE
(1884 -   )

FOUR GENERATION ANCESTOR CHART

8. Joseph Gonzales
b.
p.b. Tenneriffe, Canary Islan
m. 5 October 1795
p.m. Ascension Parish
d.
p.d.

4. Antoine Gonzales
b. Bt. 20 February 1804
p.b. Donaldsonville, La.
m. 29 June 1840
p.m. Plattenville, La.
d.
p.d. Bur. Donaldsonville

9. Andrea Caballero
b.
p.b. Canary Islands
d.
p.d.

2. Oscar Joseph Gonzales
b. 12 December 1844
p.b. Assumption Parish
m.
p.m. Donaldsonville, La.
d. 22 August 1923
p.d. Bur. Ascension Cemetery

10 Joseph Mathurin Landry
b.
p.b. France
m.
p.m.
d.
p.d.

5. Adelaide Landry
b.
p.b.
d.
p.d. Bur. Ascension Ceme-
tery

11 Marie Callegan
b.
p.b.
d.
p.d.

1. Antoine Joseph Gonzales
b. 5 December 1879
p.b. Donaldsonville
m. 15 April 1903
p.m. Smoke Bend, La.
d. 9 March 1973
p.d. Baton Rouge

12 Sebastien Gomez
b.
p.b.
m. 16 July 1825
p.m. Ascension Parish
d.
p.d.

6. Sebastien Gomez
b.
p.b.
m. 26 May 1845
p.m. Donaldsonville, La.
d. 21 October 1899
p.d. Bur. Donaldsonville

13 Marie Alpine Fernandez
b.
p.b.
d.
p.d.

3. Leonise Josephine Gomez
b. 19 March 1845
p.b. Donaldsonville
d. 26 October 1938
p.d. Bur. Donaldsonville

14 Fernando Rodrigue
b.
p.b.
m. 24 November 1817
p.m. Assumption Parish
d.
p.d.

7. Antonio Rodrigue
b.
p.b.
d.
p.d.

15 Cataline Gonzales
b.
p.b.
d.
p.d.

Jeanne Clouatre
Spouse of #1

5. Jeanne Clouatre born October 20, 1886 in McCall, As-
    cension Parish, Louisiana married April 15, 1903 in
    St. Francis of Assisi Church, Smoke Bend, Louisiana
    Antoine GONZALES (son of Oscar Gonzales and Josephine
    GOMEZ) born December 5, 1879 in Ascension Parish.
    Antoine died March 9, 1973 in Baton Rouge and is
    buried in Ascension Cemetery, Donaldsonville. He was
    a retired sugarcane farmer.

JEANNE CLOUATRE   ANTOINE (SONNY) GONZALES
(1886 -   )   (1879 - 1973)
  ADELLE, UNA, EMMA, EDDIE, LOIS, JEAN, JEANETTE

a. Beatrice Marie Gonzales born November 19, 1905 in Ascension Parish; died August 6, 1927 in New Orleans. Beatrice is buried in Ascension Cemetery, Donaldsonville.
b. Emma Marie Gonzales born November 25, 1907 in Ascension Parish married April 14, 1925 in White Castle to Allen Louis MEDINE, Sr. (son of Severan Joseph Medine and Aurelie HOTARD) born August 25, 1907 in White Castle.

   i. Andrew Graves Medine born June 17, 1926 in White Castle married June 24, 1945 to Jennie MESSINA (daughter of Philip Messina and Mary ROPPOLO) born August 27, 1927 in Iberville Parish.

      a) Andrew Graves Medine, Jr. born June 15, 195C in White Castle married October 25, 1971 in White Castle Myra GAUTREAUX (daughter of Irwin Gautreaux and Ella AMEDEE)

         i) Blake Anthony Medine born 1972

      b) Gesile Medine born January 2, 1956
      c) Grian Philip Medine born August 24, 1958
      d) Kevin John Medine born December 31, 1960
      e) Emma Jean Medine born November 23, 1963

      All children born in White Castle, La.

  ii. Allen Louis Medine, Jr. born September 2, 1929 in Iberville Parish married July 4, 1952 in Ascension Parish Joan BONIN (daughter of Elie Bonin and Eve MEAUX) born December 12, 1932 in Wright, Louisiana

      a) Deborah Ann Medine born February 9, 1953
      b) Linda Anne Medine born June 19, 1954
      c) Allen David Medine born April 22, 1960
      d) Keith Joseph Medine born September 17, 1961
      e) Romona Joan Medine born February 18, 1967
      f) Scott James Medine born February 20, 1968

      All of these children were born in White Castle

 iii. Jerrel G. Medine born March 10, 1931 in White Castle married April 30, 1951 in Plaquemine Helen ALBERT (daughter of George G. Albert, Sr. and Adele BERTRAND) born March 25, 1933 in Plaquemine

      a) Jerrel G. Medine, Jr. born February 26, 1952 in White Castle

b) Sylvia Ann Medine born August 12, 1954
c) Russell Paul Medine born August 10, 1966

iv. Curtis Philip Medine born March 3, 1933 in
     Iberville Parish married June 11, 1960 in
     Avoyelles Parish Patricia Ann LA BORDE (daugh-
     ter of Eddie Paul LaBorde and Ollie Mae
     BOURILLETTE) born November 5, 1940 in Orleans

     a) Kirt Joseph Medine born March 22, 1961
     b) Phil Patrick Medine born March 25, 1965
     c) Chad Michael Medine born June 27, 1967

     All of these children were born in Iber-
     ville Parish

v.   Calvin Anthony Medine born November 12, 1938
     in White Castle married September 29, 1960 in
     Iberville Parish Sandra Ann CALLEGAN (daugh-
     ter of Jeffery Callegan and Camilla SCHAEFER)
     born October 6, 1942 in New Orleans

     a) Calvin Anthony Medine, Jr. born February 25,
         1961 in White Castle, La.
     b) Tommy M. Medine born February 9, 1964 in
         White Castle

vi. Evelyn Ann Medine born November 18, 1941 in
     White Castle married July 30, 1960 in White
     Castle Willie A. COX (son of Brent Cox, Sr.
     of St. James Parish and Euphemie GUIDRY of St.
     Martinville, La.) born July 13, 1940 in St.
     Martinville

     a) Dwayne Anthony Cox born August 24, 1961
         in Pierre Part, Louisiana
     b) Rickey Jude Cox born January 11, 1968 in
         White Castle, La.
     c) Charlene Ann Cox born October 31, 1969 in
         White Castle, La.

vii. Donald Anthony Medine born May 22, 1946 in
     White Castle married June 15, 1964 Kathy Jane
     LIVELY (daughter of Bertrand B. Lively and
     Catherine Ella PLATT) born November 27, 1948
     in Iberville Parish

     a) Pamela Ann Medine born November 21, 1964
         in White Castle, La.
     b) Donald Anthony Medine, Jr. born June 9,
         1966 in White Castle, La.
     c) John Bradley Medine born November 25, 1970
         in Green River, Wyoming

viii. Dianne Medine born October 22, 1948 in White
      Castle married Thomas Edward BOONE (son of

153

Thomas Edward Boon and Theda ATES) born January 27, 1947 in Bogalousa, Louisiana

a) Darren Boone born August 16, 1966 in Napoleonville, La.
b) Shannon Boone born November 5, 1969 in Monroe, La.

ix. Severan Joseph Medine born December 22, 1950 in White Castle married August 21, 1971 in Plaquemine to Marion Ann PENDLETON (daughter of James Church Pendleton and Gloria Beatrice TROSCLAIR) born March 11, 1951 in Shreveport, La.

a) Shawn Elizabeth Medine born November 4, 1972 in Baton Rouge.

Severan is a druggist having obtained his degree from Northeastern Louisiana University in Monroe, La.

SEVERAN JOSEPH MEDINE
(1950 -   )

154

c. Antoine Edward (Eddie) Gonzales born January 21, 1910 in Ascension Parish married January 27, 1949 in Iberville Parish to Elsie MARTOCH.
d. Durwood Paul Gonzales born January 21, 1910; died January 26, 1910 and buried in Ascension Cemetery, Donaldsonville.
e. Adele Cecile Gonzales born November 16, 1915 in Ascension Parish married December 12, 1935 in White Castle to Durward Charles MILEY (son of Charles Durward Miley and Gladys MORALES) born August 11, 1914 in Ascension Parish.

 i. Durward Charles Miley, Jr. born July 29, 1940 in San Francisco, California married

  (1) in San Francisco to Eloise Kathleen ZANONE (daughter of Guido Joseph Zanone and Dorothy COEN)

  a) Denise Loraine Miley born August 16, 1962 in San Francisco
  b) Dawn Marie Miley born February 7, 1965

  (2) November 20, 1971 in Reno, Nevada to Diana DAVIS (daughter of Aubrey Davis, Jr. and Mary J. NEENAN) born August 30, 1942 in San Francisco.

  This was a second marriage for Diana Davis. She was previously married to John Paul GUISTI by whom she had the following children:
  John David Guisti born June 15, 1959
  Michael James Guisti born February 6, 1961

 ii. Anthony James Miley born January 24, 1942 in San Francisco married Patricia Anne SCHMIT (daughter of Francis Edward Schmit and Lola Arlene CAVE) born November 22, 1942 in Rockford, Illinois.

  a) Anne Alicia Miley born March 23, 1966 in Daly City, California
  b) Amy Jeanne Miley born April 15, 1972

f. Una Marie Gonzales born January 1, 1919 in Iberville Parish married October 18, 1938 in Iberville Parish Isaac Joseph DUGAS (son of Simon T. Dugas and Ida Marie LANDRY) born June 31, 1913 in Ascension Parish
g. Paul Gonzales born April 2, 1922 in Iberville Parish; died April 7, 1922 and buried in Ascension Cemetery, Donaldsonville

h. Lois Clotilde Gonzales born April 2, 1922 in Iberville Parish married October 31, 1954 in White Castle John Kenneth SPEEG (son of Philip Speeg and Eunice CHUTZ) born November 18, 1925 in Plaquemine, La.

    i. Lois Ann Speeg born February 1, 1956 in Baton Rouge
    ii. John Kenneth Speeg, Jr. born August 19, 1957
    iii. Terry Lynn Speeg born February 17, 1959
    iv. Gerard Wayne Speeg born May 6, 1964

i. Joseph Gonzales born April 8, 1923 in Iberville Parish; died April 8, 1923 and buried in Ascension Cemetery, Donaldsonville.

j. Jean Theresa Gonzales born March 2, 1924 in Iberville Parish married July 19, 1945 in West Baton Rouge Parish to Eugene Bennett LOAR (son of Edwin Loar and Alice KNIGHT) born July 14, 1922 in Garrison, Pennsylvania

    i. Donna Rae Loar born March 13, 1947 in Pittsburgh, Pennsylvania married August 31, 1968 in South Carolina John Alfred HERNIGAN (son of Robert Hernigan and Clare   ) born September 14, 1946 in Granite City, Illinois. John Alfred served in the Communications branch of the United States Navy

        a) John Alfred Jernigan, Jr. born May 29, 1970 in Bermerhigan, Germany
        b) Scott Michael Hernigan born July 6, 1971 in Bermerhigan, Germany
        c) Stephen Paul Jernigan born July 10, 1972 in National City, California

    ii. Eugene Bennett Loar, Jr. born October 11, 1951 in Plaquemine married March 26, 1971 in East Baton Rouge Cynthia Ann SMITH (daughter of Julian Henry Smith, Jr. and Edna Bell KYLE) born October 6, 1952 in Calcasieu Parish
    iii. Belinda Ann Loar born September 1, 1954 in Plaquemine, La.

k. Jeanette Rita Gonzales born March 2, 1924 in Iberville Parish married February 27, 1946 in Iberville Parish Alex Joseph DUGAS, Jr. (son of Alex Joseph Dugas and Evella RICHARD) born April 22, 1922 in Iberville Parish. Alex died November 13, 1964 and is buried in White Castle, La.

    i. Nancy Marie Dugas born September 27, 1947 in Eagle Lake, Colorado County, Texas married March 29, 1969 in Baton Rouge Frederick Herman KROENKE (son of Frederick Herman Kroenke and

156

Doris BROOKS) born December 29, 1947 in New
Orleans, La.

      a) Jeanne Laurance Kroenke born September 2,
          1971 in Baton Rouge, La.

  ii. Dennis Michael Dugas born November 18, 1949
       in Eagle Lake, Texas
 iii. Julie Ann Dugas born September 14, 1953 in
       White Castle, La.
  iv. Jeanette Rita Dugas born August 7, 1955 in
       White Castle, La.
   v. Alex Joseph Dugas, III born August 5, 1957 in
       New Iberia, La.
  vi. Toni Elizabeth Dugas born January 10, 1960 in
       New Iberia, La.
 vii. Jeff Anthony Dugas born April 6, 1964 in New
       Iberia, La.

6. Anna Clouatre born October 8, 1888 in Ascension Parish;
died at age 10 years and buried in Ascension Cemetery,
Donaldsonville

FOUR GENERATION ANCESTOR CHART

8 Miguel Noel Dugas
b. 25 December 1775
p.b. Ascension Parish
m. 12 February 1798
p.m. Ascension Parish
d. 25 July 1807
p.d. Ascension Parish

4. Pierre Trasimond Dugas
b.
p.b. Ascension Parish
m. 26 June 1837
p.m. Ascension Parish
d.
p.d.

9 Magdelaine Babin
b. Bt. 1 January 1777
p.b. Ascension Parish
d. 22 September 1810
p.d. Ascension Parish

2. Joseph Adam Dugas
b.   1841
p.b. Ascension Parish
m. 28 June 1869
p.m. Ascension Parish
d.   November 1909
p.d.Bur. Donaldsonville, La.

10. Pierre Deneau
b.
p.b.
m.
p.m.
d.
p.d.

5. Melanie Deneau
b.   1822
p.b.
d. 15 April 1895
p.d.

11. Marie Louise Lagrange
b.
p.b.
d.
p.d.

1 Adam Nicholas Dugas
b. 3 February 1888
p.b. Ascension Parish, Brusly McCall
m. 8 May 1912
p.m. Smoke Bend, La.
d.
p.d..

12. Fernando Rodrigue
b.
p.b.
m. 24 November 1817
p.m. Assumption Parish
d.
p.d.

6. Mathias Rodrigue
b.
p.b.
m.
p.m.
d.
p.d.

13. Catharina Gonzales
b.
p.b.
d.
p.d.

3 Azilda Rodrigue
b.   1849
p.b. Ascension Parish
d.   October 1930
p.d. Bur. Ascension

14.
b.
p.b.
m.
p.m.
d.
p.d.

7. Seraphine Falcon
b.
p.b.
d.
p.d.

15.
b.
p.b.
d.
p.d.

Philomene Clouatre
Spouse of #1

7. Philomene Clouatre born January 6, 1892 in Ascension
   Parish married May 8, 1912 in Smoke Bend to Adam
   Nicholas DUGAS (son of Adam Dugas and Azilda RODRIGUE)
   born February 3, 1888 in Ascension Parish. Adam was
   a farmer and retired from the Louisiana State Department of Highways.

<table>
<tr><td colspan="3">PHILOMENE CLOUATRE</td><td colspan="3">ADAM DUGAS</td></tr>
<tr><td colspan="3">(1892 -   )</td><td colspan="3">(1892 -   )</td></tr>
<tr><td>MILDRED</td><td>MELVIN</td><td></td><td>ANNIE</td><td>ALINE</td><td>CLAUDE</td></tr>
</table>

a. Melvin Joseph Dugas born March 18, 1913 in Ascen-
   sion Parish; employed at Exxon of Baton Rouge, La.
b. Annie Philomene Dugas born September 21, 1914 in
   Ascension Parish married December 17, 1938 in
   Baton Rouge Leonard A. TOLOUSSO (son of Marion
   August Tolousso, native of Germany and Minivere
   HORNSBY, native of East Feliciana Parish) born
   June 5, 1913 in New Orleans, La. Leonard died
   February 18, 1971; buried in Roselawn Cemetery

   i. Cheryl Lynn Tolousso born February 7, 1947 in
      Baton Rouge married September 3, 1966 in Baton

158

Rouge Paul Chester SCHOTT (son of Bernard
John Schott and Mary Isabelle RABB) born
July 7, 1946 in New Orleans, La.

   a) Brian Eric Schott born July 2, 1967 in
     Baton Rouge; died July 3, 1967 and buried
     in Roselawn Cemetery, Baton Rouge, La.

  ii. Charlott Ann Tolousso born November 30, 1952
     in Baton Rouge
 iii. Mary Ellen Tolousso born April 4, 1955 in
     Baton Rouge

c. Mildred Marie Dugas born December 2, 1919 in Ascension Parish married May 25, 1940 in Baton Rouge
William Carl RAIFORD (son of Fred Henry Raiford
and Rena BAILEY) Carl died February 16, 1971 and
is buried in Greenoaks Memorial Park. He was employed with the Baton Rouge Fire Department

  i. Sylvia Ann Raiford born April 19, 1943 in
    Baton Rouge married September 7, 1964 in
    Baton Rouge Charles Edward WYBLE (son of
    Joseph William Wyble and Verlia Madeleine
    NOEL) born September 5, 1943 in St. Landry
    Parish. Sylvia Ann died February 10, 1971
    at Oschner Foundation, New Orleans and is
    buried in Greenoaks Memorial Park, Baton Rouge

    a) Penny Gayle Wyble born October 10, 1965 in
      Norfolk, Virginia
    b) Peggy Ann Wyble born November 14, 1966 in
      Thurso, Scotland
    c) Charles Edward Wyble, Jr. born August 7,
      1968 in Baton Rouge, La.

  ii. Margo Raiford born September 21, 1944 in Baton
    Rouge married June 25, 1966 in Baton Rouge
    James Crow MURPHY, III (son of John Barrett
    Murphy, Jr. and Margaret MC KAY) born Au-
    gust 25, 1944 in Baton Rouge

    a) James Crow Murphy, IV born May 21, 1967
      in Baton Rouge

d. Aline Marie Dugas born May 5, 1922 in Ascension
Parish married November 12, 1960 in Baton Rouge
Richard Eugene ELLIS (son of Richard H. Ellis and
Rayma DEMUND) born January 24, 1925 in Phoenix,
Arizona. Richard served in the United States Air
Force from 1950 to 1954.

e. Claude Noel Dugas born December 25, 1926 in Assumption Parish married in Baton Rouge Dorothy Nell
"Sue" ARMSTRONG (daughter of Earl Armstrong and
Vallie Eugenia   ) born July 14, 1930 in Alexandria, La.

    i.   Claudette Marie Dugas born October 26, 1950 in Baton Rouge married August 23, 1969 Maurice WILSON (son of Maurice Wilson, Sr. and Lenora Frances JEROME) born March 23, 1948

        a) Maurice Wilson, III born July 19, 1970 in Baton Rouge, La.

    ii.   Saundra Louise Dugas born June 10, 1952 in Baton Rouge married Michael Don MC ALLISTER (son of O. W. McAllister and Lilly Ruth LEWIS) born August 17, 1954 in Baton Rouge, La.

        a) Scott Michael McAllister born August 21, 1972 in Baton Rouge

   iii. Sheilah Ann Dugas born September 10, 1953 in Baton Rouge, La.

    iv. Claude Noel Dugas, Jr. born August 31, 1954 in Baton Rouge

     v. Ricky Paul Dugas born August 29, 1955 in Baton Rouge

8. Leon June Clouatre born in August, 1904 in Ascension Parish; died September 27, 1910 and buried in Ascension Cemetery, Donaldsonville

LEON (JUNE) CLOUATRE
(1904 - 1910)

FOUR GENERATION ANCESTOR CHART

8. Miguel Noel Dugas
b. 25 December 1775
p.b. Ascension Parish
m. 12 February 1798
p.m. Ascension Parish
d. 25 July 1807
p.d. Ascension Parish

4. Pierre Trasimond Dugas
b.   ca. 1816
p.b. Ascension Parish
m. 26 June 1837
p.m. Ascension Parish
d.
p.d.

9. Magdelaine Babin
b. Bt. 1 January 1777
p.b. Ascension
d. 22 September 1810
p.d. Ascension

2. Pierre Trasimond Dugas, Jr.
b. 27 April 1843
p.b. Brusly McCall, La.
m. 13 January 1866
p.m. Ascension Parish
d.
p.d.

10 Pierre Denoux
b.
p.b.
m.
p.m.
d.
p.d.

5. Melanie Denoux
b.   1822
p.b. Ascension Parish
d.
p.d.

11 Marie Louise Lagrange
b.
p.b.
d.
p.d.

1. Victoria Dugas
b. 7 September 1869
p.b. Brusly McCall, La.
m. 2 October 1885
p.m. Ascension
d. 18 February 1936
p.d. Baton Rouge

12 Pierre Denoux
b.
p.b.
m.
p.m.
d.
p.d.

6. Henry Denoux
b.
p.b.
m. 29 August 1836
p.m. Ascension Parish
d. 26 September 1878
p.d. Ascension Parish

13. Marie Louise Lagrange
b. Bt. 4 June 1775
p.b. St. James Parish
d.
p.d.

3. Felicite Denoux
b.
p.b.
d.
p.d.

14. Ferdinand Capdeville
b.
p.b.
m.
p.m.
d.
p.d.

7. Felicite Capdeville
b.
p.b.
d.
p.d.

15. Elizabeth Melancon
b.
p.b.
d.
p.d.

Telasmar LeBlanc
Spouse of #1

F. Joseph Telasmar LeBlanc born April 1, 1860 in Ascension
    Parish married August 12, 1885 in Ascension Church Vic-
    toria DUGAS (daughter of Trasimond Dugas, Jr. and
    Felicite DENOUX) born September 7, 1869 in Ascension.
    Telasmar died February 10, 1940 in Baton Rouge, La. and
    Victoria died February 18, 1936 in Baton Rouge. Both
    are buried in Ascension Cemetery, Donaldsonville, La.
    Telasmar was a retired cotton and sugar cane farmer.

VICTORIA DUGAS   TELASMAR LE BLANC
(1869 - 1936)   (1860 - 1940)

FOUR GENERATION ANCESTOR CHART

<u>4. Anthony Sanchez</u>
b.
p.b.
m.
p.m.
d.
p.d.

<u>2. James Antoine Sanchez</u>
b.　　　　　ca. 1857
p.b.
m. 11 June 1877
p.m. Donaldsonville, La.
d.
p.d.

<u>5. Elizabeth Mendosa</u>
b.
p.b.
d.
p.d.

<u>1. Omere Sanchez</u>
b. 26 May 1886
p.b.Ascension Parish
m. 30 December 1913
p.m. Smoke Bend, La.
d. 1 September 1961
p.d.Bur. Donaldsonville, La.

<u>6. Raphael Rodrigue</u>
b.
p.b.
m. 7 September 1852
p.m. Ascension Parish
d.
p.d.

<u>3. Euphemie Rodrigue</u>
b.
p.b.
d.
p.d.

<u>7. Mary Gonzales</u>
b.
p.b.
d.
p.d.

<u>Delia LeBlanc</u>
Spouse of #1

<u>8.</u>
b.
p.b.
m.
p.m.
d.
p.d.

<u>9.</u>
b.
p.b.
d.
p.d.

<u>10.</u>
b.
p.b.
m.
p.m.
d.
p.d.

<u>11.</u>
b.
p.b.
d.
p.d.

<u>12. Fernando Rodrigue</u>
b.
p.b.
m. 24 November 1817
p.m. Assumption Parish
d.
p.d.

<u>13. Catharine Gonzales</u>
b.
p.b.
d.
p.d.

<u>14. Joseph Gonzales</u>
b.
p.b.
m.
p.m.
d.
p.d.

<u>15. Isabel Hernandez</u>
b.
p.b.
d.
p.d.

1. Delia LeBlanc born May 4, 1886 in Ascension Parish
    married December 30, 1913 Omere SANCHEZ (son of James
    Antoine Sanchez and Euphemie RODRIGUE) born May 26,
    1886 in Ascension. Omere died September 1, 1961 and
    is buried in Ascension Cemetery, Donaldsonville, La.

DELIA LE BLANC
(1886 -   )

OMERE SANCHEZ
(1886 - 1961)

a. Linas J. Sanchez born June 22, 1915 in Ascension
    Parish married January 2, 1936 in St. Anthony
    Church, Baton Rouge Pearl ALONZO (daughter of
    Edward Alonzo and Marie GOMEZ) born October 6,
    1914 in Ascension Parish. Linas, Sr. was inducted
    in the United States Navy on January 16, 1945 and
    served until March 11, 1946

    i.   Linas J. Sanchez, Jr. born March 11, 1937 in
         Baton Rouge
    ii. Darron J. Sanchez born June 9, 1938 married
         April 19, 1959 in St. Gerard Church, Baton
         Rouge Corine Marie FRYOUX (daughter of Houston
         Joseph Fryoux and Lena DUGAS) born March 22,
         1938 in Iberville Parish

162

> > a) Melanie Ann Sanchez born December 3, 1960 in Baton Rouge
> > b) Darilyn Marie Sanchez born December 30, 1961 in Baton Rouge
> > c) Darron J. Sanchez, Jr. born December 13, 1962 in Baton Rouge
> > d) Daniel Joseph Sanchez born March 23, 1967 in Baton Rouge

> b. Eunice Sanchez born September 2, 1919 in Ascension Parish married May 29, 1949 in White Castle Charles James FAIRCHILD (son of George D. Fairchild and Mable KING) born April 14, 1921 in Iberville Parish

> > i. Charles James Fairchild, Jr. born May 20, 1950 in Baton Rouge
> > ii. Brenda Ann Fairchild born December 7, 1951 in Baton Rouge
> > iii. Denise Sue Fairchild born August 3, 1954 in White Castle

> c. Ulysses Sanchez born June 27, 1921 in Ascension Parish married February 15, 1946 in Mobile, Alabama Lois Elizabeth LOLAND (daughter of Oleme Loland and Louisiane LE BLANC) born July 18, 1923. Ulysses was inducted into the United States Navy from Iberville Parish on May 4, 1940 and was discharged on December 23, 1946. He is now engaged in sugar cane farming. He shared with his brother, Percy, in 1969 the title Farmer of the Year in Assumption Parish

> > i. Rickey Joseph Sanchez born May 23, 1951 in White Castle married February 19, 1972 in St. Elizabeth Church, Paincourtville, Janet Marie LE BLANC (daughter of Mederick LeBlanc and   ) born in Paincourtville, La.
> > ii. Melodie Elizabeth Sanchez born August 23, 1957 in Belle Rose, La.
> > iii. Craig Gerard Sanchez born August 13, 1958 in Belle Rose, La.

> d. Percy J. Sanchez born November 26, 1922 in Ascension Parish married June 1, 1947 in White Castle Doris LAURENT (daughter of Noah Laurent, Sr. and Emily HAYDEL) born June 7, 1924. Percy served in the United States Air Force. He shared with his brother, Ulysses, the title Farmer of the Year in Assumption Parish in 1969

> > i. 'Christine Ann Sanchez born September 17, 1948 in Iberville Parish married June 14, 1967 in Assumption Parish Roy Francis TORRES, Jr. (son of Roy Francis Torres, Sr. and Joyce BLANCHARD) born March 10, 1947 in Assumption

163

　　　　　　a)　Roy Francis Torres, III born January 22,
　　　　　　　　1968 in Assumption Parish
　　　　　　b)　Paige Marie Torres born January 7, 1969
　　　　　　　　in Assumption Parish
　　　ii.　Emily Marie Sanchez born October 2, 1951 in
　　　　　　White Castle married January 15, 1972 in
　　　　　　St. Elizabeth Church, Paincourtville, Lon
　　　　　　MEYER (son of Lee Meyer and Lena POLITZ) born
　　　　　　July 3, 1951 in Assumption Parish
　　iii.　Debra Claire Sanchez born September 29, 1954
　　　iv.　Jennelle Mary Sanchez born July 13, 1958 in
　　　　　　Belle Rose, La.
　　　　v.　Dwayne Gerard Sanchez born January 13, 1963
　　　　　　in Belle Rose, La.

e.　Ruby Sanchez born August 2, 1924 in Ascension
　　Parish married September 30, 1950 in White Castle
　　Haines HALTROP (son of Harry Aries Haltrop and
　　Leda LANDRY) born September 19, 1915 in St. Mary
　　Parish

　　　　i.　Victoria Marie Haltrop born August 15, 1954
　　　　　　in White Castle, La.
　　　ii.　Mary Theresa Haltrop born August 24, 1959 in
　　　　　　White Castle, La.
　　iii.　Harry Adrian Haltrop born April 15, 1963 in
　　　　　　White Castle, La.

f.　Telasmar James (T. J.) Sanchez born October 2,
　　1925 in Ascension Parish married Gloria TULLIER
　　(daughter of　　　　　　　Tullier and Ivy LE JEUNE)
　　born November 24, 1927

　　　　i.　David James Sanchez born March 27, 1950 in
　　　　　　White Castle, La. married January 17, 1970
　　　　　　Marlene AUCOIN
　　　ii.　Marsha Ann Sanchez born June 1, 1952 in
　　　　　　White Castle, La.
　　iii.　Sylvania Marie Sanchez born June 15, 1957 in
　　　　　　White Castle, La.

g.　Elsie Mae Sanchez born February 1, 1928 in As-
　　cension Parish married November 20, 1949 in
　　Iberville Parish Evans J. MADINE, Jr. (son of
　　Evans J. Madine, Sr. and Florence MC CRACKERN)
　　born November 28, 1924 in Iberville Parish

　　　　i.　Evans Joseph Madine, III born January 31,
　　　　　　1952 in White Castle, La.
　　　ii.　Auralie Ann Madine born April 14, 1961 in
　　　　　　Morgan City, La.
　　iii.　Claude Allen Madine born January 28, 1965
　　　　　　in Morgan City, La.

ђ. Fred Joseph Sanchez born March 20, 1930 in Ascension Parish married Roselyn Ann MEDINE (daughter of Evans Joseph Medine, Sr. and Florence MC CRACKERN) born November 6, 1936

    i.   Lisa Ann Sanchez born February 12, 1957 in White Castle, La.
    ii. Fred J. Sanchez, Jr. born August 12, 1959 in White Castle, La.
    iii. Linda Leigh Sanchez born October 4, 1961 in White Castle, La.
    iv. Evans James Sanchez born April 18, 1966 in White Castle, La.

i. Shirley Sanchez born September 29, 1931 in Ascension Parish married Wilfred Joseph FREMIN (son of Ellis Joseph Fremin and Enola Mae CALLEGAN) born November 6, 1922 in White Castle, La.

    i.   Keith Omer Fremin born February 14, 1960 in White Castle, La.
    ii. Mark Ellis Fremin born April 24, 1962 in Morgan City, La.
    iii. Winifred Fremin born December 5, 1965 in Morgan City, La.

j. Delia Ann Sanchez born August 11, 1934 in St. Gabriel married Philip HYMEL, Jr. (son of Philip Hymel, Sr. and Delta LANDRY) born November 21, 1926 in White Castle, La.

    i.   Anita Ann Hymel born March 7, 1960 in White Castle, La.

2. Trasimond LeBlanc born January 29, 1887 in Ascension Parish; died in 1889 at the age of 2

FOUR GENERATION ANCESTOR CHART

```
                                              8.
                                              b.
                                              p.b.
                    4. Anthony Sanchez        m.
                    b.                        p.m.
                    p.b.                      d.
                    m.                        p.d.
                    p.m.
                    d.                        9.
                    p.d.                      b.
                                              p.b.
   2. James Antoine Sanchez                   d.
   b.          ca. 1857                       p.d.
   p.b.
   m.
   p.m.                                       10.
   d.                                         b.
   p.d.                                       p.b.
                                              m.
                    5. Elizabeth Mendosa      p.m.
                    b.                        d.
                    p.b.                      p.d.
                    d.
                    p.d.                      11.
                                              b.
                                              p.b.
                                              d.
  1 Ledonia Sanchez                           p.d.
  b. 26 August 1888
  p.b. Brusly McCall, La.
  m.  9 January 1912                          12. Fernando Rodrigue
  p.m. Smoke Bend, La.                        b.
  d.  4 May 1969                              p.b.
  p.d. Ascension Parish                       m.  24 November 1817
                    6. Raphael Rodrigue       p.m.  Assumption Parish
                    b.                        d.
                    p.b.                      p.d.
                    m.  7 September 1852
                    p.m. Donaldsonville, La.  13. Catharina Gonzales
                    d.                        b.
                    p.d.                      p.b.
                                              d.
   3 Euphemie Rodrigue                        p.d.
   b.
   p.b.
   d.                                         14. Joseph Gonzales
   p.d.                                       b.
                                              p.b.
                                              m.
                    7. Mary Gonzales          p.m.
                    b.                        d.
                    p.b.                      p.d.
                    d.
                    p.d.                      15. Isabel Hernandez
                                              b.
  Joseph George LeBlanc                       p.b.
  Spouse of #1                                d.
                                              p.d.
```

3. Joseph George LeBlanc born October 29, 1888 in Ascension Parish married January 9, 1912 in Smoke Bend, La. Ledonia Blanche SANCHEZ (daughter of James Antoine Sanchez and Euphemie RODRIGUE) born August 26, 1888 in Ascension Parish. Joseph George died December 26, 1945 and Ledonia died May 4, 1969. Both are buried in Ascension Cemetery, Donaldsonville. Joseph George was a sugar cane farmer

xxx

JOSEPH GEORGE LE BLANC
(1888 - 1945)

LEDONIA BLANCHE SANCHEZ
(1888 - 1969)

a. Herbert Lucien LeBlanc born July 7, 1913 in Ascension Parish married Edna Marie MILLET (daughter of Edward J. Millet, Sr. and Oce nie VICKNAIR), born August 15, 1915 in Montz, Louisiana

   i. John Keith LeBlanc born July 10, 1946 in Montz, La. married May 22, 1972 Helen St. Pierre ORY

   ii. Herbert L. LeBlanc, Jr. born October 19, 1949 in Fresno, California

b. Ruby LeBlanc born December 20, 1915; died at the age of 3

166

c. Joseph George LeBlanc born in 1917; died as an infant

d. Wildon P. LeBlanc born November 25, 1919 in Ascension Parish married August 18, 1942 in St. Charles Parish Juanita HALL (daughter of James Weaver Hall and Faye A. NABORS) born May 20, 1923 in Livingston, Louisiana

    i. James W. LeBlanc born June 9, 1944 married Mary Ann ANDERSON (daughter of Alton Anderson and Hazel WEIMER) born November 11, 1946. He presently makes his home in Norco, La.

        a) Michael James LeBlanc born June 3, 1967
        b) Lynn Ann LeBlanc born April 18, 1968

e. William Julius LeBlanc born November 25, 1919 in Ascension Parish married April 8, 1943 in the Chapel of the Four Oaks, Grand Coteau, Louisiana Juanita Elizabeth BROWN (daughter of Robert Peter Brown and Juanita Margaret O'DONNELL) born December 3, 1921 in Algiers, Louisiana

    i. Katherine Anne LeBlanc born June 21, 1945 in San Francisco, California married March 6, 1965 in Sacred Heart Church, Morgan City, La. Melvin Milton BARRIOS (son of Thaddeus Michael Barrios and Hattie Mae MELANCON) born August 17, 1944 in Orange, Texas

        a) Melvin Paul Barrios born February 22, 1966 in Morgan City, La.
        b) Kimberly Anne Barrios born June 15, 1969 in Morgan City, La.

    ii. Mary Elizabeth LeBlanc born March 17, 1947 in New Orleans married June 4, 1972 in Morgan City Ernest Edward OPITZ, III (son of Ernest Edward Opitz, II and Margaret Lee WELCH) born February 23, 1947 in Wisner, Louisiana

f. Calvin A. LeBlanc born September 27, 1924 in Ascension Parish married June 25, 1957 in Bay St. Louis, Mississippi Audrey Evelyn LEE (daughter of Martin E. Lee and Lula Mae MC KINZIE) born May 15, 1935 in Tylertown, Mississippi. Calvin died July 16, 1971 in New Orleans and is buried in Hollywood Cemetery, McComb, Mississippi. He was a steamship captain

    i. Calvin Joseph LeBlanc born February 2, 1958 in New Orleans; died April 14, 1966 and is buried in Hollywood Cemetery, McComb.

    ii. George Anthony LeBlanc born February 11, 1960 in New Orleans, La.

FOUR GENERATION ANCESTOR CHART

```
                                                    8.
                                                    b.
                                                    p.b.
             4. Eugene Loland                       m.
             b.          ca. 1840                   p.m.
             p.b. Ascension Parish                  d.
             m. 11 February 1861                    p.d.
             p.m. Ascension Parish
             d.                                     9.
             p.d.                                   b.
                                                    p.b.
    2. Augustive Loland                             d.
    b.          ca. 1863                             p.d.
    p.b. Ascension Parish
    m. 5 February 1885
    p.m. Ascension Parish
    d.                                              10.
    p.d.                                            b.
                                                    p.b.
             5. Carmelite Falcon                    m.
             b.          ca. 1840                   p.m.
             p.b. Ascension Parish                  d.
             d.                                     p.d.
             p.d.
                                                    11.
                                                    b.
                                                    p.b.
                                                    d.
1. Oleme Loland                                     p.d.
b. 17 December 1890
p.b. Ascension Parish
m. 13 August 1913
p.m. Smoke Bend, La.                                12. Fernando Rodrigue
d.                                                  b.
p.d..                                               p.b.
             6. Mathias Rodrigue                    m. 24 November 1817
             b.                                     p.m. Ascension Parish
             p.b.                                   d.
             m.          ca. 1848                   p.d.
             p.m.
             d.          ca. 1912                   13. Catharina Gonzales
             p.d. Ascension Parish                  b.
    3. Marie Rodrigue                               p.b.
    b.                                              d.
    p.b.                                            p.d.
    d.
    p.d.                                            14.
                                                    b.
                                                    p.b.
             7.1)Seraphine Falcon                   m.
             b.                                     p.m.
             p.b.                                   d.
             d.                                     p.d.
             p.d.
                                                    15.
                                                    b.
Louisiane LeBlanc                                   p.b.
Spouse of #1                                        d.
                                                    p.d.
```

4. Louisiane LeBlanc born April 13, 1895 in Ascension
   Parish married August 13, 1913 to Oleme LOLAND (son
   of Augustive Loland and Marie Aima RODRIGUE) born
   December 17, 1890 in Ascension Parish.

LOUISIANE LE BLANC
(1895 - 1962)

OLEME LOLAND
(1890 -   )

   a. Rena Loland born September 6, 1914 in Ascension
      Parish married November 17, 1937 in Smoke Bend to
      Elie Adam BERGERON (son of Albert Bergeron and
      Aderian WESTERMAN) born June 26, 1913. Elie died
      in a car-truck accident on November 9, 1960 in
      Morgan City. He is buried in St. Stephen's
      Catholic Cemetery, Berwick, La.

168

    i. Carolyn Ann Bergeron born August 24, 1940 in
Berwick, Louisiana married December 29, 1962
to Dale CHAISSON (son of Nolan Chaisson and
Melisa LOUPE) born September 26, 1940 in Morgan City. Carolyn graduated from Dominican
College in New Orleans with a degree in Busi-
ness Administration.

       a) Melisa Marie Chaisson born October 8, 1963
in Morgan City
       b) Dawn Elizabeth Chaisson born August 21,
1966
       c) Gary Michael Chaisson born July 29, 1970

   ii. Larry Edward Bergeron born September 15, 1942
in Berwick married January 23, 1965 in Morgan
City to Mamie Ann SIRACUSA (daughter of Sam
Siracusa and Rose CEFALU) born January 30,
1943 in Morgan City.

       a) Paul Edward Bergeron born April 3, 1966
in Morgan City
       b) Phyllis Bergeron born June 8, 1967
       c) Christopher David Bergeron born July 7,
1968
       d) Elaina Bergeron born August 8, 1969
       e) Mark Jason Bergeron born January 14, 1971

  iii. Elaine Rita Bergeron born September 20, 1945
married August 19, 1967 in St. Bernadette
Church, Bayou Vista, Louisiana to Oscar I.
LANDRY, Jr. (son of Oscar Landry and Dovey
Mae WHITE) born May 25, 1945 in Morgan City.

       a) Boyd James Landry born May 17, 1968 in
Lafayette
       b) Malise Claire Landry born June 4, 1969
       c) Alison Elaine Landry born April 10, 1972

   iv. Carl James Bergeron born August 17, 1951 in
Berwick
    v, Daniel Cornelius Bergeron born May 31, 1954
in Berwick, La.

b. Adele Loland born August 26, 1920 in St. James
Parish married Alcide Joseph ARCENEAUX (son of
Lynn Francis Arceneaux and Amy DELUCKY) born
September 23, 1923 in Morgan City. Alcide or
"Red" as he was called, served in the United State
Coast Guard.

    i. Lynn Ann Arceneaux born June 22, 1950 in Mor-
gan City married August 12, 1972 to Roger
BOUDIN. Lynn graduated from Nichols State
University with a degree in elementary education.

      ii. Ronnie Joseph Arceneaux born September 11, 1952 in Morgan City, La.

     iii. Kathy Marie Arceneaux born July 21, 1954 ,in Morgan City, La.

     iv. Jules Allen Arceneaux born December 25, 1959 in Morgan City, La.

c. Lois Elizabeth Loland born July 17, 1923 in Ascension Parish married February 15, 1946 in Mobile, Alabama Ulyssis Sanchez (son of Omere Sanchez and Delia LE BLANC) born June 27, 1921. Ulyssis served in the United States Navy from May 4, 1940 (inducted from Iberville Parish) to December 23, 1946. He served on foreign soil.

      i. Rickey Joseph Sanchez born May 23, 1951 in White Castle married February 19, 1972 Janet Marie LE BLANC

     ii. Melodie Elizabeth Sanchez born August 23, 1957 in Belle Rose, La.

     iii. Craig Gerald Sanchez born August 13, 1958 in Belle Rose, La.

d. Olda Mae Loland born December 20, 1925 in Ascension Parish married in Smoke Bend, La. Albert DUGAS (son of Simon Dugas and Ida LANDRY) born October 3, 1921 in Iberville Parish

      i. Marlene Ann Dugas born June 28, 1946 in White Castle married February 17, 1968 in White Castle James ROBBINS, Jr. (son of James Robbins, Sr. and Doris MURRY) born June 29, 1946 in White Castle. Marlene graduated from Nichols State University with a degree in lower elementary education. James served in the United States Coast Guard (inducted from Iberville Parish)

          a) Sean Gerard Robbins born December 27, 1968 in Donaldsonville, La.

          b) Rhett James Robbins born June 28, 1972 in Baton Rouge, La.

     ii. Celeste Mary Dugas born November 24, 1952 in White Castle. Celeste finished a course in business administration at a Baton Rouge Trade School

e. Edna Loland born September 17, 1929 in Ascension Parish married Vincent Paul GAUTREAUX (son of Vincent Paul Gautreaux, Sr. and Daisy TEMPLET) born January 2, 1924 in White Castle, La. Vincent served in the United States Air Force (inducted from Iberville Parish) He served in WWII

i.   Bryant Paul Gautreaux born December 22, 1956
     in White Castle, La.
ii. Glen Anthony Gautreaux born January 1, 1962
     in White Castle, La.

FOUR GENERATION ANCESTOR CHART

<u>8.</u>
b.
p.b.
m.
<u>4. Celestine Millet</u>   p.m.
b.   d.
p.b.   p.d.
m.
p.m.   <u>9.</u>
d.   b.
p.d.   p.b.
<u>2. Ulyssis Millet</u>   d.
b.   ca. 1877   p.d.
p.b. St. James, La.
m. 2 July 1901
p.m. St. James, La.   <u>10.</u>
d. March 1939, age 62   b.
p.d. St. James Parish   p.b.
m.
<u>5. Clarice Tassin</u>   p.m.
b.   d.
p.b.   p.d.
d.
p.d.   <u>11.</u>
b.
p.b.
d.
<u>1. Anna Millet</u>   p.d.
b. 2 July 1902
p.b. St. James, La.
m. 3 November 1921   <u>12.</u>
p.m. St. James, La.   b.
d.   p.b.
p.d..   m.
<u>6. Telesphore Simon</u>   p.m.
b.   d.
p.b.   p.d.
m.
p.m.   <u>13.</u>
d.   b.
p.d.   p.b.
d.
<u>3. Adele Simon</u>   p.d.
b.
p.b.
d.   <u>14.</u>
p.d.   b.
p.b.
m.
<u>7. Antoinette Trosler</u>   p.m.
b.   d.
p.b.   p.d.
d.
p.d.   <u>15.</u>
b.
p.b.
<u>Pierre LeBlanc</u>   d.
Spouse of #1   p.d.

5. Pierre Paul LeBlanc born September 26, 1897 in Ascension Parish married November 3, 1921 in St. James, La. Anna MILLET (daughter of Ulyssis Millet and Adele SIMON) born July 2, 1902 in St. James Parish. Pierre died February 14, 1959 and is buried in Ascension Cemetery, Donaldsonville, La.

PIERRE PAUL LE BLANC   ANNA MILLET
(1897 - 1959)   (1902 -   )

   a. Elma LeBlanc born January 21, 1923 on New Hope Plantation married February 23, 1941 in Smoke Bend, La. to Lazard Joseph GUILLOT (son of Michael Guillot and Lydia ALEMAN) born December 19 1920 in Pierre Part, La. Lazard died December 3, 1971 in Norco, La. He was returning from New Orleans and died of a heart attack. He is buried in Baton Rouge

      i. Lazard Joseph Guillot, Jr. born May 9, 1943 in Ascension Parish married September 19, 1964 Gwendolyn JOSEPH (daughter of Douglas Joseph and   ) of Crosby, Mississippi, born November 25, 1945

172

a) Teri Lyn Guillot born June 26, 1965 in
Baton Rouge, La.

ii. Lola Ann Guillot born August 10, 1947 married
Michel Wayne LE BLANC (son of Harry LeBlanc
and Sadie LABICHE) born July 6, 1946 in Thibodaux.

    a) Michael Wayne LeBlanc born November 25,
1966 in Baton Rouge, La.

    b) Connie Lynne LeBlanc born May 12, 1969;
died May 12, 1969 and buried in Roselawn
Cemetery, Baton Rouge

iii. Robert Pierre Guillot born January 12, 1954
in Baton Rouge, La.

iv. Ronald Michael Guillot born January 12, 1954
in Baton Rouge, La.

v. Kenneth Guillot born May 11, 1957 in Baton
Rouge, La.

b. Claude Pierre LeBlanc born June 10, 1925 in Ascension Parish; killed in World War II at the age of 18 on October 13, 1944. He entered the Army in October, 1943. At the time of his death he was stationed in Aachen, Germany. He is buried in Ascension Cemetery, date November 6, 1947

CLAUDE LE BLANC
(1925 - 1944)

c. Lottie Mae LeBlanc born August 14, 1928 on Palo Alto Plantation married September 12, 1948 in St. Francis of Assisi Church, Smoke Bend to Earl Joseph CALLAHAN (son of Philip Pierre Callahan and Clemence THERIOT) born April 23, 1926 in Plaquemine, La. Earl served in the Infantry from January 27, 1944 to September 1, 1945

   i. Cheryl Ann Callahan born November 26, 1949 in Donaldsonville, La.

  ii. Marilyn Anna Callahan born August 6, 1954 in Donaldsonville, La. Marilyn received the

American Legion Award at the Bayou LaFourche
Academy commencement class of 1972

d. Anna Lee LeBlanc born November 8, 1931 in Ascension Parish married April 7, 1951 in St. Francis of Assisi Church, Smoke Bend, La. Maurice A. GAUTREAUX, Sr. (son of Adler Patrick Gautreaux and Rosa Marie SCHEXNAYDER) born February 2, 1928 in St. James Parish. Maurice served in the United States Navy from April 26, 1946 to February 11, 1948

   i. Maurice Anthony Gautreaux, Jr. born October 23, 1953 in Ascension Parish
  ii. Claude Patrick Gautreaux born April 23, 1959 in Ascension Parish
 iii. Monique Angele Gautreaux born December 18, 1968 in Ascension Parish

FOUR GENERATION ANCESTOR CHART

8. Benjamine Desire LeBlanc
b. 14 October 1796
p.b. Ascension Parish
m. 9 June 1817
p.m. Ascension Parish
d. 30 December 1853
p.d. Ascension Parish

4. Joseph LeBlanc
b. 30 March 1818
p.b. Ascension Parish
m. 21 August 1848
p.m. St. James Parish
d. 8 May 1871
p.d. Ascension

9. Marguerite Felonise Dugas
b.
p.b.
d. 10 January 1871
p.d. Ascension Parish

2. Joseph Desire LeBlanc
b. 12 August 1849
p.b. Convent, La.
m. 18 February 1895
p.m. Smoke Bend, La.
d. 1928
p.d.Bur. New Orleans

10 Christophe Webre
b. 24 January 1799
p.b. St. John the Baptist
m. 18 September 1820
p.m. Convent, La.
d. 12 June 1855
p.d. St. James Parish

5. Amelia Webre
b. 12 March 1829
p.b. St. John the Baptist
d. 26 November 1882
p.d. Ascension Parish

11 Felicite Rome
b. 30 January 1804
p.b. St. James Parish
d. 13 November 1832
p.d. St. James Parish

1 Desire LeBlanc
b. 12 September 1895
p.b. Brusly McCall, La.
m. 22 May 1918
p.m. Bay St. Louis, Mississippi
d.
p.d..

12. Manuel Ruiz
b.
p.b.
m.
p.m.
d.
p.d.

6. Antoine Ruiz
b.
p.b.
m. 31 July 1869
p.m. Ascension Parish
d.
p.d.

13. Maria Monson
b.
p.b.
d.
p.d.

3 Jeanette Ruiz
b. ca. 1860
p.b. Ascension Parish
d. ca. 1921
p.d. Ascension Parish

14. Esteve Hernandez
b.
p.b.
m. 7 July 1834
p.m. Ascension Parish
d.
p.d.

7. Antoinette Hernandez
b.
p.b.
d. ca. 1900
p.d. Ascension Parish

15. Rosalie Ramirez
b.
p.b.
d.
p.d.

May LeBlanc
Spouse of #1

6. May LeBlanc born May 9, 1900 in Ascension Parish mar-
    ried May 22, 1918 in Bay St. Louis, Mississippi
    Desire LE BLANC (son of Joseph Desire LeBlanc and
    Jeannette RUIZ). He is a retired farmer from the
    L.S.U. Department of Agriculture. They now make their
    home in the original LeBlanc home built in 1820 in
    Brusly McCall, Louisiana

DESIRE LE BLANC   **MAY LE BLANC**
  (1895 -   )   (1900 -   )

   BETTY   BERNICE   ROMSEY

a. Romsey Joseph LeBlanc born May 5, 1919 in Ascen-
    sion Parish married September 5, 1942 in East
    Baton Rouge to Helen CAMBRE (daughter of Joseph D.
    Cambre and Helen ARCENEAUX) born July 12, 1922 in
    St. Gabriel, La.

    i. Janet Marie LeBlanc born March 16, 1944 in
        Baton Rouge married August 13, 1966 at Christ
        the King Chapel, LSU, to Luther Conley JUBAN,
        Jr. (son of Luther C. Juban, Sr. and Maxine
        PETERS) born April 7, 1943, Baton Rouge, La.

176

        a) Joan Alison Juban born June 8, 1968 in Houston, Texas
        b) Christopher Conley Juban born August 10, 1970 in Baton Rouge, La.

  ii. Randy Joseph LeBlanc born February 7, 1960 in Baton Rouge, La.

b. Bernice LeBlanc born May 17, 1920 in Ascension Parish married November 28, 1945 in East Baton Rouge Leo Leonce GUIDRY, Jr. (son of Leo L. Guidry and Ella Marie ARCENEAUX) born May 17, 1920 in Ascension Parish

  i. Wayne Edward Guidry born August 17, 1947 in Baton Rouge married April 16, 1971 in St. Pius X Church, Baton Rouge, La. Susanne HURST
  ii. Gayle Ann Guidry born April 19, 1959 in Baton Rouge

c. Mary Elizabeth (Betty) LeBlanc born September 13, 1933 in Baton Rouge, La. married November 13, 1955 Achille Paul DENOUX (son of Achille Joseph Denoux and Ella LANOIX) born September 23, 1931 in Ascension Parish

  i. Kelvin Paul Denoux born June 10, 1957
  ii. Rodney Joseph Denoux born March 3, 1959
  iii. Glenn Edward Denoux born January 29, 1962
  iv. Scott David Denoux born August, 1971

FOUR GENERATION ANCESTOR CHART

8.
b.
p.b.
m.
p.m.
d.
p.d.

4. Perique Cavalier
b.
p.b.
m.
p.m.
d.
p.d.

9.
b.
p.b.
d.
p.d.

2. Emmanuel Cavalier
b.   ca. 1879
p.b. Assumption Parish
m. 17 July 1894
p.m. St. Elizabeth Church
d.   ca.1933
p.d. Paincourtville

10.
b.
p.b.
m.
p.m.
d.
p.d.

5. Marie Domingue
b.
p.b.
d.
p.d.

11.
b.
p.b.
d.
p.d.

1. Felicie Cavalier
b. 25 April 1907
p.b. Assumption
m. 19 August 1926
p.m. Assumption
d.
p.d.

12. Henri Smith New Church
b.
p.b. England
m.
p.m.
d.
p.d.

6. Edouard New Church
b.
p.b.
m. 13 April 1869
p.m. Assumption
d.
p.d.

13. Eliza McCloskey
b.
p.b.
d.
p.d.

3. Octavie Newchurch
b.   ca. 1871
p.b. Paincourtville, La.
d. March or April 1951
p.d. Paincourtville

14. Edouard Tomalier
b.
p.b. Family from Canada
m.
p.m.
d.
p.d.

7. Felicie Tomalier
b.
p.b.
d.
p.d.

15. Arthemise Savoie
b.
p.b.
d.
p.d.

Telasmar LeBlanc
Spouse of #1

7. Telasmar LeBlanc, Jr. born June 18, 1903 in Ascension Parish married August 19, 1926 in Assumption Parish Felicie CAVALIER (daughter of Emanuèl Cavalier and Octavie NEWCHURCH) born April 25, 1907 in Assumption Parish. Telasmar is retired from Esso Standard Oil Company and now resides on Grand Bayou Road, Port Allen, La.

FELICIE CAVALIER   TELASMAR LE BLANC
(1907 -   )   (1903 -   )

    a. Clement Anthony (Snookie) LeBlanc born June 28, 1927 in Baton Rouge married April 8, 1946 in Florida Annie Laurie VERBOIS (daughter of Sidney B Verbois and Bessie ASH) born January 1, 1928 in Baton Rouge, La. Clement served in the United States Air Force in WWII

        i. Cheryle Ann LeBlanc born September 14, 1947 in West Palm Beach, Florida married December 6 1969 in Concord, California Ned Lee PRESZLER born December 30, 1939 in Steele, North Dakota

178

a) Tamara Diann Preszler born February 22, 1971 in Walnut Creek, California

    ii. Bonnie Jean LeBlanc born September 15, 1951 in Baton Rouge, La.

  iii. Randall Keith LeBlanc born December 9, 1953 in Baton Rouge, La.

   iv. Kenneth Keen LeBlanc born January 15, 1956 in Baton Rouge, La.

    v. Cynthia Sue LeBlanc born February 14, 1957 in Baton Rouge, La.

b. Lloyd Joseph (Pickey) LeBlanc born February 18, 1928 in Baton Rouge married August 26, 1949 in White Castle, La. Vera Ann VERCHER (daughter of Earl Vercher and Emma GALLION) born October 25, 1932 in Shreveport, La.

    i. David Lynn LeBlanc born May 17, 1950 in White Castle, La. married October 28, 1972 in St. George Church, Baton Rouge, La. to Brenda LANDRY (daughter of Roland Landry and   )

    ii. Darrel Joseph LeBlanc born July 7, 1951 in Baton Rouge, La. married March 17, 1973 in St. Charles Church, Baton Rouge Carolyn Theresa NOTO (daughter of Emile J. Noto and Mary Frances RAGUSA)

  iii. Robbie Ann LeBlanc born November 17, 1957 in Baton Rouge, La. married Michael Wayne MARSHALL (son of James Marshall and   )

    a) Carey Wayne Marshall born January 20, 1973 in Baton Rouge, La.

c. Betty Ruth LeBlanc born January 28, 1930 in Baton Rouge, La. married June 4, 1949 in Baton Rouge Kernan Bernell BALLARD (son of Samuel W. Ballard and Marie SICARD) born November 2, 1931 in Baton Rouge, La.

    i. Brenda Lee Ballard born April 27, 1951 in Baton Rouge married September 19, 1970 in Baton Rouge David Edwin JORDAN, Jr. (son of David E. Jordan, Sr. and Shirley Oneal HINES) born October 10, 1949. David was inducted into the United States Navy on March 20, 1972

    ii. Kernan Bernell Ballard, Jr. born November 16, 1952 in Baton Rouge married December 4, 1971 Sharon HIDALGO (daughter of Kenneth Jude Hidalgo and Althea Helen GEORGE) born August 22, 1952 at Chanute Air Force Base, Illinois. Kernan, Jr. was inducted into the Marines on March 2, 1972

    a) Christine Britney Ballard born November 6, 1972 in Baton Rouge, La.

iii. Debra Ann Ballard born December 31, 1954 in Baton Rouge, La.

d. Larkeal Agatha LeBlanc born February 5, 1934 married Roland Joseph PERAULT (son of Joseph Wallace Perault and Rachall Marie LANGLOIS) born September 11, 1929 in Baton Rouge, La.

  i. Roland Joseph Perault, Jr. born February 20, 1951 in Baton Rouge married September 30, 1972 in St. Joan of Arc Church, Bayou Pigeon, La. Gayle Marie BERTHELOT (daughter of Mc-Curley Joseph Berthelot and Ruby MICHELL) born June 28, 1954 in Plaquemine, La.

  ii. Nancy Marie Perault born June 1, 1952 in Baton Rouge, La. married April 16, 1971 Casey M. SMITH (son of James E. Smith, Jr. and Clara MAHON) born January 31, 1952 in Vivian, Louisiana

    a) Stacey Michelle Smith born November 7, 1971 in Baton Rouge, La.

  iii. Gwendolyn Ann Perault born November 8, 1953 in Baton Rouge, La. married March 25, 1972 in St. Anthony Church, Baton Rouge Edward R. ALTAZIN (son of Edward R. Altazin and Lucille Elizabeth GAUTREAUX) born November 13, 1950 in Baton Rouge

    a) Emanuel Michael Altazin born in October, 1972 in Baton Rouge, La.

  iv. Wanda Ann Perault born January 18, 1956 in Baton Rouge, La. married in 1971 in St. Anthony Church, Baton Rouge Jessie Joseph OUFNAC (son of Johnny Oufnac and Velma OUFNAC) born June 24, 1952 in New Orleans, La.

    a) Sherree Marie Oufnac born May 3, 1972 in Baton Rouge, La.

  v. RexAnn Marie Perault born December 5, 1959 in Baton Rouge, La.

e. Michael LeBlanc born November 20, 1947 in Baton Rouge, La. He died June 22, 1959 of accidental drowning at Thurderbird Beach, Baton Rouge, La. He was 12 years old and is buried in Roselawn Cemetery, Baton Rouge, La.

FOUR GENERATION ANCESTOR CHART

8. Ursin Daigle
b.
p.b.
m.
p.m.
d.
p.d.

4. Elphege Daigle
b. 20 October 1860
p.b. St. Elizabeth Church
m. 10 January 1882
p.m. St. Elizabeth Church
d. 1 March 1899
p.d. Paincourtville

9. Mathilde Therriot
b.
p.b.
d.
p.d.

2. Sidney Daigle
b. 7 October 1886
p.b. Brusly St. Martin, La.
m. 21 January 1909
p.m. St. Elizabeth Church
d. 14 January 1968
p.d. Paincourtville

10 Prudent Landry
b.
p.b.
m. 29 December 1845
p.m. Paincourtville
d.
p.d.

5. Marie Irene Landry
b. 28 November 1864
p.b. Paincourtville, La.
d.
p.d.

11 Josephine LeBlanc
b.
p.b.
d.
p.d.

1 Lonie Daigle
b. 13 August 1913
p.b. Ascension Parish
m. 18 January 1936
p.m. Smoke Bend, La.
d.
p.d.

12 Severin Dugas
b.
p.b.
m. 7 May 1857
p.m. Paincourtville
d.
p.d.

6. Desire Dugas
b.
p.b.
m. 18 May 1887
p.m. Paincourtville, La.
d.
p.d.

13 Lise Daigle
b.
p.b.
d.
p.d.

3. Agnes Dugas
b. 1 March 1889
p.b. Brusly St. Martin, La.
d. 9 October 1958
p.d. Paincourtville

14 Firmin Landry
b.
p.b.
m. 27 October 1863
p.m. Paincourtville
d.
p.d.

7. Ernestine Landry
b.
p.b.
d.
p.d.

15 Augustine Hebert
b.
p.b.
d.
p.d.

Clebert LeBlanc
Spouse of #1

8. *Clebert J. (Diddy) LeBlanc born January 12, 1907 in
    Ascension Parish married

        (1)   Anna Mae FALCON

        (2)   January 18, 1936 in Ascension
              Parish Lonie DAIGLE (daughter
              of Sidney Daigle and Agnes
              DUGAS) born August 6, 1913 in
              Ascension Parish

CLEBERT J. LE BLANC   LONIE DAIGLE
(1906 -   )   (1913 -   )

9. Octave LeBlanc born February 12, 1910; died March 10,
    1910 at the age of 6 weeks.
10. Adam LeBlanc born August 29, 1912; died as an infant

    *Clebert (Diddy) LeBlanc retired in 1972. Upon retire-
ment he was named to the Hall of Fame at the L.S.U.
Animal Farm.

FOUR GENERATION ANCESTOR CHART

8.
b.
p.b.
m.
4.   p.m.
b.   d.
p.b.   p.d.
m.
p.m.   9.
d.   b.
p.d.   p.b.
                                     d.
2. Andre Deocurro   p.d.
b.
p.b.
m.
p.m.   10.
d.   b.
p.d.   p.b.
                                     m.
5.   p.m.
b.   d.
p.b.   p.d.
d.
p.d.   11.
                                     b.
                                     p.b.
                                     d.
1. Carlotta Deocurro   p.d.
b. 4 November 1865
p.b. (at sea)   12.
m. 15 July 1885   b.
p.m. Smoke Bend, La.   p.b.
d. 31 March 1924   m.
p.d. Ascension 6. Francois Deocurro p.m.
               b.   d.
               p.b.   p.d.
               m.
               p.m.   13.
               d.   b.
               p.d.   p.b.
                                     d.
3. Elizabeth Carmelite Deocurro   p.d.
b.
p.b.
d.   14.
p.d.   b.
                                     p.b.
                                     m.
7.   p.m.
b.   d.
p.b.   p.d.
d.
p.d.   15.
                                     b.
Michel Ernest LeBlanc   p.b.
Spouse of #1   d.
                                     p.d.

G. Michel Ernest LeBlanc born February 2, 1863 in Ascension Parish married July 15, 1885 in St. Francis of Assisi Church, Smoke Bend, to Carlotta DEOCURRO (daughter of Andre Deocurro and Carmelite DEOCURRO) born November 4, 1865 at sea. Ernest died October 23, 1945; Carlotta died March 31, 1924. Both are buried in Ascension Cemetery, Donaldsonville, La.

xxx

ERNEST LE BLANC
(1863 - 1945)

CARLOTTA DEOCURRO
(1865 - 1924)

182

FOUR GENERATION ANCESTOR CHART

8. Pierre Oubre
b. 5 September 1772
p.b. St. John the Baptist
m. 7 January 1792
p.m. St. John the Baptist
d. 9 November 1829
p.d. Convent, La.

4. Alphonse Oubre
b.   1811
p.b.
m. 4 May 1837
p.m. Convent, La.
d.
p.d.

9. Felicite Pertuit
b.   1777
p.b.
d. 26 September 1837
p.d. Convent, La.

2. Joseph Florian Oubre
b.   1848
p.b. St. James Parish
m. 4 September 1876
p.m. Convent, La.
d.
p.d.

10. Valentine Gaudin
b.
p.b.
m. 30 December 1816
p.m. Ascension Parish
d.
p.d.

5. Celestine Gaudin
b.   1822
p.b.
d.
p.d.

11. Seraphine Dugas
b.
p.b.
d.
p.d.

1. Maria Louise Oubre
b. 8 December 1888
p.b. St. James Parish
m. 17 January 1910
p.m. Ascension Parish
d.
p.d..

12. Jean Gourdain
b.
p.b.
m.
p.m.
d.
p.d.

6. Jean Arsene Gourdain
b.   1819
p.b.
m. 7 April 1847
p.m. St. James, La.
d.
p.d.

13. Emelie Bergeron
b.
p.b.
d.
p.d.

3. Corinne Gourdain
b.
p.b.
d.
p.d.

14. Pierre Marcell Braud
b.
p.b.
m. 25 May 1818
p.m. St. James Parish
d.
p.d.

7. Matilde Braud
b.   1823
p.b.
d.
p.d.

15. Marie Azelie Bertaud
b.
p.b.
d.
p.d.

Louis Leon LeBlanc
Spouse of #1

1. Louis Leon "Cocoon" LeBlanc born April 11, 1887 in
Ascension Parish married January 17, 1910 in Ascension Church to Maria Louise OUBRE (daughter of
Joseph F. Oubre and Corinne GOURDAIN) born December 8,
1888 in Convent, Louisiana.

xxxxx

MARIA OUBRE   LOUIS   LE BLANC
(1888 -   )   (1887 -   )
              GRACE   CORINNE   DORIS
RICHARD   NED   WILLIAM   PERCY   CLYDE   LOUIS, JR.

   a. Corinne Marguerite LeBlanc born July 20, 1911 in
       Ascension Parish married

              (1) Dr. Tracy Thomas GATELY

       i. Corinne Anne Gately born November 25, 1935 in
           New Orleans married June 9, 1956 to Lee Tal-
           bert FREELAND (son of Nicholas Talbert Free-
           land and Ivna KUNTZ) born August 27, 1933 in
           New Orleans, La.

           a) Kathryn Corinne Freeland born October 11,
               1958 in Anniston, Alabama

183

b) Lynne Tracy Freeland born May 12, 1960 in
Orange, Texas

ii. Caroline Catherine Gately born April 20, 1938
in New Orleans married in New Orleans July 28,
1962 Philip Frances MONTE (son of Philip F.
Monte and Nellie Cornelia LIGHTSEY) born
July 2, 1932 in Atlanta, Georgia

a) Philip Frances Monte, III born August 17,
1963 in New Orleans, La.
b) Tracy Thomas Monte born July 22, 1964 in
New Orleans, La.
c) Caroline Catherine Monte born July 22,
1969 in Atlanta, Georgia

(2) Thomas Reeder SPEDDEN, native
of Cambridge, Maryland

b. Grace Rita LeBlanc born January 8, 1913 in Ascen-
sion Parish married circa 1930 James Joseph TRUX-
ILLO (son of Santiago Truxillo and Corinne
ARCENEAUX) born August 9, 1912. Grace died De-
cember 17, 1970 in Thibodaux and is buried in
Ascension Cemetery, Donaldsonville, La.

i. Grace Cecile Truxillo born October 4, 1931 in
Donaldsonville, La. married June 11, 1955 in
Thibodaux Donald Joseph GARY (son of Randolph
Camille Gary and Maude Lea GAUTREAUX) born
May 27, 1930 in Terrebonne Parish. Donald
served in the Air Force

a) Donna Lea Gary born May 23, 1956 in Houma,
La.
b) Charlotte Lynne Gary born January 4, 1958
in Thibodaux, La.
c) Anne Elizabeth Gary born October 3, 1960
in Houma, La.
d) James Randolph Gary born August 13, 1963
in Houma, La.
e) John Francis Gary born September 24, 1964
in Houma, La.

ii. Jimmie Lou Truxillo born October 30, 1932 in
Donaldsonville, La. married in October, 1954
in Thibodaux, La. Edward Theodore LAMY, Jr.
(son of Edward T. Lamy, Sr. and Vera DAVIS)
born April 13, 1929 in Orleans Parish

a) Cynthia Claire Lamy born July 28, 1955
in Baton Rouge, La.
b) Karen Louise Lamy born September 14, 1956
in Baton Rouge, La.
c) Lisa Maria Lamy born April 15, 1958 in
Baton Rouge, La.

        d) Allyson Frances Lamy born October 3, 1959
            in Baton Rouge, La.
        e) Edward Theodore Lamy, III born Novem-
            ber 25, 1960 in Baton Rouge, La.
        f) Eileen Patricia Lamy born December 3, 1961
            in Baton Rouge, La.
        g) Laura Elizabeth Lamy born December 2, 1964
            in Baton Rouge, La.
        h) James Louis Lamy born January 19, 1968 in
            Baton Rouge, La.
        i) Celeste Marie Lamy born August 20, 1969
            in Baton Rouge, La.

    iii. Roy J. Truxillo born September 8, 1936 in As-
         cension Parish married Esther SIGNORELLI
         (daughter of Joe Signorelli and Rosina GOMILLA)
         born October 18, 1938 in Hammond, Louisiana.
         Roy served in the United States Navy from
         June 11, 1954 to September 3, 1957.

        a) Roy J. Truxillo, Jr. born July 20, 1966
            in Anniston, Alabama
        b) Dawn Marie Truxillo born April 10, 1968
            in Lafayette, Louisiana
        c) Dana Lynn Truxillo born November 17, 1969
            in Hammond, Louisiana

    iv. Maria Ann Truxillo born June 8, 1938 in Donald-
        sonville married August 7, 1965 in Thibodaux,La
        to Roy PROCHASKA (son of Otto Prochaska and
        Bertha GOLDSTEIN) born May 30, 1939 in Pine-
        ville, Louisiana.

        a) Maria Ann Prochaska born May 31, 1966 in
            Baton Rouge, La.
        b) William Ray Prochaska born December 17,
            1967 in Baton Rouge, La.
        c) Kathleen Lynn Prochaska born February 1,
            1969 in Baton Rouge, La.
        d) Michael Lloyd Prochaska born August 13,
            1970 in Baton Rouge, La.

  c. Ned Louis LeBlanc born July 25, 1914 in Ascension
      Parish married September 20, 1933 in St. Anthony
      Church, New Orleans to Alma Mae HICKS (daughter
      of Samuel Thomas Hicks and Pearl HALL) born
      June 3, 1915 in Dallas, Texas.

      i. Easton Thomas LeBlanc born July 7, 1934 in New
          Orleans married October 17, 1959 in New Orleans
          to Helen Enette CLARK (daughter of Charles C.
          Clark, native of Davenport, Iowa and Alma
          Enette KUGLER, native of New Orleans, La.)
          born January 19, 1940 in New Orleans. Easton

served in the United States Army. He is presently Credit Manager at Mintz Furniture Store, Gretna, La.

   a) Clarl Louis LeBlanc born July 22, 1963 in Shreveport, La.
   b) Charne Marie LeBlanc born June 12, 1967 in New Orleans, La.
   c) Craig Peter LeBlanc born July 20, 1971 in New Orleans, La.

ii. Doris Ann LeBlanc born March 12, 1936 in New Orleans, La.
iii. Joyce Marie LeBlanc born May 17, 1937 in New Orleans married January 6, 1954 in St. Joseph Church, New Orleans Jeremiah DUKE (son of John Fulton Duke and Josephine BRUNO) born June 11, 1935 in New Orleans, La.

   a) Jeremiah Duke, Jr. born January 28, 1955 in New Orleans, La.
   b) Fay Marie Duke born May 23, 1956 in New Orleans, La.
twins c) Raymond Edward Duke born May 23, 1956 in New Orleans, La.
   d) Bradley James Duke born August 19, 1957 in New Orleans, La.
   e) Justin Paul Duke born September 7, 1960 in New Orleans, La.
twins f) Randolph John Duke born September 7, 1960 in New Orleans, La.
   g) Vivian Rene Duke born June 21, 1964 in New Orleans, La.
   h) Beth Josephine Duke born December 7, 1967 in New Orleans, La.
   i) Rebecca Ann Duke born January 31, 1970 in Belle Chasse, La.
twins j) Rachelle Angelyn Duke born January 31, 1970 in Belle Chasse, La.

iv. Janice Rita LeBlanc born July 13, 1939 in New Orleans, La. married December 12, 1959 in St. Joseph Church, New Orleans Charles P. STEIBLING (son of Charles P. Steibling and Catherine EGLOFF) born March 31, 1937

   a) Charles P. Steibling, III born August 26, 1960 in New Orleans, La.
   b) Douglas Gerard Steibling born September 10, 1961
   c) Bruce Michael Steibling born May 11, 1963
   d) Easton Gerard Steibling born April 23, 1966

    v. Ned Louis LeBlanc, Jr. born September 15, 1940 in New Orleans, La. married November 22, 1958 in New Orleans Laura Ann ARDOIN (daughter of Wallace Ardoin and Emelda BARTH) born March 14, 1941

       a) Deborah Kay LeBlanc born August 24, 1960 at Fort Huachuca, Arizona

       b) Ned Louis LeBlanc, III born August 4, 1961 in New Orleans, La.

       c) Joan Marie LeBlanc born January 26, 1964 in Ponchatoula, La.

       d) Kenneth Gerard LeBlanc born January 17, 1965 in Ponchatoula, La.

       e) David James LeBlanc born December 16, 1966 in Galliana, Louisiana

    vi. Alma Theresa LeBlanc born January 20, 1942 in New Orleans married February 1, 1962 in New Orleans to Richard John HESSE (son of Roland A. Hesse and Violet LE CROIX) born August 4, 1936

       a) Stanley Gerard Hesse born May 12, 1963

       b) Jill Ann Hesse born September 14, 1964 in New Orleans, La.

       c) David Gerard Hesse born September 14, 1964 New Orleans, La.

       d) Jan Ann Hesse born October 31, 1965 in New Orleans, La.

    vii. Mary Louise LeBlanc born September 16, 1945 in New Orleans married November 30, 1965 in St. Joseph Church, New Orleans Damon Alden DAUSSAT (son of Stirling R. Daussat and Dorothy FELIO) born November 26, 1942

    viii. James Michael LeBlanc born August 18, 1949 in New Orleans married Julie CULLEN

    ix. Barbara Ann LeBlanc born July 27, 1951 in New Orleans married William NORMAND. William is presently in the United States Navy serving in Rota, Spain

    x. Robert James LeBlanc born July 27, 1951

d. Maria Inez LeBlanc born in June, 1916 in Donaldsonville; died at the age of 1 year and buried in Ascension Cemetery, Donaldsonville, La.

e. Clyde LeBlanc born September 24, 1917 in Ascension Parish. Clyde is a Sacred Heart Brother with the religious name Brother Dacian. He is at Brother Martin High School, New Orleans

BROTHER DACIAN LE BLANC
(1917 -   )

f. Richard Joseph LeBlanc born March 10, 1919 in Ascension Parish married Rosemary DUGAS (daughter of Henry A. Dugas and Loretta MONTECINO) born July 12, 1918. Richard graduated from Louisiana State University in 1949 with a degree in Civil Engineering. He served in the United States Army from December 9, 1940 to November 10, 1945. He saw service in the Middle East Theater.

   i. Richard Joseph LeBlanc, Jr. born July 29, 1950 in Baton Rouge
   ii. Linda Claire LeBlanc born February 28, 1953

g. Percy James LeBlanc born October 11, 1920 in Ascension Parish married March 15, 1944 Clarisse

188

Elizabeth RICHARD (daughter of Albert Joseph
Richard and Lillie HEBERT) born March 13, 1919
in Paincourtville, La. Percy served in the Navy
from 1941 to 1945. He served in the South Pacific

  i. Percy James LeBlanc, Jr. born May 18, 1945
      in Assumption Parish married January 31, 1970
      in Baton Rouge Alice MAC MURDO (daughter of
      Charles MacMurdo and Genevieve LEMEE) born
      February 10, 1949 in Baton Rouge. Percy, Jr.
      graduated from Louisiana State University in
      1968 and served in the United States Army
      from January, 1969 to March, 1971
  ii. Clyde Charles LeBlanc born April 7, 1948 in
      Baton Rouge, La.

h. Doris LeBlanc born March 10, 1922 in Donaldson-
    ville married February 17, 1946 in Donaldsonville
    Lloyd Joseph LE BLANC (son of William A. LeBlanc
    and Olivia GREGOIRE) born October 22, 1920 in
    Napoleonville, La. Doris is a nurse.
i. William LeBlanc born April 6, 1924 in Donaldson-
    ville married October 18, 1952 in Our Lady of
    Mercy Church, Baton Rouge, La. Catherine Dorothy
    DUGAS (daughter of Henry M. Dugas and Marie B.
    CABALLERO) born July 14, 1925 in Donaldsonville

  i. Diane Marie LeBlanc born July 17, 1956 in New
      Orleans, La. (adopted)
  ii. Pauletta Marie LeBlanc born October 27, 1958
      in Baton Rouge, La.

j. Louis Gourdain "Boo" LeBlanc born July 3, 1930 in
    Donaldsonville married Virgie Mary BLANCHARD
    (daughter of Hubert M. Blanchard and Elloitte
    BERTHELOT) born January 4, 1932 in Assumption
    Parish

  i.   Michael Louis LeBlanc born December 29, 1955
       in Ascension Parish
  ii. David Mark LeBlanc born July 17, 1958 in
       Donaldsonville, La.
  iii. Lisa Marie LeBlanc born September 21, 1961

FOUR GENERATION ANCESTOR CHART

8 Edouard Bergeron
b.
p.b.
m. 1 September 1834
p.m. Thibodaux
d.
p.d.

4. Emile Bergeron
b. 13 April 1837
p.b. Plattenville, La.
m. 26 November 1868
p.m. Paincourtville, La.
d. 17 January 1899
p.d. Paincourtville, La.

9. Anne Pelagie Boudreaux
b.
p.b.
d.
p.d.

2. George Bergeron
b. 7 February 1874
p.b. Paincourtville, La.
m. 2 January 1894
p.m. Ascension Parish
d.
p.d.

10 Armand Faustino Blanchard
b. 10 March 1814
p.b. Plattenville, La.
m. 26 November 1836
p.m. Plattenville, La.
d. 29 June 1871
p.d. Paincourtville, La.

5. Matilde Blanchard
b. 10 February 1843
p.b. Plattenville, La.
d. 24 November 1933
p.d. Paincourtville, La.

11 Clarice Braud
b. 11 August 1819
p.b. Plattenville, La.
d. 5 September 1858
p.d. Paincourtville, La.

1 Lynda Bergeron
b. 24 October 1894
p.b. Plattenville, La.
m. 11 February 1915
p.m. Smoke Bend, La.
d. 26 September 1930
p.d. Burbank Plantation, Belle Rose, La.

12 J.B. Tertulian Boudreaux
b.
p.b.
m. 13 October 1817
p.m. Plattenville, La.
d.
p.d.

6. Emile Boudreaux
b.
p.b.
m. 23 June 1870
p.m. Labadieville, La.
d.
p.d.

13 Amelie Boudreaux
b.
p.b.
d.
p.d.

3 Agnes Broudreaux
b.   ca. 1875
p.b.
d.
p.d.

14 Neuville Boudreaux
b.
p.b.
m. 6 March 1840
p.m. Thibodaux, La.
d. 8 February 1881
p.d.

7. Emma Boudreaux
b.
p.b.
d.
p.d.

15 Aselie Dugas
b.
p.b.
d.
p.d.

Joseph LeBlanc
Spouse of #1

2. Joseph "T. Joe" LeBlanc born August 23, 1889 in Ascension Parish married February 11, 1915 in St. Francis of Assisi Church, Smoke Bend Lynda BERGERON (daughter of George Bergeron and Agnes BOUDREAUX) born October 24, 1894 in Ascension Parish. Joseph died October 16, 1971 in New Orleans and is buried in Ascension Cemetery, Donaldsonville, La. Lynda died September 26, 1930 in Belle Rose (Assumption Parish), La. and is buried in Ascension Cemetery, Donaldsonville, La. "T. Joe" made his home in New Orleans with his son, Ernest George.

LYNDA BERGERON
(1894 - 1930)

JOSEPH LE BLANC
(1889 - 1971)

JOSEPH LE BLANC AND FAMILY

ELSIE   JOSEPH   MARIE LOUISE   INEZ
   J. P.   SAMUEL   RUTH   ERNEST   GEORGE

    a. Ruth Juliette LeBlanc born January 24, 1916 in
Ascension Parish married Russell BORNE (son of
Albert J. Borne and Georgiana M. SIMONEAUX) born
March 9, 1913 in Paincourtville, La.

       i. Georgina M. Borne born June 30, 1935 in New
Orleans married April 27, 1954 in Tacoma,
Washington to William JOYNE (son of Ernest
Joyne and Minnie HOLBROOK) born January 10,
1932 in Flat Gap, Kentucky.

          a) Sue Ann Joyne born February 6, 1955 in
Tacoma, Washington
          b) Karen Lynn Joyne born April 25, 1957 in
Abilene, Texas
          c) David Ernest Joyne born April 6, 1961 in
Forest Park, Georgia

191

ii. Russell Borne, Jr. born April 29, 1941 in New
Orleans married in New Orleans Eileen MC
CLOSKEY (daughter of Andrew McCloskey and
Gladys HEBERT) born November 8, 1944 in New
Orleans, La.

a) Steven Russell Borne born November 12,
1968 in New Orleans, La.
b) Christian Andrew Borne born July 16, 1970

b. Marie Louise LeBlanc born April 26, 1917 in As-
cension Parish married February 5, 1939 Delnon
Paul TEMPLET (son of Zenon Templet and Adeline
MABILE) born October 2, 1916, Pierre Part, La.
Delnon died May 13, 1963 at age 45 and is buried
in Ascension Parish

i. Delnon Paul Templet, Jr. born January 22, 1940
in Ascension Parish married November 24, 1967
Janice Theresa SIMON (daughter of Henry Paul
Simon and Inez WAGUESPACK) widow of Albert
Joseph CAVALIER who was killed in an automobile
accident on July 14, 1964

Children of previous marriage of Janice Simon:
Jamie Marie Cavalier born May 30, 1963
Johnnie Joseph Cavalier born January 25, 1965

ii. Linda Ann Templet born February 5, 1943 in
Ascension Parish married July 9, 1966 in St.
Paul's Church, Pass Christian, Mississippi
Joseph F. HAYDEN, III (son of Joseph F. Hayden
and Dorothy SMITH) born January 9, 1943 in
Pass Christian, Mississippi

iii. Raymond Templet born June 26, 1946 in Ascension Parish married Margaret Ann HEBERT
(daughter of Robert M. Hebert and Shirley
HARP)

iv. Jeanette Marie Templet born January 7, 1949
in Ascension Parish married John Preston BECK
(son of George Preston Beck and Valerie
DE BESSONET) born September 14, 1948 in Klotz-
ville, Louisiana

a) John Preston Beck, Jr. born April 8, 1967
in Donaldsonville, La.

v. Gayle Ann Templet born January 2, 1955 in Ascension Parish

c. Joseph Pershing "J. P." LeBlanc born September 7,
1918 in Ascension Parish married

(1) Mary Hortense BARBIN

i. Ronald Joseph LeBlanc born October 28, 1939
in Orleans Parish married Mary Ann MOUTON

(daughter of Charles August Mouton and Lucille MEYER) born April 25, 1944 in Orleans Parish, Louisiana

    a)   Suzanne Marie LeBlanc born May 26, 1963 in New Orleans, La.

        (2)   Jeanne Agnes CUTRER (daughter of Simo Cutrera and Lena MANCUSO, natives of Italy) born August 19, 1925 in Plaquemine, La.

ii.   Patricia Ann LeBlanc born June 12, 1946 in Orleans Parish married July 17, 1965 in New Orleans, La. Lawrence Oral WAYNE (son of Lawrence Wayne and Muriel WILSON) born January 16, 1940 in Gassaway, West Virginia

    a)   Gina Maria Wayne born February 21, 1967 in New Orleans, La.
    b)   Lawrence Joseph Wayne born August 30, 1971 in New Orleans, La.

iii.   Charlotte Ann LeBlanc born August 1, 1950 in Orleans Parish

d.   Inez Wallace LeBlanc born January 11, 1920 in Ascension Parish married July 26, 1946 in Ascension Parish Clement Howell LANDRY (son of Levi Esneault Landry and Cloma HENY) born May 21, 1914 in Ascension Parish

   i.   Debra Elizabeth Landry born December 29, 1954 in New Orleans, La.
   ii.   Pamela Landry born July 27, 1956 in New Orleans, La.

e.   Robert Bennett LeBlanc born December 16, 1921 in Ascension Parish married April 10, 1943 in Dallas, Texas Ira Faye REAMES (daughter of Ira Dwight Reames and Della BROCK) born July 26, 1923 in Martens, Texas

   i.   Sharon Leigh LeBlanc born December 31, 1946 in Dallas married Dave Robert DU MINEL
   ii.   Robert Hoyt LeBlanc born May 10, 1951 in Dallas, Texas
   iii.   Michelle Ann LeBlanc born March 14, 1954 in Dallas, Texas·

f.   Samuel Claude LeBlanc married Juliette CASSOU

   i.   Samuel Claude LeBlanc, Jr. born September 13, 1947 in Orleans Parish married September 5, 1969 in St. Gabriel the Archangel Church, New Orleans Margaret Marie JUMONVILLE (daughter

of Harry Nicholas Jumonville and Dorothy
Huberta HUBERT) born May 4, 1947 in New
Orleans, La.

    a) Timothy LeBlanc born April 5, 1972 in New
       Orleans, La.

  ii. Linette Marie LeBlanc born November 30, 1948
      in New Orleans married in New Orleans William
      Sidney COLLINS (son of Robert A. Collins and
      Beverly RICHARD) born December 7, 1949 in New
      Orleans, La.

g. Elsie Mae LeBlanc born June 6, 1924 in Ascension
Parish married February 8, 1948 in New Orleans
Frank CZERNY (son of Frank Charles Czerny and
Louise Caroline LONG) born February 8, 1921 in
Harahan, Louisiana. Frank is a retired Air Force
Lieutenant Colonel

  i. Becky Lee Czerny born February 5, 1950 in New
    Orleans, La. married Robert CANTERBURY (son
    of Vernon Canterbury and Dorothea   )

    a) Jennifer Canterbury born February 6, 1970
       in Quebec, Canada

  ii. Karen Marie Czerny born June 24, 1957 in Mary-
     ville, Tennessee

h. Ernest George LeBlanc born September 4, 1927 in
Ascension Parish married September 23, 1950
Shirley SIMONEAUX (daughter of Ozemie Simoneaux
and Eunice KREIGER) born August 12, 1928 in
Orleans Parish

  i. Sandra Marie LeBlanc born October 31, 1951 in
    New Orleans married February 9, 1971 in Beau-
    mont, Texas Ronald BONNET (son of Louis S.
    Bonnet and Hilda Marie CRUMHORN) born Novem-
    ber 25, 1949 in New Orleans, La.

  ii. Sonya Ann LeBlanc born November 17, 1953 in
    New Orleans, La. married April 19, 1972 in
    Beaumont, Texas Donald Wayne LAWSON (son of
    Bill Lawson and Ruby ATCHLEY) born May 21,
    1952 in Knoxville, Tennessee

iii. Ernest George "Butch" LeBlanc, Jr. born Fe-
    bruary 5, 1957 in New Orleans; died April 5,
    1969 at the age of 12 and is buried in Garden
    of Memories, New Orleans

i. Unnamed boy LeBlanc born March 22, 1930 in Belle
Rose, La.; died at birth

FOUR GENERATION ANCESTOR CHART

8. Francois Carbo
b.
p.b.
m. IO May 1830
p.m. Ascension Parish
d.
p.d.

4. Francisco Carbo
b. 27 July 1835
p.b. Ascension Parish
m. 2 July 1860
p.m. Ascension Parish
d. 5 September 1925
p.d. Ascension Parish

9. Augustina Falcon
b.
p.b.
d.
p.d.

2. Louis Augustin Carbo
b. 25 August 1866
p.b. Ascension Parish
m. 4 June 1891
p.m. Ascension Parish
d. 14 August 1925
p.d. Ascension Parish

10 Antoine Manuel Ruiz
b. Bt. 1804
p.b. Ascension Parish
m.
p.m.
d.
p.d.

5. Maria Ruiz
b. 1840
p.b.
d. 1868
p.d.

11. Marie Monson
b.
p.b.
d.
p.d.

1 Laura Carbo
b. 11 May 1895
p.b. Smoke Bend, La.
m. 1 June 1914
p.m. Smoke Bend, La.
d. 27 November 1971
p.d. Baton Rouge, La.

12.
b.
p.b.
m.
p.m.
d.
p.d.

6. Eugene Loland
b.
p.b. Assumption Parish
m. 12 February 1861
p.m. Ascension Parish
d.
p.d.

13.
b.
p.b.
d.
p.d.

3. Ophelia Loland
b. 8 December 1869
p.b. Ascension Parish
d. 16 May 1955
p.d. Ascension Parish

14 Dominique Falcon
b.
p.b.
m.
p.m.
d.
p.d.

7. Carmelite B. Falcon
b. 20 September 1839
p.b. Ascension Parish
d. 9 January 1888
p.d. Ascension Parish

15. Augustine Carbo
b.
p.b.
d.
p.d.

Andrew LeBlanc
Spouse of #1

3. Andrew (Andra) LeBlanc born July 3, 1889 in Ascension
   Parish married June 1, 1914 in St. Francis of Assisi
   Church, Smoke Bend, La. Laura CARBO (daughter of
   Augustin Carbo and Ophelia LOLAND) born May 11, 1895.
   Andrew died April 22, 1969; Laura died November 27,
   1971 in Baton Rouge, La. Both are buried in Donald-
   sonville, La. Andra was a retired sugar cane farmer.
   Throughout his lifetime he farmed McCall Plantation
   (was overseer at time of retirement)

ANDREW LE BLANC   LAURA CARBO
  (1889 - 1969)   (1895 - 1971)

   a. Harry Andrew LeBlanc born February 22, 1915 in
      Ascension Parish married November 13, 1938 in
      Napoleonville, La. Sadie LA BICHE (daughter of
      Theodule LaBiche and Addie BERGERON) born March 4,
      1920 in Napoleonville, La.

      i. Harry Andrew LeBlanc, Jr. born September 5,
         1939 in Donaldsonville married March 9, 1962
         in Fayetteville, North Caroline Jo Ann COWART
         (daughter of Joseph A. Cowart and Pearl
         BROUSSARD) born March 5, 1942 in Prairieville,
         Louisiana

         a) Jeffrey LeBlanc born June 3, 1964 in
            Baton Rouge, La.

      ii. Beverly Anne LeBlanc born January 24, 1942 in
          Donaldsonville married June 27, 1968 in Baton

195

Rouge to Johnny POLITO (son of Victor Polito
and Josephine CANELLA) born July 26, 1935 in
Cheneyville, Louisiana

a)   Stephen Polito born January 6, 1970 in
     Baton Rouge, La.

LEONARD   ANDREW   RAY   MARJORIE   LESLIE   HARRY   JEANNE

    OPHELIA   LAURA   BETTY   ADELLE

iii. Sandra Ann LeBlanc born August 12, 1943 in
Donaldsonville married November 21, 1970 in
St. Anthony Church, Baton Rouge to Leon James
GRAFFEO (son of Pascal Collin Graffeo and
Nellie LANDRY) born April 27, 1945 in Napo-
leonville, La.

   a) Jaren Pascal Graffeo born August 1, 1971
   in Baton Rouge, La.

iv. Michael Wayne LeBlanc born July 6, 1946 in
Thibodaux married June 11, 1966 in Baton Rouge
to Lola GUILLOT (daughter of Lazard J. Guillot
and Elma LE BLANC) born August 10, 1947 in
Donaldsonville, La.

   a) Michael Wayne LeBlanc, Jr. born November 25,
   1966 in Baton Rouge
   b) Connie Lynn LeBlanc born May 12, 1969;
   died the same day and buried in Resthaven
   Cemetery, Baton Rouge
   c) Brett Paul LeBlanc born June 9, 1972
   in Baton Rouge, La.

v. Gregory Paul LeBlanc born May 16, 1951 in
Thibodaux, La.

vi. Veronica Jan LeBlanc born January 3, 1955 in
Thibodaux, La.

vii. Rhonda Elizabeth LeBlanc born February 1, 1960
in Baton Rouge, La.

b. Laura LeBlanc born May 3, 1916 in Ascension Parish
married January 14, 1942 in Augusta, Georgia to
Samuel Joseph Bergeron (son of Joseph Bergeron and
Corinne TALBOT) born February 4, 1918

   i. Joan Anne Bergeron born May 17, 1944 married
   August 28, 1965 in St. Gerard Church, Baton
   Rouge to John Anthony MILLER (son of William
   Miller and Mary Madeleine LUDEAU) born Au-
   gust 10, 1944

      a) Jina Angele Miller born March 16, 1967 in
      Baton Rouge
      b) Julie Ann Miller born May 27, 1969, Baton Rouge
      c) Jill Andrea Miller born July 8, 1970 in
      Auburn, Alabama

   ii. Samuel Joseph Bergeron, Jr. born April 6, 1946
   married June 10, 1967 in Baton Rouge to Harriet
   HAYNES (daughter of Thomas G. Haynes and Mary
   Louise GORDON) born March 21, 1945 in McComb,
   Mississippi

      a) Emily Bergeron born August 19, 1969 in
      Baton Rouge

iii. Elaine Marie Bergeron born November 13, 1947
      in Baton Rouge married December 29, 1965 in
      St. Gerard Church, Baton Rouge to Frank Edward
      LAMB (son of Harry John Lamb and Marjorie
      FOREMAN) born July 29, 1945

      a) Shannon Laura Lamb born November 25, 1969
          in Baton Rouge
      b) Lance Joseph Lamb born February 16, 1972

iv.   Barbara Jean Bergeron born September 24, 1949
      in Baton Rouge married October 28, 1967 in
      St. Gerard Church, Baton Rouge, La. David
      Eugene GERALD, Jr. (son of David E. Gerald, Sr.
      and Inez Ann MAYEAUX) born December 8, 1947 in
      Baton Rouge, La.

      a) David Eugene Gerald, III born January 2,
          1969 in Baton Rouge

c. Adele Marie LeBlanc born June 17, 1917 in Ascen-
    sion Parish married February 5, 1936 in St. Francis
    of Assisi Church, Smoke Bend to George Gerald
    ZERINGUE (son of Camille Zeringue and Jeanne LAR-
    ROZE) born October 3, 1913 in Vacherie, Louisiana

    i.   George Gerald Zeringue, Jr. born April 14, 193
         in Donaldsonville married February 2, 1963 in
         Our Lady of Prompt Succor Church, White Castle
         to Doris Marie MARTINEZ (daughter of Lawrence
         Martinez and Marie LE GLUE) born April 10,
         1941 in White Castle

         a) Danny Gerald Zeringue born November 9, 196
         b) Ricky Joseph Zeringue born December 24,
             1964
         c) Jeff Zeringue born April 14, 1966
         d) Glenn Paul Zeringue born in 1968

    ii. Mabel Marie Zeringue born November 13, 1938
         in Modeste, Louisiana married September 10,
         1960 in Smoke Bend to Felix F. SAVOY (son of
         Edmond F. Savoy and Bernice LANDRY) born
         November 21, 1937

         a) Charlotte Ann Savoy born September 19,
             1962 in White Castle, La.
         b) Phil Gerard Savoy born August 23, 1963 in
             Baton Rouge, La.
         c) Lynn Francis Savoy born October 13, 1964
             in Baton Rouge, La.
         d) Sherri Marie Savoy born August 12, 1965
             in Baton Rouge, La.

    iii. Jeanette Lucy Zeringue born December 14, 1939
         in Modeste married September 10, 1966 in

St. Francis of Assisi Church, Smoke Bend, La.
Joseph Larry SCHLATRE (son of Norman R.
Schlatre and Mary Maude BOURGOYNE) born
March 2, 1937 in Plaquemine, La.

    a) Joseph Larry Schlatre, Jr. born November 12, 1967 in White Castle, La.
    b) Ted Gerard Schlatre born January 13, 1969 in Baton Rouge, La.
    c) Bart Richard Schlatre born December 13, 1972 in Baton Rouge, La.

  iv. Dale Andrew Zeringue born October 15, 1956 in White Castle, La.

d. Mabel Elizabeth LeBlanc born November 2, 1918 in Ascension Parish; died January 25, 1938 and buried in Ascension Cemetery, Donaldsonville, La.

e. Jeanne Hazel LeBlanc born April 7, 1920 in Ascension Parish married April 25, 1937 Louis Mark ZERINGUE (son of Louis Victor Zeringue and Odelia LARROZE) born October 7, 1914 in St. John the Baptist Parish

  i. Louis Joseph Zeringue born March 29, 1938 in Modeste, Louisiana married January 16, 1960 in Belle Rose to Annette Marie LANDRY (daughter of Lawrence Landry, Sr. and Vivian M. WAGUESPACK)

    a) Maureen Ann Zeringue born March 26, 1961 in White Castle
    b) Alyce Ann Zeringue born March 19, 1963
    c) Liza Marie Zeringue born July 8, 1964
    d) Mark Joseph Zeringue born September 14, 1965
    e) Lynette Marie Zeringue born January 12, 1967

  ii. Lloyd Andrew Zeringue born July 3, 1939 in Modeste, La. married August 22, 1969 Joyce Ann DAVID (daughter of Wilbert Joseph David and Annie Mary JARREAU) born November 30, 1946 in Port Allen, La.

    a) Patti Ann Zeringue born August 1, 1970 in Baton Rouge, La.

  iii. Elsie Ann Zeringue born June 28, 1941 in Modeste, La. married June 19, 1965 in Plaquemine, La. Arthur J. SCHEXNAYDER, Jr. (son of Arthur J. Schexnayder, Sr. and Alice Mary Ann CHAUVIN) born January 14, 1940 in Welcome, La.

    a. Nancy Ann Schexnayder born February 21, 1966 in New Orleans, La.

      b) Beverly Marie Schexnayder born January 27, 1967 in Donaldsonville, La.

      c) Arthur J. Schexnayder, III born January 26, 1968 in Donaldsonville, La.

      d) Mary Alice Schexnayder born October 10, 1970

  iv. Audrey Ann Zeringue born January 31, 1943 in Modeste, La. married May 31, 1963 in St. John the Evangelist Church, Plaquemine, La. Sidney Joseph Schexnayder (son of Lionel Louis Schexnayder and Beatrice Ann LA BICHE) born October 15, 1936 in Welcome, Louisiana

      a) Connie Ann Schexnayder born April 20, 1964 in Donaldsonville, La.

      b) Susan Ann Schexnayder born January 24, 1967 in Donaldsonville, La.

  v. Jane Marie Zeringue born September 24, 1947 in Donaldsonville married January 28, 1967 in Denver, Colorado to Billy Robert WHITE (son of Woodrow White and Alberita CARLIN) born September 7, 1946 in New Iberia, Louisiana

      a) Jason Alan White born August 21, 1967 in Fort Walton, Florida; died the same day when only 5 hours old; buried in Grace Memorial, Plaquemine

      b) Louis Marc White born March 9, 1969 in Fort Walton, Florida

  vi. Ray Paul Zeringue born November 28, 1951 in Donaldsonville, La.

  vii. Kay Anne Zeringue born June 25, 1953 in Donaldsonville, La.

  viii. Patsy Joan Zeringue born January 18, 1956 in Donaldsonville, La.

  ix. Johnny Joseph Zeringue born January 22, 1957 in Donaldsonville, La.

  x. Debbie Anne Zeringue born July 2, 1960 in Donaldsonville, La.

f. Mary Ophelia LeBlanc born January 4, 1922 in Ascension Parish married May 14, 1939 in Smoke Bend to Lloyd Joseph BOUDREAUX (son of Eugene Boudreaux and Marie LANDRY) born April 27, 1921 in Plattenville, La.

  i. Lloyd Joseph Boudreaux, Jr. born June 6, 1940 in Donaldsonville married September 3, 1960 to Louisa Anne LEONARD (daughter of Wilton Paul Leonard and Enola NAQUIN)

           a)   Andrew Paul Boudreaux born September 11,
                1961 in Marrero, Louisiana
           b)   Phyllis Ann Boudreaux born June 20, 1963
                in Port Sulphur, Louisiana
           c)   Bret Joseph Boudreaux born November 9,
                1965 in Port Sulphus, La.

  ii. Jeanne Marie Boudreaux born May 27, 1941 in
      New Orleans married to Kenneth LASYONE of
      Alexandria, La.

           a)   Daniel Ray Lasyone born September 19, 1966
                in Marrero, La.
           b)   Darryl Joseph Lasyone born December 11,
                1968 in Marrero, La.

 iii. Ernest Joseph Boudreaux born January 31, 1943
      in New Orleans married June 1, 1965 in Belle
      Chasse, Louisiana to Karen Theresa LEONARD
      (daughter of Wilton P. Leonard and Enola
      NAQUIN) born July 6, 1941 in Thibodaux, La.

           a)   Theresa Kay Boudreaux born August 26, 1966
                in Marrero, La.
           b)   Lori Ann Boudreaux born in December, 1969
                in Marrero, La.

  iv. Diane Anne Boudreaux born December 2, 1946 in
      Thibodaux married January 30, 1965 in Port
      Sulphur, Louisiana to Richard Allen BARNEY
      (son of Charles V. Barney and Louise Faith
      STEMLER) born October 5, 1943 in Streator,
      Illinois

           a)   Richard Allen Barney born December 12, 1968

   v. Gail Theresa Boudreaux born July 13, 1948 in
      Thibodaux, La.
  vi. Carroll Paul Boudreaux born May 11, 1952 in
      Thibodaux, La. married September 18, 1971 in
      St. Patrick Church, Port Sulphur, La. Patricia
      RICHARD

g. Leslie Joseph LeBlanc born July 1, 1923 in Ascen-
    sion Parish married January 8, 1949 in St. Theresa
    Church, Gonzales, La. Shirley Theresa BRAUD (daugh-
    ter of Edward Ernest Braud and Virginia GAUTREAUX)
    born October 30, 1929 in Gonzales, La.

   i. Leslie Matthew LeBlanc born October 20, 1949
      in Ascension Parish married June 26, 1971 in
      St. Anthony Church, Baton Rouge to Deborah
      Ann DOLHONDE (daughter of Charles S. Dolhonde
      and Willa Frances BREAUX) born December 11,
      1950 in Baton Rouge

a) Willa Rebecca LeBlanc born October 22,
1972 in Baton Rouge, La.

ii. Thomas Marion LeBlanc born October 26, 1950
in Donaldsonville married June 23, 1968 in
Baton Rouge Laura Evelyn WALKER (daughter of
Frank Henry Walker and Gladys Evelyn MULLINS)
born August 19, 1949 in Texarkana, Texas

a) Christopher Thomas LeBlanc born March 4,
1969 in Baton Rouge, La.
b) Shelly Dianna LeBlanc born June 26, 1970
in Baton Rouge, La.

iii. Annette Marie LeBlanc born December 20, 1951
in Donaldsonville
iv. Patrick Joseph LeBlanc born March 18, 1953 in
Baton Rouge married November 13, 1971 in St.
Anthony Church, Baton Rouge Ruby Joette
CRUTCHFIELD (daughter of Roy Lee Crutchfield
and Amelia Mal MANNING) native of Baton
Rouge, La.
v. Ernest Paul LeBlanc born July 27, 1955 in
Baton Rouge, La.
vi. Kenneth James LeBlanc born June 20, 1957
in Baton Rouge, La.
vii. Madeleine Ann LeBlanc born January 27, 1960
in Baton Rouge, La.
viii. Louis Gerald LeBlanc born June 1, 1961 in
Baton Rouge, La.
ix. Catherine Teresa LeBlanc born July 11, 1962
in Baton Rouge, La.
x. Laura Lynne LeBlanc born September 7, 1967
in Baton Rouge, La.

h. Ray Joseph LeBlanc born October 17, 1924 in Ascension Parish married May 16, 1948 in St. Philip
Church, Vacherie, Louisiana Flora Rae GABB
(daughter of Alfred Gabb and Leah THIBODEAUX)
born December 3, 1929 in Vacherie, La.

i. David LeBlanc born April 25, 1949 in Thibodaux, La.
ii. Ray LeBlanc born September 10, 1954 in
Vacherie, La.
iii. Kevin LeBlanc born August 25, 1959 in Donaldsonville, La.

i. Andrew LeBlanc born July 4, 1926 in Ascension
Parish married January 15, 1948 in Ascension
Church, Donaldsonville Virgie TREPAGNIER (daughter
of Charles Trepagnier and Mary FALSETTA) born
October 23, 1929 in Ascension Parish

i. Andrew Charles LeBlanc born December 31, 1948
in White Castle married February 10, 1968 in

203

St. John the Evangelist Church, Plaquemine to
Carol Ann LANDRY (daughter of Ellis J. Landry
and Mabel BOUDREAUX) born May 23, 1949 in
Plaquemine

    a) Drew Anthony LeBlanc born December 31,
       1968 in Baton Rouge
    b) Nicole Carolyn LeBlanc born September 30,
       1970 in Baton Rouge, La.

  ii. Michael Anthony LeBlanc born July 28, 1951 in
White Castle married July 31, 1970 in Donald-
sonville to Diane GANN (daughter of Kenneth
Gann and   )

    a) Mace Anthony LeBlanc born December 20,
       1971 in Baton Rouge

 iii. Stephen Joseph LeBlanc born July 20, 1960 in
White Castle
  iv. Virgie Ann LeBlanc born May 21, 1967 in White
Castle, La.

j. Marjorie Ethel LeBlanc born in 1928 in Ascension
Parish
k. Unnamed son born in 1929 in Ascension Parish
l. Betty June LeBlanc born April 8, 1931 in Ascension Parish married April 5, 1951 in Smoke Bend,
La. Ewell Paul BOURGEOIS (son of Alfred Bourgeois
and Aline LEDET) born February 20, 1931 in Thibodaux, La.

   i. Sharon Ann Bourgeois born January 23, 1952 in
Donaldsonville married June 17, 1972 in St.
George Church, Baton Rouge Dr. Kenneth Comas
GREMILLION (son of Curtis Comas Gremillion
and Irene DUCOTE) born January 12, 1939 in
Moreauville, Avoyelles Parish, Louisiana
  ii. Dennis Paul Bourgeois born November 20, 1953
 iii. Gail Marie Bourgeois born November 21, 1954
  iv. Gary Mark Bourgeois born March 30, 1959 in
Baton Rouge, La.
   v. Randall Ray Bourgeois born March 24, 1961 in
Baton Rouge, La.

m. Leonard Joseph LeBlanc born September 1, 1936 in
Ascension Parish married January 18, 1958 in Wil-
kinson County, Mississippi Betty BRISTER (daughter of Donnie Royce Brister and Lois FARTHING)
born April 13, 1940

   i. Roxanna Marisa LeBlanc born September 11,
1958 in Baton Rouge, La.
  ii. Leonard Joseph LeBlanc, Jr. born August 21,
1959

iii. Donna Michele LeBlanc born June 20, 1962
iv. Bryan Paul LeBlanc born June 23, 1963

4. Adelle LeBlanc born circa 1893; died at age of 3

FOUR GENERATION ANCESTOR CHART

8. Edouard Rodrigue
b.
p.b.
m. 3 November 1818
p.m. St. John the Baptist
d.
p.d.

4. Telesphore Rodrigue
b.   1838
p.b.
m. 24 January 1856
p.m. St. Elizabeth Church
d. 17 February 1918, age 80
p.d. Paincourtville, La.

9. Anastasie Lagulann (Lagemann)
p.b.
d.
p.d.

2. Louis Thomas Rodrigue
b.
p.b.
m. 4 February 1880
p.m. Assumption Parish
d.
p.d.

10 Carville Nicholas Verrett
b. 18 October 1802
p.b. Assumption Parish, La.
m. 3 April 1826
p.m. Assumption Parish
d.
p.d.

5. Claire Verrett
b.   ca. 1840
p.b.
d.
p.d.

11. Azalie Marie Landry
b. 21 December 1808
p.b. Assumption Parish, La.
d.
p.d.

1 Henry Joseph Rodrigue
b. 8 February 1893
p.b. Belle Rose, La.
m. 27 June 1917
p.m. Ascension Parish
d. 5 January 1965
p.d. Ascension

12. Simon Francois Gianelloni
b. 23 June 1786
p.b. Rogliano, Cap Corse, France
m.
p.m.
d.
p.d.

6. Damien Gianelloni
b. 28 October 1824
p.b. Rogliano, Cap Corse
m. 4 April 1850
p.m. St. Elizabeth Church
d. 20 September 1897
p.d. Paincourtville, La.

13. Marie Bonavita
b. 15 March 1795
p.b. Rogliano, Cap Corse, France
d.
p.d.

3 Clara Marie Gianelloni
b. 4 August 1860
p.b. Paincourtville, La.
d. 25 June 1950
p.d. Paincourtville, La.

14. Simon Simoneaux
b. 9 February 1787
p.b.
m. 29 May 1809
p.m. Ascension Parish
d. 15 July 1859
p.d. Paincourtville, La.

7. Adeline Simoneaux
b. 31 December 1830
p.b. Plattenville, La.
d. 17 December 1885
p.d. Paincourtville, La.

15. Marie Reine Landry
b.
p.b.
d.
p.d.

Valerie Justine LeBlanc
Spouse of #1

5. Valerie Justine LeBlanc born December 19, 1894 in Ascension Parish married June 27, 1917 at home by the Catholic priest to Henry J. RODRIGUE (son of Louis Rodrigue and Clara GIANELLONI) born February 8, 1893 in Assumption Parish. Valerie died September 8, 1954; Henry died January 5, 1965. Both are buried in Ascension Cemetery, Donaldsonville, La.

VALERIE LE BLANC
(1894 - 1954)

HENRY RODRIGUE
(1893 - 1965)

a. Henry Joseph Rodrigue born May 1, 1919 in Ascension Parish. Henry is a Sacred Heart Brother with the religious name Brother Gasper. He is now at Vandebilt Catholic High School in Houma, Louisiana. He attended Donaldsonville High School. He entered the order on September 21, 1937 in Metuchen, New Jersey. He holds B. S. degrees in: Education, English, Medicine, and Guidance from Loyola University, New Orleans, Louisiana. He received his Master's degree in 1967 from St. Anicet, in Canada

BROTHER GASPER RODRIGUE
(1919 -   )

b. Ernest Louis Rodrigue born June 15, 1922 in Ascension Parish married January 9, 1944 in Holy Rosary Church, Taft, Louisiana to Roxie VICKNAIR (daughter of Paul Vicknair and Lena HYMEL) born June 18, 1924 in Taft, La.

  i. Ernest Louis Rodrigue, Jr. born September 29, 1946 in New Orleans married May 30, 1970 in St. Agnes Church, New Orleans to Antoinette Denise ENGERAN (daughter of Virgues Antoine Engeran and   ) born June 15, 1948 in New Orleans

c. Marion Carlotta Rodrigue born May 16, 1927 in Assumption Parish married October 25, 1952 in Ascension Parish to Peter Paul MELANCON, Jr. (son of Peter Paul Melancon, Sr. and Ella WELLS) born January 23, 1927 in Baton Rouge

  i. Marsha Ann Melancon born October 12, 1953 in Baton Rouge
  ii. Paul David Melancon born February 10, 1956
  iii. Brian Charles Melancon born November 11, 1958
  iv. Michael Louis Melancon born July 12, 1960

d. Clara Marie Rodrigue born March 27, 1935 married June 27, 1953 in Donaldsonville to Richard MILANO (son of Lorenzo Milano and Phelomine GREGOIRE) born December 23, 1930 in Donaldsonville

  i. Richard Dale Milano born March 1, 1954 in Baton Rouge, La. Died of accidental drown- in in the Comite River, Baton Rouge, La. on May 7, 1973 and buried in Resthaven Garden of Memories
  ii. Jerome Kent Milano born December 6, 1955
  iii. Charlotte Marie Milano born December 8, 1959

e. Louise Anne Rodrigue born July 26, 1937 in Ascension Parish; died September 14, 1950

6. Eursille LeBlanc born circa 1896; died at 2 months

FOUR GENERATION ANCESTOR CHART

8.
b.
p.b.
m.
p.m.
d.
p.d.

4. Ben Friend
b. 20 September 1841
p.b.
m.
p.m.
d. 9 January 1895
p.d.

9.
b.
p.b.
d.
p.d.

2. William B. Friend
b. 24 August 1872
p.b.
m.
p.m.
d. 15 August 1955
p.d.

10.
b.
p.b.
m.
p.m.
d.
p.d.

5. Berenice Burns
b. 2 February 1849
p.b.
d. 19 February 1924
p.d.

11.
b.
p.b.
d.
p.d.

1. Berenice Friend
b. 20 August 1906
p.b. Leesville, La.
m.
p.m.
d.
p.d..

12.
b.
p.b.
m.
p.m.
d.
p.d.

6. Daniel C. Webster
b. 15 February 1862
p.b.
m.
p.m.
d. 16 February 1912
p.d.

13.
b.
p.b.
d.
p.d.

3. Lula Mae Webster
b. 8 May 1888
p.b.
d.
p.d.

14.
b.
p.b.
m.
p.m.
d.
p.d.

7. Rosalie Daffan
b. 29 February 1864
p.b.
d.   1947
p.d.

15.
b.
p.b.
d.
p.d.

Francisco J. LeBlanc
Spouse of #1

7. Francisco J. "Seco" LeBlanc born February 17, 1900 in
   Ascension Parish married Berenice FRIEND (daughter of
   William B. Friend and Lula Mae WEBSTER) born Au-
   gust 20, 1906 in Leesville, Louisiana. Seco died
   March 30, 1968 in Mobile, Alabama and is buried in
   Canton, Mississippi

xxxx

BERENICE FRIEND   FRANCISCO LE BLANC
(1906 -   )   (1900 - 1968)

8. Anne Marie LeBlanc born circa 1902; died at age of
   2 months

FOUR GENERATION ANCESTOR CHART

4. Edgard Paul Drouet
b.
p.b.
m.
p.m.
d.
p.d.

2. Edmond Paul Drouet
b. 15 January 1870
p.b.
m.
p.m.
d. 25 January 1944
p.d.

5. Anai Cagnollatti
b.
p.b.
d.
p.d.

1. Lucie Marie Drouet
b. 20 March 1920
p.b. New Orleans, La.
m. 17 April 1929
p.m. New Orleans, La.
d. 19 August 1958
p.d. New Orleans, La.

6. J. Theophile Trepagnier
b.
p.b.
m.
p.m.
d.
p.d.

3. Lucie J. Trepagnier
b. 13 March 1880
p.b.
d. 28 September 1961
p.d.

7. Alix Thiberville
b.
p.b.
d.
p.d.

Ernest Joseph LeBlanc
Spouse of #1

8.
b.
p.b.
m.
p.m.
d.
p.d.

9.
b.
p.b.
d.
p.d.

10.
b.
p.b.
m.
p.m.
d.
p.d.

11.
b.
p.b.
d.
p.d.

12.
b.
p.b.
m.
p.m.
d.
p.d.

13.
b.
p.b.
d.
p.d.

14.
b.
p.b.
m.
p.m.
d.
p.d.

15.
b.
p.b.
d.
p.d.

9. Ernest Joseph "Nasy" LeBlanc born March 8, 1905 in Ascension Parish married April 17, 1929 in New Orleans to Lucie Marie DROUET (daughter of Edmond Paul Drouet and Lucie J. TREPAGNIER) born March 20, 1905. Ernest died September 26, 1971 and Lucie died August 19, 1958. Both are buried in St. Louis Cemetery, New Orleans, La.

ERNEST LE BLANC   LUCIE DROUET
(1905 - 1971)   (1905 - 1958)

   a.   Phyllis Marie LeBlanc born January 23, 1930 in New Orleans married January 12, 1952 in New Orleans to Denis J. INDUST (son of Robert L. Indust and Laurence M. ROBIN) born October 9, 1929 in New Orleans

       i.   Dennis J. Indust, III born October 24, 1952 in New Orleans
      ii.   Diane M. Indust born February 15, 1954
    iii.   Karen M. Indust born April 12, 1955
     iv.   John F. Indust born August 21, 1957
      v.   Thomas M. Indust born August 25, 1958
     vi.   Jeanne M. Indust born September 7, 1960

```
  vii.  Rachel M. Indust born April 30, 1963
 viii.  Annette Marie Indust born April 19, 1972
   ix.  Stephen Philip Indust born April 19, 1972
```

b. Marillyn Marie LeBlanc born June 26, 1932 in New
    Orleans married November 22, 1952 in New Orleans
    to Austin Joseph SICARD (son of George R. Sicard
    and Hilda DUFFEL) born May 18, 1928 in New Orleans

```
    i.  Austin Joseph Sicard, Jr. born November 27,
        1954 in New Orleans
   ii.  Clyde J. Sicard born May 4, 1956
  iii.  Denise Marie Sicard born December 22, 1958
```

c. Ernest Joseph LeBlanc, Jr. born February 9, 1936
    in New Orleans married July 8, 1957 in New Orleans
    to Mary Ellen GUILLOT (daughter of Harold Guillot
    and Ellen SCIORTINO) born May 3, 1937 in New
    Orleans, La.

```
    i.  Ernest Joseph LeBlanc, III born November 17,
        1959 in New Orleans, La.
   ii.  Harold G. LeBlanc born February 9, 1961 in
        New Orleans, La.
  iii.  Luellen A. LeBlanc born July 22, 1962 in New
        Orleans, La.
```

d. Gayle Marie LeBlanc born January 21, 1940 in New
    Orleans married June 2, 1962 Louis Albert GROSSI-
    MON (son of Peter Louis Grossimon and Rita Mary
    HOERNER) born July 15, 1939 in New Orleans, La.

```
    i.  Louis Albert Grossimon, II born March 31,
        1967 in New Orleans, La.
   ii.  Michael Patrick Grossimon born February 14,
        1969 in New Orleans, La.
```

e. Drouet Edmond LeBlanc born December 20, 1942 in
    New Orleans married February 27, 1965 in New
    Orleans Marion Dianne THOMPSON (daughter of
    Norman Augustin Thompson and Marion Patricia
    MULDRY) born August 5, 1945 in New Orleans

```
    i.  Drouet Edmone LeBlanc, Jr. born August 16,
        1967 in New Orleans, La.
   ii.  Stephen Michael LeBlanc born April 24, 1970
        in New Orleans, La.
```

FOUR GENERATION ANCESTOR CHART

<u>4.</u>
b.
p.b.
m.
p.m.
d.
p.d.

2. <u>William F. Peterson</u>
b.   1891
p.b. New Orleans, La.
m.
p.m.
d.   April 1926
p.d. New Orleans, La.

<u>5.</u>
b.
p.b.
d.
p.d.

1 <u>Doris Mary Peterson</u>
b. 21 January 1917
p.b. New Orleans, La.
m. 26 September 1970
p.m.
d.
p.d..

6. <u>Alfred Pelas</u>
b.
p.b. Buras, La.
m.
p.m.
d.   1919
p.d. New Orleans, La.

3 <u>Rose Pelas</u>
b. 15 March 1895
p.b. Buras, La.
d. 23 January 1926
p.d. New Orleans, La.

<u>7.</u>
b.
p.b.
d.
p.d.

<u>Gabriel Gardes LeBlanc</u>
Spouse of #1

<u>8.</u>
b.
p.b.
m.
p.m.
d.
p.d.

<u>9.</u>
b.
p.b.
d.
p.d.

<u>10.</u>
b.
p.b.
m.
p.m.
d.
p.d.

<u>11.</u>
b.
p.b.
d.
p.d.

<u>12.</u>
b.
p.b.
m.
p.m.
d.
p.d.

<u>13.</u>
b.
p.b.
d.
p.d.

<u>14.</u>
b.
p.b.
m.
p.m.
d.
p.d.

<u>15.</u>
b.
p.b.
d.
p.d.

10. Gabriel Gardes "Gabe" LeBlanc born December 23, 1910
in Ascension Parish married

> (1) July 7, 1936 in New Orleans to
> Ethel COMBAS (daughter of
> Jules E. Combas and Mary E.
> CARSTENS) born October 13, 1910.
> Ethel was killed in an auto-
> mobile accident on June 14,
> 1969. She is buried in St.
> Vincent Cemetery #2 in New Or-
> leans

ETHEL COMBAS   GABRIEL LE BLANC
(1910 - 1969)   (1910 -   )

a. Mary E. LeBlanc born in August, 1938; died May 14,
1939 and buried in New Orleans

> (2) September 26, 1970 in New Or-
> leans to Doris Mary PETERSON
> (daughter of William F. Peter-
> son and Rose PELAS) born Janu-
> ary 21, 1917 in New Orleans

212

GABRIEL   LE BLANC   DORIS   PETERSON
(1910 -   )   (1917 -   )

FOUR GENERATION ANCESTOR CHART

```
                                                    8.
                                                    b.
                                                    p.b.
                                                    m.
                    4. Donat Landry                 p.m.
                    b.                               d.
                    p.b.                             p.d.
                    m.
                    p.m.                             9.
                    d.                               b.
                    p.b.                             p.b.
2. Joseph Valentine Landry                           d.
b. 18 July 1813                                      p.d.
p.b. Plattenville, La.
m. 16 August 1855
p.m. Ascension Parish                               10.
d.                                                  b.
p.d.                                                p.b.
                                                    m.
                    5. Anne Elise Melancon          p.m.
                    b.                               d.
                    p.b.                             p.d.
                    d.
                    p.d.                             11.
                                                    b.
                                                    p.b.
                                                    d.
1. Valentine Landry                                 p.d.
b.  5 September 1856
p.b. Ascension Parish
m. 11 January 1883                                  12.
p.m. Ascension Parish                               b.
d. 19 July 1923                                     p.b.
p.d. Ascension Parish                               m.
                    6. Auguste Hyacinth Landry      p.m.
                    b.                               d.
                    p.b.                             p.d.
                    m.
                    p.m.                             13.
                    d.                               b.
                    p.d.                             p.b.
3. Marguerite Elina Landry                           d.
b.            1837                                   p.d.
p.b.
d.  4 April 1887
p.d.                                                14.
                                                    b.
                                                    p.b.
                                                    m.
                    7. Marguerite Eugenie Babin     p.m.
                    b.                               d.
                    p.b.                             p.d.
                    d.
                    p.d.                             15.
                                                    b.
Christine Amelie (Cecile) LeBlanc                   p.b.
Spouse of #1                                        d.
                                                    p.d.
```

H.. Christine Arselia "Cecile" LeBlanc born January 18, 1865 in Ascension married January 11, 1883 in Ascension Parish to Valentine LANDRY (son of Valentine Landry and Allina LANDRY) born September 5, 1854 in Ascension Parish. Cecile died March 29, 1929 and Valentine died July 11, 1923. Both are buried in Ascension Cemetery, Donaldsonville.

ARSELIA (CECILE) LE BLANC
(1865 - 1929)

VALENTINE LANDRY
(1856 - 1923)

I. Marie Emelia LeBlanc born October 3, 1868 in Ascension Parish; died at the age of 4

J. Benjamin Constant LeBlanc born December 12, 1870; died April 3, 1877

FOUR GENERATION ANCESTOR CHART

```
                                          8.
                                          b.
                                          p.b.
                                          m.
             4.                           p.m.
             b.                           d.
             p.b.                         p.d.
             m.
             p.m.                         9.
             d.                           b.
             p.d.                         p.b.
                                          d.
  2. William Lirette                      p.d.
  b.
  p.b.
  m.
  p.m.                                    10.
  d.                                      b.
  p.d.                                    p.b.
                                          m.
             5.                           p.m.
             b.                           d.
             p.b.                         p.d.
             d.
             p.d.                         11.
                                          b.
                                          p.b.
                                          d.
  1. Ernestine Lirette                    p.d.
  b. 3 October 1880
  p.b. Ascension Parish
  m. 27 January 1903
  p.m. Smoke Bend, La.                    12.
  d. 24 June 1938                         b.
  p.d. Ascension Parish                   p.b.
             6. Jean Marie Richard        m.
             b.                           p.m.
             p.b.                         d.
             m.                           p.d.
             p.m.
             d.                           13.
             p.d.                         b.
                                          p.b.
  3. Anastasia (Octavie) Richard          d.
  b.                                      p.d.
  p.b.
  d.
  p.d.                                    14.
                                          b.
                                          p.b.
                                          m.
             7.                           p.m.
             b.                           d.
             p.b.                         p.d.
             d.
             p.d.                         15.
                                          b.
                                          p.b.
  Joseph LeBlanc                          d.
  Spouse of #1                            p.d.
```

K. Joseph LeBlanc born April 3, 1872 in Ascension Parish
    married January 27, 1903 in St. Francis of Assisi Church,
    Smoke Bend, La. Ernestine LIRETTE (daughter of William
    Lirette and Anastasie RICHARD) born October 3, 1880 in
    Ascension Parish. Ernestine died June 24, 1938 and
    Joseph died January 26, 1967. Both are buried in Ascension Cemetery, Donaldsonville, La.

JOSEPH LE BLANC
(1872 - 1967)

ERNESTINE LIRETTE
(1880 - 1938)

FOUR GENERATION ANCESTOR CHART

8.
b.
p.b.
m.
p.m.
d.
p.d.

4. Ferdinand Collet
b.   ca. 1820
p.b.
m.   ca. 1848
p.m.
d.
p.d.

9.
b.
p.b.
d.
p.d.

2. Andrea Ferdinand Collet
b. 4 February 1854
p.b. Ascension Parish
m. 19 April 1881
p.m. Ascension Parish
d. 29 November 1926
p.d. Donaldsonville, La.

10. Valery LeBlanc
b.
p.b.
m.   ca. 1815
p.m.
d.
p.d.

5. Amalie LeBlanc
b. 27 July 1822
p.b. Ascension Parish
d.
p.d.

11. Euphrosine Dineau
b.
p.b.
d.
p.d.

1. Rene Collet
b. 21 August 1899
p.b. Ascension Parish
m.
p.m.
d.
p.d..

12. August Hyacinth Landry
b.
p.b.
m.   ca. 1820
p.m.
d.
p.d.

6. Leon U. Landry
b.
p.b.
m. 17 January 1853
p.m. Ascension Parish
d.
p.d.

13. Marguerite Eugenie Babin
b.
p.b.
d.
p.d.

3. Marie Ozilphie Landry
b.   1863
p.b.
d.   June 1936
p.d. Donaldsonville, La.

14. Simonet Landry
b.
p.b.
m.
p.m.
d.
p.d.

7. Advelina Landry
b.
p.b.
d.
p.d.

15. Bethilde Landry
b.
p.b.
d.
p.d.

Leonore Amelia LeBlanc
Spouse of #1

1. Leonore Amelia LeBlanc born November 3, 1903 in Ascension Parish married Rene Jean COLLET (son of Andrea Ferdinand Collet and Marie Olzelphia LANDRY) born August 21, 1899 in Ascension. Leonore died June 21, 1968 and is buried in Baton Rouge, La.

RENE COLLET   LEONORE LE BLANC
(1899 -   )   (1903 - 1968)

   a. Rene Jean Collet, Jr. born October 4, 1936 in Baton Rouge married November 23, 1967 in St. Gerard Church, Baton Rouge Mary Ione BURAS (daughter of Wardell P. Buras of Plaquemine, La. and

and Mabel Marie PERERES of Pierre Part, La.) born
May 6, 1939 in New Orleans

    ·i. Leonore Marie Collet born March 5, 1969 in
        Baton Rouge, La.
   ii. Kimberly Renee Collet born April 25, 1970 in
        Baton Rouge, La.
  iii. Beverly Alice Collet born November 3, 1972
        in Baton Rouge, La.

2. Sidney Paul LeBlanc born March 15, 1905 in Ascension
Parish. Sidney lives on the site of their old family
home on the river road near Smoke Bend, Louisiana.

xxx

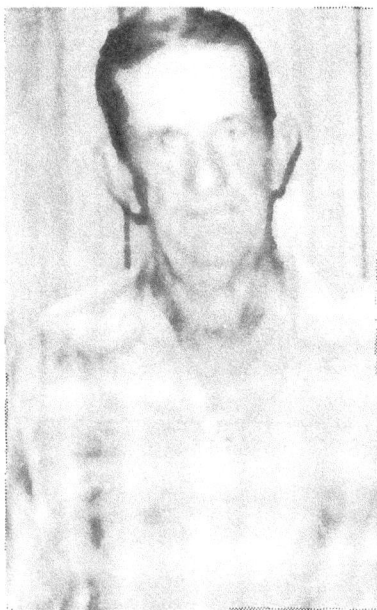

SIDNEY LE BLANC
(1905 –   )

3. Louis LeBlanc born September 3, 1907 in Ascension
Parish; died at age of 6 weeks

217

4. Louise Cecile LeBlanc born September 3, 1907 in Ascen
    sion Parish. She resides with her two brothers,
    Sidney and Paul Daniel

LOUISE LE BLANC
(1907 -   )

5. Margaret LeBlanc born in June, 1906; died as an infar

FOUR GENERATION ANCESTOR CHART

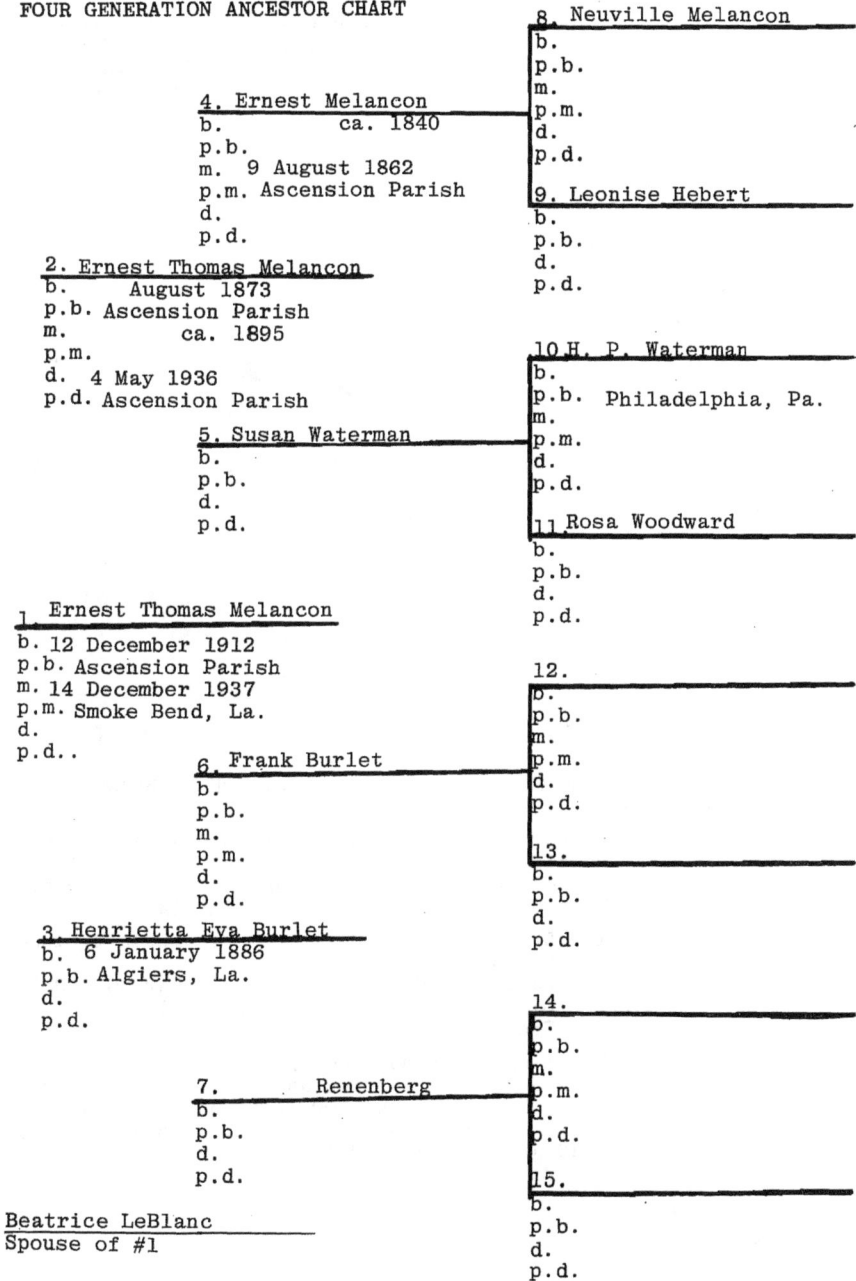

8. Neuville Melancon
b.
p.b.
m.
p.m.
d.
p.d.

4. Ernest Melancon
b.   ca. 1840
p.b.
m. 9 August 1862
p.m. Ascension Parish
d.
p.d.

9. Leonise Hebert
b.
p.b.
d.
p.d.

2. Ernest Thomas Melancon
b.   August 1873
p.b. Ascension Parish
m.   ca. 1895
p.m.
d. 4 May 1936
p.d. Ascension Parish

10 H. P. Waterman
b.
p.b. Philadelphia, Pa.
m.
p.m.
d.
p.d.

5. Susan Waterman
b.
p.b.
d.
p.d.

11 Rosa Woodward
b.
p.b.
d.
p.d.

1 Ernest Thomas Melancon
b. 12 December 1912
p.b. Ascension Parish
m. 14 December 1937
p.m. Smoke Bend, La.
d.
p.d..

12.
b.
p.b.
m.
p.m.
d.
p.d.

6. Frank Burlet
b.
p.b.
m.
p.m.
d.
p.d.

13.
b.
p.b.
d.
p.d.

3 Henrietta Eva Burlet
b. 6 January 1886
p.b. Algiers, La.
d.
p.d.

14.
b.
p.b.
m.
p.m.
d.
p.d.

7.   Renenberg
b.
p.b.
d.
p.d.

15.
b.
p.b.
d.
p.d.

Beatrice LeBlanc
Spouse of #1

6. Beatrice LeBlanc born April 6, 1909 in St. James Parish married December 14, 1936 in Smoke Bend to Ernest Thomas MELANCON, Jr. (son of Ernest T. Melancon and Eva BARLETT) born December 12, 1912 in Ascension

ERNEST MELANCON   BEATRICE LE BLANC
(1912 -   )   (1909 -   )

   a. Ernest Thomas Melancon, III born June 20, 1938 in Donaldsonville married Shirley LATIOLAIS (daughter of Antoine Latiolais and Brigett LATIOLAIS) born October 12, 1939 in St. Martin Parish

      i. Ernest Timothy Melancon born March 2, 1956 in Baton Rouge
     ii. Paula Gay Melancon born December 30, 1958
    iii. Lisa Fay Melancon born August 18, 1960
     iv. Tracey Lynn Melancon born July 2, 1964

   b. Kenneth Joseph Melancon born January 30, 1940 in Donaldsonville married July 20, 1963 in Donaldsonville to Dorothy RODRIGUE (daughter of Comey Rodrigue and Priscilla MABILE) born January 7, 1946 in Ascension Parish

219

  i. Laurie Jean Melancon born June 30, 1965 in
    Baton Rouge
  ii. Kenneth Joseph Melancon, Jr. born August 11,
    1970

 c. Larry John Melancon born January 17, 1941 in
   Donaldsonville married December 28, 1963 in Sacred
   Heart Church, Norco, Louisiana Linda Agnes
   RACHELLE (daughter of George Rachelle and Linda
   BUJOL) born June 27, 1938 in St. Charles Parish

  i. Stacy Ann Melancon born January 19, 1970 in
    Baton Rouge, La.
  ii. Renee Michelle Melancon born September 12,
    1971

 d. Margaret Ann Melancon born April 1, 1945 in Baton
   Rouge married James Earl ADAMS, Jr. (son of James
   E. Adams and Irma COOPER) born February 29, 1940
   in Baton Rouge. James was inducted into the
   United States Navy in 1958 and is still in service

  i. James Ernest Adams born September 7, 1963 in
    Baton Rouge, La.
  ii. Christina Irma Adams born February 14, 1966
    in Panama City, Florida
 iii. Melissa Ann Adams born July 12, 1968 in
    Virginia Beach, Virginia

7. Paul Daniel LeBlanc born July 30, 1910 in Ascension Parish. Paul was inducted into the United States Army on September 21, 1943 and was discharged December 22, 1945. He served in France, Belgium and Germany. Paul resides with his brother and sister, Sidney and Louise

PAUL LE BLANC
(1910 -   )

FOUR GENERATION ANCESTOR CHART

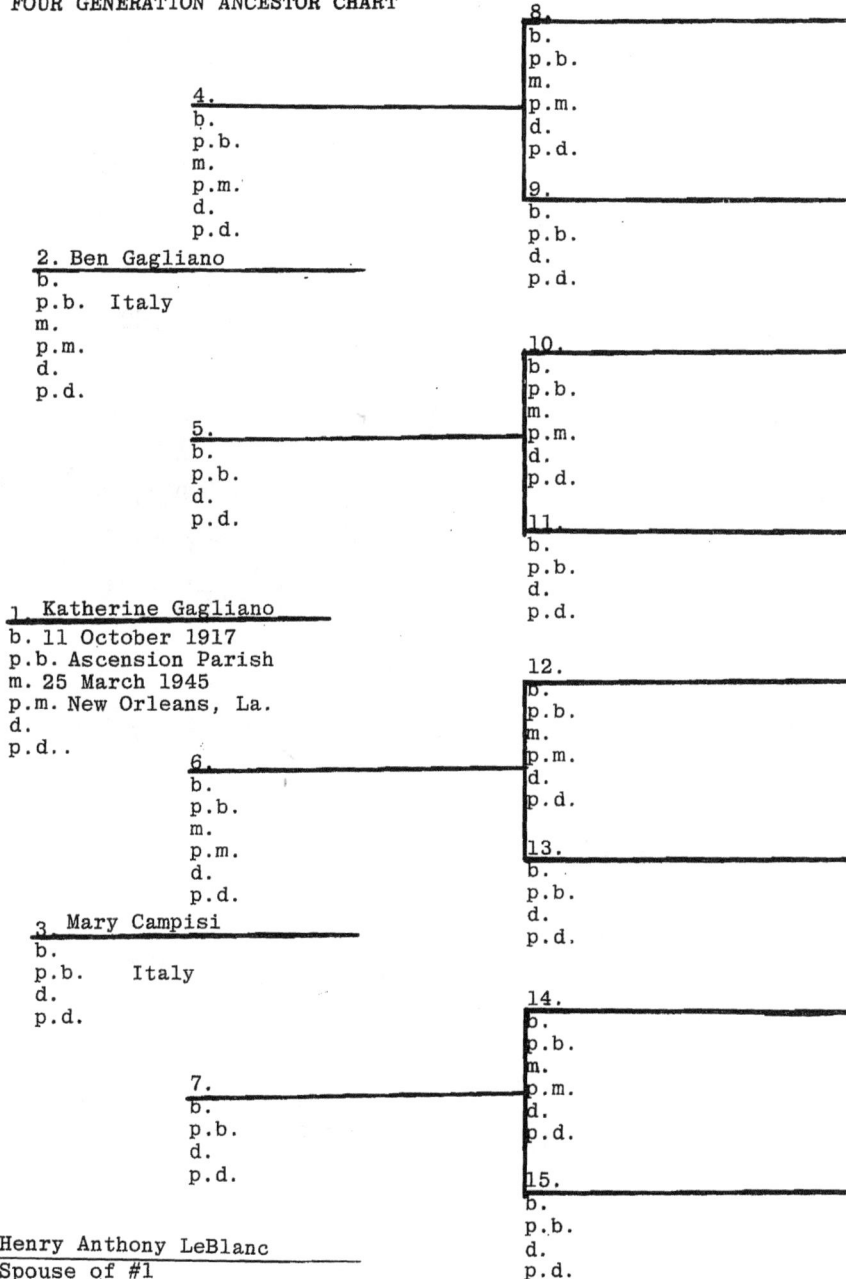

```
                                              8.
                                              b.
                                              p.b.
                                              m.
                    4.                        p.m.
                    b.                        d.
                    p.b.                      p.d.
                    m.
                    p.m.                      9.
                    d.                        b.
                    p.d.                      p.b.
     2. Ben Gagliano                          d.
     b.                                       p.d.
     p.b.  Italy
     m.
     p.m.                                     10.
     d.                                       b.
     p.d.                                     p.b.
                                              m.
                    5.                        p.m.
                    b.                        d.
                    p.b.                      p.d.
                    d.
                    p.d.                      11.
                                              b.
                                              p.b.
                                              d.
  1. Katherine Gagliano                       p.d.
  b. 11 October 1917
  p.b. Ascension Parish
  m. 25 March 1945                            12.
  p.m. New Orleans, La.                       b.
  d.                                          p.b.
  p.d..                                       m.
                    6.                        p.m.
                    b.                        d.
                    p.b.                      p.d.
                    m.
                    p.m.                      13.
                    d.                        b.
                    p.d.                      p.b.
     3. Mary Campisi                          d.
     b.                                       p.d.
     p.b.    Italy
     d.
     p.d.                                     14.
                                              b.
                                              p.b.
                                              m.
                    7.                        p.m.
                    b.                        d.
                    p.b.                      p.d.
                    d.
                    p.d.                      15.
                                              b.
                                              p.b.
  Henry Anthony LeBlanc                       d.
  Spouse of #1                                p.d.
```

8. Henry Anthony LeBlanc born August 6, 1911 in Ascension
    Parish married March 25, 1945 in St. Maurice Church,
    New Orleans to Katherine Ann GAGLIANO (daughter of
    Bennie Gagliano and Mary CAMPISE) born October 11,
    1917 in Ascension Parish.

KATHERINE   GAGLIANO   HENRY   LE BLANC
(1917 -   )   (1911 -   )

Henry was inducted into the United States Army in 1942
and was discharged in August, 1945. He saw duty in
South Africa, Sicily, Italy and France.

a. Henry J. LeBlanc born October 3, 1947 in New
    Orleans married April 14, 1967 in New Orleans, La.
    Kathleen SMITH (daughter of Walter Smith, Sr. and
    Kathleen ESCHART) born September 9, 1947 in New
    Orleans. Henry entered the United States Navy in
    New Orleans on August 25, 1967 and was separated
    May 30, 1970

    i. Renee Katherine LeBlanc born December 17, 1969
        in Brooklyn, New York
    ii. Christopher Jay LeBlanc born April 4, 1972 in
        New Orleans, La.

222

iii.　Christine Ann LeBlanc born April 4, 1972

b.　Patricia Ann LeBlanc born February 15, 1950 in
New Orleans married September 12, 1970 in St.
Maurice Church, New Orleans August Anthony DI
FRANCO (son of Anthony Di Franco and Camille
LIVICARIS) born November 20, 1948 in New Orleans.

c.　Elaine Katherine LeBlanc born July 19, 1953 in
New Orleans, La.

FOUR GENERATION ANCESTOR CHART

```
                                                         8.
                                                         b.
                                                         p.b.
                                                         m.
                         4.                              p.m.
                         b.                              d.
                         p.b.                            p.d.
                         m.
                         p.m.                            9.
                         d.                              b.
                         p.d.                            p.b.
                                                         d.
    2. Ben Gagliano                                      p.d.
    b.
    p.b.    Italy
    m.
    p.m.                                                 10.
    d.                                                   b.
    p.d.                                                 p.b.
                                                         m.
                         5.                              p.m.
                         b.                              d.
                         p.b.                            p.d.
                         d.
                         p.d.                            11.
                                                         b.
                                                         p.b.
                                                         d.
    1. Esther Gagliano                                   p.d.
    b. 15 August 1918
    p.b.  Ascension Parish
    m. 14 January 1940                                   12.
    p.m.  Smoke Bend, La.                                b.
    d.                                                   p.b.
    p.d..                                                m.
                         6.                              p.m.
                         b.                              d.
                         p.b.                            p.d.
                         m.
                         p.m.                            13.
                         d.                              b.
                         p.d.                            p.b.
                                                         d.
    3. Mary Campisi                                      p.d.
    b.
    p.b.    Italy
    d.                                                   14.
    p.d.                                                 b.
                                                         p.b.
                                                         m.
                         7.                              p.m.
                         b.                              d.
                         p.b.                            p.d.
                         d.
                         p.d.                            15.
                                                         b.
                                                         p.b.
    George Anthony LeBlanc                               d.
    Spouse of #1                                         p.d.
```

9. George Anthony LeBlanc born December 24, 1913 in Ascension married January 14, 1940 in St. Francis of
   Assisi Church, Smoke Bend to Esther GAGLIANO (daughter of Ben Gagliano and Mary CAMPISI) born August 15,
   1918 in Ascension Parish

ESTHER GAGLIANO   GEORGE LE BLANC
(1918 -   )   (1913 -   )

   a. George Anthony LeBlanc, Jr. born October 15, 1942
      in New Orleans married November 23, 1966 in New
      Orleans Betty EMBRY (daughter of Geroge Embry of
      Pennsylvania and Dorothy RICAUD of Franklin, La.)
      born August 31, 1944 in Pennsylvania. George is
      in the Naval Reserve

      i. John Joseph LeBlanc born May 26, 1970 in New
         Orleans, La.

FOUR GENERATION ANCESTOR CHART

8. Edouard Bujol
b.
p.b.
m.
p.m.
d.
p.d.

4. Edouard Bujol
b.
p.b.
m. 21 October 1857
p.m. Ascension Parish
d.
p.d.

9. Evelvina Blanchard
b.
p.b.
d.
p.d.

2. Adam Bujol
b. 15 September 1861
p.b. Ascension Parish
m.   ca. 1915
p.m.
d. 12 December 1933
p.d. Ascension Parish

10 Henri Pierre Brugere
b.
p.b.
m. 23 July 1839
p.m. Ascension Parish
d.
p.d.

5. Hermina Brugere
b.
p.b.
d.
p.d.

11 Rosalie Melancon
b.
p.b.
d.
p.d.

1. Paul Clifton Bujol
b. 10 June 1916
p.b. Ascension Parish
m. 22 December 1935
p.m. Smoke Bend, La.
d. 11 February 1964
p.d. Ascension Parish

12 Albert Medine
b.
p.b.
m. 22 April 1857
p.m. Ascension Parish
d.
p.d.

6. Lawrence Medine
b.
p.b.
m. 31 January 1876
p.m. Ascension Parish
d.
p.d.

13 Modesta Rivet
b.
p.b.
d.
p.d.

3. Rosalie Elizabeth Medine
b.   1879
p.b. Ascension Parish
d. 29 July 1951
p.d. Ascension Parish

14 Christophe Falcon
b.
p.b.
m.
p.m.
d.
p.d.

7. Antoinette Falcon
b.
p.b.
d.
p.d.

15 Catherine Carbo
b.
p.b.
d.
p.d.

Lovell Cecile LeBlanc
Spouse of #1

10. Lovell Cecile LeBlanc born September 14, 1916 married December 22, 1935 in St. Francis of Assisi Church in Smoke Bend Paul Clifton BUJOL (son of Adam Bujol and Rosalie Elizabeth MEDINE) born June 10, 1916 in Ascension. Clifton died February 11, 1964 and is buried in Ascension Cemetery, Donaldsonville, La.

CLIFTON BUJOL   LOVELL LE BLANC
(1916 - 1964)   (1916 -   )

a. Jeanette Marie Bujol born February 8, 1937 in Ascension Parish married November 26, 1955 in Ascension Parish Kenneth Dale MAHER (son of Nick Maher and Nathalie DOMINIQUE) born October 5, 1934 in Ascension Parish

    i. Kenneth Dale Maher born October 29, 1956 in White Castle, La.
    ii. Marvin Charles Maher born September 22, 1958
    iii. Mark John Maher born January 2, 1964
    iv. Karen Ann Maher born May 19, 1966
    v. Kyle Paul Maher born November 4, 1971 in Donaldsonville, La.

b. Ernestine Elizabeth Bujol born February 7, 1938
    in Ascension Parish married July 16, 1960 in
    Baton Rouge Charles Leroy CLARK (son of Otis Leo
    Clark and Ester Cordelia WELLS) born December 21,
    1936 in St. Francisville, Louisiana

    i.   Diane Marie Clark born April 27, 1961 in
         Baton Rouge, La.
    ii. Sharon Ann Clark born September 19, 1962 in
         Baton Rouge, La.
    iii. Michelle Lynn Clark born October 24, 1967
         in Baton Rouge, La.

c. Linden Andrew Bujol born November 22, 1939 in As-
    cension Parish married September 13, 1959 in Liv-
    ingston Parish Linda Carol MAHER (daughter of
    Joseph A. Maher and Barbara WHITEHEAD) born
    July 15, 1941 in Ascension Parish

    i.   Gary Lynn Bujol born July 26, 1960 in Donald-
         sonville, La.
    ii. Donna Louise Bujol born December 16, 1963 in
         Baton Rouge, La.
    iii. Barry Paul Bujol born January 1, 1968 in
         Baton Rouge, La.

d. Evelyn Ann Bujol born December 20, 1940 in Ascen-
    sion Parish married October 29, 1960 in St. George
    Church, Baton Rouge to Donald Ray COMEAUX (son o
    John Riley Comeaux and Irene AUCOIN) born July 3
    1939 in Baton Rouge

    i.   Rebecca Jane Comeaux born May 21, 1963 in
         Baton Rouge
    ii. Melissa Ann Comeaux born November 1, 1965

e. Russell Thomas Bujol born October 16, 1956 in
    Donaldsonville

226

FOUR GENERATION ANCESTOR CHART

```
                                                       8.
                                                       b.
                                                       p.b.
                                                       m.
                          4. John Gravois              p.m.
                          b.                           d.
                          p.b.                         p.d.
                          m.
                          p.m.                         9.
                          d.                           b.
                          p.d.                         p.b.
          2. James G. Gravois                          d.
          b. 11 January 1886                           p.d.
          p.b. Ascension Parish
          m.
          p.m.                                         10.
          d. 16 August 1963                            b.
          p.d. Bur. Ascension Cemetery                 p.b.
                                                       m.
                          5. Jeanne Bingy              p.m.
                          b.                           d.
                          p.b.                         p.d.
                          d.
                          p.d.                         11.
                                                       b.
                                                       p.b.
                                                       d.
  1. Lloyd Adrian Gravois                              p.d.
  b. 15 February 1919
  p.b. Ascension Parish
  m.  4 February 1939                                  12.
  p.m. Smoke Bend, La.                                 b.
  d.                                                   p.b.
  p.d..                                                m.
                          6. Louance Hymel             p.m.
                          b.                           d.
                          p.b.                         p.d.
                          m.
                          p.m.                         13.
                          d.                           b.
                          p.d.                         p.b.
                                                       d.
          3. Alice Barbara Hymel                       p.d.
          b. 18 April 1889
          p.b. Darrow, La.
          d. 11 March 1963                             14.
          p.d Bur. Ascension Cemetery                  b.
                                                       p.b.
                                                       m.
                          7. Mathilde Gross            p.m.
                          b.                           d.
                          p.b. Labadieville, La.       p.d.
                          d.
                          p.d.                         15.
                                                       b.
                                                       p.b.
  Alice Mary LeBlanc                                   d.
  Spouse of #1                                         p.d.
```

11. Alice Mary LeBlanc born June 9, 1919 in Ascension Parish married February 4, 1939 in St. Francis of Assisi
Church, Smoke Bend to Lloyd Adrian GRAVOIS (son of
James Gravois and Alice Barbara HYMEL) born February 15
1919 in Ascension Parish

LLOYD GRAVOIS   ALICE   LE BLANC
(1919 -   )   (1919 -   )

a. Irving J. Gravois born March 19, 1940 in Donaldsonville married November 22, 1959 in St. John
Church, Thibodaux to Virginia Thibodeaux (daughter
of Ouaire J. Thibodeaux and Sadie MIRE) born May 4,
1942 in Thibodaux, La.

   i. Glenn J. Gravois born October 9, 1960 in Thibodaux, La.
  ii. Glenda Faye Gravois born January 13, 1962
iii. Brian Keith Gravois born August 11, 1963

Irving served in the United States Air Force.

b. Jo Ann Gravois born July 4, 1943 in Ascension Parish married Ronald Paul ROBERT (son of Wallis Robert and Dora CAPELLO)

   i. Jeffery Robert
  ii. Chad Robert

c. Brenda Faye Gravois born July 3, 1944 in Ascension Parish married September 15, 1959 to Leo Adam HIMEL (son of Theophile Augustain F. Himel and Josephine Loula BOUDREAUX) born April 7, 1941 in New Orleans, La.

    i. Leo Adam Himel, Jr. born January 25, 1961 in Donaldsonville, La.
   ii. Bert Matthew Himel born October 7, 1962
  iii. Travis Paul Himel born August 26, 1964
   iv. Todd Jude Himel born February 21, 1971 in Baton Rouge, La.

d. Mary Alice Gravois born August 10, 1947 in Ascension Parish married July 18, 1966 in Smoke Bend to Roy Joseph GIROIR (son of Luke Giroir and Beatrice MARROY) born July 23, 1946 in Belle Rose, Louisiana

   i. Stacy Lynn Giroir born July 21, 1967 in New Orleans, La.
  ii. Nicole Beth Giroir born January 26, 1972 in Baton Rouge, La.

e. Lloyd Adrian Gravois, Jr. born February 26, 1949 in Donaldsonville married November 15, 1972 in Jackson County, Mississippi to Elizabeth Ann MINYARD (daughter of Wallace B. Minyard and Mary Alice SPURRIER) born February 28, 1952 in Harland, Kentucky.

Child of previous marriage of Elizabeth:
Stacy Alice Nottingham born January 20, 1970 in Norfolk, Virginia.

Lloyd entered the United States Air Force on August 13, 1968 and is still in the Air Force. He served in Thailand.

f. David Anthony Gravois born June 13, 1954 in Donaldsonville, La.

g. Cynthia Gravois born May 30, 1958 in White Castle, La.

FOUR GENERATION ANCESTOR CHART

```
                                                    8.
                                                    b.
                                                    p.b.
                                                    m.
                        4.                          p.m.
                        b.                          d.
                        p.b.                        p.d.
                        m.
                        p.m.                        9.
                        d.                          b.
                        p.d.                        p.b.
     2. Wilfred Toups                               d.
     b.        1900                                 p.d.
     p.b.
     m.
     p..m.                                          10.
     d. 15 October 1951                             b.
     p.d.                                           p.b.
                                                    m.
                        5.                          p.m.
                        b.                          d.
                        p.b.                        p.d.
                        d.
                        p.d.                        11.
                                                    b.
                                                    p.b.
                                                    d.
   1 Beatrice Josephine Toups                       p.d.
   b. 25 December 1925
   p.Edgerly, La.
   m.                                               12.
   p.m.                                             b.
   d.                                               p.b.
   p.d..                                            m.
                        6.      Burleigh            p.m.
                        b.                          d.
                        p.b.    Germany             p.d.
                        m.
                        p.m.                        13.
                        d.                          b.
                        p.d.                        p.b.
     3.Agnes Burleigh                               d.
     b.        1908                                 p.d.
     p.b.
     d.10 September 1964
     p.d.                                           14.
                                                    b.
                                                    p.b.
                                                    m.
                        7.      Prejean             p.m.
                        b.                          d.
                        p.b.                        p.d.
                        d.
                        p.d.                        15.
                                                    b.
                                                    p.b.
   John Darold LeBlanc                              d.
   Spouse of #1                                     p.d.
```

12. John Darold LeBlanc born January 17, 1921 in Ascension
     Parish married Beatrice Josephine TOUPS (daughter of
     Wilfred Toups and Agnes BURLEIGH) born December 25,
     1925 in Edgerly, Louisiana. J. D. served in the
     United States Army from September 2, 1943 to Decem-
     ber 2, 1945. He served in Italy and North Africa.

J. D. LE BLANC   BEATRICE TOUPS
(1921 -   )   (1925   )

    a. Jerry Lynn Anthony LeBlanc born June 13, 1948 in
        Donaldsonville
    b. John Gerald LeBlanc born May 8, 1949
    c. Joyce Marie LeBlanc born March 1, 1951
    d. Donald Paul LeBlanc born December 29, 1952
    e. Robert Lane LeBlanc born February 27, 1954
    f. Michael Allen LeBlanc born November 17, 1956
    g. Debra Ann LeBlanc born November 1, 1958

THE LE BLANC FAMILY PICNIC 1972

INDEX OF LIVING DESCENDANTS

NAME AND ADDRESS	YEAR OF BIRTH	PAGE
ADAMS, Christina Irma 4913 Deteoiter Dr., County Trailer Park Virginia Beach, Va. 23462	1966	220
ADAMS, James Ernest 4913 Deteoiter Dr., County Trailer Park Virginia Beach, Va. 23462	1963	220
ADAMS, Margaret Ann (Melancon) 4913 Deteoiter Dr., County Trailer Park Virginia Beach, Va. 23462	1945	220
ADAMS, Melissa Ann 4913 Deteoiter Dr., County Trailer Park Virginia Beach, Va. 23462	1968	220
ALEMAN, Darlene 3207 Anita Circle, Bossier City, La. 71010	1959	81
ALEMAN, Donald Robert 3207 Anita Circle, Bossier City, La. 71010	1934	81
ALEMAN, Dondra 3207 Anita Circle, Bossier City, La. 71010	1963	82
ALEMAN, Edwin J., Jr. Lake Bisteonue P. O. Box 5462, Bossier City, La. 71010	1932	81
ALEMAN, Emma (LeBlanc) 3207 Anita Circle, Bossier City, La. 71010	1913	81
ALEMAN, Gene Raymond 1802 Pollyanna, Bossier City, La. 71010	1943	82
ALEMAN, Stephanie 3207 Anita Circle, Bossier City, La. 71010	1957	81
ALLEMAN, Gladys Marie (LeBlanc) RFD Rt. 1, Box 137 A, Napoleonville, La. 70390 Phone: 369-3616	1934	102
ALLEMAN, Maria Lynne RFD Rt. 1, Box 137 A, Napoleonville, La. 70390 Phone: 369-3616	1954	102
ALLEMAN, Regina Mae RFD Rt. 1, Box 137 A, Napoleonville, La. 70390 Phone: 369-3616	1964	103
ALLEMAN, Robert Joseph RFD Rt. 1, Box 137 A, Napoleonville, La. 70390 Phone: 369-3616	1958	103
ALLEMAN, Timothy Joseph RFD Rt. 1, Box 137 A, Napoleonville, La. 70390 Phone: 369-3616	1956	103
ALTAZIN, Emanuel Michael	1972	180

231

NAME AND ADDRESS	YEAR OF BIRTH	PAGE
ALTAZIN, Gwendolyn Ann (Perault) 3656 Webb Dr., Baton Rouge, La. 70805 Phone: 357-6680	1953	180
ANDERMANN, Lawrence Joseph, Jr. Rt. 1, Box 112, Donaldsonville, La. 70346 Phone: 473-9701	1964	112
ANDERMANN, Stella Marie (Barrient) Rt. 1, Box 112, Donaldsonville, La. 70346 Phone: 473-9701	1933	112
ANDREWS, Karyn	1970	79
ANDREWS, Linda (Darmay)	1947	79
ARCENEAUX, Adele (Loland) 306 7th St., Morgan City, La. 70380 Phone: 384-5999	1920	169
ARCENEAUX, Jules Allen 306 7th St., Morgan City, La. 70380 Phone: 384-5999	1959	170
ARCENEAUX, Kathy Marie 306 7th St., Morgan City, La. 70380 Phone: 384-5999	1954	170
ARCENEAUX, Ronnie Joseph 306 7th St., Morgan City, La. 70380 Phone: 384-5999	1952	170
BALLARD, Betty Ruth (LeBlanc) 2852 Dayton, Baton Rouge, La. 70805 Phone: 357-5619	1930	179
BALLARD, Christine Britney 2852 Dayton, Baton Rouge, La. 70805 Phone: 357-5619	1972	179
BALLARD, Debra Ann 2852 Dayton, Baton Rouge, La. 70805 Phone: 357-5619	1954	180
BALLARD, Kernan Bernell, Jr. 2852 Dayton, Baton Rouge, La. 70805 Phone: 357-5619	1952	179
BARKER, Elizabeth Marie (LeBlanc) 3155 Ocean Parkway, Daytona Beach, Fla. 33435 Phone: 588-4781	1904	86
BARNEY, Diane Anne (Boudreaux) Rt. 1, Box 378, Port Sulphur, La. 70083 Phone: 564-3565	1946	202
BARNEY, Richard Allen Rt. 1, Box 378, Port Sulphur, La. 70083 Phone: 564-3565	1968	202

NAME AND ADDRESS	YEAR OF BIRTH	PAGE
BARNHILL, Barbara Ellie (LeBlanc)	1943	87
BARNHILL, Brett Talmadge	1971	87
BARRIENT, Aldridge Paul 409 Claiborne St., Donaldsonville, La. 70346 Phone: 473-9701	1935	112
BARRIENT, Christopher Joseph Rt. 1, Box 112, Donaldsonville, La. 70346 Phone: 473-9931	1971	113
BARRIENT, Deborah Rt. 1, Box 112, Donaldsonville, La. 70346 Phone: 473-9931	1960	113
BARRIENT, Deirdre Marie 409 Claiborne St., Donaldsonville, La. 70346 Phone: 473-9701	1964	112
BARRIENT, Dirk Paul 409 Claiborne St., Donaldsonville, La. 70346 Phone: 473-9701	1959	112
BARRIENT, Frank Joseph 123 Lee Ave., Donaldsonville, La. 70346 Phone: 473-9701	1950	113
BARRIENT, Hubert Joseph 426 Little Farms, New Orleans, La. 70123 Phone: 729-0467	1920	116
BARRIENT, Keely Frances 409 Claiborne St., Donaldsonville, La. 70346 Phone: 473-9701	1961	112
BARRIENT, Lawless Joseph, Jr. 2345 Yorkshire Dr., Tallahassee, Fla. 32304	1947	114
BARRIENT, Lee Jude, Jr. 715 Bayou Rd., Donaldsonville, La. 70346 Phone: 473-9701	1967	113
BARRIENT, Leo Joseph, Jr.	1937	112
BARRIENT, Leonie (LeBlanc) 230 S. Pierce St., New Orleans, La. 70119 Phone: 482-3847	1880	110
BARRIENT, Linda Marie 426 Little Farms, New Orleans, La. 70123 Phone: 729-0467	1947	117
BARRIENT, Mary Lee 715 Bayou Rd., Donaldsonville, La. 70346 Phone: 473-9701	1961	113
BARRIENT, Percy Joseph Rt. 1, Box 112, Donaldsonville, La. 70346 Phone: 473-9931	1940	113

NAME AND ADDRESS	YEAR OF BIRTH	PAGE
BARRIENT, Shelly Lynn 2345 Yorkshire Dr., Tallahassee, Fla. 32304	1971	114
BARRIENT, Steve Jasper Rt. 1, Box 112, Donaldsonville, La. 70346 Phone: 473-9931	1961	113
BARRIOS, Katherine Anne (LeBlanc) 902 Hickory St., Morgan City, La. 70380	1945	167
BARRIOS, Kimberly Anne 902 Hickory St., Morgan City, La. 70380	1969	167
BARRIOS, Melvin Paul 902 Hickory St., Morgan City, La. 70380	1966	167
BARTHE, Gail Lillian (Landry) 525 Melody Dr., Metairie, La. 70001	1936	108
BASS, Richard Lee 11120 Tams Dr., Baton Rouge, La. 70815	1966	143
BECK, Jeanette Marie (Templet) P. O. Box 14, Donaldsonville, La. 70346	1949	192
BECK, John Preston, Jr. P. O. Box 14, Donaldsonville, La. 70346	1967	192
BEHRNES, Dolores Rita (LeBlanc) 3355 Conrad Dr., Baton Rouge, La. 70805 Phone: 357-9303	1931	92
BEHRNES, Robert Gerald 3355 Conrad Dr., Baton Rouge, La. 70805 Phone: 357-9303	1953	92
BERGERON, Carl James Box 426, Berwick, La. 70342 Phone: 395-3350	1951	169
BERGERON, Christopher David 104 Carolyn St., Morgan City, La. 70380	1968	169
BERGERON, Daniel Cornelius Box 426, Berwick, La. 70342 Phone: 395-3350	1954	169
BERGERON, Elaina 104 Carolyn St., Morgan City, La. 70380	1969	169
BERGERON, Emily 1655 Marshall St., Baton Rogue, La. 70808 Phone: 927-3823	1969	198
BERGERON, Gwen RFD 1, Box 65, Donaldsonville, La. 70346	1964	97
BERGERON, Janell RFD 1, Box 65, Donaldsonville, La. 70346	1962	97

NAME AND ADDRESS	YEAR OF BIRTH	PAGE
BERGERON, Larry Edward 104 Carolyn St., Morgan City, La. 70380	1942	169
BERGERON, Laura (LeBlanc) 2938 Winbourne Ave., Baton Rouge, La. 70805 Phone: 355-9288	1916	198
BERGERON, Mark Jason 104 Carolyn St., Morgan City, La. 70380	1971	169
BERGERON, Paul Edward 104 Carolyn St., Morgan City, La. 70380	1966	169
BERGERON, Phyllis 104 Carolyn St., Morgan City, La. 70380	1967	169
BERGERON, Rena (Loland) Box 426, Berwick, La. 70342 Phone: 359-3350	1914	168
BERGERON, Samuel Joseph, Jr. 1655 Marshall St., Baton Rouge, La. 70808 Phone: 927-3823	1946	198
BERTHELOT, Anna Elizabeth (Terrio)	1946	115
BERTHELOT, Dena Ann (Clouatre) 3423 Edgemont Dr., Baton Rouge, La. 70814 Phone: 275-7144	1955	146
BESNARD, Malcom Ernest 1805 Home St., Metairie, La. 70121 Phone: 888-1918	1947	116
BESNARD, Malcom Todd 1805 Home St., Metairie, La. 70121 Phone: 888-1918	1970	116
BESNARD, Olive Ann (Barrient) 27 Joyce Ave., New Orleans, La. 70121 Phone: 831-1934	1918	116
BESNARD, Tracey Dianne 1805 Home St., Metairie, La. 70121 Phone: 888-1918	1967	116
BLANCHARD, Cynthia June 8900 Gervais, New Orleans, La. Phone: 242-9680	1960	128
BLANCHARD, David Michael 8900 Gervais, New Orleans, La. Phone: 242-9680	1961	128
BLANCHARD, Debra Jean (Clouatre) Donaldsonville, La. 70346	1954	145
BLANCHARD, Douglas Gerard 8900 Gervais, New Orleans, La. Phone: 242-9680	1964	128

NAME AND ADDRESS	YEAR OF BIRTH	PAGE
BLANCHARD, Gregory Paul 8900 Gervais, New Orleans, La. Phone: 242-9680	1963	128
BLANCHARD, Helen Marie (LeBlanc) Livonia, La. 70755 Phone: 637-2699	1924	125
BLANCHARD, John Carl P. O. Box 293, Livonia, La. 70755 Phone: 637-2780	1945	125
BLANCHARD, Linda Ann (LeBlanc) 8900 Gervais, New Orleans, La. Phone: 242-9680	1939	128
BLANCHARD, Michael Todd Livonia, La. 70755 Phone: 637-2699	1966	125
BLANCHARD, Trohn Peter	1973	125
BLANCHARD, Trudy Ann Livonia, La. 70755 Phone: 637-2699	1954	125
BOLLINGER, Donnyl Lois (LeBlanc) 11549 Catalpa Dr., Baton Rouge, La. 70815 Phone: 275-6939	1941	8
BOLLINGER, Jayme Michele 11549 Catalpa Dr., Baton Rouge, La. 70815 Phone: 275-6939	1968	8
BONNET, Sandra Marie 615 St. Patrick St., New Orleans, La. 70119 Phone: 488-0558	1951	19
BOONE, Darron Star Rt. A, Box 53 D, Franklin, La. 70538 Phone: 836-5502	1966	15
BOONE, Dianne (Medine) Star Rt. A, Box 53 D, Franklin, La. 70538 Phone: 836-5502	1948	15
BOONE, Shannon Star Rt. A, Box 53 D, Franklin, La. 70538 Phone: 836-5502	1969	15
BORNE, Christian Andrew 2148 Gibson, Gretna, La. 70053 Phone: 367-9238	1970	19
BORNE, Russell, Jr. 2148 Gibson, Gretna, La. 70053 Phone: 367-9238	1941	19

NAME AND ADDRESS	YEAR OF BIRTH	PAGE
BORNE, Ruth Juliette (LeBlanc) 500 Colledge, New Orleans, La. 70121 Phone: 833-6236	1916	191
BORNE, Steven Russell 2148 Gibson, Gretna, La. 70053 Phone: 367-9238	1968	192
BOUDIN, Lynn Ann (Arceneaux) 206 7th St., Morgan City, La. 70380 Phone: 384-5999	1950	169
BOUDREAUX, Andrew Paul P. O. Box 646, Port Sulphur, La. 70083 Phone: 564-2942	1961	202
BOUDREAUX, Brett Joseph P. O. Box 646, Port Sulphur, La. 70083 Phone: 564-2942	1965	202
BOUDREAUX, Carroll Paul Rt. 1, Port Sulphur, La. 70083 Phone: 564-3082	1952	202
BOUDREAUX, Ernest Joseph Rt. 1, Box 646, Mimosa Lane Port Sulphur, La. 70083 Phone: 564-3134	1943	202
BOUDREAUX, Gail Theressa Rt. 1, Box 378, Port Sulphur, La. 70083 Phone: 574-3888	1948	202
BOUDREAUX, Lloyd Joseph, Jr. P. O. Box 646, Port Sulphur, La. 70083 Phone: 564-2942	1940	201
BOUDREAUX, Lori Ann Rt. 1, Box 646, Port Sulphur, La. 70083 Phone: 564-3134	1969	202
BOUDREAUX, Mary Ophelia (LeBlanc) Rt. 1, Box 378, Port Sulphur, La. 70083 Phone: 564-3888	1922	201
BOUDREAUX, Phyllis Ann P. O. Box 646, Port Sulphur, La. 70083 Phone: 564-2942	1963	202
BOUDREAUX, Theresa Kay Rt. 1, Box 646, Port Sulphur, La. 70083 Phone: 564-3134	1966	202
BOUJOL, Donna Louise 1652 Webster Dr., Denham Springs, La. 70726 Phone: 665-2454	1963	226
BOURGEOIS, Betty June (LeBlanc) 1826 Denver Dr., Baton Rouge, La. 70808 Phone: 766-2848	1931	204

NAME AND ADDRESS	YEAR OF BIRTH	PAGE
BOURGEOIS, Dennis Paul 1826 Denver Dr., Baton Rouge, La. 70808 Phone: 766-2848	1953	204
BOURGEOIS, Gail Marie 1826 Denver Dr., Baton Rouge, La. 70808 Phone: 766-2848	1954	204
BOURGEOIS, Gary Mark 1826 Denver Dr., Baton Rouge, La. 70808 Phone: 766-2848	1959	204
BOURGEOIS, Randall Ray 1826 Denver Dr., Baton Rouge, La. 70808 Phone: 766-2848	1961	204
BRAUD, Abbiagale (Hebert) Pierre Part, La. 70339 Phone: 252-6978	1949	101
BRAUD, Celeste Leigh St. Patrick St., Houma, La. 70301	1971	98
BRAUD, Gerald John Pierre Part, La. 70339 Phone: 252-6978	1969	101
BRAUD, Samantha Mary Pierre Part, La. 70339 Phone: 252-6978	1968	101
BRAUD, Tiffany Ann St. Patrick St., Houma, La. 70301	1969	98
BRAUD, Trudy Ann (Thibodeaux) St. Patrick St., Houma, La. 70301	1950	98
BRIGNAC, Alice Marie (Barrient) 7820 W. Leverne, New Orleans, La. 70126 Phone: 242-2506	1916	115
BRIGNAC, Arlene Evelyn	1962	115
BRIGNAC, Ronald James, II	1961	115
BRODNAX, Barbara Jean (LeBlanc) P. O. Box 285, Maringouin, La. 70757 Phone: 625-2593	1933	119
BRODNAX, David Lynn P. O. Box 285, Maringouin, La. 70757 Phone: 625-2593	1958	120
BRODNAX, Paul Wayne P. O. Box 285, Maringouin, La. 70757 Phone: 625-2593	1964	120
BRODNAX, Roan Marie P. O. Box 285, Maringouin, La. 70757 Phone: 625-2593	1956	120

NAME AND ADDRESS	YEAR OF BIRTH	PAGE
BRODNAX, Von Allen P. O. Box 285, Maringouin, La. 70757 Phone: 625-2593	1961	120
BUJOL, Barry Paul 1652 Webster Dr., Denham Springs, La. 70726 Phone: 665-2454	1968	226
BUJOL, Gary Lynn 1652 Webster Dr., Denham Springs, La. 70726 Phone: 665-2454	1960	226
BUJOL, Linden Andrew 1652 Webster Dr., Denham Springs, La. 70726 Phone: 665-2454	1939	226
BUJOL, Lovell Cecile (LeBlanc) Rt. 1, Box 141, Donaldsonville, La. 70346	1916	225
BUJOL, Russell Thomas Rt. 1, Box 141, Donaldsonville, La. 70346	1956	226
CALLAHAN, Cheryl Ann Rt. 1, Box 256, Donaldsonville, La. 70346 Phone: 473-9366	1949	174
CALLAHAN, Lottie Mae (LeBlanc) Rt. 1, Box 256, Donaldsonville, La. 70346 Phone: 473-9366	1928	174
CALLAHAN, Marilyn Anna Rt. 1, Box 256, Donaldsonville, La. 70346 Phone: 473-9366	1954	174
CANNON, Joanne Marie (Landry) 3600 Eagle Rock Dr., Atlanta, Ga. 30340 Phone: 939-1703	1934	108
CANNON, Max Clifford, III 3600 Eagle Rock Dr., Atlanta, Ga. 30340 Phone: 939-1703	1954	108
CANTERBURY, Becky Lee (Czerney)	1950	194
CANTERBURY, Jennifer	1970	194
CAPRIOTTI, Olive Glynn (Besnard) 2629 Wilkerson Dr., Marrero, La. 70072 Phone: 347-2411	1940	116
CAPRIOTTI, Tayna Marie 2629 Wilkerson Dr., Marrero, La. 70072 Phone: 347-2411	1970	116
CARNEY, Effie Cecil Rt. 1, Jayess, Miss. 39641 Phone: 833-8616	1920	91

NAME AND ADDRESS	YEAR OF BIRTH	PAGE
CHAISSON, Melissa Marie P. O. Box 426, Berwick, La. 70342 Phone: 395-2084	1963	169
CLARK, Diane Marie 3622 Brady St., Baton Rouge, La. 70805 Phone: 766-4887	1961	226
CLARK, Ernestine Elizabeth (Bujol) 3622 Brady St., Baton Rouge, La. 70805 Phone: 766-4887	1938	226
CLARK, Michelle Lynn 3622 Brady St., Baton Rouge, La. 70805 Phone: 766-4887	1967	226
CLARK, Sharon Ann 3622 Brady St., Baton Rouge, La. 70805 Phone: 766-4887	1962	226
CLOUATRE, Amy Jane 525 Stuart (Little Farms) New Orleans, La. 70123	1970	143
CLOUATRE, Brian 18 Creamer Dr., Sayreville, N. J. 08872 Phone: (201) 254-6821	1968	146
CLOUATRE, Calvin Joseph 3423 Edgemont Dr., Baton Rouge, La. 70814 Phone: 275-7144	1930	146
CLOUATRE, Calvin Joseph, Jr. 3423 Edgemont Dr., Baton Rouge, La. 70814 Phone: 275-7144 U.S. Army presently stationed in Illinois	1953	146
CLOUATRE, Calvin Joseph, III 3423 Edgemont Dr., Baton Rouge, La. 70814 Phone: 275-7144	1971	146
CLOUATRE, Chester Joseph 3470 Winnebago St., Baton Rouge, La. 70805 Phone: 357-6173	1919	145
CLOUATRE, Christopher 3423 Edgemont Dr., Baton Rouge, La. 70814 Phone: 275-7144	1959	146
CLOUATRE, Danette 3423 Edgemont Dr., Baton Rouge, La. 70814 Phone: 275-7144	1962	146
CLOUATRE, Diane 3085 Eaton St., Baton Rouge, La. 70805 Phone: 355-0215	1963	147
CLOUATRE, Donna Denise 3085 Eaton St., Baton Rouge, La. Phone: 355-0215	1960	147

NAME AND ADDRESS	YEAR OF BIRTH	PAGE
CLOUATRE, Elmo J. 2755 Arrow Hwy. #69, LaVerne, Calif. 91750	1913	139
CLOUATRE, Gena Dianne 3471 Winnebago St., Baton Rouge, La. 70805	1969	144
CLOUATRE, Gene Raymond 3471 Winnebago St., Baton Rouge, La. 70805 Phone: 357-3070	1944	144
CLOUATRE, Gerald Ray 3724 Geronimo St., Baton Rouge, La. 70805 Phone: 357-4875	1953	145
CLOUATRE, Henry Estress 3646 Airline Hwy., Metairie, La. 70001	1940	143
CLOUATRE, Jasen Wade 3471 Winnebago St., Baton Rouge, La. 70805	1967	144
CLOUATRE, John Walter 3471 Winnebago St., Baton Rouge, La. 70805	1964	144
CLOUATRE, Miss Leonie 11522 Glenda Dr., Baton Rouge, La. 70815 Phone: 275-4035	1884	150
CLOUATRE, Leslie George 18 Creamer Dr., Sayreville, N. J. 08872 Phone: (201) 254-6821	1955	146
CLOUATRE, Leslie Joseph 18 Creamer Dr., Sayreville, N. J. 08871 Phone: (201) 254-6821	1921	145
CLOUATRE, Livingston Joseph, Jr. 11120 Tams Dr., Baton Rouge, La. 70815 Phone: 275-5289	1916	143
CLOUATRE, Livingston J., III 525 Stuart (Little Farms), New Orleans, La. 70123	1936	143
CLOUATRE, Lynn Louise 3470 Winnebago St., Baton Rouge, La. 70805 Phone: 357-6173	1961	145
CLOUATRE, Marion Leon 3085 Eaton St., Baton Rouge, La. 70804 Phone: 355-0215	1933	147
CLOUATRE, Nina Marie 525 Stuart (Little Farms), New Orleans, La. 70123	1962	143
CLOUATRE, Patricia 11120 Tams Dr., Baton Rouge, La. 70815 Phone: 275-5289	1938	143
CLOUATRE, Randel Michael 3085 Eaton St., Baton Rouge, La. 70805 Phone: 355-0215	1957	147

NAME AND ADDRESS	YEAR OF BIRTH	PAGE
CLOUATRE, Raymond 3085 Eaton St., Baton Rouge, La. 70805 Phone: 355-0215	1967	147
CLOUATRE, Reva Darleen 525 Stuart (Little Farms), New Orleans, La. 70123	1960	143
CLOUATRE, Robert Raymond 18 Creamer Dr., Sayreville, N. J. 08872 Phone: (201) 254-6821	1946	146
CLOUATRE, Sherilyn 3471 Winnebago St., Baton Rouge, La. 70805 Phone: 357-3070	1971	144
CLOUATRE, Vicki Lynn 18 Creamer Dr., Sayreville, N. J. 08872 Phone: (201) 254-6821	1948	146
COLLET, Beverly Alice	1972	217
COLLET, Kimberly Renee 3173 Calumet St., Baton Rouge, La. 70805 Phone: 355-3661	1970	217
COLLET, Leonore Marie 3173 Calumet St., Baton Rouge, La. 70805 Phone: 355-3661	1969	217
COLLET, Rene Jean, Jr. 3173 Calumet St., Baton Rouge, La. 70805 Phone: 355-3661	1939	216
COLLINS, Linette Marie 916 Stewart Ct., New Orleans, La. 70119 Phone: 486-6451	1948	194
COMEAUX, Diane Mary (LeBlanc) 403 Homestead Dr., Plaquemine, La. 70764 Phone: 687-4865	1943	134
COMEAUX, Eric George Belle Rose, La. 70341 Phone: 252-6527	1957	101
COMEAUX, Evelyn Ann (Bujol) Rt. 3, Box 481 A, Highland Road, Baton Rouge, La. 70808 Phone: 766-4887	1940	226
COMEAUX, Melissa Ann Rt. 3, Box 481 A, Highland Road, Baton Rouge, La. 70808 Phone: 766-4887	1965	226
COMEAUX, Mercedes (LeBlanc) Belle Rose, La. 70341 Phone: 252-6527	1926	101
COMEAUX, Mervin Alex Belle Rose, La. 70341 Phone: 252-6527	1949	101

COMEAUX, Nelson Joseph   1953   101
Belle Rose, La. 70341
Phone: 252-6527

COMEAUX, Rebecca Jane   1963   226
Rt. 3, Box 481 A, Baton Rouge, La. 70808
Phone: 766-4887

COMEAUX, Rhonda Mercedes   1961   101
Belle Rose, La. 70341
Phone: 252-6527

COMEAUX, Shannon Elizabeth   1969   134
403 Homestead Dr., Plaquemine, La. 70764
Phone: 687-4865

CONNON, Rhonda Jean   1958   108
3600 Eagle Rock Dr., Atlanta, Ga. 30340
Phone: 939-1703

CORIO, Denise Louise (Clouatre)   1953   146
18 Creamer Dr., Sayreville, N. J.   08872
Phone: (201) 254-6821

COUVILLON, Anna Mae (LeBlanc)   1929   126
2769 Larkspur Ave., Baton Rouge, La. 70805
Phone: 348-4448

COUVILLON, Cheryl Ann   1956   126
2769 Larkspur Ave., Baton Rouge, La. 70805
Phone: 348-4448

COUVILLON, Clifton Thomas   1952   126
2909 Addison St., Apt. 206, Baton Rouge, La. 70805
Phone: 357-9025

COUVILLON, Gwendolyn Frances   1961   126
2769 Larkspur Ave., Baton Rouge, La. 70805
Phone: 348-4448

COUVILLON, Karen Elizabeth   1953   126
2769 Larkspur Ave., Baton Rouge, La. 70805
Phone: 348-4448

COX, Charlene Ann   1969   153
Rt. 1, Box 453, White Castle, La. 70788
Phone: 545-3443

COX, Dwayne Anthony   1961   153
Rt. 1, Box 453, White Castle, La. 70788
Phone: 545-3443

COX, Evelyn Ann (Medine)   1941   153
Rt. 1, Box 453, White Castle, La. 70788
Phone: 545-3443

COX, Rickey Jude   1968   153
Rt. 1, Box 453, White Castle, La. 70788
Phone: 545-3443

NAME AND ADDRESS	YEAR OF BIRTH	PAGE
CZERNY, Elsie Mae (LeBlanc) 308 Diane Ave., New Orleans, La. 70123 Phone: 737-0447	1924	194
CZERNY, Karen Marie 308 Diane Ave., New Orleans, La. 70123 Phone: 737-0447	1957	194
DARMAY, Bryan	1954	79
DARMAY, Evelyn Mae (LeBlanc)	1921	79
DARMAY, Janis	1952	79
DAUSSAT, Mary Louise (LeBlanc) 1804 Yale Ave., Metairie, La. 70653	1945	187
DAVEZAC, Debra Marie (Landry) 7767 E. Navy Rd., Millington, Tenn. 38053 Phone: 872-0683	1953	109
DE HEMECOURT, Laura Marie (Barrient) 230 S. Pierce St., New Orleans, La. 70119 Phone: 482-3847	1904	111
DE LOUISE, Carolyn (Clouatre) % Royal Vista Motel, Hwy. 1 South Donaldsonville, La. 70346	1943	143
DE LOUISE, Lisa Marie % Royal Vista Motel, Hwy. 1 South Donaldsonville, La. 70346	1971	144
DENOUX, Glenn Edward 1107 South Park Ave., Gonzales, La. 70737 Phone: 644-4159	1962	95 177
DENOUX, Kelvin Paul 1107 South Park Ave., Gonzales, La. 70737 Phone: 644-4159	1957	95 177
DENOUX, Mary Elizabeth (LeBlanc) 1107 South Park Ave., Gonzales, La. 70737 Phone: 644-4159	1933	95 177
DENOUX, Rodney Joseph 1107 South Park Ave., Gonzales, La. 70737 Phone: 644-4159	1959	95 177
DENOUX, Scott David 1107 South Park Ave., Gonzales, La. 70737 Phone: 644-4159	1971	95 177
DI FRANCO, Patricia Ann (LeBlanc) 8531 Deerfield Dr., Chalmette, La. 70043 Phone: 271-8905	1950	223
DOMINIQUE, Bruce Anthony 1707 Bayou Circle, Bossier City, La. 71010 Phone: 742-9155	1955	111

NAME AND ADDRESS	YEAR OF BIRTH	PAGE
DOMINIQUE, Earl Joseph, Jr. 1707 Bayou Circle, Bossier City, La. 71010 Phone: 742-9155	1932	111
DOMINIQUE, Earl Joseph, III 1707 Bayou Circle, Bossier City, La. 71010 Phone: 742-9155	1953	111
DOMINIQUE, Elizabeth	1927	111
DOMINIQUE, Jason Paul 1707 Bayou Circle, Bossier City, La. 71010 Phone: 742-9155	1969	111
DOMINIQUE, Pamela Ann 1707 Bayou Circle, Bossier City, La. 71010 Phone: 742-9155	1957	111
DOMINIQUE, Penny Marie 1707 Bayou Circle, Bossier City, La. 71010 Phone: 742-9155	1956	111
DUGAS, Alex Joseph 8275 Gladewood, Baton Rouge, La. 70806 Phone: 927-6723	1957	157
DUGAS, Celeste Mary Box 94, White Castle, La. 70788 Phone: 545-3713	1952	170
DUGAS, Claude Noel 10354 Darryl Dr., Baton Rouge, La. 70815 Phone: 926-8753	1926	159
DUGAS, Claude Noel, Jr. 10354 Darryl Dr., Baton Rouge, La. 70815 Phone: 926-8753	1954	160
DUGAS, Dennis Michael 8275 Gladewood, Baton Rouge, La. 70806 Phone: 927-6723	1949	156
DUGAS, Jeanette Rita 8275 Gladewood, Baton Rouge, La. 70806 Phone: 927-6723	1955	157
DUGAS, Jeanette Rita (Gonzales) 8275 Gladewood, Baton Rouge, La. 70806 Phone: 927-6723	1924	156
DUGAS, Jeff Anthony 8275 Gladewood, Baton Rouge, La. 70806 Phone: 927-6723	1964	157
DUGAS, Julie Ann 8275 Gladewood, Baton Rouge, La. 70806 Phone: 927-6723	1953	157

NAME AND ADDRESS	YEAR OF BIRTH	PAGE
DUGAS, Julie Marie P. O. Box 239, Belle Rose, La. 70341	1964	103
DUGAS, Mary Jane (LeBlanc) P. O. Box 239, Belle Rose, La. 70341	1936	103
DUGAS, Melissa Ann P. O. Box 239, Belle Rose, La. 70341	1957	103
DUGAS, Melvin Joseph 11522 Glenda Dr., Baton Rouge, La. 70815 Phone: 275-4035	1913	158
DUGAS, Olda Mae (Loland) Box 94, White Castle, La. 70788 Phone: 545-3713	1925	170
DUGAS, Patricia Jane P. O. Box 239, Belle Rose, La. 70341	1959	103
DUGAS, Philomine (Clouatre) 11522 Glenda Dr., Baton Rouge, La. 70815 Phone: 275-4035	1892	158
DUGAS, Rickey Paul 10354 Darryl Dr., Baton Rouge, La. 70815 Phone: 926-8753	1955	160
DUGAS, Sheilah Ann 10354 Darryl Dr., Baton Rouge, La. 70815 Phone: 926-8753	1953	160
DUGAS, Toni Elizabeth 8275 Gladewood, Baton Rouge, La. 70806 Phone: 927-6723	1960	157
DUGAS, Una Marie (Gonzales) 1152 Oakley Dr., Baton Rouge, La. 70806 Phone: 924-2850	1919	155
DUHON, Darla Ann	1968	89
DUHON, Sharon Leonide (LeBlanc)	1949	89
DUKE, Beth Josephine 2119 Joseph St., New Orleans, La. 70115 Phone: 861-3354	1967	186
DUKE, Bradley James 2119 Joseph St., New Orleans, La. 70115 Phone: 861-3354	1957	186
DUKE, Fay Marie 2119 Joseph St., New Orleans, La. 70115 Phone: 861-3354	1956	186
DUKE, Jeremiah, Jr. 2119 Joseph St., New Orleans, La. 70115 Phone: 861-3354	1955	186

NAME AND ADDRESS	YEAR OF BIRTH	PAGE
DUPRE, Woodrow Joseph Pierre Part, La. 70339 Phone: 252-6555	1925	98
DURAN, Nancy Marie (Gray) 11 Boynton St., Apt. 4, Bangor, Maine	1947	106
ELLIS, Aline Marie (Dugas) 1145 Orangewood Dr., Baton Rouge, La. 70806 Phone: 926-5553	1922	159
ESKINE, Dorothy Estelle (LeBlanc) 1902 Hancock St., Gretna, La. 70053 Phone: 356-5506	1936	126
ESKINE, Rachael 1902 Hancock St., Gretna, La. 70053 Phone: 356-5506	1966	128
ESKINE, Ray Michael 1902 Hancock St., Gretna, La. 70053 Phone: 356-5506	1955	128
FAIRCHILD, Brenda Ann Rt. 2, Box 23, Sunshine, La. 70780 Phone: 642-8174	1951	163
FAIRCHILD, Charles James, Jr. Rt. 2, Box 23, Sunshine, La. 70780 Phone: 642-8174	1950	163
FAIRCHILD, Denise Sue Rt. 2, Box 23, Sunshine, La. 70780 Phone: 642-8174	1954	163
FAIRCHILD, Eunice (Sanchez) Rt. 2, Box 23, Sunshine, La. 70780 Phone: 642-8174	1919	163
FENN, Edgar James Tripple Creek Farm, Rt. 2, Box 117 Union Springs, Ala. 36089	1950	107
FENN, Eugenia Smith-T Tripple Creek Farm, Rt. 2, Box 117 Union Springs, Ala. 36089	1968	107
FENN, Helen Marie Tripple Creek Farm, Rt. 2, Box 117 Union Springs, Ala. 36089	1970	107
FENN, Helen Marie (Gray) Tripple Creek Farm, Rt. 2, Box 117 Union Springs, Ala. 36089	1919	107
FENN, Mary Helen Rt. 2, Box 117, Union Springs, Ala. 36089	1944	107

NAME AND ADDRESS	YEAR OF BIRTH	PAGE
FENN, Thomas Calvin, Jr. Tripple Creek Farm, Rt. 2, Box 117 Union Springs, Ala. 56089	1945	107
FITZPATRICK, Donna Jean (LeBlanc Chicago, Illinois	1948	129
FORTNER, Abbegail Marie (Thibodeaux) 1400 Dunn St., Houma, La. 70360	1947	98
FORTNER, Kay Marie 1400 Dunn St., Houma, La. 70360	1967	98
FREELAND, Corinne Anne (Gately) 2305 Terrace Ave., Victoria, Texas 77901 Phone: 575-4178	1935	183
FREELAND, Kathryn Corinne 2305 Terrace Ave., Victoria, Texas 77901 Phone: 575-4178	1958	183
FREELAND, Lynne Tracy 2305 Terrace Ave., Victoria, Texas 77901 Phone: 575-4178	1960	184
FREMIN, Keith Omer P. O. Box 912, Morgan City, La. 70380	1960	165
FREMIN, Mark Ellis P. O. Box 912, Morgan City, La. 70380	1962	165
FREMIN, Shirley (Sanchez) P. O. Box 912, Morgan City, La. 70380	1931	165
FREMIN, Winifred P. O. Box 912, Morgan City, La. 70380	1965	165
GARY, Anne Elizabeth 407 Woodside Dr., Houma, La. 70360	1960	184
GARY, Charlotte Lynne 407 Woodside Dr., Houma, La. 70360	1958	184
GARY, Donna Lea 407 Woodside Dr., Houma, La. 70360	1956	184
GARY, Grace Cecille (Truxillo) 407 Woodside Dr., Houma, La. 70360	1931	184
GARY, James Randolph 407 Woodside Dr., Houma, La. 70360	1963	184
GARY, John Francis 407 Woodside Dr., Houma, La. 70360	1964	184
GATELY, Corinne Marguerite (LeBlanc) 25 Oriole St., New Orleans, La. 70124 Phone: 282-3017	1911	183

NAME AND ADDRESS	YEAR OF BIRTH	PAGE
GAUTREAUX, Anna Lee (LeBlanc) Rt. 2, Box 204 B, Donaldsonville, La. 70346	1931	175
GAUTREAUX, Bennett Paul RFD, Belle Rose, La. 70341	1971	101
GAUTREAUX, Bryant Paul Box 22, White Castle, La. 70788 Phone: 525-3024	1956	171
GAUTREAUX, Charlotte Marie (Dupre) Belle River, La.	1954	98
GAUTREAUX, Claude Patrick Rt. 2, Box 204 B, Donaldsonville, La. 70346	1959	175
GAUTREAUX, Edna (Loland) Box 22, White Castle, La. 70788 Phone: 525-3024	1929	170
GAUTREAUX, Glen Anthony Box 22, White Castle, La. 70788 Phone: 525-3024	1962	171
GAUTREAUX, Janell Elizabeth 10722 Red Oaks Dr., Baton Rouge, La. 70815 Phone: 926-5825	1954	89
GAUTREAUX, Jennifer (Hebert) RFD, Belle Rose, La. 70341	1946	101
GAUTREAUX, Maurice Anthony, Jr. Rt. 2, Box 204 B, Donaldsonville, La. 70346	1953	175
GAUTREAUX, Monique Angele Rt. 2, Box 204 B, Donaldsonville, La. 70346	1968	175
GAUTREAUX, Tiffney Ann Belle River, La.	1971	98
GAUTREAUX, Velma (LeBlanc) 10722 Red Oaks Dr., Baton Rouge, La. 70815 Phone: 926-5825	1915	89
GERALD, Barbara Jean (Bergeron) Baton Rouge, La.	1949	199
GERALD, David Eugene, III Baton Rouge, La.	1969	199
GIAMBRONE, Joan Jeanette (LeBlanc) RFD 1, Box 65, Donaldsonville, La. 70346	1942	96
GIROIR, Mary Alice (Gravois) 11123 Chalice Dr., Baton Rouge, La. 70815 Phone: 926-2341	1947	228
GIROIR, Nicole Beth 11123 Chalice Dr., Baton Rouge, La. 70815 Phone: 926-2341	1972	228

NAME AND ADDRESS	YEAR OF BIRTH	PAGE
GIROIR, Stacy Beth 11123 Chalice Dr., Baton Rouge, La. 70815 Phone: 926-2341	1967	228
GONZALES, Antoine (Eddie) 8265 Royalwood, Baton Rouge, La. 70806 Phone: 924-2168	1910	154
GONZALES, Jeanne (CLouatre) 8265 Royalwood, Baton Rouge, La. 70806 Phone: 924-2168	1886	151
GRAFFEO, Jasen Pascal Rt. 1, Box 625, Plaquemine, La. 70764 Phone: 687-7561	1971	198
GRAFFEO, Sandra Ann (LeBlanc) Rt. 1, Box 625, Plaquemine, La. 70764 Phone: 687-7561	1943	198
GRAVOIS, Alice Mary (LeBlanc) Rt. 1, Box 548, White Castle, La. 70788	1919	227
GRAVOIS, Brian Keith RFD 2, Box 405 Al, Thibodaux, La. 70301 Phone: 446-1440	1963	227
GRAVOIS, Cynthia Anne Rt. 1, Box 548, White Castle, La. 70788	1958	228
GRAVOIS, David Anthony Rt. 1, Box 548, White Castle, La. 70788	1954	228
GRAVOIS, Edith Marie (Barrient) Rt. 2, Box 170 D, St. James, La. 70086 Phone: 265-3276	1902	110
GRAVOIS, Glenda Faye RFD 2, Box 405 Al, Thibodaux, La. 70301 Phone: 446-1440	1962	227
GRAVOIS, Glenn Joseph RFD 2, Box 405 Al, Thibodaux, La. 70301 Phone: 446-1440	1960	227
GRAVOIS, Irving Joseph RFD 2, Box 405 Al, Thibodaux, La. 70301 Phone: 446-1440	1940	227
GRAVOIS, Lloyd Aderian, Jr. Rt. 1, Box 548, White Castle, La. 70788	1949	228
GRAY, John James 6325 Perrier St., New Orleans, La. 70118	1917	106
GRAY, John James , Jr. New Orleans, La.	1951	106

NAME AND ADDRESS	YEAR OF BIRTH	PAGE
GREMILLION, Sharon Ann (Bourgeois) 1758 Peck Dr., Baton Rouge, La. 70808 Phone: 766-1474	1952	204
GROSSIMON, Gayle Marie (LeBlanc) 6409 Ave. B, New Orleans, La. 70124 Phone: 488-4552	1940	211
GROSSIMON, Louis Albert, II 6409 Ave. B, New Orleans, La. 70124 Phone: 488-4552	1967	211
GROSSIMON, Michael Patrick 6409 Ave. B, New Orleans, La. 70124 Phone: 488-4552	1969	211
GRYGO, Michael Edward 2629 Wilkerson Dr., Marrero, La. 70072 Phone: 347-2411	1963	116
GRYGO, Olive Glynn Ann 2629 Wilkerson Dr., Marrero, La. 70072 Phone: 347-2411	1960	116
GUERIN, Lillian (Landry) 117 Joy Ave., New Orleans, La. 70123 Phone: 729-6648	1902	107
GUIDRY, Bernice (LeBlanc) 6535 Silverleaf, Baton Rouge, La. 70812 Phone: 355-6745	1920	95 177
GUIDRY, Gayle Ann 6535 Silverleaf, Baton Rouge, La. 70812 Phone: 355-6745	1959	95 177
GUIDRY, Wayne Edward 1571 Creel Circle, Apt. E 1 College Park, Ga. 30337	1947	95 177
GUILLOT, Elma Marie (LeBlanc) 2024 N. 15th St., Baton Rouge, La. 70802 Phone: 344-8376	1923	172
GUILLOT, Kenneth 2024 N. 15th St., Baton Rouge, La. 70802 Phone: 344-8376	1957	173
GUILLOT, Lazard Joseph, Jr. 5810 Long Dr., Houston, Texas 77017	1943	172
GUILLOT, Robert Pierre 2024 N. 15th St., Baton Rouge, La. 70802 Phone: 344-8376	1954	173
GUILLOT, Ronald Michael 2024 N. 15th St., Baton Rouge, La. 70802	1954	173

NAME AND ADDRESS	YEAR OF BIRTH	PAGE
GUILLOT, Teri Lyn 5810 Long Dr., Houston, Texas 77017	1965	173
HALTROP, Harry Adrian Rt. 1, Box 118, White Castle, La. 70788	1963	164
HALTROP, Mary Theressa Rt. 1, Box 118, White Castle, La. 70788	1959	164
HALTROP, Ruby (Sanchez) Rt. 1, Box 118, White Castle, La. 70788	1924	164
HALTROP, Victoria Marie Rt. 1, Box 118, White Castle, La. 70788	1954	164
HARRIS, Julie Rita 3221 42nd St., Metairie, La. 70121 Phone: 835-0957	1967	124
HARRIS, Paul Matthew 3221 42nd St., Metairie, La. 70121 Phone: 835-0957	1971	124
HARRIS, Staci Elizabeth 3221 42nd St., Metairie, La. 70121 Phone: 835-0957	1965	124
HARRIS, Stephen George 3221 42nd St., Metairie, La. 70121 Phone: 835-0957	1965	123
HARRIS, Terrell Anne (LeBlanc) 3221 42nd St., Metairie, La. 70121 Phone: 835-0957	1938	123
HAUSWALD, Jay 402 Lynx Dr., Arabi, La. 70032 Phone: 279-0030	1962	85
HAUSWALD, Palmira (Williams) 402 Lynx Dr., Arabi, La. 70032 Phone: 279-0030	1940	85
HAUSWALD, Shawn 402 Lynx Dr., Arabi, La. 70032 Phone: 279-0030	1966	85
HAYDEN, Linda Ann (Templet) 4908 NewLands, Metairie, La. 70012 Phone: 888-9669	1943	192
HAYWORD, Douglas Spor, Jr. Rt. 1, Box 112, Donaldsonville, La. 70346 Phone: 473-9701	1955	112
HEATH, Alice Mae (Brignac) 7820 West Laverne, New Orleans, La. 70126 Phone: 242-2506	1942	116

NAME AND ADDRESS	YEAR OF BIRTH	PAGE
HEBERT, Eura Mae Pierre Part, La. 70339 Phone: 252-6156	1925	100
HESSE, Alma Theressa (LeBlanc) 2634 Cleveland Ave., New Orleans, La. 70119 Phone: 821-4715	1942	187
HESSE, David Gerard 2634 Cleveland Ave., New Orleans, La. 70119 Phone: 821-4715	1964	187
HESSE, Jan Ann 2634 Cleveland Ave., New Orleans, La. 70119 Phone: 821-4715	1965	187
HESSE, Hill Ann 2634 Cleveland Ave., New Orleans, La. 70119 Phone: 821-4715	1964	187
HESSE, Stanley Gerard 2634 Cleveland Ave., New Orleans, La. 70119 Phone: 821-4715	1963	187
HIDALGO, Ivy 10675 Gerald Dr., Baton Rouge, La. 70815 Phone: 927-9219	1941	80
HIDALGO, Karolyn Denise 10675 Gerald Dr., Baton Rouge, La. 70815 Phone: 927-9219	1965	80
HIDALGO, Kevin Allen 10675 Gerald Dr., Baton Rouge, La. 70815 Phone: 927-9219	1963	80
HIDALGO, Leonie Ann (Barrient) Rt. 1, Box 112, Donaldsonville, La. 70346 Phone: 473-8792	1947	113
HIDALGO, Robert John III Rt. 1, Box 112, Donaldsonville, La. 70346 Phone: 473-8792	1968	113
HIDALGO, Rose (LeBlanc) 478 Connell St., Baton Rouge, La. 70802 Phone: 342-0468	1903	80
HIMEL, Bert Mathew Rt. 1, Box 548, White Castle, La. 70788	1962	228
HIMEL, Brenda Faye (Gravois) Rt. 1, Box 548, White Castle, La. 70788	1944	228
HIMEL, Leo Adam, Jr. Rt. 1, Box 548, White Castle, La. 70788	1961	228
HIMEL, Todd Jude Rt. 1, Box 548, White Castle, La. 70788	1971	228

NAME AND ADDRESS	YEAR OF BIRTH	PAGE
HIMEL, Travis Paul Rt. 1, Box 548, White Castle, La. 70788	1964	228
HOLGATE, Orilia Marie (Barrient) 2429 Barracks, New Orleans, La. 70119 Phone: 821-6126	1906	111
HOLLAND, Donna Rae 542 Steele Blvd., Baton Rouge, La. 70806 Phone: 344-9072	1965	100
HOLLAND, Gaynell (Hebert) 542 Steele Blvd., Baton Rouge, La. 70806 Phone: 344-9072	1944	100
HOLLAND, Paula Marie 542 Steele Blvd., Baton Rouge, La. 70806 Phone: 344-9072	1968	100
HOLMES, Wanda Fay (LeBlanc) 1591 46th Ave., San Francisco, Calif. 94122	1930	80
HONEY, Susam Marie (Storey) 2923 Conrad, Baton Rouge, La. 70805 Phone: 357-1373	1954	89
HOOT, Dawn Marie 11120 Tams Dr., Baton Rouge, La. 70815 Phone: 275-5289	1962	143
HOOT, Scott Vincent 11120 Tams Dr., Baton Rouge, La. 70815 Phone: 275-5289	1961	143
HYMEL, Anita Ann Morning Glory Ave., Plaquemine, La. 70764	1960	165
HYMEL, Delia Ann (Sanchez) Morning Glory Ave., Plaquemine, La. 70764	1934	165
INDUST, Annette Marie 11441 Crete St., New Orleans, La. 70119 Phone: 488-4034	1972	211
INDUST, Dennis J., III 1141 Crete St., New Orleans, La. 70119 Phone: 488-4034	1952	210
INDUST, Diane M. 1141 Crete St., New Orleans, La. 70119 Phone: 488-4034	1954	210
INDUST, Jeanne M. 1141 Crete St., New Orleans, La. 70119 Phone: 488-4034	1960	210

NAME AND ADDRESS	YEAR OF BIRTH	PAGE
INDUST, John F. 1141 Crete St., New Orleans, La. 70119 Phone: 488-4034	1957	210
INDUST, Karen M. 1141 Crete St., New Orleans, La. 70119 Phone: 488-4034	1955	210
INDUST, Phyllis Marie (LeBlanc) 1141 Crete St., New Orleans, La. 70119 Phone: 488-4034	1930	210
INDUST, Rachel M. 1141 Crete St., New Orleans, La. 70119 Phone: 488-4034	1963	211
INDUST, Stephen Philip 1141 Crete St., New Orleans, La. 70119 Phone: 488-4034	1972	211
INDUST, Thomas M. 1141 Crete St., New Orleans, La. 70119 Phone: 488-4034	1958	210
JERNIGAN, Donna Rae (Loar) 2130 F. Ave., Apt. 204, National City, Calif. 92050	1947	156
JERNIGAN, John Alfred 2130 F. Ave., Apt. 204, National City, Calif. 92050	1970	156
JERNIGAN, Scott Michael 2130 F. Ave., Apt. 204, National City, Calif. 92050	1971	156
JERNIGAN, Stephen Paul 2130 F. Ave., Apt. 204, National City, Calif. 92050	1972	156
JERRIE, Donna Marie (Blanchard) P. O. Box 299, Maringouin, La. 70757 Phone: 625-2511	1948	125
JERRIE, Robert Troy P. O. Box 299, Maringouin, La. 70757 Phone: 625-2511	1968	125
JERRIE, Tami Marie P. O. Box 299, Maringouin, La. 70757 Phone: 625-2511	1969	125
JOHNSON, Carol Ann (LeBlanc)	1946	80
JORDAN, Brenda Lee (Ballard) 2852 Dayton, Baton Rouge, La. 70805 Phone: 357-5619	1951	179
JOYNE, David Ernest	1961	191

NAME AND ADDREWW	YEAR OF BIRTH	PAGE
JOYNE, Georgina M. (Borne)	1935	191
JOYNE, Karen Lynn	1957	191
JOYNE, Sue Ann	1955	191
JUBAN, Christopher Conley	1970	177
JUBAN, Janet Marie (LeBlanc) 1077 Rodney, Baton Rouge, La. 70808 Phone: 766-7592	1944	94 176
JUBAN, Joan Alison 1077 Rodney, Baton Rouge, La. 70808 Phone: 766-7592	1968	94 177
JUBAN, Randy 1077 Rodney, Baton Rouge, La. 70808 Phone: 766-7592	1960	94 177
KERR, Beryl Ann (Gray) 6325 Perrier St., New Orleans, La. 70118	1948	106
KERR, Debra Ann 6325 Perrier St., New Orleans, La. 70118	1965	106
KERR, Roy Darnell 6325 Perrier St., New Orleans, La. 70118	1966	106
KING, Chad Michael 7049 Caprice, Baton Rouge, La. 70812 Phone: 357-5681	1970	145
KING, Jacqueline Jo (Clouatre) 7049 Caprice, Baton Rouge, La. 70812 Phone: 357-5681	1949	144
KING, Troy Lynn 7049 Caprice, Baton Rouge, La. 70812 Phone: 357-5681	1969	145
KIRKSEY, Barbara Ann 1716 Tita St., Gretna, La. 70114 Phone: 367-1913	1972	131
KIRKSEY, Marsha Marie 1716 Tita St., Gretna, La. 70114 Phone: 367-1913	1947	130
KIRKSEY, Melinda Marie 1716 Tita St., Gretna, La. 70114 Phone: 367-1913	1969	130
KROENKE, Jeanne Laurance 9664 Ventura Dr., Baton Rouge, La. 70815 Phone: 927-4196	1971	156

NAME AND ADDRESS	YEAR OF BIRTH	PAGE
KROENKE, Nancy Marie (Dugas) 9664 Ventura Dr., Baton Rouge, La. 70815 Phone: 927-4196	1947	156
LAMB, Elaine Marie (Bergeron) 6949 E. Monarch St., Baton Rouge, La. 70811 Phone: 356-3955	1947	199
LAMB, Lance Joseph 6949 E. Monarch St., Baton Rouge, La. 70811 Phone: 356-3955	1972	199
LAMB, Shannon Laura 6949 E. Monarch St., Baton Rouge, La. 70811 Phone: 356-3955	1969	199
LAMBERT, Claudia Marie (Dupre) Pierre Part, La. 70339	1950	98
LAMBERT, Michelle Bernedette Pierre Part, La. 70339	1970	98
LAMBERT, Todd Anthony Pierre Part, La. 70339	1967	98
LAMBERT, Troy Joseph Pierre Part, La. 70339	1965	98
LAMY, Allyson Frances 4963 Floynell Dr., Baton Rouge, La. 70809 Phone: 937-2725	1959	185
LAMY, Celeste Marie 4963 Floynell Dr., Baton Rouge, La. 70809 Phone: 937-2725	1969	185
LAMY, Cynthia Claire 4963 Floynell Dr., Baton Rouge, La. 70809 Phone: 937-2725	1955	185
LAMY, Edward Theodore, III 4963 Floynell Dr., Baton Rouge, La. 70809 Phone: 937-2725	1960	185
LAMY, Eileen Patricia 4963 Floynell Dr., Baton Rouge, La. 70809 Phone: 937-2725	1961	185
LAMY, James Louis 4963 Floynell Dr., Baton Rouge, La. 70809 Phone: 937-2725	1968	185
LAMY, Jimmie Lou (Truxillo) 4963 Floynell Dr., Baton Rouge, La. 70809 Phone: 937-2725	1932	184
LAMY, Karen Louise 4963 Floynell Dr., Baton Rouge, La. 70809	1956	184

LAMY, Laura Elizabeth   1964   185
4963 Floynell Dr., Baton Rouge, La.   70809
Phone: 937-2725

LAMY, Lisa Maria   1958   184
4963 Floynell Dr., Baton Rouge, La.   70809
Phone: 937-2725

LANDRY, Alison Elaine   1972   169
122 Karen Dr., Lafayette, La.   70501

LANDRY, Angelic Cecile   1958   102
P. O. Box 52, Bayou Goula, La.   70716

LANDRY, Antoine Joseph   1965   102
P. O. Box 52, Bayou Goula, La.   70716

LANDRY, Boyd James   1968   169
122 Karen Dr., Lafayette, La.   70501

LANDRY, Camille Joseph   1964   102
P. O. Box 52, Bayou Goula, La.   70716

LANDRY, Carolyn Marie   1950   102
P. O. Box 52, Bayou Goula, La.   70716

LANDRY, Charles Gerard   1954   102
P. O. Box 52, Bayou Goula, La.   70716

LANDRY, David Joseph   1949   107
5354 Maribel Ct., Baton Rouge, La.   70812
Phone: 355-2969

LANDRY, Debra Ann   1952   102
P. O. Box 52, Bayou Goula, La.   70716

LANDRY, Debra Elizabeth   1954   193
Rt. 2, Box 208 A, Donaldsonville, La.   70346

LANDRY, Dennis Raymond   1951   107
5354 Maribel Ct., Baton Rouge, La.   70812
Phone: 355-2969

LANDRY, Edward Joseph   1897   105
644 Jefferson Heights, New Orleans, La.   70121

LANDRY, Elaine Rita (Bergeron)   1945   169
122 Karen Dr., Lafayette, La.   70501

LANDRY, Eloise Marie (LeBlanc)   1932   102
P. O. Box 52, Bayou Goula, La.   70716

LANDRY, Helen Marie   1896   106
6325 Perrier St., New Orleans, La.   70118
Phone: 895-1456

LANDRY, Inez Wallace (LeBlanc)   1920   193
Rt. 2, Box 208 A, Donaldsonville, La.   70346

NAME AND ADDRESS	YEAR OF BIRTH	PAGE
LANDRY, Joseph Nestor 408 Calhoun St., New Orleans, La. 70118 Phone: 899-3129	1909	108
LANDRY, Lisa Ann P. O. Box 52, Bayou Goula, La. 70716	1960	102
LANDRY, Malise Claire 122 Karen Dr., Lafayette, La. 70501	1969	169
LANDRY, Melanie Anne 5354 Maribel Ct., Baton Rouge, La. 70812 Phone: 355-2969	1955	107
LANDRY, Nestor Joseph 6124 Laurel St., New Orleans, La. 70118 Phone: 897-2471	1932	108
LANDRY, O'Neil Raymond 6070 Wilton, New Orleans, La. 70122 Phone: 283-3148	1923	105
LANDRY, Pamela Rt. 2, Box 208 A, Donaldsonville, La. 70346	1956	193
LANDRY, Shelley Clare 6124 Laurel St., New Orleans, La. 70118 Phone: 897-2471	1960	108
LANDRY, Sidney Joseph, Jr. 5354 Maribel Ct., Baton Rouge, La. 70812 Phone: 355-2969	1927	107
LANDRY, Susan Clare 6124 Laurel St., New Orleans, La. 70118 Phone: 897-2471	1957	108
LASYONE, Daniel Ray 16 Gardenia Lane, Waggaman, La. Phone: 729-7530	1966	202
LASYONE, Darryl Joseph 16 Gardenia Lane, Waggaman, La. Phone: 729-7530	1968	202
LASYONE, Jeanne Marie (Boudreaux) 16 Gardenia Lane, Waggaman, La. Phone: 729-7530	1941	202
LAWSON, Sonya Ann (LeBlanc) 2608 Missouri St., New Orleans, La. Phone: 721-6400	1953	194
LAYRISSON, Celeste Marie (LeBlanc) Rt. 2, Box 146 B, Springfield, La. 70462 Phone: 695-3622	1945	120
LE BLANC, Alfred John 465 Hamilton St., Gretna, La. 70053 Phone: 362-1775	1914	126

NAME AND ADDRESS	YEAR OF BIRTH	PAGE
LE BLANC, Charles Michael, Sr. Livonia, La. 70755 Phone: 637-2176	1939	122
LE BLANC, Charles Ray, Jr. 900 Dodge Ave., New Orleans, La. 70121 Phone: 835-6166	1961	126
LE BLANC, Charles Ray, Sr. 900 Dodge Ave., New Orleans, La. 70121 Phone: 835-6166	1927	125
LE BLANC, Charlotte Ann 713 St. Louis St., New Orleans, La. 70116	1950	193
LE BLANC, Charne Maria 836 Holt Place, Gretna, La. 70053 Phone: 367-3175	1967	186
LE BLANC, Christine Ann 1716 Redwood Dr., Harvey, La. 70058 Phone: 362-2726	1972	223
LE BLANC, Christopher Jay 1716 Redwood Dr., Harvey, La. 70058 Phone: 362-2726	1972	222
LE BLANC, Christopher Thomas 7114 N. Buttonwood, Baton Rouge, La. 70811 Phone: 357-4160	1969	203
LE BLANC, Clarl Louis 836 Holt Place, Gretna, La. 70053 Phone: 367-3175	1963	186
LE BLANC, Clebert J. (Diddy) 7502 Tipperary St., Baton Rouge, La. 70808 Phone: 766-7693	1907	181
LE BLANC, Clement Anthony 4025 Delaware St., Baton Rouge, La. 70805 Phone: 357-0818	1927	178
LE BLANC, Cleo Raye	1941	129
LE BLANC, Cleophas Joseph 930 Madison, Gretna, La. 70114 Phone: 361-1397	1916	128
LE BLANC, Cleveland Paul, Jr. 4956 Linden St., Baton Rouge, La. 70805 Phone: 356-3014	1948	124
LE BLANC, Cleveland (Tut), Sr. 3442 Greenwell St., Baton Rouge, La. 70805 Phone: 355-9924	1917	123

NAME AND ADDRESS	YEAR OF BIRTH	PAGE
LE BLANC, Deborah Kay 254 Idlewood Dr., Houma, La. 70360 Phone: 876-7977	1960	187
LE BLANC, Deborah Marie 207 Brunswick Ct., New Orleans, La. 70114 Phone: 361-0101	1963	131
LE BLANC, Debra Ann Donaldsonville, La. 70346	1958	229
LE BLANC, Delaine Michelle 4200 Mapleleaf Dr., New Orleans, La. 70164 Phone: 394-4543	1971	81
LE BLANC, Desire RFD 1, Box 108 A, Donaldsonville, La. 70346 Phone: 473-7832	1895	94 176
LE BLANC, Dian 3311 Toliver St., Houston, Texas 77016 Phone: 695-8189	1938	81
LE BLANC, Diane Marie 555 Pierce St., Baton Rouge, La. 70806 Phone: 924-1462	1956	189
LE BLANC, Dianne Pineville, La.	1941	103
LE BLANC, Dinah Lee 450 Cloud Dr., Baton Rouge, La. 70801 Phone: 927-4414	1937	122
LE BLANC, Donald Paul Donaldsonville, La. 70346	1952	229
LE BLANC, Dominique Marie Therase California	1958	124
LE BLANC, Donna Michelle 4604 Ritterman, Baton Rouge, La. 70805 Phone: 357-9927	1962	205
LE BLANC, Doris (LeBlanc) P. O. Box 161, Gonzales, La. 70737 Phone: 644-4381	1920	189
LE BLANC, Doris Ann 814 Orleans Ave., New Orleans, La. 70116	1936	186
LE BLANC, Douglas Eugene Chicago, Ill.	1950	130
LE BLANC, Douglas Philip	1942	86
LE BLANC, Drew Anthony River Rd., Donaldsonville, La. 70346 Phone: 473-3526	1968	204

NAME AND ADDRESS	YEAR OF BIRTH	PAGE
LE BLANC, Drouet Edmond, Sr. 209 W. Chester Dr, Lafayette, La. 70501 Phone: 833-9471	1942	211
LE BLANC, Drouet Edmond, Jr. 209 W. Chester Dr., Lafayette, La. 70501 Phone: 833-9471	1967	211
LE BLANC, Edith Marie (Dominique) Rt. 1, Box N-1-D, Napoleonville, La. 70390 Phone: 369-7860	1925	110
LE BLANC, Elaine Katherine 7232 Claiborne, Arabi, La. 70032 Phone: 271-8178	1953	223
LE BLANC, Elie Edmond, Jr. 5519 Laurel St., New Orleans, La. 70115	1918	86
LE BLANC, Ellis Nestor 112 Joy Ave., New Orleans, La. 70123 Phone: 729-7807	1928	107
LE BLANC, Ellis Nestor, Jr. 112 Joy Ave., New Orleans, La. 70123 Phone: 729-7807	1959	108
LE BLANC, Ernest George, Sr. 164 Garden Rd., New Orleans, La. 70123 Phone: 737-8416	1927	194
LE BLANC, Ernest Joseph, Jr. 4912 Bell Dr., Metairie, La. 70002 Phone: 887-1139	1936	211
LE BLANC, Ernest Joseph, III 4912 Bell Dr., Metairie, La. 70002 Phone: 887-1139	1959	211
LE BLANC, Ernest Paul 3636 Pasadena, Baton Rouge, La. 70814 Phone: 355-6593	1955	203
LE BLANC, Eston Thomas 836 Holt Place, Gretna, La. 70053 Phone: 367-3175	1934	185
LE BLANC, Euclid Thomas 173 Diana, Leucadia, Calif. 92024 Phone: 753-5791	1922	124
LE BLANC, Eugene Joseph Chicago, Ill.	1918	129
LE BLANC, Euzlein Paul 2933 Main St., Baton Rouge, La. 70802 Phone: 342-1081	1897	80

NAME AND ADDRESS	YEAR OF BIRTH	PAGE
LE BLANC, Gabriel Gardes 6734 Louisville St., New Orleans, La. 70124 Phone: 486-5169	1910	212 213
LE BLANC, Gary	1959	88
LE BLANC, George Anthony 333 Uvalde, Apt. 1273, Houston, Texas 77015	1960	167
LE BLANC George Anthony, Jr. 2321 Despaux Dr., Chalmette, La. 70043 Phone: 279-5853	1942	224
LE BLANC, George Anthony, Sr. 920 Forstall, New Orleans, La. 70117 Phone: 949-9220	1913	224
LE BLANC, Gregory Paul 3911 Winbourne Ave., Baton Rouge, La. 70805 Phone: 355-1250	1951	198
LE BLANC, Harold G. 4912 Belle Dr., Metairie, La. 70002 Phone: 887-1139	1961	211
LE BLANC, Harry Andrew 3911 Winbourne Ave., Baton Rouge, La. 70805 Phone: 355-1250	1915	195
LE BLANC, Harry Andrew, Jr. 1763 Mullen Dr., Baton Rouge, La. 70808 Phone: 766-6598	1939	195
LE BLANC, Heidi Lynn 936 Madison, New Orleans, La. 70014 Phone: 368-2744	1971	129
LE BLANC, Henry Anthony 7232 Claiborne, Arabi, La. 70032 Phone: 271-8178	1911	222
LE BLANC, Henry Joseph 1716 Redwood Dr., Harvey, La. 70058 Phone: 362-2726	1947	222
LE BLANC, Herbert Lucien 450 Norco St., Norco, La. 70079	1949	166
LE BLANC, Herbert Lucien, Sr. 450 Norco St., Norco, La. 70079	1913	166
LE BLANC, Hubert O'Neil 3577 Sherwood Dr., Baton Rouge, La. 70805 Phone: 356-0935	1937	120
LE BLANC, Hubert Wyley Maringouin, La. 70757	1920	124

NAME AND ADDRESS	YEAR OF BIRTH	PAGE
LE BLANC, John Keith Hester, La.	1946	166
LE BLANC, John Michael Box 231, Paincourtville, La. 70391	1971	97
LE BLANC, Jonathan Thomas 2264 Pine St., Bossier City, La. 71010 Phone: 742-5693	1945	135
LE BLANC, Jonathan Thomas, Jr. 2264 Pine St., Bossier City, La. 71010 Phone: 742-5693	1967	136
LE BLANC, Joseph Cleophas	1948	129
LE BLANC, Joseph Lee		89
LE BLANC, Joseph Pershing 713 St. Louis St., New Orleans, La. 70116	1918	192
LE BLANC, Joyce Marie Donaldsonville, La. 70346	1951	226
LE BLANC, Kathleen Belle Rose, La. 70341	1956	102
LE BLANC, Keith Michael Rt. 1, Box N-1-D, Napoleonville, La. 70390 Phone: 369-7860	1967	111
LE BLANC, Kenneth Gerard 254 Idlewood Dr., Houma, La. 70360 Phone: 876-7977	1965	187
LE BLANC, Kenneth James 3636 Pasadena, Baton Rouge, La. 70814 Phone: 355-6593	1957	203
LE BLANC, Kenneth Keen 4025 Delaware St., Baton Rouge, La. 70805 Phone: 357-0818	1956	179
LE BLANC, Kevin Rt. 1, Box 287, Donaldsonville, La. 70346 Phone: 473-9332	1959	203
LE BLANC, Kimberly Marie Rt. 3, Box 896, Morgan City, La. 70380	1956	101
LE BLANC, Laura Lynne 3636 Pasadena, Baton Rouge, La. 70814 Phone: 355-6593	1967	203
LE BLANC, Laurie Marie Box 231, Paincourtville, La. 70391	1968	97
LE BLANC, Leonard Joseph, Jr. 4604 Ritterman, Baton R(;e, La. 70805 Phone: 357-9927	1959	204

	YEAR OF BIRTH	PAGE
LE BLANC, Leonard Joseph, Sr. 4604 Ritterman, Baton Rouge, La. 70805 Phone: 357-9927	1936	204
LE BLANC, Leslie Rt. 1, Box 252, Belle Rose, La. 70341	1942	97
LE BLANC, Leslie Joseph 3636 Pasadena, Baton Rouge, La. 70814 Phone: 355-6593	1923	202
LE BLANC, Leslie Matthew 6962 Coronet Dr., Baton Rouge, La. 70812 Phone: 356-1641	1949	202
LE BLANC, Linda Claire 8846 Wakefield, Baton Rouge, La. 70806 Phone: 921-9551	1953	188
LE BLANC, Lindsey Allen 2835 Fairway Dr., Baton Rouge, La. 70809 Phone: 926-4323	1963	81
LE BLANC, Lisa Marie P. O. Box 285, Donaldsonville, La. 70346 Phone: 473-9561	1961	189
LE BLANC, Lloyd Joseph 3686 Webb Dr., Baton Rouge, La. 70805 Phone: 355-8625	1928	179
LE BLANC, Lola Ann (Guillot) 3501 Webb Dr., Baton Rouge, La. 70805 Phone: 357-6975	1947	173
LE BLANC, Loraine 709 Monroe St., Gretna, La. 70053 Phone: 361-5703	1968	128
LE BLANC, Lori Suzanne Livonia, La. 70755 Phone: 637-2176	1970	122
LE BLANC, Louis Gerard 3636 Pasadena, Baton Rouge, La. 70814 Phone: 355-6593	1961	203
LE BLANC, Louis Gourdain P. O. Box 285, Donaldsonville, La. 70346 Phone: 473-9561	1930	189
LE BLANC, Louis Leon 810 Iberville St., Donaldsonville, La. 70346 Phone: 473-8373	1887	183
LE BLANC, Louise Cecile Rt. 1, Box 144, Donaldsonville, La. 70346	1907	218

NAME AND ADDRESS	YEAR OF BIRTH	PAGE
LE BLANC, Nicole Evette 118 Sweetwood Dr., Monroe, La. 71201 Phone: 325-8940	1970	136
LE BLANC, Nolan Julien Maringouin, La. 70757	1910	119
LE BLANC, Norman Joseph 4575 E. Brookstown Dr., Baton Rouge, La. 70805	1911	121
LE BLANC, Paige Michelle 3577 Sherwood Dr., Baton Rouge, La. 70805 Phone: 356-0935	1971	120
LE BLANC, Pamela Ann Rt. 1, Box 252, Belle Rose, La. 70341	1952	97
LE BLANC, Pamela Rose 112 Joy Ave., New Orleans, La. 70123 Phone: 729-7807	1955	108
LE BLANC, Patricia 3311 Toliver St., Houston, Texas 77016 Phone: 695-8189	1944	81
LE BLANC, Patrick Joseph 2963 Brady, Baton Rouge, La. 70805 Phone: 355-4309	1953	203
LE BLANC, Paul Daniel Rt. 1, Box 141, Donaldsonville, La. 70346	1910	221
LE BLANC, Paul Michael 107 Verret St., Gretna, La. 70114 Phone: 362-9736	1945	130
LE BLANC, Paul Virginia 1591 46th Ave., San Francisco, Calif. 94122	1901	80
LE BLANC, Paulette Marie 555 Pierce St., Baton Rouge, La. 70806 Phone: 924-1462	1958	189
LE BLANC, Peggy Darlene 3442 Greenwell St., Baton Rouge, La. 70805 Phone: 355-9924	1954	124
LE BLANC, Peggy Lou (LeBlanc) 4614 Gallatin, New Orleans, La. 70114 Phone: 361-1823	1943	129
LE BLANC, Percy James, Jr. Boston, Mass.	1945	189
LE BLANC, Percy James, Sr. 463 Marion Dr., Baton Rouge, La. 70806 Phone: 927-0773	1920	188

LE BLANC, Randall Keith   1953   179
4025 Delaware St., Baton Rouge, La.   70805
Phone: 357-0818

LE BLANC, Ray   1954   203
Rt. 1, Box 287, Donaldsonville, La.   70346
Phone: 473-9332

LE BLANC, Ray Joseph   1924   203
Rt. 1, Box 287, Donaldsonville, La.   70346
Phone: 473-9332

LE BLANC, Raymond   1929   102
Belle Rose, La.   70341

LE BLANC, Raymond Michael   1952   129
930 Madison, Gretna, La.   70114
Phone: 361-1397

LE BLANC, Rebecca Ann   1965   129
4614 Gallatin, New Orleans, La.   70114
Phone: 361-1823

LE BLANC, Renee Katherine   1969   222
1716 Redwood Dr., Harvey, La.   70058
Phone: 362-2726

LE BLANC, Rhonda Elizabeth   1960   198
3911 Winbourne Ave., Baton Rouge, La.   70805
Phone: 355-1250

LE BLANC, Richard Etienne   1909   81
9578 Cal Rd., Baton Rouge, La.   70809
Phone: 937-2317

LE BLANC, Richard Etienne, Jr.   1940   81
4200 Mapleleaf Dr., New Orleans, La.   71164
Phone: 394-4543

LE BLANC, Richard Joseph   1919   188
8846 Wakefield, Baton Rouge, La.   70806
Phone: 921-9551

LE BLANC, Richard Joseph, Jr.   1950   188
8846 Wakefield, Baton Rouge, La.   70806
Phone: 921-9551

LE BLANC, Richard Patrick, Jr.   1964   128
709 Monroe St., Gretna, La.   70053
Phone: 361-5703

LE BLANC, Richard Patrick, Sr.   1945   128
709 Monroe St., Gretna, La.   70053
Phone: 361-5703

LE BLANC, Ricky Thomas   1948   125
173 Diana, Leucadia, Calif.   92024
Phone: 753-5791

NAME AND ADDRESS	YEAR OF BIRTH	PAGE
LE BLANC, Ricky Thomas, Jr. 173 Diana, Leucadia, Calif. 92024 Phone: 753-5791	1971	125
LE BLANC, Robbie Ann 3686 Webb Dr., Baton Rouge, La. 70805 Phone: 355-8625	1957	179
LR BLANC, Robert 3311 Toliver St., Houston, Texas 77016 Phone: 695-8189	1947	81
LE BLANC, Robert Bennett 138 Mink, San Antonio, Texas 78213 Phone: 342-2623	1921	193
LE BLANC, Robert Hoyt 138 Mink, San Antonio, Texas 78213 Phone: 342-2623	1951	193
LE BLANC, Robert James 861 Oakwood Dr., Gretna, La. 70053 Phone: 367-4741	1951	187
LE BLANC, Robert Lane Donaldsonville, La. 70346	1954	229
LE BLANC, Robert Neal 4404 Lake Vista Dr., Apt. A, Metairie, La. 70002 Phone: 885-9012	1948	134
LE BLANC, Robert Raymond 207 Brunswick Ct., New Orleans, La. 70114 Phone: 361-0101	1932	131
LE BLANC, Rodney Paul Rt. 3, Box 896, Morgan City, La. 70380	1954	101
LE BLANC, Romsey Joseph 367 McDonald Ave., Baton Rouge, La. 70808 Phone: 766-4724	1919	94 176
LE BLANC, Ron Vincent Livonia, La. 70755 Phone: 637-2176	1972	122
LE BLANC, Ronald Joseph 1505 Vegas Dr., Metairie, La. 70003	1939	192
LE BLANC, Ronald Philip	1946	111
LE BLANC, Roxanna Maria 4604 Ritterman, Baton Rouge, La. 70805 Phone: 357-9927	1958	204
LE BLANC, Roy James 427 Seguin St., New Orleans, La. 70114 Phone: 362-4035	1920	130

NAME AND ADDRESS	YEAR OF BIRTH	PAGE
LE BLANC, Telesmar, Jr. Rt. 1, Box 423, Old Grand Bayou Rd. Port Allen, La. 70767 Phone: 627-6619	1903	178
LE BLANC, Thomas 2262 Pine St., Bossier City, La. 71010 Phone: 742-6312	1921	135
LE BLANC, Thomas Allen 900 Dodge Ave., New Orleans, La. 70121 Phone: 835-6166	1948	126
LE BLANC, Thomas Marion 7114 N. Buttonwood, Baton Rouge, La. 70811 Phone: 357-4160	1950	203
LE BLANC, Timothy 4644 Kendall Dr., New Orleans, La. 70126 Phone: 282-1832	1972	194
LE BLANC, Tina Marie 4200 Mapleleaf Dr., New Orleans, La. 71164 Phone: 394-4543	1963	81
LE BLANC, Tracy Arthur Box 231, Paincourtville, La. 70391	1946	97
LE BLANC, Veronica Jan 3911 Winbourne Ave., Baton Rouge, La. 70805 Phone: 355-1250	1955	198
LE BLANC, Vincent Belle Rose, La. 70341	1957	102
LE BLANC, Virgie Ann	1967	204
LE BLANC, Virginia Carol 207 Brunswick Ct., New Orleans, La. 70114 Phone: 361-0101	1962	131
LE BLANC, Wayne Michael Chicago, Ill.	1952	130
LE BLANC, Wayne Micahel 4614 Gallatin, New Orleans, La. 70114 Phone: 361-1823	1964	129
LE BLANC, Wildon P. 247 Clayton Dr., Norco, La. 70079 Phone: 764-6283	1919	167
LE BLANC, Willa Rebecca	1972	203
LE BLANC, William 555 Pierce St., Baton Rouge, La. 70806 Phone: 924-1462	1924	189
LE BLANC, William Julius 900 Hickory St., Morgan City, La. 70380	1919	167

NAME AND ADDRESS	YEAR OF BIRTH	PAGE
LEE, Dana Alane	1966	89
LEE, Jeffrey Alan	1970	89
LEE, Jerilyn Lee (LeBlanc)	1945	89
LILES, Sharon Yvette (Besnard) 208 Marion Ct., Apt. B., New Orleans, La. 70123 Phone: 721-3314	1944	116
LOAR, Belinda Ann 3336 Van Buren, Baker, La. 70714 Phone: 775-3190	1954	156
LOAR, Eugene Bennett, Jr. 5103 Trisian, Baton Rouge, La. 70714 Phone: 774-1297	1951	156
LOAR, Jean Theressa (Gonzales) 3336 Van Buren, Baker, La. 70714 Phone: 775-3190	1924	156
MC ALLISTER, Saundra Louise (Dugas) 2817 Lorraine St., Baton Rouge, La. 70805 Phone: 355-1214	1952	160
MC ALLISTER, Scott Michael	1972	160
MC LAUGHLIN, Karen Ann 1535 Obier Ave., Plaquemine, La. 70764 Phone: 687-2359	1951	134
MC LAUGHLIN, Kathleen Marie 1535 Obier Ave., Plaquemine, La. 70764 Phone: 687-2359	1956	134
MC LAUGHLIN, Laurie Ann 1535 Obier Ave., Plaquemine, La. 70764 Phone: 687-2359	1960	134
MC LAUGHLIN, Mildred Ann (LeBlanc) 1535 Obier Ave., Plaquemine, La. 70764 Phone: 687-2359	1927	134
MADINE, Auralie Ann 1009 Myrtle St., Morgan City, La. 70380	1961	164
MADINE, Claude Allen 1009 Myrtle St., Morgan City, La. 70380	1965	164
MADINE, Elsie Mae (Sanchez) 1009 Myrtle St., Morgan City, La. 70380	1928	164
MADINE, Evans Joseph, III 1009 Myrtle St., Morgan City, La. 70380	1952	164

NAME AND ADDRESS	YEAR OF BIRTH	PAGE
MAHER, Jeanette Marie (Bujol) Box 4, Modeste, La. 70376 Phone: 473-7785	1937	225
MAHER, Karen Ann Box 4, Modeste, La. 70376 Phone: 473-7785	1966	225
MAHER, Kenneth Dale, Jr. Box 4, Modeste, La. 70376 Phone: 473-7785	1956	225
MAHER, Kyle Paul Box 4, Modeste, La. 70376 Phone: 473-7785	1971	225
MAHER, Mark John Box 4, Modeste, La. 70376 Phone: 473-7785	1964	225
MAHER, Marvin Charles Box 4, Modeste, La. 70376 Phone: 473-7785	1958	225
MARFORD, Fredia 917 Eleanore St., New Orleans, La. 70115 Phone: 899-8558	1924	84
MARFORD, Janice 917 Eleanore St., New Orleans, La. 70115 Phone: 899-8558	1949	84
MARFORD, John G., Jr. 917 Eleanore St., New Orleans, La. 70115 Phone: 899-8558	1950	84
MARFORD, Michael C. 917 Eleanore St., New Orleans, La. 70115 Phone: 899-8558	1947	84
MEDINE, Allen David Rt. 1, Box 143, White Castle, La. 70788	1960	152
MEDINE, Allen Louis Rt. 1, Box 143, White Castle, La. 70788	1929	152
MEDINE, Andrew Graves, Jr. White Castle, La. 70788	1950	152
MEDINE, Andrew Graves, Sr. Rt. 1, Box 392, White Castle, La. 70788	1926	152
MEDINE, Blake Anthony White Castle, La. 70788	1972	152
MEDINE, Brian Philip Rt. 1, Box 392, White Castle, La. 70788	1958	152

NAME AND ADDRESS	YEAR OF BIRTH	PAGE
MEDINE, Calvin Anthony, Jr. Rt. 1, Box 162, White Castle, La. 70788	1961	153
MEDINE, Calvin Anthony, Sr. Rt. 1, Box 162, White Castle, La. 70788	1938	153
MEDINE, Chad Michael Rt. 2, Box 69A, Marksville, La. 71351	1967	153
MEDINE, Curtis Philip Rt. 2, Box 69A, Marksville, La. 71351	1933	152
MEDINE, Deborah Ann Rt. 1, Box 143, White Castle, La. 70788	1953	152
MEDINE, Donald Anthony 8605 S. Atlanta Place, Tulsa, Okla. 74136	1946	153
MEDINE, Donald Anthony, Jr. 8605 S. Atlanta Place, Tulsa, Okla. 74136	1966	153
MEDINE, Emma (Gonzales) Rt. 1, Box 228, White Castle, La. 70788	1907	152
MEDINE, Emma Jean Rt. 1, Box 392, White Castle, La. 70788	1963	152
MEDINE, Gesile Rt. 1, Box 392, White Castle, La. 70788	1956	152
MEDINE, Jerrel G., Jr. Rt. 1, Box 290, White Castle, La. 70788	1952	152
MEDINE, Jerrel G., Sr. Rt. 1, Box 290, White Castle, La. 70788	1931	152
MEDINE, John Bradley 8605 S. Atlanta Place, Tulsa, Okla. 74136	1970	153
MEDINE, Keith Joseph Rt. 1, Box 143, White Castle, La. 70788	1961	152
MEDINE, Kevin John Rt. 1, Box 392, White Castle, La. 70788	1960	152
MEDINE, Kirt Joseph Rt. 2, Box 69A, Marksville, La. 71351	1961	153
MEDINE, Linda Ann Rt. 1, Box 143, White Castle, La. 70788	1954	152
MEDINE, Pamela Ann 8605 S. Atlanta Place, Tulsa, Okla. 74136	1964	153
MEDINE, Phil Patrick Rt. 2, Box 69A, Marksville, La. 71351	1965	153
MEDINE, Romona Joan Rt. 1, Box 143, White Castle, La. 70788	1967	152

NAME AND ADDRESS	YEAR OF BIRTH	PAGE
MEDINE, Russell Paul Rt. 1, Box 290, White Castle, La. 70788	1966	152
MEDINE, Scott James Rt. 1, Box 143, White Castle, La. 70788	1968	152
MEDINE, Severan Joseph 5700 De Siard Ave., Monroe, La. 71201	1950	154
MEDINE, Shawn Elizabeth	1972	154
MEDINE, Sylvia Ann Rt. 1, Box 290, White Castle, La. 70788	1954	152
MEDINE, Tommy M. Rt. 1, Box 162, White Castle, La. 70788	1964	153
MELANCON, Beatrice (LeBlanc) 4620 Beech St., Baton Rouge, La. 70805 Phone: 355-8401	1909	219
MELANCON, Brian Charles 14218 Carol Crest Dr., Houston, Texas 77024 Phone: 497-1868	1958	208
MELANCON, Ernest Timothy 6855 Vineyard Dr., Baton Rouge, La. 70812 Phone: 357-2013	1956	219
MELANCON, Ernest Thomas, III 6855 Vineyard Dr., Baton Rouge, La. 70812 Phone: 357-2013	1938	219
MELANCON, Kenneth Joseph, Jr. 7151 Chisholm Ave., Baton Rouge, La. 70811 Phone: 357-8074	1970	220
MELANCON, Kenneth Joseph, Sr. 7151 Chisholm Ave., Baton Rouge, La. 70811 Phone: 357-8074	1940	219
MELANCON, Larry John 6778 Vineyard Dr., Baton Rouge, La. 70812 Phone: 357-8033	1941	220
MELANCON, Laurie Jean 7151 Chisholm Ave., Baton Rouge, La. 70811 Phone: 357-8074	1965	220
MELANCON, Lisa Vay 6855 Vineyard Dr., Baton Rouge, La. 70812 Phone: 357-2013	1960	219
MELANCON, Marion Carlotta (Rodrigue) 14218 Carol Crest Dr., Houston, Texas 77024 Phone: 497-1868	1927	208

NAME AND ADDRESS	YEAR OF BIRTH	PAGE
MELANCON, Marsha Ann 14218 Carol Crest Dr., Houston, Texas 77024 Phone: 497-1868	1953	208
MELANCON, Michael Louis 14218 Carol Crest Dr., Houston, Texas 77024 Phone: 497-1868	1960	208
MELANCON, Paul David 14218 Carol Crest Dr., Houston, Texas 77024 Phone: 497-1868	1956	208
MELANCON, Paula Gay 6855 Vineyard Dr., Baton Rouge, La. 70812 Phone: 357-2013	1958	219
MELANCON, Renee Michelle 6778 Vineyard Dr., Baton Rouge, La. 70812 Phone: 357-8033	1971	220
MELANCON, Stacy Ann 6778 Vineyard Dr., Baton Rouge, La. 70812 Phone: 357-8033	1970	220
MELANCON, Tracey Lynn 6855 Vineyard Dr., Baton Rouge, La. 70812 Phone: 357-2013 .	1964	219
MEYER, Emily Marie 206 Hebert St., Thibodaux, La. 70301	1951	164
MICHELLI, Barbara Anne (Pollard) 3453 Winnebago St., Baton Rouge, La. 70805 Phone: 355-7903	1938	140
MICHELLI, John Michael 3453 Winnebago St., Baton Rouge, La. 70805 Phone: 355-7903	1959	141
MILANO, Charlotta Marie 2104 Ovide St., Baton Rouge, La. 70808 Phone: 343-0163	1959	208
MILANO, Clara Marie (Rodrigue) 2104 Ovide St., Baton Rouge, La. 70808 Phone: 343-0163	1935	208
MILANO, Jerome Kent 2104 Ovide St., Baton Rouge, La. 70808 Phone: 343-0163	1955	208
MILEY, Adele Cecile (Gonzales) 139 Wilshire Ave., Daly City, Calif.	1915	155
MILEY, Amy Jeanne 2430 33rd Ave., San Francisco, Calif. 94116	1972	155
MILEY, Ann Alicia 2430 33rd Ave., San Francisco, Calif. 94116	1966	155

NAME AND ADDRESS	YEAR OF BIRTH	PAGE
MILEY, Anthony James 2430 33rd Ave., San Francisco, Calif. 94116	1942	155
MILEY, Dawn Marie 2531 Poppy Dr., Burlingame, Calif.	1965	155
MILEY, Denise Loraine 2531 Poppy Dr., Burlingame, Calif.	1962	155
MILEY, Durward Charles 2531 Poppy Dr., Burlingame, Calif.	1940	155
MILLER, Jill Andrea 6497 Dalark St., Baton Rouge, La. 70812 Phone: 355-8227	1970	198
MILLER, Jina Angele 6497 Dalark St., Baton Rouge, La. 70812 Phone: 355-8227	1967	198
MILLER, Joan Anne (Bergeron) 6497 Dalark St., Baton Rouge, La. 70812 Phone: 355-8227	1944	198
MILLER, Julie Ann 6497 Dalark St., Baton Rouge, La. 70812 Phone: 355-8227	1969	198
MINSTRETTE, Adrienne Donaldsonville, La. 70346	1969	101
MINSTRETTE, Rita Mae (Hebert) Donaldsonville, La. 70346	1945	100
MINSTRETTA, Samuel Donaldsonville, La. 70346	1967	101
MONTE, Caroline Catherine 3466 Sunderland Circle, Atlanta, Ga. 30319 Phone: 451-0750	1969	184
MONTE, Caroline Catherine (Gately) 3466 Sunderland Circle, Atlanta, Ga. 30319 Phone: 451-0750	1938	184
MONTE, Philip Francis III 3466 Sunderland Circle, Atlanta, Ga. 30319 Phone: 451-0750	1963	184
MONTE, Tracy Thomas 3466 Sunderland Circle, Atlanta, Ga. 30319 Phone: 451-0750	1964	184
MONTZ, Barbara Ann (Terrio) 1436 Railroad Ave., Reserve, La. 70084 Phone: 536-2377	1936	114
MONTZ, Darline Ann (Carney) 6262 Dalark Dr., Baton Rouge, La. 70812 Phone: 357-7460	1946	92

NAME AND ADDRESS	YEAR OF BIRTH	PAGE
MONTZ, Khristine Ann 1436 Railroad Ave., Reserve, La. 70084 Phone: 536-2377	1966	115
MONTZ, Lisa Ann 1436 Railroad Ave.., Reserve, La. 70084 Phone: 536-2377	1960	115
MONTZ, Michelle Denise 6262 Dalark Dr., Baton Rouge, La. 70812 Phone: 357-7460	1966	92
MONTZ, Rachelle Darlene 6262 Dalark Dr., Baton Rouge, La. 70812 Phone: 357-7460	1968	92
MONTZ, Robin Ann 1436 Railroad Ave., Reserve, La. 70084 Phone: 536-2377	1962	115
MONTZ, Scott Joseph 1436 Railroad Ave., Reserve, La. 70084 Phone: 526-2377	1968	115
MOSELEY, Kathleen Margaret (landry) 2128 Robin St., New Orleans, La. 70122 Phone: 288-7304	1946	109
MOSKAU, Albert Alfred, Jr. 3425 Edenborn Ave., Apt. 136, Metairie, La. 70002 Phone: 888-3804	1944	117
MOSKAU, Albert Alfred, III 264 W. 10th Ave., Apt. 7, Mesa, Arizona	1968	117
MOSKAU, Timothy Carl 421 Celeste Ave., New Orleans, La. 70123 Phone: 729-3556	1960	117
MOSKAU, Chris David 421 Celeste Ave., New Orleans, La. 70123 Phone: 729-3556	1954	117
MOSKAU, Dorothy Carmel (Barrient) 421 Celeste Ave., New Orleans, La. 70123 Phone: 729-3556	1921	117
MOSKAU, Larry James, Jr. 312 Church St., Hammond, La. 70401 Phone: 345-6879	1972	117
MOSKAU, Larry James, Sr. 312 Church St., Hammond, La. 70401 Phone: 345-6879	1948	117
MOYE, David Alan	1967	114
MOYE, Mary Ann (Barrient)	1940	114

NAME AND ADDRESS	YEAR OF BIRTH	PAGE
MOYE, Richmond Maurice	1963	114
MOYE, Robert Michael	1960	114
MOYE, Thomas Madison	1966	114
MOYE, William Bruce	1962	114
MUNSTER, Donna Marie 6810 Curran Blvd, New Orleans, La. 70126 Phone: 241-1094	1964	115
MUNSTER, John Elvin, II 6810 Curran Blvd., New Orleans, La. 70126 Phone: 241-1094	1961	115
MUNSTER, Ruth Marie (Brignac) 6810 Curran Blvd., New Orleans, La. 70126 Phone: 241-1094	1939	115
MURPHY, James Crow, III 437 Nassau Dr., Baton Rouge, La. 70815 Phone: 275-9701	1967	159
MURPHY, Margo (Raiford) 437 Nassau Dr., Baton Rouge, La. 70815 Phone: 275-9701	1944	159
MYERS, Celeste (Clouatre) 4766 Longfellow, Baton Rouge, La. 70805 Phone: 357-8981	1948	144
NEPTUNE, Charmaine Marie (Gautreaux) 10545 Red Oaks Dr., Baton Rouge, La. 70815 Phone: 921-2324	1952	89
NEVLE, Linda (Williams) 400 Lynx Dr., Arabi, La. 70032	1945	85
NEVLE, Michael A., Jr. 400 Lynx Dr., Arabi, La. 70032	1965	85
NEVLE, Rebecca 400 Lynx Dr., Arabi, La. 70032	1967	85
NIELSEN, Leonard Lawrence 117 Aris Ave., Metairie, La. 70121 Phone: 834-1833	1944	130
NIELSEN, Mark Edward 117 Aris Ave., Metairie, La. 70121 Phone: 834-1833	1969	130
NIELSEN, Paul Christopher 117 ARis Ave., Metairie, La. 70121 Phone: 834-1833	1971	130
NIELSEN, Verlin Marie (LeBlanc) 1509 Shirley Dr., New Orleans, La. 70114 Phone: 366-3968	1925	130

NAME AND ADDRESS	YEAR OF BIRTH	PAGE
NORMAND, Barbara Ann (LeBlanc) 861 Oakwood Dr., Rota, Spain	1951	187
OLINDE, Dianna Carol 30 Elm Dr., Monroe, La. 71201 Phone: 737-6291	1964	122
OLINDE, Kurt David 30 Elm Dr., Monroe, La. 71201 Phone: 737-6291	1963	122
OLINDE, Larry Thomas 30 Elm Dr., Monroe, La. 71201 Phone: 737-6291	1960	122
OLINDE, Mary Ellen 30 Elm Dr., Monroe, La. 71201 Phone: 737-6291	1959	122
OLINDE, Norma Dell (LeBlanc) 30 Elm Dr., Monroe, La. 71201 Phone: 737-6291	1935	121
OLINDE, Roger Blaise 30 Elm Dr., Monroe, La. 71201 Phone: 737-6291	1962	122
OLINDE, Wallace Joseph, Jr. 30 Elm Dr., Monroe, La. 71201 Phone: 737-6291	1958	122
OPITZ, Mary Elizabeth (LeBlanc) Rt. 3, Box 120 A, Clinton, Ark.	1947	167
OUFNAC, Sherree Marie Pierre Part, La. 70339	1972	180
OUFNAC, Wanda Ann (Perault) Pierre Part, La. 70339	1956	180
PENNISON, Merende Theressa Rt. 3, Box 961, Morgan City, La. 70380	1952	101
PENNISON, Shawn Michael Rt. 3, Box 961, Morgan City, La. 70380	1971	101
PERAULT, Larkeal Agatha (LeBlanc) 3656 Webb Dr., Baton Rouge, La. 70805 Phone: 357-6680	1934	180
PERAULT, Rex Ann 3656 Webb Dr., Baton Rouge, La. 70805 Phone: 357-6680	1959	180
PERAULT, Roland Joseph, Jr. 3656 Webb Dr., Baton Rouge, La. 70805 Phone: 357-6680	1951	180

PIZZOLATO, Amy Lee   1972   124
4723 Castle Rose, San Antonio, Texas   78218
Phone: 653-4558

PIZZOLATO, David Joseph, Jr.   1971   124
4723 Castle Rose, San Antonio, Texas   78218
Phone: 653-4558

PIZZOLATO, Linda Diane (LeBlanc)   1950   124
4723 Castle Rose, San Antonio, Texas   78218
Phone: 653-4558

POCHE, David Paul   1965   115

POCHE, Margaret Ann (Terro)   1938   115

POCHE, Michael Shane   1962   115

POLITO, Beverly Anne (LeBlanc)   1942   195
Rt. 7, Box 89, Blount Rd., Baton Rouge, La.   70807
Phone: 775-6825

POLITO, Stephen   1970   196
Rt. 7, Box 89, Blount Rd., Baton Rouge, La.   70807
Phone: 775-6825

POLLARD, Nora Lee (Clouatre)   1915   139
3453 Winnebago St., Baton Rouge, La.   70805
Phone: 355-7903

PRESZLER, Cheryle Anne (LeBlanc)   1947   178
30 Kirkwood Court, Concord, Calif.   94521

PRESZLER, Tamara Diann   1971   179
30 Kirkwood Court, Concord, Calif.   94521

PROCHASKA, Kathleen Lynn   1969   185
1794 Denver Dr., Baton Rouge, La.   70808
Phone: 766-3984

PROCHASKA, Maria Ann   1966   185
1794 Denver Dr., Baton Rouge, La.   70808
Phone: 766-3984

PROCHASKA, Maria Ann (Truxillo)   1938   185
1794 Denver Dr., Baton Rouge, La.   70808
Phone: 766-3984

PROCHASKA, Michael Lloyd   1970   185
1794 Denver Dr., Baton Rouge, La.   70808
Phone: 766-3984

PROCHASKA, William Ray   1967   185
1794 Denver Dr., Baton Rouge, La.   70808
Phone: 766-3984

RAIFORD, Mildred Marie (Dugas)   1919   159
3376 Lone Oak Dr., Baton Rouge, La.   70814
Phone: 926-1034

NAME AND ADDRESS	YEAR OF BIRTH	PAGE
RINKER, Jerri Anne Tampa, Fla.	1968	121
RINKER, Joanne Tampa, Fla.	1958	121
RINKER, John Sanderson Tampa, Fla.	1961	121
ROBBINS, Marlene Ann (Dugas) Rt. 1, Box 95, White Castle, La. 70788 Phone: 545-3530	1946	170
ROBBINS, Rhett James Rt. 1, Box 95, White Castle, La. 70788 Phone: 545-3530	1972	170
ROBBINS, Sean Gerard Rt. 1, Box 95, White Castle, La. 70788 Phone: 545-3530	1968	170
ROBERT, Chad 117 B, St. Peter St., Houma, La. 70360		228
ROBERT, Jeffery 117 B, St. Peter St., Houma, La. 70360		228
ROBERT, Jo Ann (Gravois) 117 B, St. Peter St., Houma, La. 70360	1943	228
RODOSTA, Evella (Clouatre) 210 W. River Road, White Castle, La. 70788 Phone: 545-3940	1908	149
RODRIGUE, Ernest Louis, Jr. 3737 Diane Place, Metairie, La. 70123 Phone: 885-8147	1946	208
RODRIGUE, Ernest Louis, Sr. 329 Riverdale Dr., New Orleans, La. 70121 Phone: 833-0045	1922	208
RODRIGUE, Henry Joseph (Bro. Gasper) Vandebilt Catholic High, 209 Hollywood Rd. Houma, La. 70360	1919	207
ROGERS, Jane Lynn 920 Porter St., Gretna, La. 70053 Phone: 366-8247	1964	128
ROGERS, John Craig 920 Porter St., Gretna, La. 70053 Phone: 366-8247	1955	128
ROGERS, Scott Paul 920 Porter St., Gretna, La. 70053 Phone: 366-8247	1962	128
ROGERS, Vada Mae (LeBlanc) 920 Porter St., Gretna, La. 70053	1939	128

| --- | --- | --- |
ROME, Beryl Ann (Terrio)	1944	115
ROME, Monique Ann	1971	115
SAMSON, Christine 4005 Eleanor Dr., Baton Rouge, La. 70805	1967	80
SAMSON, Joy (LeBlanc) 6169 Dutton St., Baton Rouge, La. 70805	1922	80
SAMSON, Mary Ann 6119 Dutton St., Baton Rouge, La. 70805	1957	80
SAMSON, Pamela Ann 4005 Eleanor Dr., Baton Rouge, La. 70805	1969	80
SAMSON, Randall J. 4005 Eleanor Dr., Baton Rouge, La. 70805	1947	80
SAMSON, Valerie 6169 Dutton St., Baton Rouge, La. 70805 Phone: 355-0779	1960	80
SANCHEZ, Lois Elizabeth (Loland) Rt. 1, Box 84, Belle Rose, La. 70341 Phone: 473-7409	1923	163 170
SANCHEZ, Craig Gerard Rt. 1, Box 94, Belle Rose, La. 70341 Phone: 473-7409	1958	163 170
SANCHEZ, Daniel Joseph 4902 Baton Rouge Ave., Baton Rouge, La. 70805 Phone: 355-0770	1967	163
SANCHEZ, Darilyn Marie 4902 Baton Rouge Ave., Baton Rouge, La. 70805 Phone: 355-0770	1961	163
SANCHEZ, Darron J., Jr. 4902 Baton Rouge Ave., Baton Rouge, La. 70805 Phone: 355-0770	1962	163
SANCHEZ, Darron J., Sr. 4902 Baton Rouge Ave., Baton Rouge, La. 70805 Phone: 355-0770	1938	162
SANCHEZ, David James Ruston, La. 71270	1950	164
SANCHEZ, Debra Claire Rt. 1, Box 94, Belle Rose, La. 70341 Phone: 473-8091	1954	164
SANCHEZ, Delia (LeBlanc) Rt. 1, Box 94, Belle Rose, La. 70341 Phone: 473-7409	1886	162

NAME AND ADDRESS	YEAR OF BIRTH	PAGE
SANCHEZ, Dwayne Gerard Rt. 1, Box 94, Belle Rose, La. 70341 Phone: 473-0891	1963	164
SANCHEZ, Evans James White Castle, La. 70788	1966	165
SANCHEZ, Fred Joseph White Castle, La. 70788	1930	165
SANCHEZ, Fred Joseph, Jr. White Castle, La. 70788	1959	165
SANCHEZ, Janelle May Rt. 1, Box 94, Belle Rose, La. 70341 Phone: 473-0891	1958	164
SANCHEZ, Linas J. 2731 Huron St., Baton Rouge, La. 70805 Phone: 355-9847	1915	162
SANCHEZ, Linas J., Jr. 2731 Huron St., Baton Rouge, La. 70805 Phone: 355-9847	1937	162
SANCHEZ, Linda Leigh White Castle, La. 70788	1961	165
SANCHEZ, Lisa Ann White Castle, La. 70788	1957	165
SANCHEZ, Marsha Ann White Castle, La. 70788	1952	164
SANCHEZ, Melanie Ann 4902 Baton Rouge Ave., Baton Rouge, La. 70805 Phone: 355-0770	1960	163
SANCHEZ, Melodie Elizabeth Rt. 1, Box 94, Belle Rose, La. 70341 Phone: 473-7409	1957	163 170
SANCHEZ, Percy J. Rt. 1, Box 94, Belle Rose, La. 70341 Phone: 473-8091	1922	163
SANCHEZ, Rickey Joseph Paincourtville, La.	1951	163 170
SANCHEZ, Sylvania Marie White Castle, La. 70788	1957	164
SANCHEZ, Telasmar James White Castle, La. 70788	1925	164
SANCHEZ, Ulysses Rt. 1, Box 94, Belle Rose, La 70341 Phone: 473-7409	1921	163 170

NAME AND ADDRESS	YEAR OF BIRTH	PAGE
SAVOY, Charlotte Ann 17195 Augusta Ave., Gonzales, La. 70737 Phone: 644-1101	1962	199
SAVOY, Lynn Frances 17195 Augusta Ave., Gonzales, La. 70737 Phone: 644-1101	1964	199
SAVOY, Mable Marie (Zeringue) 17195 Augusta Ave., Gonzales, La. 70737 Phone: 644-1101	1938	199
SAVOY, Phil Gerard 17195 Augusta Ave., Gonzales, La. 70737 Phone: 644-1101	1963	199
SAVOY, Sherri Marie 17195 Augusta Ave., Gonzales, La. 70737 Phone: 644-1101	1965	199
SCHEXNAYDER, Arthur J., III Rt. 2, Box 140 A B, Welcome, La. 70093 Phone: 473-7374	1968	201
SCHEXNAYDER, Audrey Ann (Zeringue) 421 Bellvue Dr., Plaquemine, La. 70764 Phone: 687-4782	1943	201
SCHEXNAYDER, Beverly Marie Rt. 2, Box 140 A B, Welcome, La. 70093 Phone: 473-7374	1967	201
SCHEXNAYDER, Connie Ann 421 Bellvue Dr., Plaquemine, La. 70764 Phone: 687-4782	1964	201
SCHEXNAYDER, Elsie Ann (Zeringue) Rt. 2, Box 140 A B, Welcome, La. 70093 Phone: 473-7374	1941	200
SCHEXNAYDER, Mary Alice Rt. 2, Box 140 A B, Welcome, La. 70093 Phone: 473-7374	1970	201
SCHEXNAYDER, Nancy Ann Rt. 2, Box 140 A B, Welcome, La. 70093 Phone: 473-7374	1966	200
SCHEXNAYDER, Susan Ann 421 Bellvue Dr., Plaquemien, La. 70764 Phone: 687-4782	1967	201
SCHLATRE, Bart Richard	1972	200
SCHLATRE, Jeanette Lucy (Zeringue) 209 Magnolia Lane, Plaquemine, La. 70764 Phone: 687-4595	1939	199

NAME AND ADDRESS	YEAR OF BIRTH	PAGE
SCHLATRE, Joseph Larry, Jr. 209 Magnolia Lane, Plaquemine, La. 70764 Phone: 687-4595	1967	200
SCHLATRE, Ted Gerard 209 Magnolia Lane, Plaquemine, La. 70764 Phone: 687-4595	1969	200
SCHOTT, Cheryl Lynn (Tolousso) 13024 Wallis Dr., Baton Rouge, La. 70815 Phone: 275-9963	1947	158
SCHULTE, Amy Margaret 934 Madison, Gretna, La. 70114 Phone: 361-3569	1970	129
SCHULTE, Ann Elaine 934 Madison, Gretna, La. 70114 Phone: 361-3569	1962	128
SCHULTE, Antoine Joseph 934 Madison, Gretna, La. 70114 Phone: 361-3569	1968	129
SCHULTE, Ellen Marie 934 Madison, Gretna, La. 70114 Phone: 361-3569	1963	128
SCHULTE, Janet Lee (LeBlanc) 934 Madison, Gretna, La. 70114 Phone: 361-3569	1940	128
SCHULTE, Michele Rae 934 Madison, Gretna, La. 70114 Phone: 361-3569	1967	128
SEAGLES, Tiffany Angel 426 Little Farms, New Orleans, La. 70123 Phone: 729-0467	1970	117
SEAGLES, Vera Frances (Barrient) 426 Little Farms, New Orleans, La. 70123 Phone: 729-0467	1949	117
SICARD, Austin Joseph, Jr. 3037 Ivy Place, Chalmette, La. 70043 Phone: 271-4225	1954	211
SICARD, Clyde J. 3037 Ivy Place, Chalmette, La. 70043 Phone: 271-4225	1956	211
SICARD, Denise Marie 3037 Ivy Place, Chalmette, La. 70043 Phone: 271-4225	1958	211
SICARD, Marillyn Marie (LeBlanc) 3037 Ivy Place, Chalmette, La. 70043 Phone: 271-4225	1932	211

NAME AND ADDRESS	YEAR OF BIRTH	PAGE
SIMONEAUX, Ramona Ann (Dugas) P. O. Box 239, Belle Rose, La. 70341	1954	103
SMITH, Nancy Marie (Perault) 3620 Winbourne Ave., Apt. 226, Baton Rouge, La. 70805 Phone: 356-4209	1952	180
SMITH, Stacey Michelle 3620 Winbourne Ave., Apt. 226, Baton Rouge, La. 70805 Phone: 356-4209	1971	180
SPEEG, Gerald Wayne 6344 Celia Dr., Baton Rouge, La. 70811 Phone: 775-1616	1964	156
SPEEG, John Kenneth 6344 Celia Dr., Baton Rouge, La. 70811 Phone: 775-1616	1957	156
SPEEG, Lois Ann 6344 Celia Dr., Baton Rouge, La. 70811 Phone: 775-1616	1956	155
SPEEG, Lois Clotile (Gonzales) 6344 Celia Dr., Baton Rouge, La. 70811 Phone: 775-1616	1922	155
SPEEG, Terry Lynn 6344 Celia Dr., Baton Rouge, La. 70811 Phone: 775-1616	1959	156
STEECE, Anne Louise 11120 Tams Dr., Baton Rouge, La. 70815 Phone: 275-5289	1965	143
STEECE, Theressa Ann New Orleans, La.	1957	143
STEIB, Charles Daniel, Jr. 119 Modock, Destrahan, La. 70047	1925	84
STEIB, Charles Daniel, III 199 Modock, Destrahan, La. 70047	1951	85
STEIB, Courtney Andrew 119 Modock, Destrahan, La. 70047	1961	85
STEIB, Edna (Landry) 1725 Abundance St., New Orleans, La. 70119 Phone: 944-3557	1902	84
STEIB, Jill Elaine 199 Modock, Destrahan, La. 70047	1959	85
STEIB, Julie Elizabeth 199 Modock, Destrahan, La. 70047	1959	85
STEIBLING, Bruce Michael 1212 N. Hullen, Metairie, La.	1963	186

NAME AND ADDRESS	YEAR OF BIRTH	PAGE
STEIBLING, Charles P. 1212 N. Hullen, Metairie, La.	1960	186
STEIBLING, Douglas Gerard 1212 N. Hullen, Metairie, La.	1961	186
STEIBLING, Eston Gerard 1212 N. Hullen, Metairie, La.	1966	186
STEIBLING, Janice Rita (LeBlanc) 1212 N. Hullen, Metairie, La.	1939	186
STOCK, Adele (Landry) 915 Eleanore St., New Orleans, La. 70115 Phone: 897-0928	1897	84
STOCK, Conrad, Jr. 915 Eleanore St., New Orleans, La. 70115 Phone: 897-0928	1930	84
STOCK, Elizabeth 915 Eleanore St., New Orleans, La. 70115 Phone: 897-0928	1926	84
STOCK, Mary Louise 915 Eleanore St., New Orleans, La. 70115 Phone: 897-0928	1922	84
STOLTZ, Christopher Stephen 525 Melody Dr., Metairie, La. 70001	1957	109
STOLTZ, Martin Edward 525 Melody Dr., Metairie, La. 70001	1960	109
STOLTZ, Wayne Ernest 525 Melody Dr., Metairie, La. 70001	1955	109
STOREY, Jenny V. (LeBlanc) 10945 Red Oaks Dr., Baton Rouge, La. 70815 Phone: 926-3791	1922	89
STOREY, Lorreta Ann 10945 Red Oaks Dr., Baton Rouge, La. 70815 Phone: 926-3791	1960	90
TEDDER, Ernestine (Aleman) Park Manor, 511 2nd St., Denham Springs, La. 70726 Phone: 665-8340	1938	82
TEDDER, Walt Bryant Park Manor, 511 2nd St., Denham Springs, La. 70726 Phone: 665-8340	1967	82
TEDDER, Warren Dean Park Manor, 511 2nd St., Denham Springs, La. 70726 Phone: 665-8340	1964	82

NAME AND ADDRESS	YEAR OF BIRTH	PAGE
TOLOUSSO, Annie Philomine (Dugas) 13024 Wallis Dr., Baton Rouge, La. 70815 Phone: 275-9963	1914	158
TOLOUSSO, Charlott Ann 13024 Wallis Dr., Baton Rouge, La. 70815 Phone: 275-9963	1952	159
TOLOUSSO, Mary Ellen 13024 Wallis Dr., Baton Rouge, La. 70815 Phone: 275-9963	1955	159
TORRES, Christine Ann (Sanchez) 614 Evangeline St., Ville Platte, La. 70586	1948	163
TORRES, Paige Marie 614 Evangeline St., Ville Platte, La. 70586	1969	164
TORRES, Roy Francis, III 614 Evangeline St., Ville Platte, La. 70586	1968	164
TRUXILLO, Dana Lynn 1013 Belvedere Dr., Mobile, Ala. 36606 Phone: 471-4874	1969	185
TRUXILLO, Dawn Marie 1013 Belvedere Dr., Mobile, Ala. 36606 Phone: 471-4874	1968	185
TRUXILLO, Roy J. 1013 Belvedere Dr., Mobile, Ala, 36606 Phone: 471-4874	1936	185
TRUXILLO, Roy J., II 1013 Belvedere Dr., Mobile, Ala. 36606 Phone: 471-4874	1966	185
TURNER, Betty Joyce (LeBlanc)	1933	88
VERRETTE, Brian Paul 517 Melody Dr., Metairie, La. 70001 Phone: 833-3898	1957	97
VERRETTE, Craig J. 517 Melody Dr., Metairie, La. 70001 Phone: 833-3898	1955	97
VERRETTE, David A., Jr. 517 Melody Dr., Metairie, La. 70001 Phone: 833-3898	1950	97
VERRETTE, Mary Lee (Dupre) 517 Melody Dr., Metairie, La. 70001 Phone: 833-3898	1924	97

WATTS, Betty Joyce (LeBlanc)   1935   120
11411 Katy Freeway, Apt. 133, Houston, Texas   77024
Phone: 461-9396

WAYNE, Gina Marie   1967   193
4885 Sierra Madre Dr., New Orleans, La.   70127
Phone: 242-5779

WAYNE, Lawrence Joseph   1971   193
4885 Sierra Madre Dr., New Orleans, La.   70127
Phone: 242-5779

WAYNE, Patricia Ann (LeBlanc)   1946   193
4885 Sierra Madre Dr., New Orleans, La.   70127
Phone: 242-5779

WHITE, Jane Marie (Zeringue)   1947   201
P. O. Box 137, Plaquemine, La.   70764
Phone: 687-3458

WHITE, Louis Marc   1969   201
P. O. Box 137, Plaquemine, La.   70764
Phone: 687-3458

WILLIAMS, Carolyn Fay (Barriet)   1938   114
P. O. Box 44, Lake Park, Ga.   31636

WILLIAMS, Edwin LeGrand III   1960   114
P. O. Box 44, Lake Park, Ga.   31636

WILLIAMS, Frank Wilfred   1912   85
4649 Werner Dr., New Orleans, La.   70126
Phone: 242-3188

WILLIAMS, Joseph Cason   1962   114
P. O. Box 44, Lake Park, Ga.   31636

WILLIAMS, Virginia Grace   1972   114
P. O. Box 44, Lake Park, Ga.   31636

WILLIAMS, Walter Thomas   1914   85
404 Lynx Dr., Arabi, La.   70032
Phone: 279-0388

WILLIAMS, Walter Thomas, Jr.   1952   85
404 Lynx Dr., Arabi, La.   70032
Phone: 279-0388

WILSON, Claudette Marie (Dugas)   1950   160
2817 Lorraine St., Apt. 25, Baton Rouge, La.   70805
Phone: 355-1214

WILSON, David Lawrence   1968   144
454 Finchley Dr., Baton Rouge, La.   70806
Phone: 927-7139

WILSON, Margie Louise (Clouatre)   1946   144
454 Finchley Dr., Baton Rouge, La.   70806
Phone: 927-7139

NAME AND ADDRESS	YEAR OF BIRTH	PAGE
WILSON, Maurice 2817 Lorraine St., Apt. 25, Baton Rouge, La. 70805 Phone: 355-1214	1970	160
WILSON, Vicki Lynn 454 Finchley Dr., Baton Rouge, La. 70806 Phone: 927-7139	1967	144
WILSON, William Lloyd, Jr. 454 Finchley Dr., Baton Rouge, La. 70806 Phone: 927-7139	1966	144
WYATT, Arlene Ann (Gautreaux) 10764 Red Oaks Dr., Baton Rouge, La. 70815 Phone: 926-5825	1947	89
WYBLE, Charles Edward, Jr. 3376 Lone Oak Dr., Baton Rouge, La. 70814 Phone: 926-1034	1968	159
WYBLE, Peggy Ann 3376 Lone Oak Dr., Baton Rouge, La. 70814 Phone: 926-1034	1966	159
WYBLE, Penny Gayle 3376 Lone Oak Dr., Baton Rouge, La. 70814 Phone: 926-1034	1965	159
ZERINGUE, Adele Marie (LeBlanc) Rt. 1, Box 595, White Castle, La. 70788 Phone: 473-4729	1917	199
ZERINGUE, Alyce Ann P. O. Box 572, Plaquemine, La. 70764	1963	200
ZERINGUE, Dale Andrew Rt. 1, Box 595, White Castle, La. 70788 Phone: 473-4729	1956	200
ZERINGUE, Danny Gerald Rt. 1, Box 448 A, White Castle, La. 70788	1963	199
ZERINGUE, Debbie Anne P. O. Box 137, Plaquemine, La. 70764 Phone: 687-3458	1960	201
ZERINGUE, George Gerald, Jr. Rt. 1, Box 448 A, White Castle, La. 70788	1937	199
ZERINGUE, Glen Paul Rt. 1, Box 448 A, White Castle, La. 70788	1968	199
ZERINGUE, Jeanne Hazel (LeBlanc) P. O. Box 137, Plaquemine, La. 70764 Phone: 687-3458	1920	200

NOTES

NOTES

NOTES

NOTES

NOTES

NOTES

NOTES

www.ingramcontent.com/pod-product-compliance
Lightning Source LLC
Chambersburg PA
CBHW060325100426
42812CB00003B/879